D0768805

Tabloid Prodigy

MARLISE ELIZABETH KAST

RUNNING PRESS
PHILADELPHIA • LONDON

© 2007 by Marlise Elizabeth Kast
All rights reserved under the Pan-American and International Copyright Conventions
Printed in the United States

This book may not be reproduced in whole or in part, in any form or by any means, electronic or mechanical, including photocopying, recording, or by any information storage and retrieval system now known or hereafter invented, without written permission from the publisher.

9 8 7 6 5 4 3 2 1

Digit on the right indicates the number of this printing

Library of Congress Control Number: 2006934603

ISBN-13: 978-0-7624-2970-7
ISBN-10: 0-7624-2970-4

Cover design by Whitney Cookman and Bill Jones
Back cover design by David Serrano
Interior design by Alicia Freile
Typography: Minion and Trade Gothic

This book may be ordered by mail from the publisher.
Please include $2.50 for postage and handling.
But try your bookstore first!

Running Press Book Publishers
2300 Chestnut Street
Philadelphia, PA 19103-4371

Visit us on the web!
www.runningpress.com

Back cover photos:
Top Left: Marlise and famed paparazzo, James Churchill*
Top Center: Sharmin Bryles
Top Right: Marlise and paparazzo Randal Traub* in Egypt
Center: Sharmin Bryles' wedding in 2006: Sharmin Bryles, Karen Glaser*, Ryann, and Marlise
Far Right: Pete Trujillo, Marlise, Adam Edwards*, Sharmin Bryles, Ryann, and Karen Glaser* at *Globe* charity race
Left Center: Sharmin Bryles and supermodel, Tyson Beckford
Bottom Center: Sharmin Bryles and Pete Trujillo
Bottom Left: Pete Trujillo, Sharmin Bryles, Adam Edwards*, Marlise, and Karen Glaser* celebrating Halloween

* Fictitious names used to protect the anonymity of tabloid personnel and paparazzi

Front cover photograph by John Chapple
Black and white photograph by Thomas Gurnee

Dedication

To my heavenly Father, in whom I put my trust.
You alone are my rock and my refuge.

Contents

Author's Note

To retain the integrity of *Tabloid Prodigy*, none of the names of celebrities have been changed. All of the events recorded in this book actually took place. Details of those events are excerpted from the journals that I have maintained throughout my life. I have gone to great lengths to ensure the accuracy of my story by drawing on external research as well as on my personal archives.

The names of all my sources have been changed to protect their anonymity. The names of paparazzi and tabloid personnel have also been changed, with the exception of Pete Trujillo and Sharmin Bryles—both of whom requested that I use their real name. Fictitious names have been substituted for all of my friends.

CHAPTER 1

Spinning on the Axis of *Globe*

I t wasn't as if I intentionally set out to work for one of the lowest forms of media. It just sort of happened. As a 21-year-old communications and English major, I longed to carry a business card that would label me as a high-profile reporter. I envisioned that I would be surrounded by ringing cell phones, my hair tied in a loose bun with a stylish pair of gold-rimmed glasses dangling from my lips. I wanted to be the one searching frantically for the taped interview for tomorrow's cover story. I wanted to be Katie Couric.

After all, I hadn't exactly popped out of the womb singing "Hollywood" or even had a desire to see my face on the big screen, for that matter. But somehow I ended up in Los Angeles, smack dab in the middle of the tabloids. In a city where people blend together like salt crystals in a shaker, there I was, a single speck of pepper, trying to fight my way out of the spout.

As the daughter of a minister, I was encouraged to walk the "straight and narrow path." Each generation of my family tree had produced dedicated preachers and foreign missionaries. By sprouting off in my own direction, I was determined to avoid becoming just another typical branch in my heritage.

After graduating early from Westmont College, I moved to LA to share a condominium with my sister, Heidi. Although she is only two years older, we are as opposite as siblings can be. Heidi excels in math and science, while I always rely on calculators. She has blue eyes, fair skin, and lives under a layer of SPF 35. My eyes are green, I live to surf, and I chase the sun. Heidi is sensitive and compassionate with a desire to deliver medical supplies to third-world orphans. I am raw and spontaneous and take risks as if I were indestructible. Considered "grounded and brilliant," Heidi brushes those labels aside and insists that our dissimilarities bring balance to our wobbly spirits. I think she's right. Over time, my sister and I have developed a common understanding of our roles. I will continue to live the way I want and Heidi will make sure nothing falls apart. Yet, for all her years of damage control, Heidi will never forgive herself for introducing me to her campus Web site. Using her student code, I gained access to the UCLA job board.

"Would you look at this?" I said, pointing to our computer screen. "*Globe* magazine is hiring celebrity reporters. Maybe I should send in my resume."

"Maybe," Heidi suggested apprehensively, "you should think about getting your teaching credential instead."

Ignoring her concerned pleas, I spontaneously sent my resume to *Globe*. Later that week, I received a call to interview with the magazine, a publication I had never read or even purchased. Eight days later, I was scheduled to meet with *Globe*'s West Coast bureau chief, Madeline Norton.

During the week prior to that fateful meeting, my family and I went on vacation to Hawaii. The first day of our holiday ended painfully with my family lying flat on the floor, charred to a crisp after naively believing that our base tans could brave the tropical rays. There we were, side by side on our bellies, looking like bright, pink sausages lined up on the rotating spit of a 7-Eleven hot dog warmer.

Our faces buried in the carpet, we were only vaguely aware of the background noise of CNN's world news coming from a television in the corner of our rented condo. Suddenly, regular programming was interrupted by a special report announcing that Princess Diana had just been involved in a serious car crash. At the time, the extent of her injuries remained unknown.

Without making the correlation between my upcoming interview and the historic events unfolding on the screen, I remained absorbed in my own burnt suffering. It was agonizing to peel away my sun-pasted bikini. "More aloe," I motioned to the lifeless bodies around me. Responding to my tormented call, my mother began rubbing the green goop on my back.

As CNN's coverage continued, one expert after another began to blame the paparazzi for the accident, naming them as the primary culprits. Breaking away from the horrific scenes in the French tunnel, live footage cut back to the CNN studio as the anchorman introduced yet another guest.

"Here, to speak on behalf of the tabloids," he was saying, "is Trenton Freeze, editor in chief of *Globe* magazine."

I lifted my inflamed face long enough to take notice of Mr. Freeze. It was my first introduction to the man who would later become my boss. With slightly graying hair and coaster-sized glasses, he spoke with a thick British accent.

"Oh, how splendid," I said, mimicking his English pronunciation. "It appears my future boss is defending the tabloids on the telly."

My mother stopped rubbing my back. "Marlise, please don't tell me this man runs the magazine where you'll be interviewing on Monday."

"Calm down," I said, dropping my head between my burning arms. "I don't even have the job yet."

"But how could you even think about working for those people?" my mother asked. "Princess Diana may very well be dead."

"Well," I snapped, "I didn't kill her."

And that was the end of our discussion. The next week, I stormed the doors of the great American tabloid. In retrospect, it is a wonder that the editors even granted me an interview. My journalistic background was far from comprehensive. It consisted of two summer internships at a Monterey, California, tourist publication, where I did everything from layout to writing copy and selling ads. After college graduation, I spent fourteen months working at a stock footage library in Hollywood. As a production assistant, I helped film everything from street scenes and buildings to taxis and airplanes. Production companies would order these specific stock shots to be spliced into movies and television shows.

That Hollywood exposure, combined with my journalistic experience, was apparently enough to get me through the tabloid doors.

With a portfolio of my writings in hand, I entered the lobby of *Globe* magazine. Because of my limited background in celebrity reporting, I had little confidence I would get the job. Watching the Oscars® was about as close as I had come to the private lives of Hollywood's rich and famous. At the time, however, *Globe*'s desperation was my ticket to employment.

I was escorted into the office of *Globe*'s West Coast bureau chief. Noticeably absent were the customary questionnaires, clipboards, and editing exams. Our interview was brief and direct. My fate was ultimately determined by my answer to a single question:

"What would you do," Madeline asked, "if you believed that Tom Cruise was cheating on Nicole Kidman?"

At that moment, all I could think about were my sweaty palms and how they might reveal my insecurity. Phone lines on the editor's desk were lighting up like a Christmas tree at Nordstrom.

"Excuse me for a moment," she murmured, pressing her manicured nail onto a blinking light. Placing the call on hold, she ordered someone in the other room to "bring the JonBenet rewrite." I wiped my damp hands on the arm of the chair before folding them tightly in my lap.

The walls around me were studded with paparazzi photos encased in gold frames. Like trophies on display, each photograph represented another life that had been changed by a single flash and a probing lens. There they were, all those well-known images: Michael Jackson covering his burnt face, a pregnant Farrah Fawcett sweeping her garage, and a young Liz Taylor romancing in Rome. I felt as if their freeze-framed eyes were begging me to reconsider.

"Stop it," I pled silently to the desperate celebrities screaming in my head. "I'm making a decision here and I can do it without your help."

The editor slammed down the phone. "So, where were we?"

Picking up where we had left off, I blurted, "I would follow him."

The editor leaned over her desk with a look of confusion. "Excuse me?"

"Tom Cruise," I answered. "I would follow him."

Standing up, she walked toward me and extended her hand. "So, we'll be seeing you on Monday then." It was an announcement, not an invitation.

Monday? Do I have to come back for another interview or did she just offer me the job? What is the job? Can I ask her? No, Marlise, you can't ask her that. Act confident.

"You know, it's nothing official," she continued with a saccharine smile. "We'll just take it one day at a time and see how it goes. But I must admit I have a good feeling about this."

Easy, Turbo. This is going way too fast.

"Actually," I mumbled, trying to cover the damp handprints on my skirt, "could I have a little time to think it over?"

The editor seemed stunned to have a 21-year-old challenging her game. Regaining control, she slipped me her card. "You have exactly twenty-four hours."

The interview was officially over.

That evening I phoned my parents, who habitually tell me what I need to hear rather than what I want to hear. "Mom, Dad, I'm becoming a tabloid journalist."

Silence.

"What do you exactly mean when you say 'tabloid journalist'?" my father asked. I told them everything I knew about the position, which was not very much. I understood their hesitation, but I was unwilling to pass up this opportunity.

"Do you really have to write for a tabloid?" my mother asked. "What about working for CNN or *National Geographic*? If you take the job at *Globe*, you won't be climbing the corporate ladder. You'll be climbing the corporate footstool." She was probably right. After all, how could a tabloid reporter ever become a respected journalist?

By this time, the death of Princess Diana had been officially confirmed. It seemed as if the whole world were in mourning. The tabloids in general, and paparazzi in particular, were under fire for their alleged roles in her untimely death. The tragic passing of the internationally adored princess only worsened the infamous reputation of the tabloids. The timing could not have been worse for my career change from production assistant to tabloid journalist.

Consistent with my reputation for spontaneity, I picked up the phone and called Madeline. Without fully realizing where it would take me, I accepted the position as a tabloid reporter.

The transition was rough.

Day one at *Globe* felt like an eternity. After leaving my car in underground parking, I signed in with building security and took the elevator to the ninth floor. Walking down a long, narrow corridor, I made my way to suite 925. I knocked and waited. The heavy blue door was flung open.

Standing there was an attractive African-American woman who appeared to be in her early thirties. "You must be Marlise," she said, reaching out her hand. "I don't think we've officially met. I'm Sharmin."

"It's nice to meet you, Sharlin," I responded, giving her a firm grip.

"No," she said, letting go of my hand. Turning away, she led me into the lobby and continued. "It's Sharmin, as in, 'Don't squeeze the Charmin.'"

I smiled, wondering which had come first, the toilet paper or her birth.

Dramatically waving her arm over the couch like a game show model, she asked me to take a seat. Rather than receiving a traditional office tour or a formal introduction to the staff, I was handed a stack of magazines and told someone would be with me shortly. For the next forty-five minutes, I sat there flipping through the pages of *Globe*, wondering what on earth I had gotten myself into.

Fortunately that moment marked the only time I would ever sit on the "outsider couch," reserved solely for sources and the endless string of auditioning reporters. The lobby was a cold and forsaken place, with more of the intimidating paparazzi photos covering the walls. The furnishings were sparse. In addition to the uncomfortable loveseat, the room held a black slate reception desk. That desk remained empty throughout my years at *Globe*, during which the magazine never hired a receptionist.

Instead, those duties were performed by Sharmin, who informed everyone that she was the "senior assistant to the bureau chief." Over and over, we could hear her sexy telephone voice echoing from around the corner, "Thanks for calling *Globe*. This is Sharmin. How may I help you?"

Despite her claims of being overworked and underpaid, Sharmin was the office favorite. Everyone adored her, especially the FedEx man, who blushed when she dropped enticing lines like, "Do you make after-hour deliveries?" She flirted with the men and befriended the women, wrapping nearly everyone in the industry around her little finger.

Somehow, Sharmin had even convinced upper management to grant her paid vacation time for any day related to minorities: Martin Luther King Jr. Day, Slavery Abolition Day, *Cinco de Mayo*, Rodney King Conviction Day, and even the anniversary of Tupac Shakur's death. She loved to joke, "Whose idea was it to put cotton in the top of a medicine bottle anyway? I say leave the cotton pickin' to the white man. Set my people free."

With a mastery of multitasking, Sharmin could talk on the phone, write up leads, file her nails, and play computer solitaire, all at the same time. Ultimately, my friendship with Sharmin was one of the reasons I stayed in the industry. But day one was another story. From the beginning, she had mentally written me off as "some rich white girl who won't last a week."

Almost immediately, I sensed that I was disliked by the staff. Teamwork was nonexistent, and there was little opportunity to get to know one another. We only worked together when a predecessor had failed, or, on those rare occasions when assignments required us to blend as partners.

The editors constantly reminded the reporters that they could not "afford" to have us sitting around. This seemed odd, given the fact that the publishers were selling more than two million magazines each week. Yet we all knew that any reporter who did not produce regular leads would be fired. We were set up to become competitors, not teammates. It was a dog-eat-dog world and we were the dogs. It was that simple.

Naturally these realizations only became clear to me over a period of time. From the moment Sharmin escorted me to my section, there were clues that I was entering a company of quick employee turnover. Empty desks and barren bulletin boards hinted at a staff that could never completely settle into the system. The office was surprisingly quiet. There was little movement, except for the sound of typing and the occasional ringing phone. My long-anticipated visions of a frenzied newsroom, perfumed with the smell of cigarette smoke and black coffee, would have to remain a stereotypical image inside my head.

White walls and black desks made the place look stark. In the main section, there were six desks, with three on each side of the open room, lined up one behind the other. The small tabloid family was made up of only five staff reporters, nine editors, and three assistants. Head of the LA household was the Los Angeles bureau chief, Madeline. There was very little to know about her personal life, particularly since she didn't seem to have one. Commuting three hours from Santa Barbara every day, Madeline dedicated herself to *Globe* as if she also lived in fear of the tabloid guillotine. She came in early and left late.

About five feet tall, she wore flat dress shoes, tan nylons, and bland skirts that hit directly below the knee on her pear-shaped body. Her auburn hair was styled in a pixie cut, but I thought she was far from the magical Tinkerbell. Although her normal practice was to stay inside her office, she occasionally paced up and down the center aisle of the open room like a flight attendant, making sure that seat belts were fastened and tray tables were in their upright position. During these periodic appearances, she sprinkled her fairy threats of, "Leads, people! Where are your leads?"

She had hired me on a risk and could have fired me on a dime. Oddly enough, I felt indebted to her for employing me without journalistic credentials, tabloid experience, or an extensive portfolio. Countless complaints bounced off the office walls, but none of them could accuse Madeline of a lack of commitment. Typically, this would be the appropriate time to say she took me under her wing and taught me everything I know about journalism. But that would not be true. In reality, Madeline pushed me off the edge of *Globe* and forced me to fly alone.

That first day should have given me a clue of what was to come. After sitting alone in *Globe*'s lobby for almost an hour, I timidly walked around the corner to Sharmin's desk. "Excuse me," I said, wondering if they had forgotten about me. "Was I supposed to be meeting with someone or doing anything in particular?"

Sharmin's expression showed me that I had, in fact, been forgotten. "Oh, right," she answered. "Why don't you follow me?"

As we walked through the office, the handful of reporters did not even glance up from their desks long enough to make eye contact. No words, waves, or smiles were exchanged. Sharmin led me to an empty desk at the back of the office. She handed me a second stack of magazines, including the latest issues of *Globe*, *National Enquirer*, and *Star*. "Read through these," she said. "They'll give you an idea of what we're about."

Within that first hour, I read everything Sharmin had given me from cover to cover. Naïve to the world of weekly publications, I came face to face with stories such as JonBenet Ramsey's murder, Princess Diana's death, and Kathy Lee's marriage to Frank Gifford.

At the time I had no way of knowing that the *National Enquirer* would soon publish a story alleging that *Globe* had paid $250,000 to a former flight attendant to lure Frank Gifford into a hotel room. The *Enquirer* further claimed that the encounter had been taped with a hidden camera. But on my first day, I knew none of that.

As a novice tabloid reporter, I had no idea what it meant to find "a source." The fact that the magazine bought stories was meaningless to me. Eager to start writing, I was desperate for some sort of direction.

"Excuse me," I said, spinning my chair toward a young, blond reporter. "Could you possibly tell me what I should be doing? It's my first day. I'm a bit clueless, to be perfectly honest."

Biting into his tuna sandwich, the reporter paused to finish his mouthful. "It's noon," he said. "You can take your lunch break if you want."

"No, I mean as far as work goes," I continued with embarrassment. "What do we all do?"

He wheeled his chair toward me and whispered. "Listen, it's only my second day at *Globe*. If you want to keep your job, I suggest you try to look busy." Pointing toward a rack of publications, he added, "Grab a mainstream magazine and start looking for a buried quote. Maybe you can create a story from something a celebrity said in another interview."

"Thanks," I whispered back. "By the way, I'm Marlise."

He wiped his mayonnaise-smudged mouth with the front of his sleeve. "I'm Adam, Adam Edwards, from New York."

Other than Sharmin, Adam was the only person who spoke to me all day. From time to time, Madeline would pass my desk on the way to the conference room, but she never acknowledged my existence. I was beginning to wonder if I were invisible.

At Adam's direction, I spent the next five hours flipping through the pages of *Time*, *People*, *USA Today*, and *Elle*. Although I was far removed from the world of celebrity gossip, everything seemed to be old news, even to me. One by one, the other reporters shut down their computers and left the office, calling it a day.

"It's six o'clock," Sharmin said, reaching for her purse. "You can leave now."

Fearing my days at *Globe* were numbered, I drove home deep in thought. When people asked me how it had gone, I had no idea how to respond. It was one of the strangest days I had ever experienced in an office.

Day two was even worse. No one spoke to me, helped me, or guided me. The only change was on my desk, which now bore two pencils and a stenographer's notepad. After skimming through twenty magazines, I compiled a list of five story ideas pertaining to everything from "Madonna's Beauty Secrets" to "Charlie's Angels, Where Are They Now?" By five o'clock, I had worked up enough courage to knock on Madeline's door.

"Yes?" she murmured without looking up from her desk.

"Sorry to bother you," I said shyly. "I came up with a few possible story ideas."

Speed-reading through my list, she handed it back without giving me any direction. "Not bad, but keep trying."

I walked out of her office feeling more defeated than encouraged. Day three was a repeat of the initial two, except for the appearance of a reporter seated in the desk beside me.

"Well hello, luv," he said brightly with a strong British accent. "No one told me we were getting a new bird in the office."

Reaching out his hand, he introduced himself as Patrick Kincaid.

"Marlise," I said, relieved to have a bit of conversation. "I didn't realize anyone sat in that desk. Do you have Mondays and Tuesdays off?"

He laughed at the absurdity of my question. "There are no days off here. I've been on assignment in Texas. Do you know how much beef they have over there? I've never seen so many fat people in my life."

He had lost me.

"I've been doing a story about Oprah supposedly destroying the beef industry," he continued. Pantomiming the headline in the air, he added, "'Farmers Rage: Oprah Ruined Our Lives!' It's a brilliant story, really. But I can't bother being tied up in here all day. Especially with that witch looking over my shoulder every five seconds. I would have left *Globe* long ago, but I'm signed on for a year."

Patrick tapped his pencil on the desk. "Whatever you do, never get involved in contracts. The tabs brought me over from the British papers a few months ago. Supposedly I'm a roving editor, but I don't like that title. It makes me sound like a bit of a wanker."

"Well, at least you know your job," I said, leaning over to whisper. "I have no idea what I'm doing here."

"You're not much different from the rest of us then," Patrick laughed, lifting the cover of his laptop. "See if you can get one of these beauties. Then you can actually pretend to be busy."

I glared at the enormous computer that was on my desk, similar to the one I had used in elementary school. It looked like it operated on the DOS system, controlled with turtle-slow arrow configurations rather than by a mouse.

Booting up the tank, I wondered aloud, "Do these things actually work?"

"Well, you can type on them," Patrick explained. "But you can't check the bloody football scores now, can you?" He turned his laptop screen toward me with a little victory shove to show me the sports Web page.

I was surprised to learn that most of the office computers lacked Internet access. Looking back, this made the research process of tabloid journalism that much more remarkable. Further into the job, I was told that we were expected to rely on a file room for our data gathering. Filled with newspaper clippings and magazine articles, it contained a file on nearly everyone in the entertainment industry. If the file library lacked the specific information we needed, we were to call Marsha Powell in the Florida office. She would then fact check everything from celebrity birth-dates to their past flings. Marsha was amazing. She single-handedly faxed reporters all of the requested information within minutes.

Most of the time, tabloid journalists relied on sources for gathering information. At this point, I had not yet established any useful contacts. Lacking sources, I used my lunch breaks to research current celebrity Web pages from my home computer. Some time later, *Globe* installed dial-up Internet, which gave me an added level of job security. Oddly enough, in this office of old-school veterans, anyone who knew how to operate e-mail was considered computer savvy. In their words, the Internet was "much too technical." Apparently Patrick and I were on our own when it came to the world of Yahoo.

"So, how do you like the job so far?" he asked, looking up from his screen.

"Well, there isn't too much to like, really," I said. "To be honest, I'm a bit frustrated at the moment."

Patrick turned off his computer as if calling it a day. "Keep your chin up, luv. I reckon you'll be the star of *Globe* in no time."

Day three had ended without making any progress. That evening, I watched *Inside Edition, Access Hollywood, Entertainment Tonight, Extra,* and the E! channel, determined to get a sense of celebrity reporting. I had to get up to speed in the world of gossip. My hope was to capture a line that I could develop into a story. The following morning I typed out a list of possible ideas and placed it on Madeline's desk. Nearly an hour passed before she made any reference to my efforts.

"Marlise," she called from inside her office. "Come in here for a mo-ment, please."

Holding my pad and pen in jotting-ready position, I practically ran to her office. Madeline began talking even before I entered the room.

"I like your enthusiasm. But you've got to think headlines. Headlines, Marlise! Like here, for example." She pointed toward my idea to interview Anthony Hopkins about his upcoming role in *The Edge.*

"Obviously Hopkins is not going to give us an interview, nor would we want one. Find out something else that is going on around him. I think you're headed in the right direction."

She handed me back my list and continued about her work. Although I had absolutely no idea what she was talking about, it seemed pretty clear that I dare not ask. During my lunch break, I raced home and researched *The Edge* on the Internet. The leading stars in the film were listed as Anthony Hopkins, Alec Baldwin, and Bart, the bear. The name of the bear's publicist and contact information were listed below the animal's film credits. Dialing the management firm, I explained that I was a reporter who was interested in interviewing the animal's owner. Viewing the exposure as harmless publicity, the bear's publicist organized a telephone interview with Bart's owner, Doug Seus, for later that afternoon.

Back at the office, I composed a series of questions similar to what one might ask an actual actor. How does the bear stay in shape? How many hours of sleep does he get? What are the bear's favorite foods? Does he have a girlfriend? Has he been to acting school? Does he ever get moody? I then called the bear's owner. Midway through my telephone conversation, Madeline walked past my desk and motioned me into her office. After I hung up the phone, I knocked on her open door and entered.

"Who were you talking to?" she asked, somewhat puzzled to see me using the phone.

"The bear," I responded. "Well, not the actual bear, but the bear's owner."

She looked annoyed. "What bear?"

"You know, the bear as in *the bear.*"

"Marlise," she said, shaking her head. "We are a tabloid magazine. We want scandal."

"Well," I nodded. "I just thought it might make an interesting lifestyle piece on the wealthiest pet in Hollywood."

It was the first time I had seen her smile in four days. "So, what did he say?"

"It turns out the bear is quite a spoiled star." I waited for visual feedback from Madeline, but she gave me nothing. "He's appeared in over twenty movies. He eats Oreos, sits at the dinner table, swims laps with his personal trainer, sleeps in his own bed, makes ten thousand dollars a day—"

She stopped me before I had a chance to continue.

"Write it up. Two pages double-spaced, twelve point, Times New Roman. Have it on my desk first thing tomorrow."

I smiled the entire way back to my desk. As a so-called celebrity writer, it was somewhat humiliating to be reporting on the beauty secrets of a grizzly, but the following day, I realized that this single story saved my job. With hardly any editorial corrections, Madeline signed off and faxed my story to Florida headquarters. The article was published as a full-page spread with my byline.

It took me only one week to adjust to tabloid lingo. "Tone down your vocabulary a bit," Madeline scolded. She claimed that my writing style sounded like it was addressed to an educated audience. She explained that I needed to target the trailer-park readers who thrive on stories like "Oprah Battles the Bulge." Within a few days, I learned to incorporate catch phrases into my articles. Among the tabloid favorites were "hunky beau," "love nest," "tragic heartbreak," and "secret romance."

It was quite a week. Adam from New York barely made the cut. He survived only after aggressively assisting a veteran reporter on a *Brady Bunch* update. Unable to make the same deadline, another rookie reporter whom I never met was fired the following day. That Friday, Sharmin distributed a memo announcing staff happy hour at LA's Westwood Brewing Company.

"Remember to bring extra flow for the less fortunate," she added, holding out her hand. "I'm not too proud to beg for money."

After work, I drove to the bar where the majority of reporters were already well into their pints and cocktails. Madeline and Sharmin were there. Patrick Kincaid showed up but ignored the entire bunch in exchange for being able to watch televised sports on ESPN. Adam sat across from me, looking just as relieved as I felt to still be employed.

"Have you met the staff?" Madeline asked, pointing her wine glass toward the others around the table.

"No, just Patrick and Adam," I replied.

One by one they welcomed me to the team.

"I'm Karen," said one who looked rather pale. "I specialize in covering soap opera gossip."

Over time, I discovered that Karen was somewhat timid and introverted, most likely as a result of some chronic health issues. Then there was Pete, a 350-pound bundle of pure tabloid bliss. Digging into the nut bowl, he threw back a handful of almonds and introduced himself as "the unorganized one of the bunch."

Like Sharmin, Pete was adored by everyone. Suffering from severe narcolepsy, he was notorious for two things: falling asleep at his computer and stashing candy wrappers inside his desk. Pete's chocolate fetish was the root of all ant problems at the office. When he typed, he used an unorthodox two-finger punching method, but still managed to write as fast as the rest of us. After a year at *Globe*, Pete had already mastered the tabloid formulaic jargon and was viewed as the greatest wordsmith in the industry.

The rest of the LA staff was made up of a handful of freelance reporters like me. We had no binding contracts, no benefits, and no formal proof of our relationship with the tabloid. As freelancers, we received a flat day rate of $200 and knew that *Globe* could drop us at any moment. One such freelancer introduced herself as Ronda and appeared to be in her early fifties. Turning to the mustached gentleman by her side, she said, "This is my husband, Jacques Pierre."

"So, are you both reporters?" I asked, turning toward Jacques Pierre.

"No," Ronda answered, speaking for him. "He's a photographer."

Maybe it was the language barrier, but by the end of the evening, I realized that Ronda did all the speaking for both of them. The couple was seldom seen in the office and predominantly worked from home as dedicated freelancers. Then there was Jason, the smooth operator. He kissed the back of my hand and explained that he dealt with the dirty side of the business. Throughout the evening, he inched his chair closer and closer toward mine. Jason had a habit of winking at the end of each sentence and repeatedly suggested another toast to "new beginnings." I found him a bit creepy.

Pete leaned over and whispered, "Jason digs in celebrities' trash cans in search of anything that might lead to a story."

Nodding, I excused myself and went to the restroom to scrub my hands. Returning to the group, I asked, "So where is the rest of the staff?"

"This is it," Madeline explained. "At least on the West Coast. Most of the news comes out of our LA office even though *Globe*'s headquarters are in Florida."

Everyone seemed much more relaxed in this setting than they had been at the office. I was stunned to learn that there were seldom more than five full-time staff reporters, plus freelancers, working from Hollywood at any time. It was amazing that these reporters could produce as much as they did each week. By the end of the evening, I began to realize that life behind the walls of *Globe* was not what might be expected from one of the world's most scandal-filled magazines. My fellow journalists were not evil or malicious, nor were they on a mission to destroy lives. They simply wanted to write and get paid for it.

They were an unusual bunch. Although they made a living from delving into the details of celebrities' lives, they neither asked nor shared information about their own. Sometimes they made jokes I didn't get and had sayings I didn't understand. At other times, the office was awkwardly quiet, the silence only broken by the sound of an air bubble rising to the top of the water cooler.

As far as I could tell, no one had any enemies that they knew of, until of course those cyclic days when Madeline would invite a reporter into her office and close the door. One by one we would lower our heads, sensing we were about to lose another solider from the battlefield. We came to think of the simple act of that closed door as the tabloid guillotine, ready to behead another reporter at any moment.

The industry itself was structured on a well-defined hierarchal scale. There were distinct levels of seniority on the tabloid pen. Madeline reigned somewhere on the cap while the rest of us clung to the sides of the pocket clasp for fear of sliding onto the page and smudging the ink. Above the LA bureau chief was the Florida staff. That team consisted of a cluster of executives who generally communicated through the chain of command. Never once did I meet the faces behind those ominous voices, nor did I ever visit the headquarters in Boca Raton. To this day, it remains a corporate Neverland, where people dream that someday, they too might be able to fly away from the tabloids to become respectable writers.

Our brave Peter Pan was Trenton Freeze, whose name was at the top of the masthead with the unpretentious title of editor. The man I had first encountered through CNN secretly gained the nickname of "Freezy" among the rest of the staff. Most considered him to be king of the tabloids, with a history linking him to leadership at the *National Enquirer* and some of England's best-known dailies. Trenton Freeze was the equivalent of our feared father, seldom pleased with the work we produced.

There were, however, a handful of memorable times that his calls were patched through to my personal line. Always notified prior to his calls, I was coached on how to respond to his comments.

"Excellent work on your latest cover story," he would say. "Keep it up." There would be an awkward silence, before a burst of "Cheerio!" would precede the final hang up.

Sandwiched between Freezy and Madeline was the Florida-based managing editor, Cathy Tidwell. Again, I had very little direct contact with Cathy, although it was significantly more than I had with Trenton Freeze. Occasionally I would receive one of her "not too bad" phone calls, accompanied by a pep talk to keep me going in the game. I never met Cathy or saw a photograph of her.

I constantly felt as if I had fooled everyone, successfully turning out stories with circumstantial luck rather than skill. My fear of the tabloid guillotine kept me furiously typing away. The turnover among reporters was staggering. Some entered the doors only as hopeful prospects. Others were viewed as potential contributors hired to help the magazine grow. As one of the few who had survived the critical first week at *Globe*, I was granted access to the secret vault of tabloid journalism.

Each day, I was handed more responsibility and given more insider tips. The fact that information was being revealed gradually seemed to cut down on the overall shock value of the industry's tactics. My job was saved by a series of column fillers, on everyone from Roman Polanski to Alyssa Milano. Column fillers were short, three-inch reports based on longer articles that had appeared in other periodicals.

By the close of the second week, I had been given a proper tour of the file room. I had also been introduced to *Globe*'s research tools and data banks, such as Faces of the Nation. I was taught how to "run faces" by plugging in celebrities' Social Security numbers to access credit reports, former addresses, and lists of phone numbers of their neighbors and relatives. The starting point for all data gathering was getting the correct Social Security numbers for celebrities. All it took for reporters was a written request to Cathy Tidwell at *Globe*'s Florida office.

We were never told how she obtained those numbers and, at the time, I was too naïve to ask. Rumor had it that *Globe* paid $150 for each Social Security number. The identity of that source was top secret and we never learned how Cathy worked her magic.

In time, the other reporters started to accept me as a colleague. They began to casually drop phrases that were common to tabloid insiders. These included terms such as "pulling numbers" and "running plates." When throwing a term my way, reporters were always careful to protect the secrets behind their surreptitious tactics.

With the assistance of paid sources at various phone companies, *Globe* could pull numbers. It was then a routine matter of using celebrity phone bills and viewing the numbers they had been calling to gain insight into their private lives. "Running plates" meant contacting the Department of Motor Vehicles to determine car ownership and driving records. Eventually I was asked to perform the dreaded "door-stepping," which involved showing up unannounced on the front steps of celebrities' homes.

There were other commonly used phrases flying around the office, such as "leads" and "cold calls." The latter term referred to unsolicited tips from unconnected sources who would spontaneously call *Globe*. All of this information would appear on the source sheet that the editors required for every article. These sheets, seen only by editors and *Globe*'s legal department, documented the actual names of informants who might appear in articles as "an insider" or "a pal." The source sheets were faxed to Florida separately from the related article in order to protect the identity of our sources.

As the newcomer on board, I envied the bulging Rolodex of my co-workers. They regularly turned in leads from their roster of paid contacts. Lacking sources, I lacked stories. Hungry for another byline,

I asked Sharmin to patch through any new call-ins to my line.

"I'm supposed to pass them out equally," she replied. "But, considering you're new, I guess I'll make an exception." Smiling, she added, "By the way, bribes are accepted."

Flipping through a stack of new magazines, I anxiously waited for the phone to ring. *Globe*'s phones had remained eerily silent due to increased suspicion of the tabloid's following the recent death of Princess Diana. The only exception was the occasional angry call from someone whose loathing of the tabloids had intensified over the past weeks.

Unfazed, Sharmin would reply to those callers with a polite, "Well, thank you for those kind words. I'll be sure to pass on your message."

Between the dual curse of silent phones and my lack of sources, I feared that I was about to lose my job. With mortgage payments to be made, I dreaded the possibility of being unemployed. Fortunately, a lead sheet from Madeline was waiting on my desk the following morning. Lead sheets were single pages that listed story ideas in the form of potential headlines. They could either be submitted for approval from reporters to editors or could be assigned by the editorial staff. This one read, "Patsy Ramsey auctions off JonBenet's pageant dresses." Across the lead sheet Madeline had written, "Check it out."

Madeline suggested I start by calling Christie's auction house. Lacking guidance on how to proceed, I independently decided to play the role of an interested shopper.

"I would like to buy all of JonBenet's dresses and donate them to charity," I said, creating my first fake identity.

Grudgingly checking the system, the woman on the line informed me that the dresses of a murdered child would probably never be auctioned at Christie's. It had seemed a bit odd to be inquiring about such a lead. But then again, almost anything was possible at *Globe*. Although that lead sheet turned out to be a false tip, it introduced me to the world of phone scams.

Note:

At the time of writing, JonBenet's killer remains unidentified. Patsy Ramsey passed away from cancer in 2006.

CHAPTER 2

William Shatner's Uninvited Wedding Guest

As the baby of the tabloid family, I had crawled out of the playpen of gossip onto the wobbly stage of reporting. My efforts would end in taking either my first successful step or a humiliating tumble.

I was still branded as a tagalong reporter, assigned to work with tabloid veterans. Despite this, I began to see lead sheets as games to win rather than stories to investigate. Prior to joining the tabloids, I had seldom noticed the row of celebrity magazines in checkout lines. Now, I started to see them as the faceless competition I longed to defeat.

Even my senses started to change. My eyes adapted to scanning rooms in search of targets, while my ears tuned into trigger words that carried me toward untold secrets. In restaurants, I learned how to block out my dinner conversation to plug into the one beside me. Gossip was everywhere and I wanted it. I didn't actually care about scandal, or celebrities for that matter. I was simply addicted to getting leads.

Hollywood's core is not the films themselves, but rather the faces that make up those films. Naturally, this breeds celebrity exposure, and with exposure comes fame, and with fame comes *Globe* magazine. This was my job.

Contrary to common belief, tabloid reporters do not sit around a conference desk creating a list of lies for an upcoming issue. Printing scandalous accusations has huge legal risks, even if those accusations are proven true. When going up against power, fame, or fortune, the judicial system tends to side with the best-known faces. As reporters, this reinforced the necessity to cover our backs.

The tabloids do not create stories—they create headlines. Given the nature of our business, legal letters and threats came across our desks on a regular basis. Since legal action was seldom taken, we proudly tacked these letters on our bulletin boards like progress reports, right next to our favorite tabloid clippings.

Living in a Hollywood-hungry environment, it is nearly impossible to stand in the checkout line without flipping through the pages of a celebrity publication. We all do it. It is cheap shock value at its best, like driving past a car accident without the guilt of being caught staring at tragedy. We follow celebrity success, but that's not what we want to read about. Naturally, we enjoy attending their films, listening to their music, or watching them on TV. What we really want to know, however, is that celebrities are just as human as we are. Although they may look flawless in front of the camera, we want to see them first thing in the morning on a bad hair day. We want to see them before and after plastic surgery. We want to see them fall in love, get married, and file for divorce six months later.

The majority of celebrities cannot seem to lead normal lives. Oddly enough, most of us envy them, and at some level, we take a demented satisfaction when they fail, whether in marriage, in fame, in finances, or in appearance. *Globe*'s cover price is an inexpensive way to feel better about ourselves. Our own failures become minimized when we see celebrities cry under the spotlight.

One of *Globe*'s most successful issues featured a close-up of Goldie Hawn's cellulite thighs. From that point forward, reporters were sent on a quest for anything that was Goldie-related. Admittedly, the tabloids sensationalize stories to the point that a tear becomes a "sob" and an insult becomes a "vicious battle." In every tabloid story, however, there is a nugget of truth, although sometimes one must dig deeply to find it. *Globe*'s legal department required that high-risk articles be supported by three sources. They either had to have eye witnessed the event or be somehow connected to the celebrity. The greater the potential legal risk, the more solid the support needed to be. Our sources were often subjected to lie detector tests, recorded interviews, signed contracts, and background checks. *Globe* was legally protected by the language in the source agreement, which provided that the source would agree to testify in court should a legal challenge occur.

Most of our sources received payment for their information, generally within a month of publication. On many occasions, we independently uncovered stories without any tips from outside sources. Being a rookie without established contacts, I had to uncover stories on my own if I was to stay in the game. The greater the challenge, the more I was willing to risk. After a few mundane research assignments, my editor felt it was time to lift me out of the playpen and let me learn to crawl.

I was ready for my first celebrity wedding.

"How do you feel about going to Santa Barbara this weekend?" Madeline asked. The distance from LA was a mere two hours, but at that stage in my career, I considered anything outside of the office as a business trip.

"Lauralee Bell is getting married to Scott Martin this weekend." She paused and waited for my response. "You do know who Lauralee Bell is, don't you?"

I was ashamed to admit I didn't recognize her name.

"*The Young and The Restless,*" she answered, even before I had a chance to respond.

She explained that my assignment was to accompany Karen Glaser, *Globe*'s reporter who specialized in covering soap opera stars.

"Now look, don't try to do anything at the wedding. I just want you to watch Karen and see how a skilled reporter handles the job. Take a few notes and try to get a feel for the business. Blending in is key in this sort of situation. You still might want to take a camera in case you can snap a shot on the outside."

She looked up at the clock and saw that it was 4:30. "Since you're going to be working all day Saturday, why don't you take the rest of the day off."

Grabbing a copy of *Soap Opera Digest* on my way out of the office, I spent the evening educating myself on the private lives of soap stars. That night I could hardly sleep, hoping that the techniques I was about to learn from Karen's three years of experience would gain me access to the team.

The following day, I drove to Santa Barbara early to check out the exact wedding location. Karen and I had arranged to meet two hours before the ceremony at All Saints-by-the-Sea Church. As I loaded my camera with film, I heard two small honks from a car behind me. It was Karen.

"Follow me," she said from her car window.

We headed to a Starbucks in Montecito, an upscale community near Santa Barbara. Dressed in a floor-length pleated skirt and white blouse, Karen calmly explained that we should both try to get a photo of the bride.

"I'll work from the inside and you stay on the outside," she ordered.

"Don't we have a photographer working this assignment as well?" I asked, a bit puzzled.

"I thought so, but I haven't heard any word from her yet," Karen said between sneezes.

"Do you have a cold?" I questioned.

She reached for a crumpled tissue and blew her rose-cornered nose. "Oh, well, yes. It's a chronic illness, more of a severe case of sinus infection. There isn't too much that can be done other than break my nose and clear my nasal passages. I'm still trying to get the surgery covered by insurance, but Madeline doesn't want to give me the time off." She sneezed again.

"Bless you," I said.

"Thanks . . . You know this nose thing doesn't bother me as much anymore. The only problem is that my watery eyes tend to blur my vision during stakeouts."

Cradling the cup with my hands, I blew into the steaming blackness. "Hopefully you won't sneeze during the wedding," I joked.

Ignoring me, she patted the corner of her nostrils and then sneezed again.

"I suppose we better take our places," she said in a nasal voice. "Good luck, and remember, lay low."

I parked my car at the back of the church, entered through the choir loft, and poked my head between the blue silk curtains. Rather than waiting outside as instructed, I thought that I might at least be able to divert attention away from Karen while she took pictures inside. This was my first real assignment and already I was breaking orders. Greed had taken control.

There was still an hour before the ceremony began and only a few guests had arrived. Shoving my camera into the base of my sleeve, I backed out of the choir loft, opened the side door, and walked straight toward the restroom. This was a typical Episcopal church, fitting the blueprint of many chapels where I had been before. Hiding in the handicap stall, I sat on the toilet for forty-five minutes until I heard the wedding music. Leaving the bathroom, I adjusted my floor-length, cream-colored dress and moved toward the sanctuary.

Pushing open the heavy wooden door, I spotted two ushers escorting members of the bride's family to their seats. Trailing closely behind the pack, I squeezed onto the end of a pew, fourth row from the back. There was Karen, two rows in front of me. We never made eye contact.

Eventually the "Wedding March" began and we all rose to our feet. Unfortunately, my visible location made me an easy target. Lauralee looked in my direction, and I smiled boldly as if we were long lost friends. I believe it was my confidence that caused her to smile back.

Other than the professional wedding photographer, not a single person was holding a camera. And then, I saw a small flash from the corner of my eye. In front of me, Karen had aimed and taken a shot. A woman seated beside her grabbed the camera and motioned Karen toward the exit. By now the bride was only halfway down the aisle.

Karen rushed toward the side door. Others around me took notice of her quick escape. "Imagine that," whispered a man beside me. "No respect for a person's privacy."

Turning to their songbooks, the entire congregation began to sing a hymn as instructed. Rather than the guilt I should have been feeling, the music brought flashbacks of Christmas pageants and Sunday-school plays. I felt as if I belonged. Had I been questioned, I imagine that I could have confidently defended my presence.

The ceremony lasted less than an hour, with a typical three-second kiss to seal the deal. The couple looked faultless, perfect molds replicated in the image of the plastic figurines perched on the third tier of a wedding cake. And then, my moment arrived. There they were, hand-in-hand, marching straight toward me down the aisle. Sliding the camera from my sleeve, I raised the lens and snapped a single shot. I knew I had nailed it. By that stage, everyone was focused on the bride and groom and cared less about a flash in the distance.

I was in no hurry to leave. I felt as if I had reached a position of importance among the chosen few. Row by row, guests trickled out of the church, commenting on how stunning the bride looked in her satin gown.

"Excuse me," said a voice behind me. There stood the same woman who had taken Karen's camera. Prepared to run if necessary, I clutched my purse firmly and took a step back.

"Do you know how to get to the reception?" The woman pointed toward her invitation, which read, "Rancho Carinoso Resort."

"It's easy, really," I said, taking out a pen. Having attended college in Santa Barbara, I knew the area well. On the back of her invitation, I drew a map from Santa Barbara to Carpinteria, where the reception was located.

"See you there," I said, shoving the pen back into my purse with relief. From my car I dialed Karen, who didn't seem overly enthused about spending her Saturday afternoon chasing soap stars to dinner parties.

"What do you think is the best way to get into the reception?" I asked, waiting for my orders.

"It's your call if you want to go or not," Karen replied between sniffles. "We've got the shot you took, plus the pictures taken by *Globe*'s photographer outside the wedding. There's really no need to push your luck. Soap weddings never run more than half a page."

"Okay," I said, rather disappointed to end the adventure so soon. "See you at the office on Monday then."

She sneezed. "See you."

As I started back toward Los Angeles, I decided on a whim to drive past the Rancho Carinoso Resort. It was only a short drive through town and perhaps I could snap a picture from the exterior. Perched on the hill was an enormous white tent surrounded by a fence. Security guards were stationed at each corner of the grounds, leaving only one entrance into the resort. The highly secured grounds also happened to be the location of a Westmont ball that I had attended two years prior.

As I approached the gate, the security guard asked for my name and ID.

"I'm Amy Meyer," I said, dropping the real name of a former Westmont student body president. "I'm ASB president of Westmont College in Montecito. We're planning to have our next formal event take place here and I'm scheduled to check out the facilities today."

He looked down at his list. "I don't see you mentioned anywhere here. Can you possibly come back tomorrow? There is a private party taking place this evening."

I shook my head as if there were no other option. "But our planning committee is meeting tomorrow," I whined. "Today is all I have."

Stepping away from the car, he spoke into his radio and waited for a static reply. "You've got five minutes," he said, pointing toward me with his radio antenna.

Parking my car, I walked directly toward the tent and approached a waiter who appeared to be in his early twenties. Dressed in a white uniform, he lowered his tray and offered me a glass of champagne.

"So what's on the menu?" I asked grabbing a glass.

"I believe we'll be serving beef tenderloin with a Cajun pepper crust and wild mushrooms," he said with a smile. "I'm not exactly sure about the wedding cake, but I can ask if you'd like." He gave me a look over. "May I ask, are you a friend of the bride or groom?"

"Both actually," I answered, quickly changing the subject. "Umm . . . do you know what type of music they are having tonight?"

"They have a band," he answered. "So, why all the questions?"

Sensing the waiter's suspicions, I walked toward my car and hollered back, "I'm just a curious girl, I guess."

That night I phoned Karen and told her everything I had seen. This gave her more than enough data to complete her article. On Monday morning, Madeline walked toward my desk and said, "I heard you did okay on Saturday."

I spun around in my chair, smiling as Madeline continued.

"If you're up for it, there's a big wedding coming up this weekend. Do you want to tag along? Some of our best reporters and photographers will be working the story. It might be good for you to see how a big operation comes together."

"Who's getting married?" I asked curiously.

"Well, do you want to do it or not?" she asked again, ignoring my question.

"Sure," I nodded. "I'll go."

Throwing a thick file onto my desk, she added, "Don't make any plans for the weekend. This assignment is top priority."

As she walked away, I opened the file and read the name—William Shatner. With little interest in science fiction, I had never watched an episode of *Star Trek* and had no idea why *Globe* was going to such lengths to cover a man best known as Captain Kirk.

The next day, freelance reporter Ronda explained, "People who read the tabloids are the same people who watch sci-fi." Ronda was in charge of the eleven-person team, which included her photographer husband, Jacques Pierre. Also included were pudgy Pete Trujillo, four British freelance photographers, and Sharmin. She was paired with photographer Frank Black as her pseudo date. Rounding out the team was Kaylee, the girlfriend of a photographer named Radford, and Adam Edwards from New York, with whom I was paired.

In preparation for the assignment, I headed to Rodeo Drive in Beverly Hills to pick up a Tiffany's box. "Sorry," the saleswoman told me, "but we cannot hand out boxes unless you intend to purchase something." Despite the fact I bought a small pickle dish, I convinced her to wrap it inside a box large enough to hold a punch bowl. I was determined to make a grand entrance.

Two hours before the scheduled ceremony, I met the *Globe* team in room 304 of the Hyatt Hotel, a little place we called "base camp." It was the closest we could get to the Pasadena mansion where the wedding was being held. Proud of my Tiffany's box, I walked into the room and introduced myself to the new freelance faces.

"Great minds think alike," said Ronda, pointing toward a stack of gifts wrapped in the signature turquoise boxes from Tiffany's.

"We filled our boxes with rocks," said Adam. "What's in yours?"

Embarrassed to ask how they had managed to obtain empty Tiffany's boxes, I responded under my breath, "A pickle dish."

"Don't be getting all starstruck on us now," scolded Sharmin.

"Listen up, everyone," interrupted Ronda. "We need a game plan. Shatner has tight security covering the grounds and already he's blocked off a pack of media from approaching the front gate. The wedding will be inside an enclosed tent far off from the main road. It's unlikely that a tele-photo lens will work. We don't have too many options."

"Pete, I want you and another photographer to head to the house and search for a lookout point. Try to shoot from the exterior and maybe we'll get lucky if the inside lighting is bright enough. Give us a call and let us know what you find."

The fact that Pete was a 350-pound Puerto Rican made blending in something of a challenge. Usually he was given in-house writing assignments while other staff members headed to the streets to do the ground work. On this occasion, Pete picked out his photographer of choice and they were off.

"Good luck," Sharmin said as she smacked Pete on the back. "Come back alive. My baby needs a daddy."

Eyeing the team, Ronda pointed toward her photographer husband. "Jacques Pierre, you stand near the front gate and get whatever you can. It won't be anything exclusive, but you might be able to capture the arrival of the *Star Trek* co-stars."

Adam stood to grab a Coke from the mini-bar. Still labeled as rookie reporters, Adam and I remained silent and waited for our cues.

"Okay, Adam," Ronda continued. "Sorry, but you'll have to go in as bait. Most likely you'll get caught, which hopefully will make them think we tried and failed. That's when we'll send in our next batch."

"What do you want me to do exactly?" he asked in a shaky voice.

"I don't care," she added. "Just try not to get arrested."

Turning to me, she directed, "Okay, Marlise, you go in the limo with Adam. You'll basically do the same thing he does, but just a few minutes later after the dust settles. Maybe you could circle the block a few times, so they'll think it's a new limo."

Though entirely confused, I nodded as if I understood. By now Sharmin was busy unwrapping the complimentary chocolates that rested on the pillow. Pointing toward her, Ronda ordered, "Then Sharmin and Frank will go in as a couple."

"Pairing me with Frank is the worst form of prejudice," Sharmin joked, referring to the fact that they were the only African Americans in the group. Between mouthfuls, she added, "I'm charging overtime for this sort of work."

Ignoring Sharmin, Ronda scribbled a few notes on her legal pad. "Okay, let's start with that and see how it goes."

While several of us studied maps of the area, others flipped through Shatner's personal file and discussed the probable guest list. Suddenly Ronda's phone rang.

"Hello?" she answered. "Pete? What's going on?"

The room fell silent as we all impatiently waited for an update.

"Well, I guess there isn't too much else you can do then," she said into the phone. "Stay put and call if you get anything."

Ronda hung up and quickly briefed us. "Pete has bribed some construction workers next door to the wedding. Apparently the neighbor's roof is being repaneled, so they are letting us shoot pictures from the top level. The only problem is that the lighting is much too dark. Pete says the only way we can get a good photo is if our camera shoots at the exact same time as a another flash goes off in the tent. To make matters worse, we'll be shooting through plastic windows."

Everyone looked discouraged.

"Adam, you and Marlise are up," Ronda added. "Call me from the limo."

"Or from jail," Sharmin hollered, as we walked out the door. "Remember, you only get one call."

Adam and I didn't say a word until right before we reached the red carpet. "What are you going to do?" I asked nervously.

"Wing it," he answered.

Crawling toward the back of the limo to hide, I watched as a pack of paparazzi moved toward us. Adam reached for the door handle to open it himself.

"No!" scolded the driver in a whisper. "You're doing my job. Now they'll know you're not an invited guest."

Even before Adam made it down the red carpet, he was turned away by security. After a brief exchange with a guard, Adam awkwardly handed him his wedding gift and returned to the waiting limo.

"What happened?" I asked, shocked by the brevity of his absence.

"Those people are so freaking intimidating," Adam explained. "They threatened to arrest me for trespassing, so I told them I was a *Star Trek* fan and wanted to deliver a gift."

"Good thinking," I said. Adam's hands were shaking. Tossing him a water bottle from the mini-bar, I leaned over the seat and told the driver, "Let's drop Adam back at the hotel. We'll circle the block and I'll try and get in the same way."

En route, I phoned Ronda to give her the update. I could hear Sharmin singing in the background, "Go, white girl! Go, white girl!"

The limo circled the block one last time as we waited behind the string of Porsches, Mercedes, and luxury SUVs. Moments before we reached the front of the line, I reapplied my lipstick and flipped my head back and forth to give my hair a tousled look. The driver looked puzzled.

"And what do you want me to do?" he asked.

"Stand by until you see what happens," I begged. "If I get in, try and stay in the area in case I have to make a run for it."

Parking briefly in front of the mansion, the driver walked to my side of the car and opened the door. It was still light enough to justify wearing sunglasses. Pushing them over my eyes, I adjusted my black skirt and reached for his outstretched hand. As gracefully as possible, I stepped out of the limo one extended leg at a time, just as I had seen celebrities do at the Oscars®. Focusing directly on the security table, I avoided eye contact with everyone. This was my first experience of walking the red carpet.

Suddenly a series of flashbulbs went off around me. "Who is she?" photographers were asking each other.

I overheard one of them reply, "I don't know. Probably no one, but shoot her just in case. We can always caption her as 'a friend of the bride.'"

Without removing my sunglasses, I placed my Tiffany's box on the table and peered over the guest list, which consisted of fifty elite names.

"And you are . . . ?" asked the security guard.

"Martha Klad," I said boldly. "I'm the daughter of the minister. My dad's doing the wedding."

The similarity between my true identity and my fake one somehow helped to boost my confidence.

He looked down at his list. "Mmm . . . . I don't see your name here."

"Call Nerine Kidd," I said, dropping the bride's name. "She's the one who invited me during yesterday's rehearsal."

He spoke into a walkie-talkie and we both waited for the static answer.

"Wait," I offered. "I have my invitation back at the hotel. Will that help?"

He smiled politely and assured me that it would be enough to get me in. Somehow I had to escape before security could check my ID. Walking away, I hoped that my shaky legs would make it back to the waiting limo.

"I told you she's a nobody," mumbled one photographer as I passed by.

Back in the limo I reluctantly called Ronda to tell her of my defeat. "Sorry I didn't get in," I apologized. "But I did manage to get two names off the guest list for Sharmin and Frank to use for their identities."

"Brilliant," she said, enthusiastically. "I'll send them to the hotel lobby to meet you."

As I stepped from the limo, I heard Sharmin barking orders at Frank. "Just because we're supposed to look like a couple doesn't give you a license to fondle me. Hand-holding is about as far as I'll go with this disguise."

Ignoring her comments, Frank shook his head and started loading a roll of film.

"Okay, here are the names I got for you to use," I said, slipping them a piece of paper. "I'll see you guys back at the hotel."

Pushing her way past me, Sharmin stepped into the limo and sprawled out on the leather seats. "Ohh . . . just look at this. Nobody told me this bar was stocked," she said, reaching for a bottle of champagne.

"Move over here," Frank snapped. "How the hell are we supposed to look like a couple if you don't let me get close to you?"

"Hell no," Sharmin said, as the driver slammed the door.

"Good luck!" I hollered through the tinted glass.

Returning to the hotel room, I joined the others who were waiting impatiently for new developments. Suddenly the door flew open. There stood Pete and his photographer, both completely out of breath and dripping with sweat.

"I'm not cut out for this," Pete said reaching for a can of soda.

"What happened?" Ronda asked in total shock. "I thought you were taking pictures from the neighbor's roof."

"We were, until security spotted our flash," Pete explained. "That stupid thing went off by accident. The security ran toward the house, hollering into their radios for backup and police support. There are cops everywhere."

Pulling back the curtain to peer out, Adam asked, "They didn't follow you here, did they?"

Pete was still panting heavily from his two-block run. "No, we hid in the bushes and then saw our limo driver pass. He had just dropped off Frank and Sharmin. You should have seen us, running down the street behind the limo, with our arms flailing in the air. We're lucky we didn't get caught."

"So what's going on with Sharmin and Frank?" Ronda asked. "I don't want to call them in case someone hears their cell phones ringing."

"They got in," Pete said laughing. "It was hilarious to see those sworn enemies holding hands."

Just then, Ronda's phone rang. "Sharmin, where are you? . . .Calm down . . . Just stay put and we'll send the driver to come find you."

Slamming down the phone, Ronda said, "We're dropping like flies. Sharmin and Frank got busted. When the actual guests with those names showed up, they found their seats already taken. Security called the police and Sharmin and Frank had to make a run for it. They're hiding in the bushes, but they don't know exactly where they are."

Dialing the number of the limo driver, Ronda held up her hand to quiet us down. "Hello?" she said into the phone. "Yes, this is Ronda. I need you to find two of my reporters somewhere in the bushes. Yes, that's right, the bushes. I have no idea, really. Yes, I realize there are police everywhere. Just find them!"

Ronda dropped her face into her hands. "Okay. Who's up?"

Radford Thayer, one of the freelance photographers, stood to his feet. "Kaylee and I will give it a go if you like," he said in a thick British accent. "Any bright ideas?"

Radford stared around the silent room. No one had any suggestions and his little blonde girlfriend looked terrified.

"Smashing," he said sarcastically. "What a bunch of useless tossers. We'll give you a buzz if we need your help."

Taking his girlfriend's trembling hand, he nearly dragged her from the room.

Five minutes later Ronda's phone rang. "Sharmin . . . What do you mean the limo keeps passing you by? Can't you give the driver a signal or something? Take out a lighter and flick it as he passes. I'll call him back to give him the signal. Do you know where you are? Well, what do the bushes look like? . . . No Sharmin, I'm sure it's not poison ivy. . . . Yes, I know 'the 5-0' are everywhere. Just stay put, the driver's on his way."

Ronda's phone rang again between her call to the driver and telephone scoldings from the LA and Florida editors. With a discouraged expression, she turned to the group and explained, "That was Radford. A reporter from *Star* recognized him from a story they had worked on together. She tipped off security and Radford and Kaylee never made it down the red carpet."

There was silence. "We're all going to get lashings on Monday for missing this story," said Pete quietly.

"Nobody here answers any cell phones until I figure out how to handle the editors," Ronda ordered.

Suddenly the door flung open. It was Sharmin and Frank, looking rather frazzled. "What's a black woman got to do to get rescued around here?" Sharmin slammed the door. "For thirty minutes you people forgot about me. Do I have to remind you about the abolition?"

Frank reached over to pick a leaf from Sharmin's hair. "Don't you touch me," she said, pulling back.

"What did I do, woman?" he asked, laughing.

Sharmin shook her head in disgust. "Oh, please! How dare you caress my back inside the wedding ceremony? That was not part of our deal."

Pete started laughing hysterically.

"See what happens when you try to lead an honest life?" Sharmin asked of no one in particular. "I'm just a law-abiding secretary with benefits. It's bad enough my baby's daddy is in jail."

There was a knock at the door as Jacques Pierre entered. Tossing a finished roll of film on the bed, he shook his head and said, "Nothing special there. All I got were a few shots that the rest of the media will also have."

Ronda looked around the room at *Globe*'s beaten eleven. "Okay," she said, defeat in her voice. "I'll call Florida and tell them the bad news."

"No, wait," I said, standing up. "I'm going back in."

The *Globe* team looked at one another in disbelief. "Who let Lois Lane into the room?" Sharmin joked.

I didn't laugh.

"Are you sure about this?" Ronda asked, covering her smirk with a quick sip from her soda.

"Sure, I'm sure," I said, trying to convince myself. "But I'm going to need to change my outfit. Can someone call room service and order me a wine glass? I'm also going to need a camera, a tape recorder, and a pair of high heels." I shortened my skirt by rolling it up at the waist, pulled up my hair, and started to apply heavy mascara.

While I was putting on my makeup, Sharmin commented, "You don't have to do this, you know?"

Smacking my glossed lips together, I applied one last coat of lipstick and threw the tube into my purse. "Is that concern and compassion I sense in your voice?"

"Now, don't get all 'Ebony and Ivory' on me," Sharmin replied while stashing a bottle of hotel lotion in her pocket.

As I walked down the hall, the rest of the team waved goodbye as if I were heading off to school. Sharmin called out as a parting shot, "If you see my baby's daddy, tell him I'm still waitin' for child support."

Twenty minutes later I was squatting in the bushes outside William Shatner's wedding tent. Admittedly, it was an odd tactic, but it worked. Within seconds, security had spotted me.

"Excuse me, Miss," said a guard. "You might want to use the toilet inside. There are all kinds of paparazzi out tonight. What are you trying to do? Get yourself on the cover of *Enquirer*?"

Gazing up toward his offered hand, I let out an awkward giggle.

"Sorry," I said, slurring my words. "Can you point a lonely lady in the right direction?" With my tilted glass in one hand and my stilettos in the other, I stumbled toward the bridal tent pretending to be a tipsy wedding guest. My guise worked. The security guard personally ushered me toward the reception as he spoke into his radio, "West grounds are clear."

By this stage, the ceremony was long over and guests were mingling throughout the house and the adjoining tent. Blending into a crowd of fifty was not an easy task, especially considering the age gap between the guests and me. Never lingering too long in one place, my strategy was to look as if I had a clear destination.

Between the house and the tent was a small area where several potted plants and floral arrangements had been placed. There I stood, sheltered behind a vase of orchids hoping that no one would notice my presence. Quickly slipping the miniature camera from my sleeve, I held it waist high and rapidly started snapping shots. Knowing I could not use a flash under the circumstances, I hoped at least one of my pictures would be useable. My hands were shaking uncontrollably as I walked into the reception tent. Hoping to remember as many details as possible, I made a mental list of the menu. "Lobster, grilled vegetables, stuffed mushrooms, asparagus . . ."

Light-headed, I was on the verge of fainting. I was terrified that if I kept moving, it might result in a call to the paramedics. Already I could imagine the headlines: "Novice Reporter Passes Out at William Shatner's Wedding." Back-pedaling, my knees hit the base of a chair and I collapsed like a rag doll. I started hyperventilating near the wedding cake. I had to get out.

"Honey, let's go already," called a woman from the back of the room. "I'm so exhausted and my feet are killing me."

"Okay," answered a familiar voice. "Let me just find my suspenders."

Turning slowly in my chair, I glanced up and saw Captain Kirk looking me straight in the eye. I stared blankly at the *Star Trek* legend, realizing that my worst nightmare was playing out in front of me.

"That is, of course," he said, still staring at me, "unless you want them?"

It was obvious that he knew that I did not belong there. Here I was, inside his very private wedding reception, which was accessible only to close friends and family. In my panic, I had mistakenly sat down at the head table and was now perched on the groom's chair, of all places.

"Why would I want your suspenders?" I said in a quaking voice.

"Well, you're sitting on them." Reaching beneath me, he snapped the suspenders toward him like a bungee cord. Suddenly the bride appeared behind him.

"Darling, the guests are waiting for us to cut the cake." She grabbed him by the hand and pulled him into the small crowd.

"Hey," he called back to where I was sitting. "Come here."

Letting go of his bride's hand, he walked toward me. Ignoring him, I backed away from the table as fast as my legs could move. Panic-stricken by now, I realized that if I stopped, I would be arrested. Ducking under the plastic tent wall, I sprinted through the rose garden and ran toward the waiting limo. Until then, I had always thought that getaway cars existed only in movies.

The door flew open. "Quick, get in!" The *Globe* eleven were packed inside the limo like sardines.

"We all decided to come along for moral support," said Pete.

"And for the free booze," added Sharmin, passing out wine glasses.

"Does *Globe* pay for dry cleaning?" I asked, examining my torn threads. "I just sacrificed my body in a thorn bush for sci-fi fans."

Sliding the camera out of my sleeve, I handed the film over to Ronda and apologized in advance for the shaky photos. No one seemed to care. They considered me the hero of the hour. Oddly enough, two out of the ten pictures I had taken were actually good enough for publication.

"Pop the bubbly," Pete declared. "We've got ourselves a tabloid prodigy!"

Note:

William Shatner's third wife, Nerine Kidd, accidentally drowned in the pool of their Studio City home on August 9, 1999. Shatner married his fourth wife, Elizabeth Anderson Martin, on February 13, 2001.

CHAPTER 3

The Real Star Wars

Two weeks had passed since the Shatner wedding and things were changing at *Globe*. I could sense it the moment I pulled into the underground parking garage. Pushing the red button, I snatched the parking ticket as it spat out from the machine. Before the arm gate had completely lifted, I peeled out and listened as the song on my radio faded into static. Submerging from level P1 to P2, I sang the lyrics as far as my memory would take me before giving up and just humming the melody.

Whizzing past a shimmery string of cherry Porsches, I spiraled out of the VIP zone and entered the land of Toyotas, Hondas, and Volvos. My 1971 convertible Karmen Ghia fit nowhere in this club. Lost somewhere between comfort and reliability, my tinfoil gumdrop of automotive character had a tendency to backfire—setting off car alarms—and leave oil puddles behind like an untrained puppy.

In the distance, I could make out the sound of a two-fingered whistle echoing in the garage. "Hey, stop," cried a voice. Glancing in my rearview mirror, I noticed the parking attendant running toward me. I slammed on the brakes and the Ghia hiccupped to a stop. Out of breath, the attendant reached for my door handle and asked me to step out of the car.

Over the chorus of beeping car alarms, I yelled, "Did I do something wrong?"

The attendant was fidgeting with my door handle. "Oh no," he replied, handing me an electronic parking card through the window. "Your company has authorized assigned parking for you on P2. In the future, you can just wave this card over the sensor rather than taking a ticket. Would you like me to park your car for you, Miss Kast?"

He knows my name. The parking guy knows my name! Good-bye P9 parking. Hello one more hit on the snooze button!

"Sure," I said, tossing him the keys. "Just so you know, she can be a bit moody at times." Motioning for him to back away, I threw my shoulder into the door and hung suspended for a split moment between my seat and the door handle. "Piece of cake."

It was 9:10 by the time I reached the office. Ringing the buzzer, I waved at the security camera and waited for one of Sharmin's sarcastic greetings.

She didn't disappoint me. "Tardiness equals grounds for termination," she said through the speaker.

Passing the glass walls of Madeline's office, I lifted my workbag above the level of the window blinds, hoping she would not notice that I was arriving late.

"She can see your feet, Einstein," Sharmin reminded me.

"I realize that," I whispered. "But maybe she'll think I'm going back and forth to the file room."

"Good morning, Marlise," Madeline called from behind her desk. "Glad that you could join us. I need to see you in my office."

Pointing at me, Sharmin mouthed, "Busted."

"Quick, take this," I said, shoving my bag at Sharmin. I grabbed a notepad and pen off her desk.

Unzipping my bag, Sharmin replied, "As caretaker of this property, I will not be held responsible for the loss of any stolen goods. . . ."

"Marlise?" Madeline yelled again.

"Yes, here I am," I said, shuffling into her office. Sitting down on the black leather chair, I assumed the writer-ready position and waited for her command.

"In this morning's editorial meeting, Trenton was discussing the Shatner wedding. He was particularly impressed with your determination on that assignment."

"Oh yes, well," I fumbled, "it was a team effort, really. You know the

Globe crew wore down the security so that by the time I went around—"

"We are prepared to offer you a full-time staff position," she interrupted. "The salary breakdown equals the standard day rate you are currently earning, plus benefits."

She paused as if waiting for some sort of response. Noticing my silence, she continued. "Nothing changes really, except that you will have a bit more security within the company." Sliding a two-page document across her desk, she directed, "Sign at the bottom."

Scanning over the legal jargon, I asked about specific hours.

"Well, we don't offer overtime, if that's what you're getting at. You're expected to keep a record of the extra hours accumulated outside of the basic forty-hour workweek. At some stage you can claim some of those hours as a day off if necessary."

I looked up, waiting for a translation.

"Sharmin will give you all the *Globe* equipment you'll need on the job. She'll also explain the expense reports. Make sure you keep your receipts for reimbursement."

I shrugged and mumbled an agreeable, "Okay."

Tapping the air with her manicured nail, Madeline repeated, "Sign, right there at the bottom."

Scribbling my signature on the document, I handed it back to her with a smile.

Madeline lifted her phone and punched two digits. "Sharmin, please assign Marlise a laptop, tape recorder, cell phone, office key, credit card . . . you know, the usual."

"I'll get right on it," I heard Sharmin respond through the phone and through the door. It seemed ridiculous to use an intercom system in such a small office.

"Follow me," Sharmin said, popping her head into our meeting.

"I've taken the liberty of ordering your business cards," Sharmin continued, as we walked through the office. "I've included your middle name: 'W-H-I-T-E-Y.'"

Rolling my eyes, I joked, "Sounds like reverse discrimination to me."

Handing me my LAPD Press Pass, she added, "I'm just warming up, girlfriend."

The phone rang. "Answer that, will you?" Sharmin ordered while fanning her hands. "I have to get back to drying my nails."

In my best Sharmin voice, I answered, "Thanks for calling *Globe*. How may I assist you?"

There was a long pause before a shaky voice whispered, "Yes, I have a tip about Carrie Fisher." Without revealing her identity, the caller claimed to have attended group therapy at a mental clinic with the actress. Just as I began to ask the when, where, why, and how, the nervous caller said, "I'm sorry, this was a huge mistake. I never should have called." Then she hung up.

I had no contact information or any way to follow up. This was not going to sit well with Madeline. The moment I told her the news, she ordered me to call Florida's research department.

"Go through the list of Carrie Fisher sources they'll send you," Madeline suggested. "Start by talking to her friends and family. Maybe they'll know what this is all about."

Oddly enough, the research team could only come up with one number related to Carrie Fisher. Pulled from the archives in Florida, it was an unidentified number scribbled on a piece of paper. The tabloid research department carefully maintained every scrap of celebrity information, no matter how insignificant it might appear on the surface. Knowing this, I decided to dial the unidentified number.

"Hello?" answered a soft, gentle voice.

Why does that voice sound so familiar?

"Hello," I stammered. "This is Marlise. I'm not sure if I have the right number. With whom am I speaking?"

"This is Debbie," she replied.

For a moment I was caught off guard, startled to realize that the unidentified number had led me to Debbie Reynolds, Carrie Fisher's mother. Shaking my head in disbelief, I regained my composure and continued. "Oh, hello. I'm looking for Carrie. Is she around?"

"No, not right now," she answered. "Who is this?"

"I'm a friend of Carrie's from the clinic," I said, spontaneously. "Umm, do you know where I can reach her?"

"Carrie is out shopping," she said. "But why don't you try her cell number? I think I have it here somewhere."

This was entirely too easy. It didn't seem like the appropriate time to tell Ms. Reynolds of my fondness for *Singin' in the Rain*. I thanked her and dialed the number she had given me.

Another familiar voice answered. "Hello?"

I decided to take the honest approach. "Carrie? Hi. You don't know me, but I hear you've been treated for depression at Cedars-Sinai's Thalian Clinic this past month and—"

"Who is this?" She demanded. "How did you get my number?"

"Actually, your mother gave it to me," I said, trying to gain her trust.

"What?" she yelled.

"Wait, please don't hang up," I begged, anticipating her next move. "I honestly want to know how you are. I mean, if what I heard is true, then perhaps you need someone who'll listen."

There was silence.

"Ms. Fisher?"

"Yes, I'm still here," she replied. "So what did you hear?"

Realizing that I was basically trying to verify the information we already had, I explained my purpose for calling, whom I worked for, and how I was trying to determine the truth behind her illness.

"Let's get one thing straight," she said. "I'm not a drug addict."

Carrie's unrelated denial came out of nowhere. I felt a need to defend myself. "I never said you were."

"Well, you said I was manic-depressive," she rebutted. "You probably assume I'm on drugs."

"Are you?" *Whoa, that was sudden. Think before you speak, Marlise.*

"Am I what? Manic or on drugs?" Our conversation was beginning to sound like "Who's on First."

I took another swing. "Both."

"Yes, I'm manic-depressive. Right now I'm taking lithium and a few other psychiatric medications for my bipolar disorder, but everything I'm taking is supervised."

My pen was dancing across the notepad. "Are things getting any better?" I asked.

"Not really." This conversation seemed frighteningly candid. "One of the side effects to my medication is weight gain."

I didn't know what to say next. "Everyone has issues."

"I know," she agreed, "but yours aren't magnified by the media."

"Think of it as a favor to your fans," I assured her. *What in the world am I saying?* "I mean, they are people who have the same, if not worse, problems than you do."

She laughed as I continued. "No, it's true. We sit around waiting for celebrities to succeed and then fail and then succeed again. It's your complex private lives that make us feel okay about our simple ones. Am I making any sense?"

I knew I was rambling but I couldn't seem to stop.

"Sort of," she said, hesitantly.

"Look," I continued. "I've got a fair amount of depression in my family. Knowing that we are both dealing with the same problem makes me feel, I don't know . . ."

"Not so alone," she completed.

"Exactly," I said.

"This isn't something new for me," Carrie continued. "I've been manic-depressive since I was twenty-four. And now I'm trying to explain all this to my daughter, who really doesn't understand what is happening to me."

I listened, scribbling notes on everything she was saying.

"Have you thought of traveling?" I suggested. "Sometimes it's good to get away. Physical separation and mental separation seem to go hand in hand. Most of the time when I travel, I return home a lot stronger than when I left."

She laughed again. "Marlise, how old are you?"

"Nearly twenty-two," I answered. "Why?"

"Well, you seem like a really sweet girl. If you want my advice, I suggest you get out of the tabloids before they poison your innocence."

"Oh, don't worry about me, Ms. Fisher," I told her. "There's not too much that can change me. I'm a pretty stubborn girl. Just ask my dad."

It was a quick good-bye. There was no "I'm a huge fan of your work" or "let's keep in touch." Carrie Fisher wished me luck and I did the same. Considering I was probably one of the few people who had never seen

Star Wars, I was more impressed with her honesty than with her celebrity status. I felt that Carrie and I were friends.

Well, sort of.

As I hung up, I envisioned becoming the revolutionary voice behind the tabloids, uniting celebrities and rag mags as honest partners. I walked into Madeline's office to tell her the news.

"So the caller was right," I said. "Carrie was in a psychiatric clinic."

"And where are you getting this information?" she asked doubtfully, removing her glasses.

"Carrie told me herself," I answered.

"What do you mean she 'told' you?" Madeline smirked.

"Well, I had her home number but she wasn't there, so then Debbie Reynolds told me to try Carrie on her cell. We just had a nice conversation about her depression and—"

"Fabulous," she interrupted, trying to seem unimpressed. "Type it up. Have it on my desk by the end of the day."

Sincerely moved by Carrie's situation, I wrote a completely sympathetic story, making it as optimistic as possible. Three days later, I showed the published article to my sister, Heidi. She had never read a tabloid magazine until I began writing for one.

"Check this out," I said, throwing the magazine on the foot of her bed.

Heidi's eyes scanned the headline: "*Star Wars* Beauty's Candid Revelations about Her Visit to Psycho Ward."

"This makes me so sad," she said reflectively. "For one thing, this is not your writing style. For another, how do you think Carrie Fisher is going to feel about this?"

"Well, I don't know," I said, snatching away the magazine. "Maybe you should ask her yourself."

As a newly published journalist, I was embarrassed to admit that the article did not contain my own words or my sentiments. The copy I had submitted was sympathetic toward Carrie and contained information we had discussed over the phone. The published article however, emphasized the extremes of her condition, using terms like "psycho ward," "crippling depression," and "mental illness." The editors had also inflated the story by adding that "Carrie's mental health deteriorated after hubby Bryan Lourd reportedly left her for another man." All of these words appeared over my byline.

The whole incident left me confused. In the back of my mind, I had always associated editorial changes with insufficient copy or correcting typographical errors. It had never occurred to me that editors would be so drastic in the way they changed the actual content of articles. After tabloid writers submit a story to the editors, they never see the copy again until it is in print. This was my twelfth published story in seven weeks and every one had been altered at some level. As the newcomer to the team, I dared not question this practice or complain for fear of losing my job.

My co-worker Patrick Kincaid explained that tabloid reporters never have control over their photos or headlines and that they are seldom given copy approval. Those decisions are left to the editors.

"Well, I don't think the editors like my writing," I told him, trying not to take it personally.

"Sure they do, luv," Patrick assured me. "They always make a little twist here and a little stretch there. They do it to the best of us." He grabbed the issue off my desk and rolled it into the shape of a tube. "If you want to survive in this business, you need to keep your head down and your chin up." He lightly tapped my head with the rolled up magazine. "Fighting back will only lead to an empty desk, my dear."

Patrick was right. If I was going to climb this corporate ladder, I had to separate myself emotionally from the story-behind-the-story. Celebrities had to become products rather than individuals. I had to grow a tough skin and learn to laugh in the face of rejection. I had to push away anyone who caused me to question what I was doing. I had to break down the righteous walls that had formed my spiritual edifice. This enticing new profession was twisting my morals. Born and raised in a house of integrity, I was now willing to lie and assume false identities to advance my career.

It was time to cut free of this ethical knot. It wouldn't be easy, especially considering that my conservative family had begged me to use my writing for good. I kept telling myself, it's just a job, right? This is not about moral convictions.

I was feeling torn between the devil and an angel jumping up and down on my shoulders. Inside, I pleaded with them. *Slap me with a wing or poke me with a rod, but for heaven's sake, somebody make a move.*

"Hey, daydreamer," Sharmin called from her desk. She awakened me from my mental slumber with the landing of a well-placed paper airplane. Unfolding the flaps, I read the memo, "Attention *Globe* employees: Show your Halloween spirit by wearing a costume to work. Your involvement is mandatory!"

Although Sharmin was just three desks away, I picked up the phone and dialed her extension. "This is a joke, right?"

Sharmin's laugh was in stereo. "Hell no. Come on, girl. Where's your Halloween spirit?"

"Sharmin," I whined. "I haven't dressed up since I was eight. I swear, if this is some kind of prank . . ."

"Don't worry," she assured me. "Everyone is dressing up. I give you my word."

The following morning I entered underground parking to find the attendant dressed in his regular uniform. His lack of a costume made me nervous.

"Good morning, Miss Kast," he said, offering me a packet of Halloween candy-corn. "I hardly recognized you as a blonde, and those glasses really suit you. What are you exactly, if I may ask?"

"Isn't it obvious?" I said, hiding behind the latest issue of *Globe* that I was using as a prop. "I'm an undercover tabloid reporter. By the way, have you seen my co-workers yet?"

"Don't worry," he said. "They dressed up, too. Just follow the debris."

I wasn't quite sure what he meant until I noticed a ring of straw just inside the elevator. As the doors opened onto the ninth floor, I followed the trail of hay that led directly to our office. Having forgotten my newly assigned key, I rang the buzzer and spoke into the intercom.

"Either Hansel and Gretel are inside there or else we have a shedding scarecrow," I said. "Which is it?"

"Just get your white ass in here," Sharmin said. "You're not going to believe this."

The first thing I noticed when I rounded the corner was that Sharmin was dressed in a Hawaiian grass skirt with a coconut shell bikini top.

"Like my nuts?" Sharmin asked enthusiastically, arching her back. "You would never guess they're hollow, would you?"

"But Sharmin," I said, pointing down at the hay remnants, "the foliage doesn't match your skirt. Who's the culprit?"

"Happy Halloween," Adam cheered as he wheeled his chair across the floor. Popping up, he twirled in his robe and announced his identity as the Pope.

"Ohh, forgive me father, for I have sinned," Sharmin said, smacking him on the rear.

"Where's Pete?" I asked, glancing at the straw leading to his corner of the office.

"I'm back here," a nasally voice said in the distance.

Sure enough, there was Pete, all three hundred fifty pounds of him, dressed as a tribal aboriginal. Wearing a straw skirt, he had a bone through his nose. He sported a feathered headpiece, and rattled his painted maracas in the air as I approached.

"Pete, it looks like a stall back here," I said, picking up the loose strands from his shedding skirt that had formed a ring around his chair. "Madeline is going to kill you."

He bopped me on the head with his maraca. "As leader of this tribe, I must gather gossip for the enemy chief. She has blown her conch from the one-oh-one freeway, demanding 'The Wedding Secrets of Will Smith and Jada Pinkett.'"

"What's your deadline, oh brave and fearless leader?" I asked, digging into his jack-o'-lantern candy bucket. Without waiting for me to make my selection, Pete reached for a Mini Snickers and peeled back the wrapper.

"The deadline was yesterday," he said, biting into the caramel chew. "Can you help me, Squatting Eagle?" Chocolate bits fell from his mouth onto the keyboard.

"You know I would, Pete," I said, blowing between the keys, "but I haven't turned in any leads this week."

"Look, if you help me with the Will Smith story, I'll give you one of my leads," he said.

"Are we talking A-list or B-list celebrities?" I negotiated.

"How does Brooke Shields sound?" he said between bites.

"I don't know," I hesitated. "Is lead swapping against company policy?"

"Please," he begged. "Madeline has me writing about everything from the flavor of Will Smith's wedding cake to the size of Jada's ring. The problem is I don't even have a source yet."

"Trick or treat," Karen sang, offering us a handful of Jolly Ranchers. She was dressed in a black robe with a mask and a pointed witch's hat. Sharmin followed close behind, snatching the candy cubes from Karen's open palm.

"Oh, look," Pete said. "It's Little White Fish and Saber-Toothed Boar, all the way from Land of Hemp. How goes your clan?"

Sharmin slid the rock candy into her mouth and pegged the wrapper at Pete. "I wouldn't be talking if I were you, oh Foolish and Chubby Hippo."

Circling around Karen, I complimented her witch's costume, with its warted nose and broomstick. In contrast to the blackness of her outfit, Karen's skin looked even more milky than usual.

"Does Madeline know you are borrowing her clothes?" I wondered aloud.

Just then the door flung open. "What the hell is going on in here!" It was Madeline, holding a leather briefcase and dressed in a cream business suit with matching flats. We looked so ridiculous; the five of us huddled around Pete's straw-littered desk, shoving Halloween candy down our throats.

"Imagine if Trenton Freeze walked in here right now," she screamed. "How on earth would I explain that this, yes this, is, in fact, my winning LA team?"

Adam adjusted his pope's hat and mumbled under his breath. "I guess she didn't get the office memo."

"And Pete, where is my Will Smith copy?" she yelled. "It's next week's cover story and I need it now. You haven't even started yet, have you?"

We all parted like the Red Sea as Madeline approached Pete's computer. His screen was blank.

"Marlise, I want you to work with Pete on this story. You dictate and Pete will type. Just write as fast as you can. I'll find the sourcing to back it up before deadline. I want it on my desk in forty-five minutes." This unrealistic deadline was typical of the way everything operated in hyper-mode at *Globe*. Tabloids were the bullets of journalism and the editors were the powder that made them explode. "Karen," Madeline continued, "I need soap opera catfights from you right away, and Adam, where are your leads? Sharmin, in my office, now. I need updates on this morning's calls." Clapping her hands twice, she added, "Everyone, get to work."

Just when Madeline was out of earshot, Sharmin whispered in her best slavery voice, "Yes suh, mastah suh."

The next forty-five minutes were crammed with creative writing at its worst. We found ourselves clinging to every wedding cliché imaginable. Candles, roses, a string quartet, and a tropical honeymoon getaway were generally used as the tabloid wedding script. Fortunately, Pete was a master at fabricating detailed copy without getting overly specific. In this case, even before Will and Jada had made an official engagement announcement, we were "reporting" on the details of the bride's Badgley Mischka beaded-silk gown, the five-carat diamond ring, and her elaborate bouquet of pink and white roses. We painted a verbal picture of Will planning a secret wedding rap and his son, Trey, holding the rings. We even included a list of wedding guests like Will's first wife, Sheree Smith, and Afeni, the mother of the late rapper Tupac Shakur.

Despite having overworked our creative license, we still didn't have even an imaginary location or alleged date for the ceremony. That's where Sharmin came in. As *Globe's* one and only African American, she was considered to be the magazine's ethnic specialist. The editors routinely pulled her away from her secretarial duties to cover such events as the BET Awards or Tupac's funeral. She complied of course, on the condition she would receive the going $200 day rate in addition to her regular salary.

"Pray for a miracle," Sharmin said as she passed Pete's desk. "I've got fifteen minutes to find the location of Will and Jada's wedding."

"Please tell me you have a source on this story," Pete begged. "We are wading in serious legal waters here."

"I wish I did," Sharmin hollered, entering the conference room. As she shut the door behind her, we knew she was about to embark on one of the many phone scams that took place within our company. Little did we know that she was phoning the home of Afeni Shakur, claiming to be Jada's personal assistant. Sharmin had been Tupac's most dedicated fan and knew every detail of the rapper's life, including the fact that he had dated Jada while attending Baltimore's School for the Arts. Only a short time had passed since Tupac's murder, giving Sharmin that much more to discuss during her sympathy call to his mother.

During their heartfelt conversation, Sharmin managed to ask two essential questions: Where should she send Tupac's memorial flowers from Will and Jada, and would Afeni be attending the couple's upcoming wedding?

Afeni candidly responded, "I would love to, sweetheart, but I just don't know if I'm going to make it to Baltimore five days after Christmas."

Afeni's comments gave us both the date and the location of Will and Jada's upcoming wedding. Sharmin walked out of the conference room and dramatically collapsed onto Pete's desk. "Bless her soul," she said, fanning her face with a magazine. "So many lives have been touched by the gift of her womb."

"What are you talking about?" Pete said, flicking at Sharmin's head like a bothersome fly.

"I'm talking about the woman who shoulda' been my mother-in-law," she said, sitting up. "Tupac's mamma."

Madeline came running out of her office. "Pete, Marlise, Sharmin," she yelled. "The copy should have been on my desk ten minutes ago."

Sharmin knew the only way to calm down our editor was to give her some good news. "Madeline," she said, distracting her. "You won't believe what I just found out. I got the place and the date of Will and Jada's wedding."

"That's great," Pete interjected. "But we still need a source to support the wedding details."

"Pick up line two," Madeline said, pointing toward me. "Nick's got sourcing for you."

Reporters seldom shared the identity of their sources with anyone else in the office. This was our way of maintaining a caller's anonymity. The only ones permitted to see the source sheets we submitted were the editors and members of *Globe*'s legal team.

One exception to this rule was Nick Royce, otherwise known as "Rent-a-Quote Man." As a longtime executive at Sony, Nick seemed to have a connection to virtually every major name in Hollywood. Sometimes it was just a "friend of a friend of a friend," but it was always close enough to pass the sourcing requirements. From three to six times per week, *Globe* paid Nick an assist fee for his credible sourcing on low-risk stories. Nick always came through in times of desperation. This happened to be one of those times.

"Nick, it's Marlise," I said picking up the phone. "What do you have for us?" As I scribbled down the names of his sources, I realized we were dealing with five degrees of separation.

"Let me get this straight," I said, tracing over the list. "These quotes are coming from Jada Pinkett to the woman who tailor-makes Jada's miniature shoes, to the shoe designer's sister, to you, and then finally to me."

"And don't forget to add Pete to that list," Nick laughed.

I looked over at Pete, who was too busy typing to notice the absurdity of this call. "Sorry, Marlise," Nick said. "But that's the closest I could get without putting myself at any legal risk."

"No, that's fine Nick," I assured him. "I'll make sure you get payment on this one."

Hanging up the phone, I looked at the computer screen and read the words, "The sexy couple is already planning a romantic get-awayyyyyyyyyyyyyyyuuuiiioiiooioipp. . . ."

There was Pete, fast asleep on the keyboard with his forehead rolling back and forth across the letters. "Pete, wake up," I said with a nudge of my elbow. He let out a little snore as he came to. Pete's sudden bouts of narcolepsy had become so commonplace in the office that eventually we viewed them as just another unfortunate habit.

"I have the sourcing," I bragged.

"Okay," he said, wiping a chocolate stain from the corner of his mouth. "Lay it on me. It's Jada Pinkett to whom?"

"Get ready for this," I said with a smile on my face. "We are sourcing this story back to Jada Pinkett's cobbler." Falling into hysterics, Pete began to type those very words onto the source sheet: "Source: Jada Pinkett's cobbler, reliable shoemaker to the stars."

Just then, Madeline came running over to Pete's computer. "Quick, send it to the printer," she demanded, pushing the print button herself. "I don't care if it's done. Florida is screaming for copy. We've got to give them what we have."

Oddly enough, Pete and I were never questioned about our dubious sourcing on the Jada story, and thankfully, neither was the cobbler. The success of that assignment led us to tag-team victory in several other stories. One was a piece titled "The Bedroom Secrets of Barbra Streisand and James Brolin," for which Nick Royce was once again our go-to source guy.

The Streisand article caught the attention of radio personality Howard Stern, who read our embarrassing text on air: "Sources say that Babs teases her hubby by dangling juicy mangos above his puckered lips." On several occasions, I would drive to work listening as Stern praised my latest exclusive on national radio. In an odd sort of way, I felt that my work was making an impact. Howard was killing airtime, *Globe* was landing publicity, and I was getting published. Even more important to me was the prospect of covering out-of-town stories.

Unlike my colleagues, I was primarily driven by the possibility of travel rather than by the promise of a paycheck. My ultimate goal was to land stories in tropical locations or in mountain resorts. Ironically, my first solo road trip took me back to my hometown.

"Marlise, pack your bags," Madeline ordered. "You're going to Monterey. We think Tim Allen had an affair there with Patricia Richardson."

Monterey wasn't exactly Maui, but it would do. Famous for golf courses, fried calamari, and the Lone Cypress Tree, it also happened to be the town where my family had lived for the past eleven years. Picking up the phone, I dialed my parents and told them to meet me at the Doubletree Hotel. I figured they could enjoy my vacant room while I was out chasing the story.

"No, Dad," I whispered into the phone. "You can't come on assignment with me. I don't even know what's involved yet." I didn't have the heart to tell him that I would probably be trespassing and might be participating in questionable activity.

My dad whispered back, "Mom wants to know if we should bring our swimmies?"

As it turned out, I only saw my parents for about twenty minutes. It was just long enough to check in and explain the rules. "Room service and movies are on *Globe*. Everything else is on your own tab. And whatever you do, do not pick up the phone."

As I retreated from the lobby, my dad saluted farewell as my mom blew a series of dramatic kisses into the air. Considering that this was my first assignment involving flight travel and an overnight stay, I felt an added pressure to deliver the story, but I was off to a bad start. Budget Rent-a-Car had refused to rent me a car after learning that I was under twenty-five. Embarrassed, I phoned Madeline and told her I was too young to rent a car.

"I don't have time to deal with that sort of issue," she told me. "Try all the companies in the phone book and get back to me." After a few calls, I managed to get approval from Dollar Rent-a-Car on the condition I obtained extra insurance coverage. It would have been easier to phone my parents and ask them for a ride, but my pride was at stake.

Now, in my rented Toyota, I took a deep breath and thought about the financial loss to *Globe* if I were to come back to LA empty-handed. The expense meter was already ticking. Later that afternoon, I met my parents at Carmel's Hog's Breath Inn, owned by Clint Eastwood. Dirty Harry Burgers served with horseradish and garlic potatoes left me with some serious indigestion and no game plan.

According to Madeline, *Globe* had received an extremely unreliable tip that Tim Allen had been seen in Monterey kissing his co-star, Patricia Richardson. That lead came from a cold caller who panicked and hung up before giving any specific details. Considering the growing popularity of Tim Allen's show, *Home Improvement*, the editors decided the rumor was worth probing.

I had no idea where to begin. Monterey was a tranquil fishing paradise, seldom visited by celebrities except for weddings and golf tournaments. My dad motioned for the bill while I peeled back the cellophane wrapper from a toothpick.

"May I take a look at the story file?" my mother asked hesitantly. Sliding the Tim Allen folder across the table, I watched as she began thumbing through article clippings and photographs. My mom seemed torn between trying to help her daughter and taking a stand against unethical conduct. I snapped my toothpick into bits while my dad chomped on ice cubes.

"Look here," my mom said, holding up a blurry photograph. "He's a race car driver. I bet he was here visiting the Laguna Seca racetrack."

Grabbing the photo from her hand, I took a closer look at the picture of Tim Allen's Mustang emblazoned with the number 75.

"Nice work, Sherlock," I said, giving my mom a high five. "So how do I get to the track?"

My dad drew a map on the table with his finger. "Stay on highway sixty-eight and you can't miss it."

Hugging them both good-bye, I wished they would tell me they were proud of me. They never did.

"Be safe," my mom said. "Good-bye." My dad told me to call when the story was done. By late afternoon, I had confirmed that Tim Allen had in fact visited Laguna Seca and attended the Skip Barber Racing School. The only problem was that the dates I was given did not coincide with the actor's alleged fling. Pretending to be a prospective racing school student, I had no problem hanging around the track, especially considering that the majority of employees were male.

"The three-day racing course will cost you around four thousand dollars," said one employee. Adjusting his greasy baseball cap, he slid me a company brochure and a two-page liability waiver. "Sign here."

"Oh no," I said, refusing his outreached pen. "I'm not ready to commit to the racing thing quite yet. I was just thinking about it as a way to someday overcome my fear of speed."

The explanation sounded rather plausible.

"Sign here," he repeated, placing the pen into my hand. "This is only a form stating that you won't sue us if a car flies out of the track and kills you on the sideline."

"I probably won't sue you if I'm dead," I snorted. *Stupid, stupid. Just sign the freaking form, Marlise!*

Taking a helmet off the counter, he put it on my head and said, "Good. Now follow me."

Before I had a chance to argue, we were inside the gated area. As he took his place behind the wheel, I found myself climbing into a cherry-red Dodge Viper.

"When I told you 'someday,' I didn't intend for it to be this soon," I yelled over the roaring engine.

"Don't worry," he responded, consolingly. "You'll be safe with me. Plus, this is a ninety thousand dollar car. If anything happens, it's my butt."

In less than three seconds, we went from zero to sixty and then punched to a solid 170 miles per hour by the end of the first lap. Orange cones, tire-walls, and checkered flags melted past my shaking head. I wanted out but couldn't seem to form the words between my elastic lips. Three laps seemed like a road trip. The end was my refuge. I felt queasy and lightheaded as the Viper hugged the final corkscrew turn. Almost as fast as we had peeled out, the car screeched to an abrupt stop.

"Want to go again?" he asked enthusiastically.

Wobbly and unbalanced, I slowly stepped from the death machine. "No, I think that about cured my fears. Thanks."

I leaned on the hood, pretending to look sexy when in reality, my equilibrium was completely off. Suddenly my cell phone rang. It was Madeline. "You need to come home," she said.

I am home.

"We just found out Tim Allen was taping his show during the exact dates of the alleged affair," she added.

I realized I was still wearing my racing helmet. "But I think I'm onto something, Madeline—"

"Marlise," she interrupted. "There is no 'other woman.' Don't worry, it's not your fault. These false leads happen all the time."

The driver pantomimed for me to unfasten the helmet.

"This job is all trial and error," Madeline explained. "You'll just have to get used to it."

Closing my phone, I handed the helmet to my driver. "Thanks for the ride," I told him. "I'll give the racing school some thought." He was gorgeous and I knew I would definitely be giving him some thought.

As he tucked the helmet under his arm, he asked if I wanted to meet up for a drink later that night. The timing could not have been worse.

"Believe me, I would love to," I said, sincerely. "But unfortunately, I have to fly home."

He nodded. "So, where's home for you?"

There was a slight hesitation, and then I told him the truth. "Los Angeles."

Returning to *Globe* empty-handed made me feel as if I had failed. By nature, I was accustomed to having something to show for my efforts and now I had nothing. I wanted a story. My need to belong to this empowering ring intensified more each day. My list of occasional sources was growing, but not as fast as it needed to. I wanted a consistent flow of leads. Other reporters like Patrick Kincaid and Karen Glaser seemed to be on the phone the better part of each day, screening calls and checking out tips from their sources. When I asked Patrick how he had created such a solid group of confidants, he told me that it takes a good deal of money to get such a following.

"Entertain," he told me. "Entertain everyone you can. Target bartenders, security guards, nannies, family members, anyone you think might be connected to a celebrity. Treat them to a martini. If you think they'll take the bait, hand them your business card. If you sense any hesitation, keep them as 'friends' and never tell them what you actually do."

"This method must cost you a fortune," I said, eyeing Patrick's three-piece suit.

"Oh, *Globe* picks up the tab," he said, fumbling in his drawer. Pulling out a manila envelope, he opened the flap and emptied a mound of receipts onto his desk. "This is one of the only perks in this business. It's called 'checkbook journalism'—everyone gets paid."

The idea of including alcoholic beverages on my expense report somehow seemed corrupt.

"Come on," Patrick continued, sensing my hesitation. "The tabloids have an editorial budget of fifteen million a year. If they can pay O.J.'s maid eighteen thousand dollars for a measly interview, then they can bloody well pay for your margarita on the rocks."

That night I decided to give source-shopping a try. After all, LA was my new home, and so far, there was very little I knew about the city. Considering that most celebrity sightings took place in Hollywood, I figured Sunset Boulevard would be the best place to start. The only question was, who would be my partner in crime?

My sister Heidi was busy feeding her cells at UCLA's biochemistry lab. She swore midnight was the best time to research the gene phospho-choline. Her latest discovery was that "cytidylyltransferase (CT) encodes the rate-controlling enzyme in the phosphatidylcholine biosynthesis pathway." That probably meant that she would not be able to proofread my latest tabloid feature, "Pill-Popping Demi's Marriage on the Rocks."

Realizing Heidi wasn't available, I picked up the phone to call Sharmin. Her first question gave me an instant answer. "You think they'll let my baby into that nightclub?" My search for a cohort was not going very well. The majority of my friends were still living in Santa Barbara and no one was willing to drive to LA on such short notice. Heidi suggested that I ask our neighbor Manuela Perez to go with me.

With wide, brown eyes and spindly legs, Manuela reminded me of a fawn. Based on her daring wardrobe, it appeared that she stayed perpetually ready for a night on the town. Without any hesitation, Manuela accepted my invitation to Billboard Live, a three-storey nightclub I had seen on Sunset Boulevard. As arranged, I knocked on her door at exactly 10:30.

"Hello," she said, handing me a glass of wine. "Come on in. I'm almost ready." Manuela was Peruvian, moved like honey, and had skin as smooth as butterscotch. Despite her colorful appearance, my eyes were drawn to Manuela's exposed belly button. Her abnormally large outtie had an uncanny resemblance to a wad of half-chewed gum. Dressed from head to toe in lavender, she was wearing skintight pants that flared at the ankle like miniature Eiffel Towers. Completing her outfit was a halter-top adorned with sequins and feathered shoulder straps.

I was dressed in brown.

"Let's give you a little color," she said, grabbing my hand as we ran up the stairs. We were like preteens playing dress up. Fortunately, I couldn't fit into her size three clothes and I refused to wear any of her stilettos.

"Weak ankles," I explained, pointing to my surgery scar. I was too embarrassed to tell her that it was the result of a recent skateboarding accident.

"How about these?" she asked, tossing me two balls of compacted jelly. There, in the palm of my hand, sat two perfectly formed silicone breasts.

"They are only a C cup," she added. "I figured the D might look unrealistic." The warm mounds looked frighteningly natural. I placed them nipple side up on the bed and excused myself to wash my hands.

"I've been thinking about getting implants," she continued. "These are sort of like training boobs."

This was fast becoming an uncomfortable one-way conversation. "Umm, Manuela . . . the guest list closes at eleven," I said awkwardly. "Otherwise we'll have to pay the fifty dollar cover charge."

In one swoop, she managed to grab her patent leather pumps, her lavender sweater, and her two jiggling mounds of pinkish blobs. Considering that the club was my idea, I agreed to drive. I merged onto the 405 freeway as Manuela placed the finishing touches on her eye shadow.

"Marlise," she began, fishing beneath her seat. "Have you seen my boobs?"

The bizarre question hung unanswered in the air. Finally I managed to say, "Last I saw them was when you were getting into the car." Suddenly we both realized that the silicone twins were probably still sitting on the roof.

"Stop the car," she screamed. "These are one hundred and fifty dollar breasts we are talking about."

The maneuver was clearly dangerous. Here we were, weaving in and out of LA traffic for the sake of a little cleavage. Somehow I made it safely to the shoulder before Manuela jumped from the passenger seat. Like a sea anemone clinging to corral, one jelly mound was suctioned precariously onto the roof of the car. The other had gone astray.

"We've got to go back," she demanded, utter desperation in her voice. Exiting at the next off ramp, we retraced our steps from the condo back to the 405.

"There it is," she cheered, as I flashed my high beams into the fast lane. This time I was forced to stop on the left hand side of the freeway. Jumping from the car, Manuela waited for a two-second break in traffic before swiftly rescuing the lonely breast. Covered with tire marks, the once perky mound looked more like a grilled hamburger patty.

Suddenly I was distracted by the flashing lights of a police car approaching behind us. I easily talked my way out of the humiliating experience by substituting the word "wallet" for the word "boob." The officer let us off with a minor scolding.

On that first night, it became clear that every outing with Manuela would turn into an adventure. That initial club experience only reinforced my image of Hollywood's blonde, plastic-inflated stereotypes. Despite all my effort, I was ending the evening without a source. But as we reached our car, a man handed Manuela his card and invited us to an after-hours party.

"It's at the Scorpions' house," he added.

Manuela's eyes lit up. I reminded her that the Scorpions were a heavy metal band from the seventies named after anthropods in the arachnida class. We went anyway.

While Manuela mingled happily with the long-haired, leather-clad musicians, I explored the house. Gold records lined the downstairs hallway, eventually leading me directly toward the recording studio. I turned the door knob. It was open.

In the center of the foam-paneled room sat the most enormous drum set I had ever seen. I'm still not quite sure what came over me, but suddenly I felt an impulse to play the drums. Settling into the swiveling chair, I picked up two wooden sticks resting on the snare and knocked them together three times, as I had seen drummers do on MTV. Then, I drummed my heart out. It's probably a blessing I never found the headphones or I would have made even more noise. The crash cymbal was definitely my favorite, adding that extra zing after my bass drum solo. That did it.

I was politely escorted out of the house by a friend of the band, Shane Woods. "Sorry to have to kick you out," he said, adjusting his blonde ponytail. "But these guys don't want people snooping around their house."

My sympathetic apology turned into a lengthy conversation. I had a good feeling about Shane, so I told him what I did for a living.

"Well, I happen to be an assistant at the William Morris Talent Agency," he said. "We might just become very good friends."

As he handed me his card, I realized I had just landed my first real source.

The following Monday, Shane phoned to tell me that Jodie Foster was pulling out of the film *Double Jeopardy*.

"Why?" I asked excitedly. "Is she sick?"

"I don't know," he said. "You're Miss Wonder Spy. Isn't that what you guys are supposed to figure out?"

Although I felt a small twinge of guilt, I immediately phoned Paramount, the film's production studio. Introducing myself as a freelance journalist, I asked for an update on the status of the film. I was told it would be on hold for nearly a year, or until they could find a replacement for Jodie Foster. Based on the suspicious timing of that single tip, I wrote an article claiming Jodie was pregnant. During my follow up comment call to Jodie's representatives, they refuted my claim. It was *Globe*'s policy to make a comment call to celebrities or their publicists before printing any article. These comment calls were to notify them of the pending articles, thereby protecting the tabloid's legal interests.

The denial of Jodie's representatives caused *Globe*'s lawyers to consider my story to be a legal risk. The article was cut in half and appeared under the diluted title "Jodie Foster's Mystery Illness."

As it turned out, my assumption had been correct. Month by month, the world watched as Jodie Foster's belly grew. Although I was disappointed that my superiors had refused to back up my original story, I felt vindicated that the facts had proven me right. Meanwhile, Shane was pleased with the $150 check he received for having simply picked up the phone to call me. His initial lead triggered a three-article series involving the actress.

My second Jodie Foster article touched on the extent of her relationship with Cydney Bernard, her production coordinator. By this time, speculation about Jodie's sexuality had been rumored for more than a decade. While she neither confirmed nor denied the assumptions, Jodie's brother, Buddy, later labeled her a lesbian in his biography, *Foster Child*.

Despite her successful resume, Jodie Foster managed to remain one of Hollywood's most private celebrities. *Globe* wanted to change that. The fact that she was officially reported as being pregnant was no longer a headline. Editors now wanted to determine the identity of the father and prove that Jodie was a lesbian. Unfortunately, I was in charge of confirming the latter.

By this time, nearly a month had passed since my article had run about Jodie's mystery illness. My colleague Patrick had uncovered the fact that Jodie had been artificially inseminated. He also had received evidence suggesting that the donor was Jodie's close friend, Randy Stone. *Globe* sent a photographer to follow the actress. He had snapped pictures of Jodie and an unidentified female companion with a dog outside a veterinary clinic.

"Marlise," Madeline said, handing me an address. "I need you to go to this veterinary clinic in Culver City." She slid an accompanying photo across her desk. "Find out who this other woman is, and what she and Jodie were doing there. Ask about their body language, conversation, details, anything about their relationship."

None of this sounded very romantic to me. It wasn't some magical island that they were visiting. It was an animal hospital.

"Give me details," Madeline continued. "Maternal instincts, anything you can find that will insinuate the women are more than just friends."

I nodded, as if this were a logical idea. "Um, one problem," I said doodling on my notepad. "I'm pet-less."

"I don't have time for your excuses," Madeline said, pointing me toward the door. "The article runs tomorrow so I need it by five o'clock today." I stood up as she added, "And don't come back until you have something."

As usual, time was of the essence. The clock now read 3:00. I had exactly two hours to find a pet, get an appointment at the veterinary clinic, find sources, convince them to talk about Jodie's alleged lesbian lover, and write the story. Once again, I found myself turning to my next-door neighbor for help.

"Manuela," I pleaded into my cell phone. "I need to borrow your cat."

"You mean Precious?" she asked. "Why? What are you going to do with her?"

"It's only a checkup," I stammered. "Look, I don't have time to explain. It's for a story I'm working on. I promise I'll get her back to you healthier than when she left."

"I don't know about this," Manuela said, hesitantly. "I mean I hardly know you, except for the fact that you destroyed my silicone boobs, got us kicked out of the Scorpions' mansion, and work for the tabloids."

"None of those things are my fault," I pleaded. "Except, maybe, the tabloid part."

There was a long pause. "Well, okay," she said between sighs. "As long as you bring Precious back in one piece. There's a key in the potted plant to the left of the front door. Call me when you get my cat back home."

It took nearly fifteen minutes to find the furry thing that Manuela later identified as a Himalayan Persian cat. Before moving to LA, I had owned dogs and was used to the concept of them responding to my calls. Now, here I was, forced to crawl on my hands and knees in search of the hidden feline. "Here kitty-kitty-kitty," I called. "Precious, where are you?"

Finally I peeled back the lid of a Fancy Feast can and began fanning the odorous substance into the air. It did the trick. Precious shoved her furry face directly into the mush, giving me just enough time to grab her and carry her to the car. Instantly she clawed the leather seats of my Ghia, hissing every time the tailpipe backfired.

Luckily Sharmin had called ahead to the vet to schedule an appointment. "You better do some minor damage to the cat," Sharmin warned. "I told them it was an emergency and you had to get in today."

After battling LA traffic, I ran through the door of the veterinary clinic and plopped frantic Precious on the counter. The smell of medications, urine, aluminum tables, and nervous pets permeated the air.

"Hi," I yelled over the sound of barking dogs. "I have an appointment for my cat, Precious."

"Oh yes," the receptionist said, glancing at her books. "Your assistant said it was an emergency."

On the Formica countertop, Precious's paws slid out from under her like Bambi on ice. I headlocked her into place. "Well, isn't every day an emergency, really?"

The receptionist looked confused. "Actually," I continued. "Precious really needs her shots. She's long overdue."

Solidly built, the assistant reminded me of Nell Carter. I was heartened to see that an open copy of *People* magazine sat beside her computer. I filled out routine paperwork and she escorted me into the examination room.

As her hand reached for the door, I blurted, "You know, I was referred to you through my friend, Jodie Foster."

She stopped in her tracks and nodded. "Oh, yeah, she was in here the other day with her dog."

"And with her girlfriend," I interjected. The assistant came closer and we both began petting Precious. As I whisked away clumps of fur from the shedding feline, I continued, "I forget the name of Jodie's friend. You know, the woman she's been dating recently?" I made it sound like a question.

Without realizing she was divulging client secrets to a tabloid reporter, the assistant confirmed my suspicions that the actress had in fact been at the vet "with her partner." Although it was difficult to read the chatty assistant, I decided to go for it.

"I'm actually here to find out if . . ." Suddenly my spiel was interrupted by the doctor's entrance.

"So, who do we have here?" asked the cheery veterinarian. The talkative assistant exited the room and I was left without a name to complete my story.

After the exam and immunizations, I paid the bill and asked the assistant to help me carry the cat to the car. I purchased a twenty pound bag of gourmet cat food to make my plea seem even more convincing. "Sorry, my hands are full," I explained, lifting the heavy sack.

On the way to the car, I gave the assistant my true identity and explained the purpose of my visit. "There could be some serious money in this for you," I hinted, slipping her my card.

She shook my hand. "They signed in under the name of Cydney Bernard," she mumbled. "I'll call you soon with more details."

For the price of a $300 vet bill, *Globe* got another breaking story, Precious got a clean bill of health, and I met my five o'clock deadline.

Naturally, I was expected to do the follow-up story when Jodie gave birth to a seven-pound, eight-ounce son named Charles. At that point, all we knew was that the baby had been born at Cedars-Sinai Medical Center. Using a flamboyant floral arrangement as a decoy, I made my way to the nurses' station.

"Delivery for a Ms. Foster," I said, glancing down at my prop clipboard. Unfortunately, I only got as far as private suite #3129 before being turned back by the intimidating security guards.

"But, I've been asked to deliver these to her personally," I insisted.

"Just put them there with the others," he said, pointing toward the garden of bouquets. "I'll make sure she gets them."

Bending toward the pile, I scanned the flowers, cards, stuffed animals, gift boxes, and balloons that declared, "Congratulations! It's a boy!" I paused at the doorway trying to overhear anything I might include in a story. Ultimately, however, I was forced to rely on Rolodex sources to fill in the gaps.

The magnitude of willingness I had displayed on the Jodie Foster stories labeled me a reporter of compliance. The editors milked my optimism, pushing me on to other assignments that seemed virtually impossible to complete. Inwardly, I thanked them. I thanked them for setting the bar so high. I thanked them for assigning unreachable goals. I thanked them for the adrenaline that kept me going.

With time, I longed to become indispensable to the tabloids. I wanted the editors to feel that the magazine could not survive without me. I was notorious for pushing people away and for giving the impression that I needed no one. But now, I needed *Globe* and *Globe* needed me.

Ironically, this warped desire was birthed out of my religious background. I come from a "yes" family, one of service that habitually over-commits until there is nothing left. We give more than one hundred percent. We demonstrate the martyr syndrome, willingly suffering for the sake of others' survival.

Now I was willing to suffer for *Globe*. This job was the ultimate lure for an adrenaline junkie. I thrived on deadlines and bylines. I liked the idea of being in Hollywood but not of it. No other profession could provide this combination of thrills for someone my age. For *Globe*, I was prepared to jeopardize my morals, abandon the voice of ethics, embrace perilous risks, and somehow justify it all through the use of my pen.

Note:

Carrie Fisher spoke to thousands of psychiatrists in May 2004 at the American Psychiatric Association's Annual Meeting about her diagnosis of bipolar disorder.

Will Smith and his second wife, Jada Pinkett, were married on December 31, 1997, and are the parents of two children.

Barbra Streisand and James Brolin have been married since July 1, 1998.

Tim Allen divorced his first wife, Laura Diebel, in March 2003. They have one child. On October 7, 2006, he married Jane Hajduk.

Jodie Foster has been in a serious relationship with Cydney Bernard since 1993. She has never revealed the identity of the father of her two children.

CHAPTER 4

The Writer from Glasgow

Workdays were getting longer at *Globe*. Had it not been for the sun sinking below the base of the window, my mind would never have noticed the time. The hands of the clock kept rotating through a typical nine-to-five cycle, yet for some reason, I always left the office hungry for more.

News never took a break. Like everyone else on staff, I was expected to work one weekend each month. Celebrity tragedies and romances always seemed to peak after hours and during holidays. *Globe* compensated employees with time off during the work week rather than awarding overtime pay. As the new girl, I was the only staff member willing to surrender weekends. I accepted overtime assignments on the condition that I could accrue those hours toward an extended vacation. Word quickly spread that I was a willing candidate for overtime. Being young, single, and childless made me an easy target for schedule manipulations.

For the rush of chasing a Hollywood rumor, I routinely traded my Saturdays and Sundays without objection. "Sure, I'll cover for you," I echoed, time and again. There was only one problem: I never had enough time to cash in my accumulated days off.

The editors knew I was hooked. As my responsibilities increased, so did their demands. Each week I felt as if I were passing another test, my grades awarded through my growing collection of bylines. In the three months since I had begun my job, two other reporters had already suffered the tabloid guillotine. One of them was my desk-neighbor, Patrick Kincaid.

No one knew exactly why Patrick had been fired. We were all afraid to ask. Karen thought he had lost his job because his intelligence threatened Madeline in the pecking order. Sharmin said it was his overindulgence, like the way he submitted receipts for his dry cleaning or three meals a day of "source entertainment."

Ignoring all that, I was just grateful to belong. Rather than questioning the reasons behind my newly-found acceptance, I felt indebted to *Globe* for actually paying me to write. It was almost as if the magazine were a higher power, a divine being that I both embraced and feared. Faithfully, I paid my penance by working longer hours, landing more leads, and gaining weekly bylines. Ultimately, I was the only one to blame for my obsession. The pressure to excel came from within.

Nearly every evening, I stayed awake watching Jay Leno and David Letterman, hoping that just one interview would reveal a celebrity lead. My research library became the E! channel, *Extra*, Howard Stern, and celebrity Web sites. These time-consuming habits quickly replaced my former hobbies of drawing, language study, and creative writing. Those parts of my personal life were stored on the shelf just below friendship, religion, and family.

Exercise was my one remaining passion. In retrospect, I'm not sure how I managed to fit marathons, biking, and yoga into my schedule. Like my job, these became addictive rituals. At the end of each workday, I would change into my gym clothes at the office to avoid "wasting time" by going up to my condo. Leaving my car in underground parking, I would jog straight from the garage to the beach, running as if I were being chased and stopping only after completing eight miles. In my mind, even pausing to greet my sister after work would have slowed down the system. And so I ran, further and further from the place I now called home.

One of my regular routes took me to Venice Beach, where street performers, artists, athletes, and the homeless mingled with the *Baywatch* crew for the sake of the sun and freedom. Like them, I too had become a boardwalk regular, exchanging greetings with shop owners and musicians like Harry Perry, the famous turban-wearing guitar player on roller skates.

No one would have guessed that I, the little jogger with fire on her heels, had secretly convinced a handful of hippies to become my beach spies. On occasion, they would tip me off to celebrity surf lessons or star mommies playing at the beach. One of their leads alerted me to a beach party that Melanie Griffith was planning. Another tip resulted in *Globe* capturing a picture of Arnold Schwarzenegger pushing a jogging stroller.

There were moments, however, when I just happened to be at the right place at the right time. During one of my daily runs, I passed an older man who looked vaguely familiar. Shuffling along the sandy boardwalk, he suddenly grabbed onto a lamppost and began wheezing.

"You okay?" I asked, stopping beside him.

Slowly looking up, he waved me away and mumbled, "Fine, fine." Drops of milky whiteness were crusted in the corners of his eyes. His shirt was blotched with perspiration rings.

I pointed toward a beachside café. "Do you want some water?"

Again, he waved me away. As I continued on my run, I overheard a man on Rollerblades commenting to his friend, "Hey, did you just see Rodney Dangerfield back there?"

Suddenly, I realized why the ailing man had looked so familiar. The following morning at *Globe*, I decided to follow up on what I had seen. Digging into the office file cabinet, I pulled out a blank lead sheet and scribbled the following headline: "Comedian Rodney Dangerfield suffering from mystery illness. Let's check it out. Sourcing: Marlise Kast, who eyewitnessed the sickly star on the beach."

By now, I had become quite bold with submitting leads. When I first started working for *Globe*, only about one out of five of my leads received approval. Each morning, I would type out two or three ideas I had come up with between closing time the night before and my morning shower. I would carefully overlap those lead sheets in a tidy, single row, smack dab in the middle of Madeline's desk to welcome her like a cup of coffee. One by one, the lead sheets would find their way back to my desk. They would either have a red-inked X of rejection across the page or the initials "MN" scribbled in the approved box. Her approval was the equivalent of getting the gold star from the toughest teacher in elementary school. I lived for those initials.

It had taken me a while to figure out the system. It wasn't always the actual storyline that earned the stamp of approval, as much as the way a story was pitched. My score was improving. I now was averaging three approved leads out of every five I submitted. The Rodney Dangerfield lead was one of those. Considering that the idea was based solely on my personal observation, the editors did not give it much stock. Therefore, I was given less then seventy-two hours to turn the story.

By the end of day one, I had obtained the comedian's medical history from previously run articles. I was also able to get his home phone number from our Florida office. At that point, I was still lacking a credible source that would be able to identify Dangerfield's health problem. In the world of mainstream journalism, it might take several days to obtain the information I needed. At *Globe*, however, my efforts at data gathering involved shouting one simple question across the office: "Anyone have any Dangerfield sources?"

"Sure, he's my next-door neighbor." It was Keith Harden, the latest addition to the West Coast office. As soon as Patrick's desk became vacant, Florida executives had put Keith on the next plane to LA. Trenton Freeze had immediately approved Keith's transfer to California for the simple reason that no one in Florida wanted him around. In his late fifties, Keith was a hard-hitting reporter who had been in the business for years.

It was probably Keith's personal life rather than his professional skills that bothered most of the editors. Habitually late, he wore business suits that were a couple of sizes too small and always seemed to have breakfast stains on his mismatched ties. Keith never walked over to the desk of a fellow reporter. Rather, he would wheel around the office in his desk chair, throwing down story files with such force that they made our hair blow. Tapping his pen to a secret beat, Keith constantly whistled songs nobody else knew. Most of his time was spent on the phone. It drove Madeline mad.

"Confidential source," he would whisper mysteriously while covering the receiver. Over the years, Keith had accumulated a lengthy list of reliable sources. Despite this, some of us wondered why his lengthy calls seldom produced major leads. Keith was a nervous chair twirler, constantly spinning as the phone cord wrapped around his body like a string of Christmas lights. Coffee was his water and sugar was his vitamin. Keith twitched. His handkerchiefs were used and reused—always shoved into his right pocket, deep enough to stay inside, yet never far enough to be completely hidden. Lacking any legitimate grounds for firing him and reluctant to lose his list of sources, the editors were forced to keep Keith around. Perhaps they hoped that one day they could find a reason to let him go. It was just a matter of time.

I liked Keith. Unlike the rest of us, he was not a chameleon. He treated Madeline as his equal, or so he thought. Refusing to respond to her calls of superiority, he ignored her status and simply hollered back when she called his name. He overrode all of her decisions by going straight to the top.

Although Keith had been in Los Angeles less than two weeks, he had already settled into the same beachfront apartment building as Rodney Dangerfield. The actor had no idea that he was living next door to a tabloid veteran. At *Globe*, we were all judged by those we befriended, and we were often found guilty by association. No one realized that I respected Keith. Now, wheeling over to my desk with his Rolodex in tow, he flipped to the "D" section and pulled out a card on Dangerfield.

"I had a conversation with his wife, Joan, the other day," he said, slamming down the card with the flat of his palm. "She said Rodney twisted his ankle or something. I didn't even think it was newsworthy, but feel free to call her yourself."

After what I had seen at the beach, I was convinced Dangerfield was suffering from something more than a limp. I dialed the number Keith had given me. A woman answered.

"Hello," I said, boldly. "My name is Kelly and I'm writing a piece on Mr. Dangerfield's recent illness." Hoping the woman on the line would bite the bait of my trigger words, I waited. There was an uncomfortable pause before I continued. "Does he have any comment that he'd like to share with our readers?"

She laughed dismissively. "What magazine are you with?"

"I'm freelance," I lied. "I'm not sure where I'll be selling the story yet."

"Well, Rodney's not here right now," she said. "This is his wife. But honestly, I don't think there's too much he'd have to say. Rodney tore a ligament in his right ankle."

Things were not going as I had planned. This was fast becoming another routine mystery illness story. I was losing my health-crisis headline. Falling into the tabloid mindset, I found myself wondering if perhaps Dangerfield had been injured in a nasty love quarrel or maybe he had tumbled down a flight of stairs in a drunken rage. There was still hope I could make something of this story.

"How did it happen?" I blurted.

"In his sleep somehow," she explained. "He went to an orthopedic surgeon at the Kerlain-Jobe Clinic. That's about it. You can tell your readers that Rodney is doing just fine."

My headline had virtually melted into nothingness. As it turned out, Dangerfield's maladies were nothing more than a combination of foot surgery and hay fever. At least I had found a credible source for my article. I walked into Madeline's office to break the news.

"Write it up as a page filler," she said coldly. "Maybe Florida can squeeze it into a hole somewhere. Otherwise we'll throw it on the gossip page."

Gossip page! Did she just say "gossip page?"

The gossip page was the tabloid graveyard. It was the valley of humiliation, where stories-gone-bad fought for their last breath of life. It's where "Jodie Foster's Mystery Illness" had landed rather than on the front cover where it belonged.

For the next hour, I wrote the Dangerfield story, squeezing out every bit of juice I could get from the brief phone call. Several days later, I was flipping through the latest issue of *Globe*, vainly searching for my byline. Just then Madeline passed my desk, throwing down her copy of the published story titled "At Last! Rodney Dangerfield Gets Respect—From His Foot Doctor."

"You're lucky your story made it in," she said. "Hopefully next time you can get more than just a single column on the back cover."

I had been warned. It was now officially time to get aggressive. I had to take my dedication to a higher level. A few days later I got my chance. It was just after five in the morning when Madeline jump-started my day.

"Marlise? It's Madeline," she said, sounding frighteningly awake. "Sonny Bono is dead."

It took a few seconds before my brain caught up with the rest of my body. "What happened?" I asked, squinting toward the clock.

"He hit a tree," she answered. "It was some freak skiing accident.

Don't worry about that right now. I need you to drive to his daughter's home in West Hollywood immediately."

I grabbed a pen, preparing to scribble down her barked commands. By this stage, Madeline had rightly assumed I was out of touch with celebrity identities.

"Her name is Chastity," Madeline continued. "I'm guessing she's about your age. She lives in West Hollywood with her girlfriend, Laura LeMastro."

Based on the reported time of Sonny's death, it was safe to assume that Chastity would have just learned of her father's accident. I didn't want to be the one to break the news to her. Occasionally, the tabloids would learn about situations even before the celebrities themselves. For instance, Geena Davis first heard of her husband's infidelity and love child from reading one of my *Globe* articles, according to one of her associates. As pleased as I had been with getting the Davis exclusive, I still felt a twinge of guilt that it had contributed to Geena's divorce from Renny Harlin. I wanted to avoid a repeat of those emotions.

My thoughts were interrupted by Madeline's voice still droning into the phone. "Florida wants the headline, 'Cher Collapses in Tears.' See if you can get Chastity to discuss her mother's reaction. Try to build your story around that."

Madeline never said good-bye or wished us luck. She simply closed every assignment with the words, "Keep your phone on."

After she hung up, I realized she had just given me the dreaded task of door-stepping at Chastity's place. One of the worst parts of being a tabloid reporter was door-stepping. It ranked right up there with making comment calls or sleeping in a car. Those duties were generally reserved for freelance reporters like Adam from New York. By now he was clearly on his way out, his days in the office having been reduced to only Tuesdays and Thursdays. Consequently, this particular door-stepping assignment was on me.

Of all the staff reporters, I lived the closest to Chastity's West Hollywood home. I was also the only one foolish enough to answer the phone at five in the morning. I cross-checked the address in my Thomas Guide. I had learned to rely on this detailed map directory containing every street, avenue, and alley in LA County. At this dawn hour, it led me straight to a small, brick, box-style home that seemed ideal for young college grads. I knocked and waited nearly five minutes before someone finally answered. In front of me stood a woman who apparently had not been awake long.

"Can I help you?" she asked, tightening the belt of her tattered bathrobe. She had blondish hair and wore terry cloth slippers that seemed too big for her feet.

"Good morning," I said, preparing myself for a verbal beating. "Sorry to bother you at this hour. I'm a writer and was hoping to speak with Chastity about her father's accident."

The whole time I was delivering my prepared speech, I kept thinking about the absurdity of this exchange. No one in her right mind would talk to a reporter about something so personal.

Suddenly a hand appeared from behind the door and yanked it open. From the pictures in the Bono file, I immediately recognized that I was looking at Chastity. Holding a mug of strong-smelling coffee, she was already fully dressed.

"Get the hell out of here," she said through the rising steam. Her eyes were watery and her neck was blotched with redness. "How can you people be so insensitive?"

You people? How dare she throw me into a general tabloid category?

Backing away from the porch, I stared down at the cracked cement and apologized for my intrusion. Before I could finish my sentence, the door slammed as I heard the words, "Get out of here, you bitch."

Fair enough. I'll leave.

In cases of rage, persistence is always futile. It was still dark. From the glow of my watch, I could see it was ten minutes to six. I phoned Madeline from the car.

"How'd it go?" she asked.

"Well, Chastity didn't exactly sob in my arms," I explained.

I pulled down my visor and glanced into the mirror. The deep circles beneath my eyes looked like tattoos.

"What did she say about Cher?" Madeline asked.

"I didn't quite get that far," I continued. "She slammed the door in my face."

Madeline let out a sigh of disappointment. "Chastity's probably still angry that we outed her in 1990."

These are the sorts of details that the editors often failed to mention before we knocked on celebrities' doors. Now, in the distance, I could see a figure walking out of Chastity's house. Grabbing a pair of binoculars from my glove compartment, I informed Madeline, "Wait. She's leaving, and she has luggage." Too late, I realized I had just volunteered to pursue the story further.

"Forget about her," Madeline ordered. "We know she's heading to her dad's house in Palm Springs. Right now, I need you to call Florida and dictate Chastity's reaction over the phone."

Already, I could visualize my verbal copy, "Chastity heartbroken over father's tragic death."

"Why can't I just type it up once I'm in the office?" I asked, still gazing through the binoculars. Automatically I grabbed a pen and scribbled down Chastity's license plate number to add to the Bono file.

"Because you need to be in Palm Springs in exactly two hours." Madeline made it sound as if she were reminding me of a plan to which I had already agreed.

Unsure of what the new assignment entailed, I asked her if I should pack a bag.

"We've talked about this before, Marlise," she snapped with exasperation. "You should always have a packed bag in your car at all times."

I was too embarrassed to explain that my entire wardrobe could fit into a single suitcase. Her suggestion would have forced me to live out of my trunk.

"Move quickly," she added. "We don't have a lot of time."

I started my car and waited for her to tell me to keep my phone on. She did.

During the drive to Palm Springs, I thought about the entire story and the way it would be covered. I felt certain that I would be able to write exactly what the editors wanted, even without a single interview, source, or photo to back up the Cher headline. Could I prove that Cher had collapsed? No. Did she? Probably. Was there any legal risk? Absolutely not. Celebrities are eager for any publicity that shows them in a sympathetic light. I grabbed my tape recorder and dictated the story while I drove.

Considering it was now just after eight in the morning, I figured I would be one of the first reporters to reach Desert Memorial Park in Century City, near Palm Springs. To my surprise, the funeral site was already packed with camera crews, satellite vans, and paparazzi. I phoned Madeline and told her I was one of many. This should never be the case for a tabloid reporter.

"Leave the cemetery," she demanded. "I want you to stay parked at the Bono house. At some point you'll see Cher either coming or going from the property."

The heavily guarded house sat on a hill at the end of a long road. More media vehicles were parked outside the Bono estate. Feeding mainstream news to *Globe* from the funeral site was "Rent-a-quote Nick," who was also covering the story for talk radio. He and I stayed in constant communication by cell phone throughout the day. That evening we regrouped over drinks at the downtown Hyatt.

"There's nothing *Globe*'s going to get that everyone else doesn't already have," Nick said, deflating my hopes for an exclusive.

For three days, I stood in front of the Bono home in the pouring rain. By Sunday the TV cameras were gone, leaving me as the lone reporter still waiting at the base of the driveway. The security guards took pity on me and brought me an umbrella from the house.

"Maybe we can put in a good word for you," one guard said. "You say you're freelance?"

I nodded and told him I was a journalism major looking for my big break. Sure, it was a lie. And yes, I was prepared to crush this family in its darkest hour. But none of that crossed my mind at the time. The only thought I had was to get the story.

"I'll go talk to Mary," the guard continued. "Maybe she'll agree to meet you in the garage for a few words."

It wasn't a Cher interview, of course, but a comment from Sonny's widow would be better than nothing. I watched the guard as he slowly walked up the long driveway, his walkie-talkie clipped to his back pocket. He never returned.

Recognizing defeat, I finally gave up and started to walk away. Three days had passed since Sonny's death and there had been no sign of Cher near the Bono house. Just as I reached my car, a black Mercedes sped past, splashing dollops of mud onto my shoes and pants. The car stopped and slowly reversed through puddle-filled potholes.

"You just don't give up, do you?"

Instantly I recognized the familiar voice speaking through the top of the tinted window. As I took a step closer, the window dropped an inch further. There was Cher in all her straight-haired notoriety, stopping to give a young journalist the time of day. I was stunned.

Focus, I told myself. Remember the headline: "Cher Collapses." Should I ask her if she collapsed? Who told her that Sonny hit a tree? Is there anything she would have wanted to tell him before he died? How is she holding up? Yes, that's it! Aim soft and then throw the tough punches.

Now was my chance. I could almost taste the exclusive.

"Well . . .?" Cher was still waiting.

Suddenly my mind went blank. I was flustered, nervous, exhausted, and caught off guard.

Before I could stop myself, I blurted, "What are your thoughts on the wedding?" The moment I uttered the words, I knew I had blown my chance.

Cher looked at me in disbelief. "What did you just say?"

Trying vainly to recover, I muttered, "I mean, uh, the . . . funeral."

It was too late. Cher shook her head and rolled up the window and the car drove away. Mortified, I was beyond humiliation. Did that actually just happen? The car exhaust hit the cold air, leaving behind a trail of smoke. If only I could have another chance. There I stood in the pouring rain, cold, wet, alone, and left without a printable quote.

Looking down at my muddy clothes, I made a pledge never to mention my encounter to anyone. And I didn't, until now. The shame alone cured me of future failures, marking the last mistake like that I would make at *Globe*.

Back in the safety of my car, I dialed the LA office. Keith answered the phone.

At the sound of his voice, I joked, "Wow, Sharmin, you really need to lay off those steroids."

"Well, well. If it isn't the tabloid wonder," Keith responded cheerfully. I could hear the familiar tapping of his pen in the background. "How wonderful of you to call."

"What are you doing answering the phones?" I asked. "Demoted already?"

"No," he explained. "Sharmin's in a meeting with the witch. How on earth can you guys work with that woman? She's driving me absolutely insane."

"Get used it," I said. "She's not going anywhere."

"Maybe she's not," he whispered. "But I am. It looks as if Florida is sending me to Boulder to work on the Ramsey case."

"Congratulations," I responded. "Maybe you can actually find the killer. I believe *Globe* has already pinned the murder on everyone from the parents and the brother to the milkman and the dog."

Keith laughed. "I heard this week's headline is going to be 'JonBenet Committed Suicide.'"

Suddenly there was a thud on the line. "Keith?" I asked. "Are you still there?"

His chair-twirling must have gotten out of control. Keith finally came back on the line. "Sorry about that," he explained. "I dropped you on your head."

"No harm done," I said. "Listen, can you tell Madeline that I'm leaving Palm Springs? She can call me if she needs me."

"Sure," he agreed. "Drive carefully and watch out for those trees."

Less than five minutes later, my phone rang. I knew it was Madeline even before glancing at the number.

"I need you to come into the office tonight." she ordered. "Your Bono text needs to merge with the copy from Caelan Dunmore. He's in Lake Tahoe covering the ski accident. Here, take down this number."

Madeline started rambling digits as if I could steer, shift, talk, and write all at the same time. "Got it," I lied.

"Florida needs the story faxed by midnight," she continued. "I don't have time to edit your work, so make sure it's clean before you send it off."

The line went dead. I assumed that was good-bye. Once again, I called the office.

"Thanks for calling *Globe.* This is Sharmin. How may I direct—"

"Sharmin," I interrupted. "Glad I caught you. Can you do me a favor and call this Caelan guy? Ask him to type up his info on Bono's skiing accident and fax it to the office."

"There's nothing that would bring me greater pleasure," she responded cheerfully.

Puzzled by her willingness to help, I asked, "Let me guess, is Madeline standing next to you?"

"Hell no," she responded. "This just gives me an excuse to call my Scottish lover."

"Who? Caelan?" I interjected. "Please don't tell me you slept with him, too."

Although Sharmin was never one to keep quiet about her conquests, her voice suddenly got quieter. "Girlfriend, you know I would, but I don't think he could handle a black woman like me. I've got more caboose than the Orient Express."

I was intrigued. "So what makes this guy so special? Is it the fact that he's unattainable?"

"No," Sharmin continued. "Just picture Edward Norton with a Scottish accent. He came to LA last year for the Christmas party. I still don't know him too well, but I intend to change that with my special wooing powers. You know I ain't one to gossip, but I hear he might transfer to our LA office."

Suddenly I felt threatened. Would this Caelan person be replacing me? "Who told you that?" I demanded.

"Nosy, nosy," she scolded. There was a brief pause. "Well, all I know is that it has something to do with a broken engagement."

I gasped. "Did he call it off, or did she?"

"Damn girl, you startin' to sound like a reporter!" Sharmin's voice was muffled now. "I call dibs on his bagpipes."

"You're horrible," I said between laughs.

"I want to see what's under his skirt," she added.

"Sharmin, they're called kilts," I corrected.

"Don't get all culturally sensitive on my ass now," she blurted. "Look,

I gotta go. You comin' in or what?"

"Yeah, after five," I answered. "Will you still be there?"

Sharmin had a habit of answering questions with a question. "Does the black man have equal rights?"

"See you Monday then," I said.

"Hold up," she said. "I almost forgot. A new source called in today but said she would only talk to a woman. You want her number?"

"Sure. Lay it on me." I grabbed a pen from my purse. Suddenly I was becoming a multi-tasker. After hanging up with Sharmin, I dialed the barely legible number.

"Hello," I said. "This is Marlise from *Globe* magazine. I'm returning a call."

The woman on the line had a sensual voice and introduced herself as Abbey Barnett.

Sources often failed to understand that tabloid journalists are required to hear a story before they can ascribe it a value. When I explained this process to Abbey, she sounded extremely reluctant to proceed.

"How do I know you're not going to steal my information without paying me?"

"I can fax you a confidentiality agreement if you'd like," I assured her. "But, in all honesty, that would just slow things down. It's up to you."

She was breathing heavily on the line. "God, I can't believe I'm actually doing this," she mumbled. I could sense her hesitation.

"Why don't we meet for a drink?" I suggested. "You might feel better if you can see who you'll be working with."

There was silence, so I continued, moving in quickly. "Let's meet at ten tomorrow night at Barfly on Sunset."

"Well, okay." She still sounded unsure. "How will I find you?"

She had a point. Everyone at Barfly wore black. "I've got brown hair down to my waist. I'll be sitting at the bar near the entrance. Call my cell phone if you can't find me."

"I'll be the blonde wearing bright red lipstick," she replied, narrowing it down to ninety percent of the Barfly clientele. "I guess I'll see you tomorrow night then."

Suddenly I felt as if I had just arranged a blind date.

It was seven o'clock that evening by the time I arrived back at the office. Everyone was still hard at work except Sharmin and Karen. It had been three days since I was last at my desk, yet no one seemed to notice I had returned.

On my desk, Sharmin had placed the copy that Caelan had faxed from Lake Tahoe. A note was scribbled on the cover letter, "Call if you need my help," signed, "Caelan." I could almost picture him running around the ski slopes wearing his kilt. Placed beside the fax were two new lead sheets, neither of which I had submitted. One lead stated, "Donny and Marie Osmond starring in a talk show. Find a story." The other lead sheet read, "Steve McQueen's daughter in health crisis. Check it out."

Always eager to prove myself to the editors, I hated the idea of stories piling up on my desk. Even if the stories were not time sensitive, a growing stack of leads made my heart beat a little faster. It was going to be a long night. I needed coffee.

"Welcome home!" Pete Trujillo greeted me in the lounge. Dumping a handful of sugar cubes into his hot cocoa, he asked, "How was Palm Springs?"

"Wet and cold," I answered, "not at all what I expected."

"Don't worry," he said. "You'll have plenty of time to see the desert on a sunny day. No one else wants to cover stories out there. It's a haven for senior citizens, but a nightmare for anyone with a social life."

I nodded. "So, what are you doing here so late?"

"Oh," he responded casually. "I'm doing a follow-up on the Chris Farley overdose."

Before Sonny Bono's skiing accident, comedian Chris Farley had become the latest tragedy from the *Saturday Night Live* alumni. "I'm heading to Chicago tomorrow," Pete continued, "to buy a photograph that we probably won't even publish."

I was shocked. "You're kidding me. Dare I ask, how much?"

Without hesitation, Pete responded. "Twenty-five thousand dollars. The source threatened to sell the picture to the *Enquirer* if we didn't act fast."

I was confused. "That doesn't make any sense. Why wouldn't we use a photo that cost so much?"

"Too graphic I guess," Pete explained. "I haven't seen it yet, but apparently it was taken by one of the investigators. They said Chris Farley looked as purple as Barney. He had blood dripping from his nose and some frothy fluid pouring from his mouth."

Pete wasn't being callous. He had simply mastered the tabloid journalist's ability to disassociate from his subject. Nevertheless, the description made me nauseous. I threw out my coffee.

"The tabloids do this sort of thing all the time," he continued. "It's better to buy the milk and let it spoil, than let the neighbor have a taste." He dropped another sugar cube into his cup and licked the crystals off his chubby fingers.

Our conversation ended the moment Madeline entered the room. "Come on, you two," she said with a double clap. "Get back to work. Florida's waiting for your copy to close the issue. It's almost midnight there."

Suddenly an air bubble floated to the top of the water cooler, breaking the silence. We all looked at one another as if someone had farted.

That night, I was the last to leave the office. Despite the fact that I had never landed the Cher interview, I was still able to complete my story from an eyewitness perspective. Combined with quotes from other sources and the ski resort details from Caelan, my cover story appeared under the title, "The Secret Behind Cher's Moving Funeral Tribute." There was an odd sense of accomplishment when I finally locked the office door that night, a sort of grown-up mentality that I associated with being a career woman. I was exhausted, but it was worth it.

That night I had difficulty falling asleep. The Osmond lead sheet kept me as awake as a shot of espresso. I needed a headline. That is where my stories often started. I would hear a rumor, think up a headline, and let it set the tone to help structure the direction that my investigations would take.

Getting out of bed, I tiptoed to my sister's bedside and whispered as loudly as I could. "Heidi . . . you awake?" Still wearing her glasses, she had fallen asleep with an open chemistry textbook on her chest. She chewed at the air like a dreaming baby. "Heidi?"

Her eyes still closed, she turned away from me, mumbling, "How do we link apolipoprotein metabolism to bile acids synthesis?" My sister was talking about her research project in her sleep.

And I thought my *job was all consuming.*

"What was that?" I prodded. "I didn't quite catch that." Grabbing my Dictaphone machine, I pushed the record button.

"Bile acids transcriptionally regulate FXR," she continued, as if teaching a bio-chem class.

Trying to contain my laughter was absolute torture. "How do we do that?" I probed. Apparently my question was much too basic. Slowly opening her eyes, Heidi looked like a hospital patient coming out of a coma.

"What's going on?" she asked, rubbing her head.

"You really need to spend less time in that chemistry lab of yours," I said, playing back the taped proof.

"Please," she begged. "Let me get some sleep."

We were both still whispering. "Okay," I agreed, lifting the glasses off her face. "But not until you give me an Osmond story."

She sat up and closed the textbook. "What?"

"You know," I continued. "Donny and Marie Osmond. Weren't you into their music at some stage?"

"Oh, come on, Lise." Heidi sounded annoyed now. "I was like five and we were forced to listen to gospel music."

"They're Mormons, by the way," I pointed out.

"Whatever." Lying back down, she pulled the covers over her head. "All I know is that Marie sells dolls on infomercials and Donny was a virgin till his wedding day."

Enthusiasm overpowered my inside voice. "Yes! That's it! I'll pitch the virgin thing."

I knew the lead would be approved, especially considering I had just published a story called "Pint-Sized Gary Coleman Still a Virgin at 30." It had been an easy turn-around story, predominately based on Coleman's own statements. In contrast, sourcing for the Osmond story would became an issue. There was no way I could credit the information back to my Hollywood-detached sister. "Where did you hear about this virgin thing?"

"I think it was on Howard Stern," she explained. "You listen to him every single morning, remember?" Since starting to work for *Globe*, Howard's celebrity interviews had become a part of my daily ritual.

"Hopefully I can pull the Stern transcript," I said, thinking about the time involved in that process. "This virginity line might work. It's such a rarity these days."

"Welcome to the Kast family," Heidi said. "If you and I don't get married soon, we're going to dry up like old wells."

"Good luck finding yourself a virgin husband," I told her. "We are a dying breed, you know."

She threw a pillow across the room that hit the wall behind me. "Do we really need to be having this conversation at one in the morning?" she asked. "Please, just go to sleep."

"Okay, okay. I'm going." I stood up. Stopping at the door, I turned back toward her. "Sweet dreams, Heid. I love you."

She rolled over toward the wall and whispered, "Good night, Little One. Love you, too."

I am not a morning person. That's never been a secret. Term papers, nightclubs, movies, or conversation can easily keep me awake until four in the morning. Yet the moment my head hits the pillow, it is best to consider me a lost cause. Growing up, my mother tried to awaken me with everything from rooster alarm clocks and bright lights to licking dogs and breakfast in bed. I'm convinced that a few too many early mornings have helped shape me into a woman of perpetual tardiness.

"Lise!" It was Heidi, putting an abrupt end to the annoying sound of static music. "This thing has been going off for the last hour." My alarm clock now read 8:45. I had exactly fifteen minutes to dress and get to work on time. But first, I needed my coffee.

Heidi was in the kitchen, sealing two sandwiches into plastic Baggies. She opened the fridge and grabbed two sodas.

"Predicting a hearty appetite, are we?" I asked, accidentally bumping into the refrigerator door. My equilibrium was still a tad off. I held the Baggie up to my nose and whiffed tuna on rye.

"Give me that," she said, grabbing it from my hand. "For your information, they are not both for me. One is for a man, a friend, a—"

"A man friend?" I interrupted.

Heidi rolled her eyes. "No . . . Actually, he's a homeless guy I pass on my way to UCLA. He always asks for money, but I just give him food instead."

Conversations with Heidi often made me feel like the evil sister. "Well, look out Mother Theresa," I joked sarcastically.

Throwing her backpack over her shoulder, Heidi headed toward the door. "See. That's exactly why I didn't want to tell you. Go ahead, mock me."

"I'm not mocking you," I defended myself. "I just can't believe you would make the time to do that for someone you don't even know."

Heidi was as awkward at receiving compliments as I was at giving them. Looking at her watch, she said, "Speaking of time, aren't you late?"

Without answering, I downed my coffee in one gulp and ran past Heidi, who was still standing in the doorway. It wasn't until I was in the car that I became aware of my coffee-burnt tongue. What a miserable way to start off the day.

If anyone in the office noticed that I was half an hour late, no one mentioned it. The night before, I had purposely left the fax confirmation sheet in the file room to prove that I had still been working after eleven. My long hours were by no means editorial consent for habitual tardiness. Those hours did, however, justify my reason for hitting the snooze button one time too many.

By noon my Donny Osmond lead was approved. Two hours later I had the Howard Stern transcript, and by five o'clock the Florida editors had their article, "Hunky Donny Was a Virgin at the Altar." The piece ran as part of *Globe*'s series, "The Investigation of Hollywood Love Lives." Although far from groundbreaking, my Osmond article showed the editors that I could turn a full story from concept to completion in less than twenty-four hours.

For a change, I was out of the office by five. That would give me enough time to exercise, cook dinner, and still make it to Sunset Boulevard for the meeting with my new source, Abbey Barnett. When I arrived there, Barfly had a lengthy guest list as usual. Bouncers kept out anyone who did not fit "the look," which I was learning to mimic. For presentable women who arrived early, the bouncers' list was meaningless. This night, I was late. Fortunately, so was Abbey.

She showed up just as I was paying for my cocktail. With her bouncy blonde hair, blue eyes, black dress, and clearly enhanced breasts, I spotted her immediately. Abbey wore lip liner that traced her smile far outside cosmetic boundaries.

"Can I buy you a drink?" I asked after introducing myself.

She ordered a martini and scanned the room. The timid woman on the phone seemed to have vanished completely.

"David Boreanaz is here," she commented, popping the pimento olive onto her outstretched tongue.

"Who?" I asked, scanning her scan.

Before taking a sip, she licked the rim of her martini glass to keep her lipstick from sticking. She frowned when it left behind a puckered imprint. "You know," she continued, "the guy who is on *Buffy*. He is getting his own show, called *Angel*."

I still had no idea whom she was talking about. "Oh. Oh right. David . . . Dave . . . Angel."

She kept shifting from one leg to another at the bar, as if posing. "And there's Mickey Rourke," she added. As she flipped her hair, a mouthful of her blonde locks stuck to my freshly glossed lips. I tasted Aqua Net blended with cheap perfume. The name Mickey Rourke sounded vaguely familiar, but I probably couldn't have picked him out of a lineup.

"Come on," she said, grabbing my hand. "Let's go meet him." Her abrupt movement caused my gin and tonic to splash all over my hand. "He'll love you," she continued. "You look just like his ex-wife Carre Otis."

Somehow I had completely lost control of the situation. "Abbey, wait . . . hold on. . . ."

Ignoring me, she reached out her hand. "Hi, Mr. Rourke."

Suddenly I recognized him: the greased hair, the creviced face, and the hard features. His black leather jacket brought the look together. A plume of smoke floated from his lips, toward the ceiling. Surrounded by friends, he sank deeper into the velvet booth as if relaxing in a Jacuzzi.

"My name is Abbey," she said, "and this is my girlfriend, Marlise."

I was still blotting gin off my hand with a cocktail napkin when I heard my name and looked up. "Oh, nice to meet you." As he shook my hand, I wondered if he would think it was wet from sweat or just from the condensation of my glass.

"Doesn't she look familiar?" Abbey asked with a giggle.

Utterly embarrassed, I felt as if we must seem like groupies obsessed with chasing celebrities. Without saying a word, Mr. Rourke motioned me over with a single nod of his head. Nudging me from behind, Abbey pushed me toward the table. I was reluctantly submissive.

"You have eyes just like my ex-wife," he said, taking another drag from his cigarette. "It's unbelievable."

At that point, I was unsure what to say. Since I reminded him of his former wife, he might not have intended his statement as a compliment.

"Thanks," I said hesitantly. "I think."

Like a member of the mafia, he gave me another silent nod. For an uncomfortable moment, Abbey and I stood there before realizing that this signal meant we were dismissed.

Confused about my next move, I lied to Abbey in a whisper, "I have to go to the restroom." I backpedaled for fear someone at the table would analyze the size and shape of my rear.

Thankfully, Abbey was still waiting at the bar when I returned from the restroom. It was becoming apparent that our meeting was going nowhere.

"I don't mean to be rude, Abbey," I said, ordering another round. "But what is this all about? I thought you had a story to sell."

"I do," she said, summing it up in four simple words as she closed her compact. "I'm a star fucker."

My ears did a double take. Here I was, the daughter of a minister, having drinks with someone who appeared to be far from a virgin. "What?" I asked, nervously poking at the lime in my drink with a straw. "You mean that really is your honest profession?"

She reached across the bar to grab another olive. "Well," she answered matter-of-factly, "I don't know how 'honest' it is. But it sure pays the bills."

"You mean like a call girl?" I blurted.

She pressed her finger to my lips, a flirtatious move she probably used with her clients in the bedroom. "Shhhh . . . not so loud."

Forgetting the original purpose of our meeting, I suddenly began rambling. "Don't you feel dirty? Do you really love these men? What do you charge? Do you pay taxes? Who are your clients?"

"Slow down," Abbey said, starting to sound annoyed by my ignorance.

Insisting she never asked clients for money, she claimed to operate on a donation basis. "They are sort of like my secret sugar daddies."

When those "daddies" refused to feed her candy, however, Abbey said she had "no choice" but to sell them out.

"I'll tell you who I sleep with, but it will cost you," she continued.

"I already told you," I explained. "We don't work that way. First, you tell me the story and then I'll let you know if we're interested."

"Fine," she said between sips. "Let's start off with Jack Nicholson. If you guys want that story, then I'll reveal more details."

The next day I typed up the lead sheet, "Jack Nicholson sleeps with hookers." I was surprised when it came back from Madeline crossed out with a big X and the editorial comment: "That's not news."

Pete later explained that in the arena of reporting, uncommitted celebrities can sleep with whomever, whenever, and wherever they want. The tabloid goal, however, is to catch the married ones, even if they have to be trapped like Frank Gifford was with the flight attendant.

When I called Abbey to say we were not interested in her Nicholson story, she was still convinced her bedroom accomplishments could earn her a fortune.

"Okay, what about David Boreanaz?" she asked.

Knowing he was married, I was sure Abbey was lying. "You mean the *Buffy* guy we saw at Barfly last night? That's impossible. You don't even know him."

"Well, I got to know him pretty well after you left," Abbey explained. "I slipped him my number and he called."

There was no way this intimate process could have been so simple.

"Prove it," I demanded. "What's his number?"

There was a pause before she answered. "I never got it."

"And photos inside the house?" I continued.

She was hesitant to reply. "Ummm . . . no."

As a celebrity reporter, the process of providing substantiating proof now seemed basic to me.

"Can you give me a love note, a business card, a message on your phone . . . anything?"

There was silence on the line.

"Look, Abbey, there's a certain way of doing things at *Globe*. I know it's hard to believe that a tabloid magazine actually supports its claims, but we need some hard evidence here. Next time, call me and we'll have a photographer waiting outside the house. You'll have to kiss the celebrity on the doorstep or something, but a picture like that could potentially be worth a lot of money."

"What if I give you the used condom?" she asked earnestly. "Can you run a DNA test or something?"

Bile was rising in my throat. "We are a tabloid, Abbey, not a forensic lab."

Her calls became incessant. Communicating in code, Abbey often scheduled "emergency" meetings at some of the best restaurants in Beverly Hills, like Morton's Steakhouse or Spago's. By the second course, she would have confessed her latest fling and by the time dessert arrived, I would have told her we just weren't interested in her story. Abbey's black book was filled with the names of single men, each one laced in fame with a wild reputation to match.

In an effort to provide hard evidence, Abbey showed me her collection of sexual souvenirs. Together, we dug through her shoe box, stuffed with everything from tape-recorded messages to phone numbers on cocktail napkins. Despite Abbey's frantic efforts, *Globe*'s editors refused to publish her stories unless she was willing to go on the record.

"Keep my name out of it," she would insist. Time and again, I delicately explained that there simply was no "it." Occasionally, however, there were one-page headlines based on tips Abbey had generated that had nothing to do with her bedroom antics. As a result of Abbey's dwindling income, *Globe* covered David Boreanaz's divorce from his first wife, Ingrid Quinn, and did short pieces on Yasmine Bleeth and Don Johnson.

"I hate to sell these people out," she said, trying to justify herself. "But I really need the money."

Approaching her mid-thirties, Abbey was struggling to keep pace with the Heidi Fleiss call girls. Pushed out of the celebrity pleasure-ring, Abbey was desperate to profit off her lustful experiences. Often calling me from the bathroom of a celebrity's home, she became a kiss-and-tell woman, selling her sins to anyone who would buy them.

Madeline encouraged me to cut Abbey loose, claiming she was costing the tabloids more in entertainment than she produced in leads. I never complied. Abbey remained one of my most committed sources throughout my time at *Globe*.

By now I had added Abbey to my list of sources. In that pre-Palm Pilot era, my Rolodex of contacts had begun to grow noticeably.

My inside line rang. "Hey girlfriend." It was Sharmin, sitting two desks away. "Meet me in the bathroom for some office gossip." Sixty seconds lapsed before I casually headed down the hall to meet her. Like a teenager skipping gym class, Sharmin was propped up on the counter-top flipping through *Ebony* magazine. I stayed close to the sink in case Madeline walked in.

"Guess who got married last night?" she asked in a guarded whisper. "I'll give you a hint. It's someone in the office."

My mind raced through images of all the staff members now sitting at their desks. "Is it Pete?"

Sharmin gave me a look of shame. "Girl, last I checked, Congress ve-toed gay marriage in the state of California."

It seemed I was always the last to know. "You've got to be kidding me, Pete's gay?"

Jumping off the counter, Sharmin peered under the stalls to check for feet. She nodded. "We'll save that topic for another day. The one I'm talking about is Keith Harden."

"I didn't even know he had a girlfriend," I said.

"Neither did I, until I read this," Sharmin said, handing me the lat-est issue of the *National Enquirer*. The gossip section announced the sudden wedding of Keith Harden to the widow of a famous television actor, whose series had been popular a few decades ago.

"I'm curious to see how long their marriage will last," Sharmin added. "You know I ain't one to gossip, but I hear she's been known to tip the bottle."

Having made friends with nearly everyone in the office, I was starting to feel like an insider among the insiders. Sharmin even included me in the morning bagels and coffee she bought compliments of *Globe*'s petty cash fund. It was nice to belong.

Returning to my desk, I discovered a Post-It note stuck to my computer screen: "See me in my office—MN." Next to it was another Post-It, obviously forged in Pete's unmistakable handwriting: "I'll give you a bonus if you lick my neck—MN." Grabbing the second of the two, I walked toward Pete and stuck it on his forehead. "I'm watching you, Trujillo," I said with a laugh.

As I suspected, Madeline was waiting to inform me of my latest assignment: *Globe* had received word that Steve McQueen's daughter, Terry, was in the hospital. That was all we knew. Considering the importance of the story, Madeline felt it essential to have Caelan Dunmore working on the assignment, too. The editors had flown Caelan in from San Francisco and had sent him to the McQueen home in Pacific Palisades.

"Just stay in your car and watch how Caelan works," she ordered, handing me the address. "Get a feel for the neighborhood. A fair number of celebrities live over there, so you'll need to know your way around."

I was offended that the editors had so little faith in the LA office that they had to send in reinforcements from San Francisco. Making my way to the parking garage, I was humiliated to realize that, again, I was reduced to being nothing more than a tagalong reporter. As I waited to get the car keys from the valet, the elevator bell rang and there stood Pete.

"It's a *Globe* field trip," he cheered, jiggling his keys. "Madeline caught me playing solitaire and told me to make myself useful. Want to go to Starbucks?"

"Sure," I said. "Your car or mine?"

In Pete's 1988 Nissan Maxima, we looked like the Flintstones, the car tilted to one side due to our uneven weight distribution. While Pete parked curbside, I ran into Starbucks to grab us two blended Frappuccinos.

"With extra cream," Pete shouted from the window. As I paid for the order, there was an incessant honk coming from the street. Running outside, I found Pete fast asleep, his head on the steering wheel. His narcolepsy was becoming increasingly worrisome.

"Okay, one Mocha Frappuccino, extra cream," I said, waking him with a slam of the car door.

Pete grabbed the plastic cup as if nothing out of the ordinary had happened. "Did you keep the receipt?" he asked, taking a deep sip. "You know you can expense all caffeinated products as a key ingredient of efficient reporting."

I shook my head, admitting that I had never given it much thought. We were well into a sugar high by the time we reached the McQueen house.

"That must be Caelan's rental car," Pete said, pointing toward a Buick. "They all look the same."

Considering this was not officially our assignment, there wasn't too much we could do except wait for Caelan. "Some of these homes are gorgeous," I said, pointing at one with my Starbuck's straw.

Pete nodded. "I know. I've door-stepped all over this neighborhood." Slipping his drink into the cup holder, Pete started counting on fingers. "Let's see . . . Tom Cruise, Billy Crystal, Anthony Hopkins, Steven Spielberg, Bill Cosby, Whoopi Goldberg . . ."

While his list grew, I reached for the binoculars and focused into the distance. "Quick, duck!" Grabbing the back of Pete's neck, I pushed his head into my lap, covering it with my arched body. "We've been spotted. Someone is running down the street toward us."

Pete fought my grip and whispered, "If they know we're here, why are we hiding?"

Before I could answer, there was a hard tap on the window with the back of a cell phone. My heart danced the samba. "Pete, don't look now, but there's a man standing directly behind you."

The face came closer to the glass. "Whit are yers' messin' aboot in there fer?"

Recognizing the voice, Pete freed himself from his hiding place. "Caelan! Long time no see."

Rolling down the window, Pete leaned back so we could shake hands over his belly. "Marlise, meet Caelan. Caelan, meet Marlise."

When Caelan poked his head inside the car window, I notice the Joaquin Phoenix-like scar above his left lip and caught the aroma of his tobacco-stained clothes.

He smiled without showing his teeth and had a brown speck in the ring of his hazel eyes. "Pleasure tae finally meet ye, luv," he said.

Did he just say "love?" It seemed odd that anyone could use the word so flippantly as a noun rather than a verb. I thought "love" was a verb. I loved my family and my dog. I loved cookie-dough ice cream. But I had never batted that term at a man, romantically or even platonically, for that matter. How dare he abuse it so poetically? Both my love and sexuality were items of power I intended to save for the man I was to marry.

With his forearm resting on the window frame, Caelan continued, "I've already heard an awful bit aboot ye." At least, that's how it sounded to me.

Saying nothing, I took a sip of my blended Frappuccino. The straw caught air, making a dreadful slurping sound as I inhaled the last drop of slushed coffee.

I must look infantile to Caelan, like a milkshake junkie devoid of table manners.

He smiled again, instantly destroying my Scottish stereotype of *Trainspotting* crudeness chased down with a shot of malt whisky. He seemed unprocessed, a social fusion of Ewan McGregor trapped inside the body of Edward Norton.

Pete's voice interrupted the drumming of my thoughts. "How's the story turning out, Caelan? Did you get an interview?"

"Ah had a wee bit o' luck with the mother," he explained in his thick accent. "A rather dark story, 'tis. She tells me the poor child nearly passed from liver failure. The lassie's dyin' cus of her father. 'E carried the gene, ye know."

Pete rattled the base of his drink. "Anything we can do to help out with the story?"

"I've aboot got it," Caelan said, tapping the roof of the car. "Ye two go on ahied. Ah may pop by the office a wee bit later."

To my horror, I could hear my overly peppy voice entering the fleeting conversation. "It was so wonderful to meet you!"

Pete glanced at me oddly, as if he didn't recognize the person sitting beside him. My voice had left me sounding like a cheerleader when all I wanted to be was a sultry librarian.

"And ye as well, luv. And ye as well," Caelan replied, looking back through the window.

Caelan never did come into the office that day, instead faxing his article from the hotel. The cover story he sent to Florida was titled "Steve McQueen's Girl Cheats Death."

It was months before Caelan and I spoke again. This time, it was to discuss my tragic follow-up story, "McQueen's Daughter Fought to the End."

As *Globe*'s leading freelance reporter, Caelan had already rejected several offers to permanently sign with the company. The fact that he was a dedicated worker seemed to be enough reason for the editors to leave him alone for the time being.

Unlike most of those on the tabloid staff, Caelan could not be labeled or summed up in a single sentence. It was like defining Jell-O. Any descriptions of Caelan were limited to his physical traits rather than those of his character. It seemed there was very little that I, or anyone else, knew about the elusive writer from Glasgow.

Note:

In 1997, Rodney Dangerfield became outspoken about his persistent bouts with depression. He died on October 5, 2004, after falling into a coma after surgery. At the time of his death, he was married to his second wife, Joan.

CHAPTER 5

Affairs to Forget

Hello," I said, answering my cell phone. "Can I help you?"
"Yeah, it's me, Abbey. Don't speak, just listen." I could hear ringing on the line. "I'm calling Jack's house," she continued. "You'll be on three-way with us. Don't say a word or he'll know you're there."

She seemed to have lost her mind. "You mean you're calling Jack Nicholson right now? No, Abbey. I beg of you—"

"Hello?"

My voice was silenced by that of the *Batman* Joker.

"Hi, baby." Suddenly my source had transformed into a seductive temptress. "It's me, Abbey."

The raspy laugh I recognized from the big screen was now coming through my private line. It was like watching *The Shining*.

"Abbey . . ." His words lingered. "What can I do for you?"

"Well, Jack, I was hoping I could do something for you," she said. I had to admit, she was smooth. "Do you miss me, baby?"

He belted out his infamous evil laugh as Abbey continued with her pitch. "I could come over if you'd like."

Pete noticed my hand cupping the receiver. "Who're you talking to?" he asked. Shooing him away, I stood up and ran into the conference room cradling my cell phone. I could hear Pete yelling in the background, "Since when did the tabloids start keeping secrets?"

Thankfully, Jack Nicholson could not hear the invasive commotion.

"You are one naughty girl," I could hear him saying. "Do you need a spanking?"

"Yes." Abbey sounded overly excited at the prospect of being beaten. *Do people actually talk like this?*

"I've been a bad, bad girl Jack. I need a scolding from the cyberspace god."

I had to cover my mouth to keep from laughing.

There was a pause before he responded, "I hope you're talking about me."

"Of course I'm talking about you, baby," Abbey cooed. "You're all over the Internet now. It's like you're a total cyberspace god."

Abbey had perfected the art of petting celebrity egos. My heart was beating as I listened to his heavy breathing.

"I guess I am now, aren't I," Nicholson said.

"How 'bout you get that velvet nightstick ready for your naughty girl? I can wear my French maid costume and be over there in an hour."

"Why the hell not?" He laughed one last time.

And then, the line went dead. I remained silent, shocked at what I had just overheard.

"Marlise? You still there?" It was Abbey, sounding utterly normal once again.

I exhaled deeply. "Yeah, I'm here."

"Now do you believe me?" she asked.

"Abbey, I never doubted you," I explained. "I know you have sex with celebrities. Unfortunately, *Globe* just doesn't care."

Abbey was silent, probably because I had just insulted her pastime. "Do me a favor, Abbey. Call me when you have a really good story to sell."

She hung up without saying good-bye. Knowing I had offended her, I thought about the advice from my former colleague Patrick Kincaid: "Never become friends with your sources."

By now I was as consumed by the ethical warfare of my job as I was by the pressure for headlines. The latest addition to my list of worries was the hunt for new roommates. As the financial adviser of the family, Heidi had decided to help underwrite our mortgage by renting out our spare bedroom. A simple ad in the UCLA newspaper brought in a flood of prospects. We had narrowed the selection down to two Japanese students. One of them had yet to learn English and the other dreamed of joining Cirque du Soleil. We decided to rent them the room.

They were a unique pair, generally keeping to themselves except when our schedules happened to overlap. Each week I would give them copies of the latest *Globe* and, in return, they gave me a bowl of sticky rice. Green tea, tofu, sashimi, and sake graced our kitchen. Forks and knives were replaced with porcelain chopsticks, which eventually found their way to the top of my head as fashionable hair accessories. My roommates didn't seem to mind my insensitivity.

This was a strange time in our lives. Heidi and I felt we were bursting with cultural awareness. Yet, no matter how good the sushi, four girls living under one roof ultimately led to problems. One of our roommates never did learn English, nor did we learn Japanese. This was fine, but it did hinder the prospect of female bonding. The other roommate had hygiene issues. She also turned the living room into her circus training center and insisted on practicing her routine at all hours of the night. Her inverted-juggling act habitually began at three in the morning. Heidi and I were ultimately forced to re-evaluate the situation. Before long, my sister and I were again on our own.

Meanwhile, life inside the office continued to improve. I began to lose my feelings of insecurity, guilt, and doubt. Despite the fact that my parents considered my profession a "temp job," I had no intention of going anywhere else anytime soon. As long as my sources remained loyal, my byline would remain intact. Even my very first source, Shane from the William Morris Agency, stayed in close contact. He, too, was notorious for including me on three-way calls with clients such as Clint Eastwood and Jodie Foster. Like many sources, however, he could not seem to understand the concept that the better the information, the better the pay.

"I've got a hot one for you," Shane said in a whisper. He was convinced his office phones were being tapped. "A big name actor is having an affair."

"You're going to have to give me more than that," I demanded.

"Clue number one," Shane continued. "Actor starred on *The Electric Company*. Clue number two, mistress has the same name as a hotel."

I hated playing his games. "Shane, do we really have to go this route? Come on already. You know how this works."

His whisper became louder. "As a committed employee of William Morris Agency, I refuse to name names."

"Fine," I agreed. "Let me start with clue number two. Marriott, Ramada, Sheraton—feel free to stop me anytime—Radisson, Doubletree, Hilton—"

"You're getting warmer," he interrupted.

". . . .Hyatt."

"Bingo," he cheered.

I wondered what had become of his stealth whisper. "What? Her name is Hyatt? Shane, if I'm going to move forward with this story, I'll need a first name."

"D-E-B-O-R-A-H," he spelled out, as if that held him less liable for breaking confidentiality.

I was getting angry now. "Shane, I don't have time for these childish games. Now give me the actor's damn name!"

"*The Electric Company*," he repeated. "Afro-American."

Then he hung up.

Spinning in my chair, I shouted across the office, "Anyone know a black actor who was on *The Electric Company*?"

Adam from New York was famous for his knowledge of TV trivia. "Morgan Freeman," he called back. "From nineteen seventy-one. He played the Easy Reader."

"Oh yeah," Karen added, pausing to sneeze. "He played Count Dracula."

Pete looked up from his computer. "Or, it could actually be Bill Cosby. He was a regular on that show, too."

Keith tapped his pencil twice and pointed at Adam. "Wasn't Morgan Freeman also in *Pulp Fiction*?"

Never one to miss a racial slur, Sharmin shook her head in disgust. "You think we all look alike, don't you?"

"Actually, that was Samuel L. Jackson," Pete corrected politely.

The conversation had digressed. "So, it was Morgan Freeman then?" I repeated, trying to nail my lead.

Sharmin and Pete simultaneously started singing the educational nursery rhyme, "Conjunction Junction, what's your function?" Grabbing a magazine off her desk, she rolled it into a tube and sang, "Come on boys and girls! Everybody together now!—Conjunction Junction, what's your function?"

Keith started tapping his pencil to the beat as Adam stood up from his chair to join the choir. "Chug-a-chug-a-chug-a-chug-a . . ." he repeated in the background.

Karen clapped her hands to the beat of Keith's pencil and cheered, "It's like *Soul Train!*"

Adam linked onto Sharmin and Pete, who had already formed a two-person conga line. Joining in, I swung my legs back and forth as if wearing a pair of bellbottoms and made my way to the back of the line. "Wait for me, my sistah!"

"What the hell is going on in here?" Suddenly the chorus line fell silent as we noticed Madeline standing in the doorway of our musical tabernacle. Adam threw his hands in the air like a criminal caught red-handed.

"What is this, some sort of joke to you people?" Color was quickly rising from Madeline's neck into her face. "We have a paper to run here and you need to take this job seriously."

Like a classroom of scolded children, we all gazed down at the floor and stood in silence.

"Marlise!" I was still holding onto Adam's belt loops when she called my name. "Other than dancing, what are you working on?"

Under the circumstances, trying to sound professional was quite a challenge. "My source just informed me of an alleged affair involving a celebrity," I said, already dreading her next question.

The other staff members slowly returned to their desks while the focus remained on me. "Who's the celebrity?" Madeline demanded.

"Well, umm, it seems more research needs to be done before I can write up a lead sheet." I hoped my answer would buy me some time.

"Hurry up, otherwise I'll need you to write up some shorts," she threatened.

Shorts? I hated shorts.

Shorts were page fillers, void of bylines. They typically ran no more than a quarter of a column in length. Each one came with a catchy title and pictured the head of a celebrity inside a dime-sized circle. These miniature articles were generally based around a single celebrity comment that had been previously quoted in another publication. We would then effortlessly reshape the interview and type it up as a short. This kind of task often filled my slow news days.

"I'll have something to you right away," I promised.

As Madeline turned to walk away, Keith let out a cheery little "Toot-toot!" Thankfully, we were the only ones who heard his belated conclusion to our song.

As soon as Shane was able to leave his desk at William Morris, he called me from an outside line to confirm that the targeted celebrity was, in fact, Morgan Freeman. According to Shane's tip, the actor would be attending the premier of *Kiss the Girls* with Ms. Hyatt, his assistant and alleged mistress. Considering that Morgan Freeman had been happily married to Myrna Colley-Lee since 1984, the editors thought the story was a waste of time and gave me exactly one day to determine the truth.

My assigned photographic partner was the 27-year-old freelance paparazzo James Churchill. British-bred, James loathed celebrity chases and only participated in them for the ridiculous amounts of money they generated. Like me, James's ultimate dream was to break into respected journalism. For the moment, however, we were both making enough money and having too much fun to think beyond the tabloids. Rumor had it that James was notorious for missing shots by milliseconds and apologizing to the stars whose pictures he did capture. Despite these shortcomings, James's nocturnal reputation to accept all-night stake-outs made him a hot commodity with tabloid editors.

Globe's head office had drastically reduced James's work hours. They were convinced that his pierced tongue, his Austin Powers greeting of "Yeah, Baby!" and his platinum spikes were anything but discrete. It took exactly five minutes for me to determine that James and I would become lifelong friends.

On this particular assignment, we knew that the film premiere for *Kiss the Girls* would serve only as a launching point for the Freeman story. At media-covered events, celebrities tend to be overly cautious and never publicly display affection unless they want their romances to become known. Our plan was to determine if Freeman's alleged romance with Ms. Hyatt did, in fact, exist.

Stepping from a limo, Morgan Freeman and an attractive brunette made their way onto the red carpet at Mann's Village Theater in

Westwood. A string of actors posed as flashbulbs blinked from all directions. "Mr. Freeman," James called. "May we snap a nice photo of you and your beautiful wife?"

Keeping her distance, the brunette took a step backward while Morgan Freeman explained, "Oh, she's not my wife, son. She's my assistant."

Without missing a beat, James asked, "Does she have a name for our photo caption?"

Turning away from the crowd of screaming fans, the pair ignored James's question and walked inside the doors to safety. We knew we had our woman. After a drink at nearby Maloney's Pub, James and I headed back to the theater and waited for the couple to exit. Again, there was no public display of affection. From what we could tell, there was only a professional link between the two.

Contrary to the stereotypical image of tabloid tactics, James and I casually followed the trail of cars to the after party held at Flint's. There was no chase or aggressive behavior on our part. We were just two journalistic partners waiting patiently for something to happen. From our car, we watched as lavishly dressed VIPs entered the speakeasy bar.

"What do we do now?" James asked.

I looked down at my worn Levi's, Yankees T-shirt, and Adidas tennis shoes. "We go inside and get a drink," I said. James's clothes were stained and torn and he looked worse than I did.

As expected, the security guard took one look at us and said, "Sorry. Guest list only." For the next hour, James and I sat curbside, looking more like street punks than professional journalists. He told me some of his paparazzi tales and talked about the famous photographers with whom he had worked. On high-risk stories, the tabloids would generally assign two or more photographers to guarantee at least one print-worthy picture. I listened intently to James, wishing that I had something equally exciting to share.

"My best work was definitely the Brooke Shields and Andre Agassi wedding," James explained. "They were planning to get married in Monterey and had arranged for tight security protection. *Globe* partnered me with Paul Radley, who is borderline psychotic. That man will absolutely not quit until he gets his best shot."

By this stage, I had heard countless horror stories about Paul Radley. Although we had never met, I learned that he was undoubtedly the most successful paparazzo of all time. Known as "the terror of Hollywood," Radley began his photographic stint in the late '60s with his New York-based partner, Randal Traub. The struggling freelancers shot for the *National Enquirer*, which was then owned by Generoso Pope. The team's popularity grew after they broke the story of Burt Reynolds's romance with Loni Anderson. At the time, money was still minimal for celebrity photographers.

In 1982, Johnny Carson had publicly belittled the *National Enquirer* on *The Tonight Show*. His comment triggered a revenge assignment straight from the desk of Generoso Pope, who hired Radley and Traub to tail Carson. For days, the duo parked in front of Carson's house, hoping to catch him with another woman. Even after Pope suspended the fruitless assignment, the determined paparazzi persisted on their own. One month later, the team captured Johnny Carson and Sally Field relaxing on Carson's balcony, drinking champagne. Knowing the potential worth of such photographs, Radley sold the pictures, initially priced at $200, for a total of $20,000. This sale marked the beginning of the celebrity gossip explosion.

Their success was continuing to climb when, in 1984, the two hopped on a plane in pursuit of Elizabeth Taylor. Uncertain of where she was headed, Radley and Traub spontaneously followed the actress on a six-week global vacation that took them through four Asian countries. Years later, Radley made tabloid history by renting a submarine for $16,000 to track Princess Diana. He submerged the vessel in the Caribbean and was able to photograph the late princess sunbathing on Necker Island.

Although I had heard many of these anecdotes before, James was holding me spellbound. Still sitting on the curb waiting for Morgan Freeman to emerge, James tried to keep me awake by describing how he had managed to get shots of Brooke Shields's wedding.

"Before the wedding, Radley and I scouted the grounds from a helicopter, but realized there was no way we could get close enough to shoot pictures," James explained. "So I decided to rent a cherry picker."

"A what?" I interrupted.

"A cherry picker. You know, to pick cherries. My grandfather owned one when I was a kid so I knew exactly how they worked."

James's story seemed highly improbable. "How did you find a cherry picker in the middle of Monterey?" I asked.

"In the Yellow Pages," he responded. "We rented a forty-five-footer from an equipment company for six hundred dollars a day. In foreign sales alone, the pictures brought in a fortune."

I couldn't help thinking how my experiences paled in comparison to James's. "And you didn't get caught?"

He shook his head. "Nah . . . there were police surrounding the cherry picker but the controls for the machine were inside the bucket. I just pretended that I couldn't hear them down below. It was brilliant."

Just then, the familiar voice of Morgan Freeman brought me back to the present. "The sky is so clear tonight," he was saying. "Look at those stars."

Nudging James, I pointed toward the actor, who was standing in the street holding the hand of his alleged mistress. "Hurry James," I whispered. "Take the shot!"

Unprepared and clearly flustered, James strolled toward the couple and politely called out Mr. Freeman's name. The sound of his approaching steps caused the pair to immediately separate in opposite directions.

Lowering my head into my hands, I knew we had just lost our story.

James disagreed with my assessment. "I'll get the car and we can follow them. It's not too late to get a shot."

He was right. Well, sort of. From a discrete distance, we followed the pair to the Four Seasons Hotel. We spent the next ten hours sleeping in two hour shifts. This was the one and only time I ever camped overnight in a car for the sake of a celebrity story. It was obvious that James made this a regular habit, judging from the sunflower seeds, blankets, pull-down shades, and crumpled cigarette packs littering his car.

At nine a.m., the alarm on my watch sounded to announce another two-hour tradeoff. The timing could not have been worse. At that exact moment, Morgan Freeman and Ms. Hyatt exited the hotel together. Although there was no public display of affection between them, the suspicious hour and hotel backdrop would have been enough to justify an accusation.

Just then, my cell phone rang. "You've got to be kidding me," I muttered, pulling the phone from my pocket.

"Don't answer that," James ordered.

Noticing that the call was from the LA office, I ignored him. "Hello?"

"Why aren't you in the office?" It was Madeline.

"Well, I'm still working on the Morgan Freeman story," I explained. "James and I are outside the Four Seasons. Freeman is leaving right now with his assistant."

"Marlise," she said, sounding annoyed. "I gave you one day to work on that story. If you don't have any proof of an affair—and I'm talking about solid evidence with a photo—then I want you back in the office in thirty minutes. Do you understand me?"

Before I could respond, the line went dead. James aimed his lens through the window. "We're too far to get anything," he said. "Let's call it quits." I knew James had mentally given up long before. He had already earned his $200 day rate and would not earn a cent more, even if he did capture the photograph. There was no incentive for him to succeed.

I watched as Morgan Freeman's chauffeured car exited onto the street. "Come on James, let's follow them."

He was already taking apart his camera equipment. "No, Marlise, there's no story."

"There's no story because you don't give a damn," I said. Suddenly I realized how rude I sounded.

James just lit up a cigarette and inhaled deeply. "In case you haven't heard, Marlise, the photographer is never to blame. If a story fails, it's because the reporter lost control. Reporters are the ones supposedly in charge of each assignment." James started the engine and continued. "I probably shouldn't be telling you this, but you really need to learn how to be a bit more aggressive."

"Really?" I said, somewhat taken back. I gave him a fake glare, pretending to practice my evil look. "I suppose I can do aggressive." I punched the air like a boxer before a fight. "What do you think?"

James ashed his cigarette and pointed with the stub. "Oh yeah, baby! A bitch is born."

By early afternoon I was back in the office, embarrassingly defeated and empty-handed. Other than Karen and Sharmin, the place was empty and void of action.

"Where is everyone?" I asked.

Sharmin looked up from her magazine. "Madeline's getting her nails done, and Keith and Pete are with a bunch of transvestite prostitutes." These unusual explanations were becoming commonplace. I was too exhausted to probe, but Sharmin volunteered further information. "They're interviewing drag queens who were supposedly picked up by Eddie Murphy."

I nodded absentmindedly. "Did anyone call for me?"

"Just Abbey," Sharmin said, handing me the number. Rolling my eyes, I wished my day would take a turn for the better. I wasn't in the mood to hear another story about Abbey's latest celebrity fling.

"Who did you sleep with this time?" I asked sarcastically.

"Very funny," Abbey said. "Actually, on this one, it's my sister Gloria with Sonny Bono."

My exhaustion faded from one second to the next. "You're kidding me. You're going to sell out your own sister?" The fact that Abbey and I had become borderline friends made me feel I could ask such a direct question.

"Aren't you supposed to be encouraging me on this?" she asked. "Besides, my sister and I are estranged and I'm totally broke. I need the money."

Over a late lunch, Abbey showed me photos of her sister Gloria with Sonny in Palm Springs. She claimed they had been having an affair while he was holding office as a member of the U.S. House of Representatives. I rushed back to the *Globe* office with Abbey's photograph in hand.

"First off," Madeline said. "The pictures don't prove anything except that Gloria and Sonny knew each other. Secondly, Sonny Bono is dead. The only way this story will ever run is if you can get a firsthand account from the mistress."

Having given a vow of confidentially to Abbey, I phoned Gloria directly in Palm Springs. Naturally, she hung up the moment I mentioned Sonny's name. Calling back, I told her that *Globe* was going to run the story with or without her cooperation. "Your willingness would also give you more control over the outcome of the story," I coaxed.

Although it wasn't about the money for Gloria, I threw in the verbal offer of $3,000 to sweeten the deal. Slowly, Gloria began to open up about her relationship with Sonny. "The fact that Sonny is gone makes this so much harder," she said. At one stage, Gloria seemed to forget that she was talking to a tabloid reporter. I had deliberately tapped into her emotions. I kneaded Gloria's memory, convincing her that a public confession would help free the guilt she had been carrying for years. There were tears and then moments of uncontrollable heaving as she told me about her destroyed friendship with Mary Bono, Sonny's widow.

According to Gloria, her ex-husband had partnered with Sonny in the early '90s to create the Palm Canyon Resorts and, in the process, had introduced his wife to the Bonos. Mary became Gloria's workout partner, while Sonny became her secret lover. Their three-year romance continued even after Sonny became a U.S. congressman. Suspecting that Gloria and Sonny were having an affair, Mary confronted Gloria in Washington, D.C. Gloria was there, visiting her dying grandfather. That was the last time Gloria had ever spoken to either of the Bonos.

Unbeknownst to Gloria, I was secretly recording our entire phone conversation, despite the fact that *Globe* forbids reporters to tape interviews without consent. I was willing to break the rules as long as I could gain an exclusive. It was only at the end of our call that I tried to insert a belated disclaimer by asking, "Do you mind if I record this?"

Gloria immediately became ballistic. It was obvious that she had considerable personal experience with California privacy laws. "Who are you?" she screamed into the phone. "I don't know what you're talking about." She hung up.

Walking into Madeline's office, I told her that the story was rapidly slipping away. Furious that I had disobeyed company policy, Madeline confiscated the tape and told me never to mention what I had done. She demanded that I drive directly to Palm Springs to try to repair the damage. Three hours later, I was knocking on Gloria's door.

"Are you Gloria?" I asked, slipping her my card. "We spoke on the phone earlier today. I'm Marlise."

Gloria was naturally stunning, just as she had appeared in the pictures. She looked like a soccer mom who bakes brownies but never eats them. Her eyes were puffy and I could tell she had been crying. She did not invite me in.

"I'm afraid I said too much," she admitted. "You know, I started opening up and I didn't think about the permanent consequences. This would devastate my family and ruin Mary's political career. I beg of you, please leave."

I placed my hand on the door frame and fought to gain eye contact. "Gloria, the editors decided to run the story without your help," I lied. "I just thought you might want to get the three thousand dollars I promised."

She looked past me and onto the street. "Look, my husband is coming home soon. I really don't want to pursue this any further."

I was running out of ideas. Speaking in a whisper, I asked, "Can I use your bathroom?"

She nodded and opened the door without saying a word. Taking out the source agreement, I placed it on the counter and added, "You should at least get something out of this."

When I returned, she was holding a pen and her eyes were welling up with tears. I pointed at the blank line where she needed to sign her name. Suddenly, the kitchen door flew open. A man, whom I assumed was her husband, reached for the contract and began reading the fine print.

Turning to Gloria, he asked, "Who the hell is this?"

Gloria tried to put on a fake smile. "Hi, honey. This is my friend Marlise." Her hands were trembling. "Actually, she was just leaving." Tears formed rivulets down her cheeks. I realized her husband had noticed them, too.

"I don't know who you are," he said, finally looking at me. "But I want you out of my house now."

Gloria's efforts to diffuse the situation were futile. Her husband reached for the phone and dialed the police.

"Yes," he said, into the phone. "I want to report an intruder."

An intruder? Two hours earlier I was practically a therapist and now I'm an intruder?

I was more insulted than I was frightened, but I knew this guy was serious. Running to my car, I drove around the block and stopped to phone Madeline.

"Well, it's all rather unfortunate, isn't it?" she commented, coldly. I told her that Gloria would have signed the contract had it not been for her husband's untimely arrival. "It doesn't matter anymore," Madeline continued. "I'm killing the story. You've already wasted enough time and money."

"But Madeline," I pleaded. "It's all there. Please just give me one more day to nail the story."

By that point, *Globe*'s money and time didn't matter to me. I had put every ounce of effort into getting this story and I wasn't about to throw it away because of some tabloid budget.

"I know I can get her to sign the contract—"

"Stay away from that house," she interrupted. "I want you to go home and get some rest. Really, Marlise, you are becoming way too personally involved in your assignments lately. *Globe* is about quick turnarounds, not about long therapy sessions, and definitely not about tears. Monday morning, I expect you to bring in some new leads. I think you're overdue for a headline."

After ending my call with Madeline, I dialed Abbey to explain what had transpired. Having been cut out of her $2,000 lead fee, Abbey was angry and threatened to sell the story to our competitors.

"Be my guest," I told her. "You won't be able to sell this story anywhere else."

Before leaving Palm Springs to head back to LA, I took one last look through the Sonny Bono file. Thumbing through the published articles of his death, I realized that the press had overlooked Sonny's mother, Jean. Inside the file was also a list of related phone numbers and addresses, including one belonging to Sonny's mother. Making my way to Jean Bono's house, I knocked on the door and told her I was writing a story about her late son.

Jean invited me in and offered me milk and cookies, as any ordinary grandmother might do. Her mantelpiece was covered with pictures of Sonny, his children, and his string of ex-wives. Noticeably absent were pictures of his widow, Mary.

"Are you and Mary friends?" I probed, knowing very well that I was on the hunt for a story. Jean confirmed my assumption about her strained relationship with Mary. This ultimately helped give me the headline for my resulting story, "Cher Caught in Catfight with Battling Bonos."

The following week, Abbey realized she had been unable to sell out her sister to any of our competitors. As a result, she agreed to sell herself to *Globe*. The price was $2,000. This led to my article titled "I Bedded Sex-Hungry Stars." The two-page spread exposed the details of Abbey's romances with Charlie Sheen, Jack Nicholson, Ian Ziering, Mikhail Baryshnikov, and Nicolas Cage. The story was later syndicated to Britain's leading tabloids, *The Daily Mirror* and *The Sun*. All benefits from syndication went directly to *Globe*'s publishers. As reporters, we received neither bylines nor remuneration of any kind when our stories were syndicated.

Despite the fact that my success was at the expense of someone else's confession, an odd satisfaction came over me. I had turned a negative into a positive and had regained lost ground in Madeline's eyes. The thing that frightened me most was not that I was participating in these devious acts, but that I was comfortable doing so. I could easily sleep at night, wake up, and repeat the cycle the following day. Finally, my guilt had been quelled. All it had taken was something as simple as a tabloid byline.

Note:

Since 1984, Morgan Freeman has been married to his second wife, Myrna Colley-Lee.

Mary Bono has represented the 45th congressional district in the U.S. House of Representatives since 1998. From 2001 to 2005, she was married to businessman Glenn Baxley. The mother of two children,

Mary Bono has been romantically linked recently with Florida Congressman Connie Mack IV.

CHAPTER 6

The Innocent Sinner

After six months and thirty-four bylines for *Globe*, my social life was in desperate need of a perm. Understandably, Manuela had stopped calling, instead focusing her energy on an acting career. At least that was her plan. When not occupied as a social worker, she attended drama classes and spent hundreds of dollars on headshots. Like many aspiring actors, Manuela settled for working as an extra, for which she earned $60 a day as a body prop for sitcoms and movies. All that was about to change, or so she thought.

"Look what I've got," Manuela said, waving two tickets in front of my face. Although we lived in the same complex, almost two months had passed since I had last seen her. With golden skin, she looked rested and much more toned than before. Her abs had formed a four-pack on either side of her bubble-gum outtie.

"Well hello, Abs of Steel," I said, poking her exposed stomach. "What's your secret?"

She had obviously just worked out. There was sweat dripping from the center of her violet sports bra down to her spandex shorts that cut midway at the calf. Despite my workout regimen, I could never obtain her sculpted calves.

"Step aerobics in the morning and running in the evening," she explained, still somewhat out of breath. "It's the perfect high-impact workout. I'm burning like negative calories now."

Her leg was propped vertically on my door frame in some sort of standing split. I was afraid she might snap.

"So, what are these tickets for?" I asked, directing her back to the purpose of her visit.

She switched legs. "Oh, right. Well, there was this guy on the beach who saw me jogging. He's like this really big casting director who works with MTV."

I knew where this was headed. Sooner or later, nearly every semi-attractive female in Hollywood comes in contact with an "agent" or "director." The majority of these men prowl the nightclubs, caressing the arms of women and wave-pointing at men. They deal out business cards Vegas-style before mouthing the words, "Call me."

Manuela handed over the tickets. "This guy wants me to be on MTV's *Singled Out.* Can you believe it? I mean, I don't have the main part yet, but at least it's an in to the show."

Singled Out had to be the worst game show ever created. It was MTV's version of *The Dating Game*, in which two contestants find love and another ninety-eight walk away feeling ugly and rejected. As the show's host, former *Playboy* Playmate Jenny McCarthy became better known for her facial contortions and burping sounds than for her mind.

"Why two tickets?" I asked, fearing her answer.

"Because you, my dear," she said, touching my nose, "are coming with me."

Manuela was the essence of optimism. She had a glimmer of hope that I vowed to support even if it killed me. As expected, the show was torturous. Literally hundreds of bikini-clad ladies stood in line, each waiting for her chance to reach the casting table. In fashion protest, I had worn my overalls. Manuela was furious, convinced that my drab style would influence the outcome of her career. Nearly two hours after arriving, it was our turn to be questioned.

"Breast size?" asked the MTV employee.

I looked down at my flat chest. "32B."

She knew I had lied, yet continued through the entire list of body measurements.

"Okay," she said. "Whaddaya lookin' for in a man?" I could tell this girl wasn't from around Hollywood. Her East Coast accent had yet to misuse such grammatical intensifiers as "totally" and "majorly," commonly heard around LA.

Manuela was standing on a scale in front of me. Dozens of sun-bleached contestants were behind us, applying and reapplying three shades of lip gloss. There was no way I was going to pursue this superficial survey any further.

"I'm sorry, but I really shouldn't be here." My voice dropped to a whisper. "You see, I'm actually just supporting my girlfriend." Pointing toward Manuela, I hoped her appearance alone would let me off the hook.

"Fugeddaboutit," said the woman behind the desk. "I'm not supposeda be here either. I'm jus' volunteerin' so I can break in ta the production world." Her nails were bitten short and she wasn't wearing any makeup.

"You mean they aren't paying you to be here?"

Leaning across the table, she spoke back in a whisper. "Can you believe it? I move out here a week ago from back East. Just like that. I pack my car and end up in Hollywood. I don't even have an apartment yet."

She looked surprisingly calm considering her circumstances. "By the way, the name's Chantal."

I shook her hand. "I'm Marlise. It's nice to meet you."

Setting down her clipboard, she stood up from the table. "Do ya' wanna grab a coffee?"

I pointed toward the ladies who were becoming increasingly impatient as they waited in line to be interviewed by her. Chantal just shrugged her shoulders. "What are they gonna do, fire me?"

That afternoon Chantal and I relaxed at the food table while Manuela bounced in the studio audience. Sadly, nothing came from her efforts other than another party invite. I, on the other hand, had just found myself a new roommate in Chantal.

One week later, Chantal moved into our townhouse without any baggage, literally or figuratively. She was exactly what Heidi and I needed—simplicity with panache. Chantal baked with chocolate, danced in the living room, worked on puzzles, and played Natalie Merchant. She applied green mud masks and cucumber eye patches. Her room was fragranced with incense that made your nose perk, yet never made you feel like you were living with a hippy. She sewed her own party dresses, slept in silk sheets, painted her toes red, and had bunions that stretched the sides of her shoes. I liked her because she didn't judge me. Heidi liked her because she listened.

"*Globe* isn'cha lifelong career," Chantal used to tell me. "So stop ya worryin' about all them pointin' fingers and just enjoy ya' life."

And so, I did. Thanks to the encouragement of my new friend, I decided to capitalize on my twenties. My wardrobe adapted accordingly. I began to have weekly manicures and facials. My brows were plucked, my skin was bronzed, my teeth were bleached, and suddenly, I felt like a woman. As my confidence climbed, so did my social life. Casual dates became routine, sometimes four or five different guys in one week. It was dinner and dancing, or drinks and a movie. Whatever the combo, it was always at night and only went as far as my front doorstep.

Nearly every second date ended in a kiss. And then I never called them again. I provoked with my lips, over-glossing and brushing four times a day, becoming a mouth tease without morning regret. It was like *Sex and the City* minus the sex.

I dated some strange ones, like an Iranian oil tycoon who drove a yellow Lamborghini and tipped our waitress $100 at California Pizza Kitchen. Our second date ended abruptly after he caught me waving at a male bartender and threatened to chop off my fingers.

Then there was the MTV editor, Sebastian Steel, a party boy who was intrigued by my paradoxical background. He had *Playboy* magazines on the coffee table, a hemp garden on the balcony, and a basket of feminine products next to the toilet. Sebastian believed that Pamela Anderson was sent to this earth to serve as his mental pastime. This made it even more remarkable that we were together at all. Our three-month on-again, off-again relationship was more off than on. He never understood why I wouldn't sleep with him.

"Because I don't love you," I explained honestly.

"And that's okay," he would respond. "I don't love you either."

I told him about Jesus and he told me about threesomes. He offered to buy me a boob job on the condition he could touch them post-surgery. Neither of us understood the other. And so, we broke up unemotionally, realizing that, in our case, opposites don't necessarily attract.

Blind dates were never my thing, unless of course I had previously seen the date on TV. Such was the case with *Days of Our Lives* actor Bryan Datillo. Unfortunately, our date didn't work out very well. He held my hand, bought roses, and sang love songs in the car. It was all a bit overwhelming. I constantly felt trapped inside a dramatic soap opera and, one time, accidentally called him by his television character's name, Lucas.

Match Game host Michael Burger was another unfortunate knot in my string of dates. He wore three-piece suits, drove a gold Mercedes, and placed his hand on the small of my back. Every question he asked made me want to push a buzzer or go for the Daily Double. The twenty-year age gap limited our dates to lunch at Chin-Chin and dinner at Jerry's Famous Deli. He stopped calling after I changed his car's radio station from jazz to hip-hop during one of our dates.

And then there was John Ritz, a film producer who was intrigued by my virginity and labeled me the "Big V." He thought he could "break me," yet never made it to my lips. Eventually, we settled on a platonic relationship based on superficial events and shallow conversation. Together we attended the Emmy® Awards, cocktail parties, and a Hugh Hefner party. Terrified of being associated with a tabloid reporter, he insisted that I tell everyone I was studying law. For three months, I became his paraded show pony while he remained my ticket in.

Sadly, none of these men made a lasting impression on my life. I was beginning to wonder who, in fact, ever would. Noticing my frustration, Chantal suggested we balance out the party scene with an occasional night at a comedy club. That's when I met Ahmed Ahmed, an Egyptian-born standup comedian who grew up in California. The fact his name repeated itself should have been some sort of sign that he was a little too exotic for my taste.

Ahmed wasn't overly attractive, or always funny, for that matter. In fact, he used me as a mock audience to test out his new material. I never let on that I realized what he was doing. He was an across-the-room pointer, an annoying habit that I associated with agents and club promoters. After six months, he came to terms with my "no premarital sex" policy, most likely finding liberation outside the relationship.

Known for his friendships, Ahmed roamed Hollywood with a group of struggling actors, all of them longing to one day get beyond local theater and open mic night. They "chased the scene," as Ahmed called it, searching for a showbiz connection to pull them from the abyss of anonymity and into the zone of "members only." After seven years of rejection, this persistent pack made its debut in the film *Swingers*. The group included Vince Vaughn, Jon Favreau, Ron Livingston, and film producer Peter Billingsley, the former child star who played Ralphie Parker in *A Christmas Story*. Ahmed, on the other hand, was generally typecast as a terrorist in films like *Passenger 57* and *Executive Decision*. Long after discovering our incompatibility, I continued to date him.

I truly enjoyed spending time with some of these men, yet never longed for them. Turning the tables on the roles of dominance, I began to use them. Like a temptress, I taunted and begged and enticed with my virginity, giving a glimpse of hope that they just might be "the one." I seldom returned calls. I canceled at the last minute and was always late. I handed out fake numbers and took on false identities. I cheated with my lips and made conversation with my eyes. Yet there was never a chastity belt or purity ring to keep me in line. My mind alone became my voice of accountability. Determination and the thought of losing my sexual prominence saved me in fits of passion. Playing games had now become an integral part of every aspect of my life. I enjoyed the control and power and thrill of being in charge.

This mentality was difficult to comprehend. I was both pure and polluted at the same time. My real identity was lost somewhere between a minister's daughter and a tabloid reporter. The two sides of me never seemed to mesh. I danced on Saturdays and prayed on Sundays. As a reader of scripture and a writer of gossip, I was a spiritual contradiction. I cursed God for not making me strong enough to stand or weak enough to fall. The more I embraced my job, the more my faith wavered. My mother told me they were praying for me, but I was too busy shaking hands with evil to care. Inwardly, I blamed my parents for being too consumed with the next life while I was living only for this one. And so, I danced in the garden and juggled forbidden apples.

Apparently I wasn't the only soul going astray. Around this time, I received a call from an acquaintance, Ron Haler. Three months before, we had met through a mutual friend and had remained in contact. In the '60s, Ron had made a fortune by designing mirrors that looked like album covers. Apparently, the hippy generation had taken a liking to his mirrors, which could double as cocaine cutting boards. His clients paid a fortune to snort lines on the images of the Rolling Stones or the Grateful Dead.

At fifty-two, Ron had made a clean break from this lifestyle and was reinvesting his fortune. He had gray hair that touched his shoulders and wore silver-rimmed glasses much too big for his face. His lips seemed to hang like the snood of a turkey and he wore cashmere sweaters with jeans and loafers. Until recently, his hair had been pulled back into a slick ponytail. Overall, Ron was a lonely man, jumping from one Internet romance to another and regretting his actions later. An overflow of finances functioned as Ron's therapy, and the more he spent, the better he felt.

Now working as an investment manager, he was in town on business to promote his latest client, Vonda Shepard. The singer had launched her career with Ron's financial backing. (Only later, after Vonda became a regular on the TV show *Ally McBeal*, did her career really take off.) Prior to his LA arrival, Ron had mailed me two tickets to Vonda's concert to be held at the Troubadour. I decided to take Manuela with me.

As soon as I introduced Manuela to Ron, it was a case of hunter meets the hunted. Batting her Bambi eyes, Manuela knew exactly what she was doing. I warned Ron, telling him that at eighteen years his junior, Manuela was all about the money. He just ignored me, biting the air and mouthing the word "juicy."

I don't exactly know what happened after the concert. Manuela never told me and I never asked. All I know is that the following day, she and Ron went to Malibu's Colony Plaza and Manuela returned home with ten designer dresses.

Had I wanted to, I knew that I could have been holding those shopping bags. But that is where selective morality robbed me of my worldly pleasures. Somehow I had no problem justifying unethical means to better my career. When it came to sexual or financial gain, however, I wanted no part of it. After that weekend, Manuela and I never again discussed Ron or their shopping spree.

When Vonda's album became a success, Ron was cut out of the profits from his former protégé. Out of revenge, he begged me to write a story that would expose the singer. He got his wish and I got another byline. Soon, the lack of love and money caused Ron to relapse into drugs. I found myself reluctantly providing him with telephone therapy.

Shortly thereafter, Manuela became pregnant by a nightclub bouncer. It was a miracle he hadn't crushed her. The guy had legs like tree trunks and an embrace that could crack a spine. He called every woman "Baby" and every man "Bro." Despite the fact that he stamped hands for a living, he managed to win over Manuela for a one-night stand. When she phoned him about the baby, he responded, "Who are you again, exactly?"

Although he offered to pay for an abortion, she insisted on keeping the child. Manuela miscarried in the first trimester, and one month later returned to her family in Lima, Peru. That was the last time I saw her.

After Manuela's departure from the neighborhood, I had even more time to dedicate to *Globe*. My attention shifted to scandal in the White House, where America's president had been caught with his pants down. Naturally *Globe* wanted to find the woman who had made them drop. Initially the magazine's owner had refused to cover the scandal out of respect for the nation's leader. During *Globe*'s two-week Clinton ban, however, sales had dropped by fifty percent. That's when the editors decided it was time to spread the news of the Cigar-Lover-in-Chief.

My assignment was to interview as many celebrities as possible who would comment in support of Clinton. My four-column article included statements from Whoopi Goldberg, Geraldo Rivera, Candice Bergen, Barbra Streisand, Alec Baldwin, Montel Williams, Walter Matthau, Sidney Poitier, Angie Dickinson, and Lauren Bacall. It was a relatively simple process to get positive quotes from Clinton supporters for my story, titled "Hollywood Stands by Its President."

Although I was far from politically savvy, *Globe* gave me three follow-up assignments related to the Clinton scandal: 1) get Chelsea's reaction to her father's affair, 2) locate a duplicate of the infamous "blue dress," and 3) find dirt on Monica Lewinski.

In the end, getting Chelsea's reaction was the easiest part. Armed only with the knowledge that Chelsea was a Stanford student, I contacted one of my former classmates who was now attending Stanford's grad school. Ironically, he also turned out to be one of Chelsea's private tutors. My resulting article reported that although Chelsea was upset with the situation, she was still defending her dad. I delivered the entire article in less than four hours.

More difficult to accomplish was finding a replica of "the blue dress." My workday was spent Gap-hopping from Santa Monica to the Beverly Center Mall. Finally I found the dress and a black Donna Karan beret, both of which *Globe* later used in a photo layout. Even more humiliating than buying the garments was returning them, slightly used but unstained, to save the magazine $102.89.

The third and final task was definitely the most arduous. The entire *Globe* staff was sent on a mass expedition, heading in different directions to try to unearth new angles on the Lewinski story. After reviewing Monica's records, I discovered that she had attended high school in Portland. I flew to Oregon and knocked on the door of one of her former classmates. I had already gone through a lengthy chain of people and three door slams to find the right girl. This time, my youth proved to be an advantage. Lewinski's classmate admitted that she had, in fact, received e-mails from Monica during her White House internship. However, she was unwilling to share them with us out of respect for her friend.

Realizing the value of those letters, I offered her $50,000 for the Lewinski e-mails. I knew *Globe* would consider it money well spent. The girl turned me down without any hesitation. Obviously, there are some things neither money nor *Globe* can buy. As much as I regretted not making the conquest, I was inwardly impressed by her profound loyalty to her friendship with Monica. From my car, I phoned Madeline to tell her I had been unable to buy the e-mail letters.

"Go back and offer her thirty thousand dollars," Madeline demanded.

I took a deep breath and admitted, "I already offered her fifty thousand and she turned me down cold."

"No offense," Madeline told me. "But I would sell you out for five."

My job in Portland was complete. Ultimately, Barbara Walters was the only one able to get close enough to Monica for an interview.

It was Friday, and for the first time in months, I had a free weekend. Rather than flying directly back to LA, I drove to Seattle to visit my old friend, Darin Leverett. We had first met while attending Westmont College and had remained close despite his transfer to Washington State University. His father intended to groom Darin to become a lawyer in the family's Seattle firm. Darin's liberal arts education was not about to stand in the way.

About twice a year, Darin would fly back to California to rekindle our friendship. Permanently stuck in that "love you like a sibling" stage, we were mentally more than friends yet physically less than lovers. Darin was like no other man I had ever met, operating in his own world of discovery and contemplation. Often I would clap my hands in front of his face just to bring him back to the conversation at hand.

He played the piano with his eyes closed, nodded politely when people spoke, and wore wigs at respectable events just to get a reaction from the elite. Neither I nor anyone else seemed to understand Darin's sense of humor. In college, he would run from room to room, hiding textbooks inside bedsheets, and then, for his grand finale, set off stink bombs in the hallway. He practically lived in the library, only rewarding himself with "free time" once his studies were completed. He became consumed with the stock market, eight hours of sleep, memorizing five SAT words per day, and salsa dancing.

After Darin broke my toe on the dance floor, everyone knew to stay clear of his unpredictable moves. He habitually stepped on feet and snapped his fingers out of sync, yet it was always everyone else who needed to find the rhythm. With cotton balls shoved in his ears, Darin would point at his head and scream over the music, "I'm prolonging my hearing!"

He never owned an alarm clock or a camera, claiming the sun would be his buzzer and his memory would be his film. Neither of us was very good at communicating our feelings, and so our friendship never progressed to the next level. There was little doubt that Darin actually cared.

Every evening at college, he would call my room and play Elvis songs in the background.

"Darin, is that you?" I would ask.

My roommate was convinced that the mysterious music-lover was some eerie campus stalker. I hoped it was Darin. Sadly, the music stopped when he left for Seattle. When I drove him to the airport from campus, he closed his eyes tightly and then opened them again. "I'm taking a picture with my mind," he explained.

Now, thanks to *Globe*, I had the entire weekend to give Darin a new photograph. It had been six months since we had last seen one another. He hadn't changed much. After an awkward hug, he began walking around my hotel room, pulling back curtains, knocking on wooden beams, and peeking inside closets.

Words were limited and shallow. In general we saved our deeper thoughts for late-night phone conversations. For the most part, Darin was passive, except when it came to racquetball. Our skills were perfectly matched, to the point that every game ended in a final deuce. "You wanna play a game of racquetball?" he asked. "For old time's sake?"

I gave him a single nod. "Sure. What are we betting?"

He held out his hand for the agreement shake. "Lunch at Taco Loco."

On the way to the courts, we stopped at 7-Eleven for vanilla cappuccinos. It was Darin's first exposure to any caffeine other than Coca-Cola. "My taste buds are dancing," he said, sucking from the plastic stick. Holding up a copy of *Globe*, Darin told the checkout clerk that I was the magazine's top reporter.

"So, is she rich?" the guy asked. Darin nodded and said I was his sugar momma.

I walked outside to fill the car with gas while Darin engaged in a lengthy conversation indoors.

"Darin, let's go," I yelled, poking my head inside. I could hear him discussing stock options and IPOs with the clerk. Darin claimed the man was an investment genius. Back in the car, we rambled about all sorts of things, neither of us really listening to the other. It was mayhem, but I loved it, because it was us.

Once we hit the racquetball courts, my game was on, winning both sets 15-13. I kept expecting him to smack my rear with his racquet like he used to do in college, but he never did. That's when I knew he had a girlfriend.

Darin kept his part of the bet with a stop at Taco Loco. Over lunch, he explained his plan to study tax law and eventually intern in New York. Like me, Darin was a breathing oxymoron, except that he was a naïve genius and I was an innocent sinner. He longed to try pot brownies in Amsterdam and buy a motorcycle to defy his father. Darin's latest act of benign rebellion was his refusal to purchase car insurance, claiming he would drive with caution and save $7 a day.

"That means our burritos were free," he said, balling up the empty foil wrap. The girls at the taco stand knew him by name. Apparently he ate there three times a week, stocking up on their famous chocolate chip cookies. Insisting they were better than Mrs. Fields cookies, he was furious that the restaurant staff would not divulge their secret recipe. Staring into oblivion, Darin rubbed his chin and sat silently. I noticed neither of us had spoken in a while.

"Well, they probably just reduce the amount of eggs or add extra brown sugar," I said offhandedly, biting into the chewy treat. With a snap of his fingers, Darin pointed toward me as if I had just solved a groundbreaking riddle.

"So Darin, are you dating anyone?"

He was still nodding from the cookie revelation. "Yes. Yes I am."

I waited for a name, description, identity, anything that would bring me closer to the woman who had captured Darin's heart. "In fact," he continued. "I'm gonna ask her to marry me."

A spray of cookie crumbs shot out my mouth.

"Her name's Marlene." He wiped off the front of his shirt.

Marlene? Did he just say Marlene? Silently, I sat there waiting for him to comment on the similarity of our names. He never did.

"She's a twenty-eight-year-old law student, studying criminal defense."

Now I nodded. "Sounds like quite a woman."

Darin unzipped his backpack and pulled out a can of Pringles. We were still at the restaurant. Popping the top, he tilted the can toward me. "Pringle?"

I told him that the taste of salt so soon after a chocolate chip cookie tends to destroy the pleasure of both flavors. Shrugging his shoulders, he reached inside the half-empty can and pulled out a stack. They broke in his grip.

"So, are you dating anyone?"

I found myself wishing I had a relationship to brag about. "Well, not really," I confessed. "Just a few guys here and there, but no one to bring home to the parents."

I crunched on ice while Darin, now trying to reach the chips at the bottom of the can, got his hand stuck inside. I could hear the Pringles breaking into pieces. This conversation was frustrating me. Yanking the tube off his arm, I flipped his hand and dumped the remaining bits into his palm. "Just tilt the freaking can, Darin!"

He looked shocked. "Jeez, Marlise, bite my head off, why don't you? What's wrong with you? You're acting weird. I swear, you've completely changed."

"I've changed? Darin, you're the one getting married."

"Why are you so upset?" he asked. "I thought you'd be happy for me."

I did sound rather upset, borderline jealous, in fact. I had to back-track. "I'm not upset," I lied. "I'm just surprised, that's all. You're like my brother, Darin. I would expect you would tell me these things sooner." *Oh no, did I just drop the brother line?*

"Well, I only met her four months ago." His explanation made matters worse. "It's just not the type of news you want to shove in an e-mail. And besides, I haven't officially asked her yet. It's just something we've been discussing lately." Darin looked at his watch. I knew he wanted to change the subject. "Look, I actually have to be going now. The bar exam is coming up soon and—"

"It's fine, Darin. I have to get back to LA anyhow."

We drove in silence, only commenting on Seattle's architecture and the smell of Pike Place Market.

"It was nice seeing you again," I said, giving him a series of unemotional pats on the back.

"Yeah, you too." His hand was already on the door handle. "Next time we meet will probably be at my wedding."

The thought nearly made me cry. "Can hardly wait, Darin."

Stepping from the car, Darin closed the door and began talking through the glass.

"I can't hear you," I said rolling down the window. "What was that?"

He shook his head. "Oh, never mind. It was nothing important."

I was dying to know what he had said, but I didn't want to seem too desperate. "Okay. Well, good-bye then."

For a split second, he closed his eyes tightly and then opened them again. Darin had gotten his picture after all. And, so had I.

For the first time since I had begun working at *Globe*, returning to the office was something of a challenge. I had never been fond of Mondays, especially this one, considering the weekend I had just experienced. Both my personal life and professional life were undergoing some major adjustments.

Adam from New York had been replaced by Jared Schooner, a 23-year-old freelance reporter who introduced himself as a "private investigator." Despite his age, I never felt threatened by his position on staff. Jared wore camouflage gear, hid in trees, flashed his press pass, and worked off duty. He watched sci-fi movies, read *Mad* magazine, loved to hunt, and tried to solve crimes for stories to which he was not assigned.

Tolerated by many and liked by few, Jared's days at *Globe* were clearly numbered. Rumor had it that Trenton Freeze had hired him straight out of college as a favor to Jared's uncle, who also happened to be Freeze's neighbor. Jared had been assigned to work on the Ramsey case. Plunked down in the middle of Boulder, he had been given $1,000 a week, plus a rental car and living expenses.

Jared's plan had been to go undercover as a neighbor of JonBenet's older brother, John Andrew Ramsey. He had also become a regular at the Episcopalian church the Ramsey family attended. Like many others who met Jared, the Ramseys became suspicious of the young reporter and were adamant about keeping their distance from him.

Everyone sensed there was something odd about Jared. Like some character in a bad TV movie, he called himself "JonBenet's avenging angel" and made a pact to capture the killer.

Moving his focus from the Ramseys to the authorities, Jared had used his tactics to gain access to Detective Steve Thomas and District Attorney Alex Hunter. Interestingly enough, these major figures had taken a liking to Jared and, despite his profession, confided in him. Ultimately, however, he lost the trust of these prominent sources.

Having burned nearly every other bridge, Jared then turned the tables on *Globe* by recording eighty hours of conversation with his editors about their take on the Ramsey case. His plan was to submit those tapes to the FBI and become a national hero. To his surprise, no one seemed to care. Eventually CBS picked up the tapes, which were briefly aired on *48 Hours*.

For his underhanded actions, Jared was slapped on the wrist and sent to *Globe*'s LA office to finish out the year. Openly loathed by his West Coast co-workers, Jared was obsessed with finding his way back to Boulder. In the meantime, Keith Harden had replaced Jared on the Ramsey case. Unlike Jared's stealth-like tactics, Keith marched straight up to the door of the Stine home, where the Ramseys were living. When Keith flashed his ID, Ms. Stine grabbed his wallet and slammed the door in his face. She then called the police to report a stalker on her property. By the time officers arrived, Keith was so worked up that they had no choice but to arrest him. Like Jared, Keith was also shipped back to LA.

Despite having been relocated, Jared still felt he was on a divine mission to help the little blonde princess. Madeline tried to keep him busy in the office, knowing he was a liability every time he stepped outside the door. Apparently, Jared had once left his rental car in a no-parking zone at the Denver Airport. His negligence forced *Globe* to pay more than $2,000 in parking violations and late rental fees.

Surrounded by celebrity news, Jared's passion for investigative journalism had dwindled along with his hopes of finding JonBenet's killer. Depressed and lonely, Jared shared his story with me one night over pizza. I listened to his endless tales of torment and revenge. After that day, Jared seemed to consider me his closest friend. He lent me techno CDs, which I never played, and *Star Wars* movies, which I never watched.

On a whim, I decided to invite Jared home for Easter. It was a bold move. Maybe it was a carryover from my childhood practice of bringing home stray kittens and lonely classmates. When relatives did a double take as we entered the house, I introduced him as "my co-worker Jared Schooner, only my co-worker."

Jared's plaid, button-down shirt was tucked inside his snug jeans, and the entire ensemble was pulled together with a braided belt. There he was, in the midst of a family reunion, boasting about his reputation as an FBI informant. Dinner conversation was interspersed with his conspiracy theories, his take on the O.J. Simpson trial, and his obsession with the Ramsey case. In the midst of coloring Easter eggs, Jared suddenly cried out, "We must find justice for JonBenet!"

I held my head in shame, wondering how I had gone from bringing home stray pets to bringing home mentally unstable reporters. That was the last time I ever saw him.

Apparently the editors couldn't hold out long enough to allow Jared to finish his *Globe* contract. The following week he was shipped back to Florida, along with the unforgettable chair twirler, Keith Harden.

Undoubtedly, someone would be filling their empty desks soon enough. That's when I saw the office memo announcing the arrival of *Globe*'s new roving editor, Caelan Dunmore.

Note:

Ahmed Ahmed went on to become a regular on MTV's *Punk'd*. He headlines a specialty show at The Comedy Store called "Arabian Knights," which features Middle Eastern comics.

Bryan Dattilo was married to Jessica Lahm from 1999 to 2001. They have one son.

JonBenet Ramsey's case returned to the news in August 2006 when John Mark Karr confessed to her murder. When Karr's DNA failed to match that at the crime scene, no charges were filed against him.

CHAPTER 7

Identity Crisis

'll admit it. *Globe* was changing me. I had been with the tabloids less than a year and already I had lost sympathy for celebrities. Working behind the scenes had given me a whole new perspective on the term publicity. Madeline used to say, "Good publicity or bad publicity, it's still publicity." I was beginning to understand what she meant.

There was no time for guilt or remorse in the tabloid world. Our goals were simple: Grab the headline, publish the story, and move on. As long as people kept buying the tabloids, *Globe* would keep selling them. And, as long as I could keep creating them, I would survive.

If it meant gaining another byline, I would wear the disguise, talk to the neighbor, tell the lie, and sleep in the car. I had no illusions about being a tabloid journalist. I knew I was not being paid for my ability to write, but rather for my ability to expose, and I was okay with that.

Still trying to refine this ability, I was looking forward to the arrival of Caelan Dunmore. Having worked under his direction while he was still freelancing out of San Francisco, I knew that I could learn a lot from his experience. As our staff roving editor, Caelan would still spend most of his time on the road even though he would be officially based out of the LA office. His latest assignment was a health-related story on Michael J. Fox.

Globe had purchased a series of photos of Fox taken in Central Park. The exclusive photographs showed him sitting alone on a park bench, studying his shaky hands, and "breaking down" in tears. Caelan consulted a medical expert who theorized that the actor was suffering from Parkinson's disease. Although an enormous legal risk was involved, Caelan located three sources and boldly ran the health crisis story with the photos.

As expected, Michael J. Fox denied the claim and called the tabloid article a complete farce. Apparently he was still bitter over a previous tabloid escapade in which paparazzi disguised as llamas had shown up at his countryside wedding in Vermont.

One week after *Globe* first broke the news of the actor's ill health, *People* magazine featured as its cover story, "Michael J. Fox's Brave Battle with Parkinson's." The actor had granted *People* an interview and they had landed another "exclusive." CNN covered the feature article and stated: "Fox, 37, made the revelations in an interview with *People* magazine." This only served to further fuel my anger toward the mainstream media for scooping what we, in the tabloids, had slaved to uncover.

During this same period, I had been assigned a "Where Are They Now?" story on the cast members of the '80s television show *Growing Pains*. I began my research by calling the home of Tracey Gold, who had played the role of Carol Ann Seaver in the show. Her answering machine announced, "You've reached Roby, Tracey, Sage, and our new bundle on the way. We're not home, so leave a message."

My editors felt that Tracey's own admission was enough to print a story about her pregnancy. Typically, we would tie the story to a past event and link it with an emotional headline. For example, *Globe* might print something along the lines of "Tracey Battles Anorexia Demons with Pregnancy." The week after we published our story, *People* magazine featured the exact same news.

One question remained unanswered. If numerous publications reported the same news, why were the tabloids, and only the tabloids, so loathed? It seemed that much of that hatred was launched shortly after the death of Princess Diana. Erroneous reports had originally linked her accidental death to her driver's high-speed attempt to escape from aggressive reporters. Even after further investigation determined that the driver's blood-alcohol level was three times the legal limit, the paparazzi were still viewed as the real cause of her death.

Until I began working for the tabloids, I too had blamed the paparazzi for invading the private lives of celebrities with their stalker-like tactics. One month into my job, Pete explained that there are no tabloid paparazzi as such. Every published image that runs in the papers is actually snapped by freelance photographers. They are seldom commissioned to capture a specific image. Rather, photographers independently stake out celebrities in the hopes of snapping world exclusives. This happened to have been the case with Princess Diana.

My defense of the tabloids was weak. I needed a reason to justify not only my own job, but the industry as a whole. It seemed unlikely that any good could come from celebrity journalism, apart from its entertainment value. Six months into the job, I finally discovered one bit of information that helped subdue my guilt. I learned that a great deal of celebrity publicity is a setup. Remarkably, the loathed paparazzi are covertly embraced by the very ones who pretend to yearn only for peace and privacy.

In an effort to restore a damaged reputation, publicists would often notify the tabloids of their clients' whereabouts. It was not uncommon to hear an actress cry out "please don't shoot," when, in fact, that same voice had just informed the paparazzi of her location. Other stars would either subdue or minimize privacy invasion by voluntarily giving photographers the poses they wanted. These mutually beneficial partnerships enabled celebrities to gain publicity and photographers to gain financial profit. Such pre-emptive strikes were a brilliant use of the symbiotic relationship between celebrities and the paparazzi.

As tabloid journalists, we routinely covered phony fights or fake romances, especially for celebrities whose careers were on the decline. Roseanne Barr was a regular tabloid contributor, tipping us off to everything from her public breakups to the renewal of her vows with her husband, Ben Thomas.

Some celebrities used the tabloids to promote such products as their new books or the release of their latest albums. That was the case with Diahann Carroll, Joan Collins, and Suzanne Somers. In general, celebrity stories fell into one of four categories: cooperative and compliant, resistant and resentful, purely accidental, or staged.

It was a welcome change to work with stars who just didn't take the headlines all that seriously. One of them was Enrico Colantoni, who played the photographer on *Just Shoot Me*. I had scheduled an at-home interview with Enrico, but had yet to come up with a suitable headline. Jumping into the tabloid spirit, Enrico jokingly asked, "Can you tell the world that I have an alien baby?" That afternoon, I got acquainted with his wife, whom he had met when she was working as his nutritionist. That single piece of information provided my headline: "*Just Shoot Me* Star's Amazing Love Diet."

Of course, some celebrities choose to simply make a deal with the tabloids. On numerous occasions, Jay Leno would trade sugary interviews as a substitute for information he did not want published. This led to one of my rather bland headlines, "Jay Leno: My Secrets to a Happy Marriage."

Stars like Jane Seymour, Lorenzo Lamas, Eric Estrada, Jean-Claude Van Damme, and Stefanie Powers fell into this category. Quenching the thirst for publicity, they offered the tabloids everything from "at-home" interviews to photographs of their new babies.

Also included on *Globe*'s "safe list" were Clint Eastwood, Arnold Schwarzenegger, and Sylvester Stallone. In 1997, Schwarzenegger pressed battery charges against two paparazzi who were later convicted and sentenced to three months in jail. Along with Eastwood, the actor was considered a legal risk and off limits to *Globe* reporters, no matter how big the potential headline might be. It wasn't until Schwarzenegger became California's governor that the public learned he had signed an $8 million contract with *Globe*'s owner, David Pecker. By contributing to our tabloid's sister publication, *Muscle & Fitness*, the governor was safe from the danger of any scandal hitting the tabloids. The editors soon realized that this arrangement would ultimately cost more than they had bargained for. Two days after the actor announced his candidacy, *Globe* reportedly paid a woman named Gigi Goyette $20,000 to keep silent about her alleged affair with Schwarzenegger.

The more I learned about the devious motives of celebrities, the easier it became to justify my position as a tabloid reporter. I felt as if everyone were evil. Some were only slightly more evil than others. The skin of my conscience had been stripped of remorse, allowing me to freely explore the profession I had entered so hesitantly just months before. This worked to the benefit of my editors, who had no intention of letting me go. Their plan was to groom me for upward mobility, meaning that sooner or later, I too might reach the top of the tabloid totem pole. For now, I was content to simply watch the shifting taking place around me.

This movement was accelerated when *Globe* decided to withdraw from its emphasis on the JonBenet murder case. After nearly three years, *Globe*'s readers had justifiably lost interest in weekly coverage of that exhausted topic. Consequently, all the magazine's Boulder-based reporters returned to Florida headquarters for their new assignments. The only problem was, their Florida desks had since been filled by new staff members who had proven that their talents were worth keeping.

In many ways, the West Coast office never entirely knew what was going on at Florida headquarters. We just kept to ourselves, working feverishly and going through the motions until the day we would be fired. No one had ever voluntarily quit. It was very much a case of them and us.

Despite the strained atmosphere in the office, we always found ways to diminish our tension. The mood would become noticeably lighter whenever Madeline went out of town. It was like attending school without the presence of a principal or teachers. On one occasion, I brought three abandoned kittens into the office, hoping my co-workers would give them adoptive homes. Instead, the feline trio took over the bureau, batting at phone cords, disconnecting computer cables, and running across the editor's vacant desk. In her absence, Sharmin took a picture of one of the kittens on top of Madeline's desk, cradling her business cards. Sharmin threatened to use the photo as blackmail if I ever got out of hand. By the time Madeline returned, the kittens were gone, only leaving behind enough dander to stir up Madeline's allergic reactions.

Meanwhile, things continued as normal on this particular Monday. Sharmin greeted me with a hint of sarcasm. Karen typed away in an antisocial mode. Pete was well into his third Costco muffin. By now, we were the only four who had survived from our original LA team.

"Morning, people," I waved with my cup of coffee. Before working for *Globe*, I had sworn I would never fall victim to caffeine addiction. It was still early enough to poke my head into Madeline's office and say hello.

"Morning, Madeline."

The back of her leather chair was facing me and I could hear the sound of paper being ripped from the fax machine.

"And howdy to y'all too, Sweetheart."

The deep southern drawl sounded nothing like Madeline's demanding tone. Suddenly her chair twirled 180 degrees. In her place sat a rugged-looking man who appeared to be somewhere in his mid-forties. He flashed a set of teeth perfectly aligned like sugar cubes in a box. Somewhere inside that Texan mouth was a wad of gum, snapping and popping. Leaning back in the chair, he stretched his arms over the head-rest, exposing a fading farmer's tan beneath the sleeves of his white T-shirt. It was only nine o'clock and already Madeline's usually organized desk was a scattered mess. This definitely was not Madeline.

"Hey, you're not Madeline," I thought out loud.

"And we can all thank the good Lord for that." He crossed his legs on top of the desk and shot a basket with a wad of paper. Dressed in cowboy boots and faded blue jeans, he looked like the Marlboro Man gone corporate. He motioned me over with a wiggle of his finger. I approached slowly.

"Where's Madeline?"

"She's under my desk," he said, "demoted to office intern." I could tell he was trying to read my reaction. I gave him my poker face.

"Actually," he continued, "she's attending meetings in Florida for a couple of days, and I've been assigned to cover her desk while she's gone." He held out his hand. "Greg Logan is the name."

"Oh yeah," I interrupted. "You're the editor who handled the team in Boulder, right?"

He nodded with a smirk, most likely because everyone knew that the Ramsey assignments had always gone awry.

"So, you must be the tabloid wonder." Leaning over the desk, he grabbed my hand and jokingly kissed my knuckles.

I meant to giggle, but all that came out was a single, awkward, bellowing, "Ha!" I could tell my mouth had opened abnormally wide.

"As your respected substitute editor, I'm first going to ask you to dinner. Then, I'm going to tell you to make friends with Sharon Stone."

Perhaps I should have been insulted by his straightforwardness, but I wasn't. The tabloid industry was virtually rule-free, both on the streets and in the office. As far as I was concerned, sexual harassment only existed if I defined it as such. I wasn't quite sure how to respond. Was this some sort of trap?

He interrupted my thoughts. "Actually, I was just kiddin' about dinner."

I let out a sigh of relief. Walking from behind the desk, he came toward me with a new lead sheet. He was now standing uncomfortably close.

"Let's do lunch instead," he said.

I grabbed the lead sheet from his hand and read the words, "Sharon Stone to wed Phil Bronstein on Valentine's Day." I changed the subject. "Who's on duty this weekend?" Considering I had filled my monthly quota for weekend hours, I assumed the editors would not expect me to work.

"Caelan Dunmore is flying back in time to cover the Stone wedding," Greg explained. "Have you met him yet?"

The writer from Glasgow? The man who called me "Luv"? I nodded casually. "I believe we've met."

"Well, it's only two days until the weddin' and all we have is Stone's home address. I need you to buy up some sources—caterers, florists, security, neighbors, anyone who will talk."

"But I'm in the middle of a Nick Lachey story," I countered.

Greg popped his bubble gum. "Nick who?"

"You know, the guy from the band 98 Degrees. He's dating some blonde named Jessica Simpson. She's the daughter of a minister and says she's saving herself for her wedding day."

Greg was busy shuffling through a pile of papers. "Oh yeah," he said, locating the approved lead sheet. "You're calling her the next Britney Spears in this lead sheet, huh?"

I nodded, waiting for him to let me off the hook on the Stone wedding.

Grabbing a red pen, he drew a diagonal line across the page. "I'm killin' that Jessica Simpson story. It's sourced as a T.O.H. and it's not time sensitive. And besides, no one really cares about this Simpson gal or Nick Lachey, for that matter."

T.O.H. stood for "top of the head," meaning the reporter had personally created the lead rather than learning about it through the usual paid-source route. The only reason I knew about this "unknown singer," Jessica Simpson, was because of my connection to the church.

Greg handed me Sharon Stone's address. "So, it's settled then. Go out to her house and work your magic. By the way, you should probably know that only credentialed weddin' staff and neighbors have access to the area. Good luck."

Despite what Greg had said, I had no magic or fairy dust to sprinkle over the heads of celebrities. Luck alone landed me the headlines I was producing. But, as the saying goes, luck eventually runs out.

On this assignment, all I had to do was to get near the house. A few ideas came to mind, like roaming the neighborhood with an empty leash, asking if anyone had seen my lost dog. But, as with my previous disguises, I tried to stay close to my true identity. And so, I decided to go jogging in Sharon Stone's neighborhood.

Wearing black Adidas sweatpants and a white tank top, I pulled my hair into a ponytail and threw on a set of headphones as a prop. I intentionally left the volume off. By the time I reached the targeted street, I had been jogging for thirty minutes, long enough to break a sweat. Two security guards were standing on either end of her street, which was blocked by orange cones. With such limited options, I decided to run directly through the barricade and past the two guards. My actions triggered an unexpected response.

"Looking good," said one.

I had noticed him all along, a stereotypical security guard dressed from head to toe in black. Standing with his legs shoulder-width apart, he held an empty water bottle in one hand and a walkie-talkie in the other. Both men came toward me. They appeared to be melting in the afternoon sun.

As they approached, I was jogging in place but quickly stopped for fear my masquerade was a bit over the top. "I'm sorry, did you say something?" I asked, removing my silent headphones.

"Yeah, we were admiring your form," added the second guard. Extremely well-groomed, he had trimmed dark hair, chiseled features, chocolate eyes, and thick brows. He was the Brawny man minus the flannel shirt and ax.

I wasn't sure what to say next. "Oh, well . . . you know . . . got to stay in shape."

Segue, Marlise, you need a segue, I coached myself.

Stretching my arm across my chest, I stalled, trying to think about the best way to handle this situation. "So, are you guys FBI or something?"

Perhaps that was a bit too forward.

They looked at one another, each waiting for the other to answer. "You think I don't know?" I joked. "It's like one hundred degrees out here, you're dressed in black, and you're wearing Top Gun sunglasses. And your earpieces are a dead giveaway."

"Brawny" gave "Water Boy" a single nod, as if my naiveté was reason enough to engage in harmless conversation.

"Actually, we're here for a celebrity wedding," he said. "But we aren't at liberty to divulge any information."

Standing on one leg, I pulled back on my other ankle, pretending to stretch my thigh muscle. "Oh, come on, look who you're talking to here. I won't say a word, I promise."

Brawny moved a step closer and whispered behind his hand, "Okay, Sharon Stone is getting married."

I tightened my ponytail. "Wait . . . is she that chick from *Basic Instinct*?"

He nodded.

"Get out! How random is that? I live just up the road and had no idea that she was my neighbor. So, who is she marrying? Anyone famous?"

"Some newspaper editor, I think," said Brawny.

Water Boy seemed agitated by his partner's openness. "You do realize that this is private information. Our job is to protect Ms. Stone from media intrusion, especially the paparazzi."

I nodded enthusiastically. "Oh, of course, of course. I completely understand." The conversation had to be prolonged, especially now that I was making progress. "Does that mean I'm invited?"

Suddenly two hands cupped my eyes and a familiar voice answered, "Absolutely not."

Grabbing the delicate fingers, I removed them from my face and felt them drop to my shoulders. Terrified to turn around, I knew that whoever it was had not been softened by my flirtatious tactics.

And there she stood, Sharon Stone, looking every bit as porcelain as she did on the screen. Her tall, slender frame seemed fragile compared to her defined features and empowering voice. Wisps of blonde hair flared from her untamed pixie cut, youthfully framing her soft cheeks and sapphire eyes. Her forehead was smooth and glowing, her jawbones sloping down to shape her oval face. Pedicured toes peered from beneath her faded jeans, showing signs of recent pampering. A ribbed tank top hung slightly below her thin charcoal sweater, draped loosely as if for fashion rather than warmth.

Of all the people who could have confronted me on that day, I had never expected to come face to face with the bride. We were all standing in a ring now. Sharon was smirking, like a parent who had just caught her child in a devious act. "Guess who?"

"Oh hi, I mean, congratulations!" I fumbled for words as the actress put her arm over my shoulder. "I was just jogging and saw these two nice men standing here and—"

"Don't trust this girl," Sharon said, playfully squeezing me around the neck. "You know she's an undercover reporter."

We all laughed, but I laughed the loudest, hoping that her joke would not be taken seriously. My mind was racing, trying to decide which house I would claim was mine if she did, in fact, ask where I lived.

I pulled her arm further over my shoulder. "Oh come on, I was just having a chat with these handsome men."

"I know," she interjected. "I saw the whole thing from the window. But you see, I'm paying these 'handsome men' to do a job, which they aren't doing very well." She pretended to give them a kick. "Seriously guys, no one else gets past this road." She tucked her hands into her jeans and looked toward me. "And you . . . where are you off to, exactly?"

I pointed past her house. "Up the road and then around the block. I'm not quite done with my workout."

Instantly catching on that I had no idea what I was talking about, Sharon chided me, "It's a cul-de-sac, you know."

I nodded. "Yep. That's where I stretch." I pointed in the opposite direction. "And then I go back down and around. . . ." I knew I was rambling.

She didn't care. "Well, I have a wedding to plan. Guys, I'm not going to tell you again. No one else gets through here."

The two guards nodded in unison. With her back toward us, she waved good-bye.

Of course my "loop" comment would now force me to stretch at the end of her road and then pass the guards yet a second time. I said good-bye, knowing that I would have to repeat the farewell process minutes later. Once I reached the end of the street, I leaned on the hood of a florist's van and pretended to stretch my legs.

Stashed inside the cassette holder of my Walkman were several of my *Globe* business cards. Opening the case, I slipped one of them under the windshield wiper of the florist van. I did the same thing on a catering truck and again on a neighbor's car, awkwardly stretching my limbs on a series of parked cars. My hands were shaking uncontrollably as the guards looked toward me and waved. Undoubtedly, my actions looked suspicious.

I jogged past them one final time. "Sorry I got you guys in trouble earlier."

Brawny hollered back. "Bring us some lunch and we might just forgive you."

Waving to them, I finally turned on my Walkman. This time, I heard music. Back at the office, I told Greg, the substitute editor, what had happened.

"Go back and bring them some lunch," he demanded.

He had to be joking. "I can't go back," I whined. "My business card is on every windshield on that block. I'll get nabbed the second they see my face."

Greg repeated his orders in detail. "Go to the deli across the street and pick up two of their best sandwiches. You've made it this far. Maybe you can buy them up."

The chance that I could bribe the guards directly in front of Sharon's home, or "buy them up" as Greg put it, was highly unlikely. One thing *Globe* had taught me was to weigh the consequences of my decisions. Sometimes it was better to only act submissive than to actually comply with an order. As a compromise, I had Domino's deliver pizza to the two guards.

Returning to Sharon Stone's neighborhood, I waited further down the road for someone from the wedding staff to pass. I needed to approach them off of her property. When the florist's van passed by, I flagged down the driver. He acknowledged that he had, in fact, received my card and more or less knew what I wanted.

"We are talking about thousands of dollars here," I explained. "And all you have to do is take one picture of the bride."

Although he didn't agree to the task, he passed the assignment on to another insider. Less than six hours before the wedding, *Globe* paid a caterer $5,000 for letting us put a video camera inside his cummerbund. The plan was to pay the source five thousand in advance and ten thousand upon receiving the recorded tape. *Globe* had gotten the source it wanted and the guards had gotten the lunch they deserved.

That weekend I was off duty, yet was still mentally consumed with the assignment. Although it was not technically mine, I rushed into Madeline's office for updates on Monday morning. Expecting that Greg would still be lounging at Madeline's desk, I could immediately see that he was gone, as was the disarray he had created. This was becoming a game of corporate musical chairs.

Sharmin was on the phone, engaged in a conversation about obtaining child support. "That bastard owes me three years of wages. I don't care if I have to kill him to get it—"

"Where's Greg?" I mouthed.

She scribbled on a sheet of paper, "Sun Valley Idaho—Bruce and

Demi story. Caelan is in charge."

My whisper went up a few notches. "Caelan? As in the new guy, Caelan?"

"Well, that's aboot as welcomin' as a plate of haggis." It was Caelan, the new roving editor we had all been expecting.

"Oh, I'm sorry," I explained. "I just thought you would be starting after Madeline came back from Florida." I reached out my hand. "Welcome."

Shifting his armful of story files to his left side, he shook my hand. He looked professional yet approachable, wearing khaki pants and an ice blue collared shirt.

"You're right, o'course. That was me plan. But I'm finding meself here a bit early on account o' the Stone wedding."

"How did it go with the cummerbund?" To anyone outside the office, my question would have seemed absurd.

Caelan shook his head. "'Twas a wee bit of a mess, I'm afraid. The source turned out to be something of a head case. 'E ran off with me camera."

Despite the fact I had been off duty, I somehow still felt responsible for the outcome of the assignment. "Sorry to hear that."

"'Tis nobody's fault, ye know." His voice sounded consoling. "Florida 'ardly gave it a thought. The important thing is the other papers got nothing either. I reckon that saved us from getting a beating."

Caelan still spoke in terms of "us" and "them," despite the fact that he had officially obtained management status. He seemed to be the link bridging the two worlds of master and slave.

Suddenly Sharmin's voice interrupted our conversation. "Kirstie Alley source on line three. Who wants it?"

"I'll pass," Pete hollered. "I'm up to my ears in 'Ticker Trouble for Schwarzenegger.'"

I looked at Caelan. "I thought Arnold was off limits."

"We've got plenty o' proof on this story," he explained. He turned toward Karen. "What would you be workin' on then?"

"I'm typing up my date with George Clooney," she answered. I was still jealous over Karen's latest assignment. At a recent charity event, she was the highest bidder to win a date with the actor. She kept her identity a secret throughout the entire evening, and only on publication day would Clooney discover the truth.

"They're still holding. . . ." Sharmin reminded us.

Grabbing the phone, I took the call without waiting for approval to do so. "This is Marlise. How can I help you?. . . When did she arrive?. . . Okay, someone will be there within fifteen minutes…. Right now I'm going to pass you over to our editorial assistant, who will take down your information so we can arrange payment."

Caelan stood there waiting for the details. I began to explain. "Kirstie Alley is at Gourmet Grub in Santa Monica. We've been looking for a story to tie in with the success of her show, *Veronica's Closet.*"

He nodded. "Very well, then. Let's try to focus on findin' out just 'ow many stone the lass has actually gained. Take a peek inside her shopping cart. See if Kirstie nibbles a wee bit on her food before she pays fer it. Meanwhile, I'll send a photographer 'round to wait outside the shop to shoot a snap from across the way."

The plan sounded simple enough. Unfortunately Kirstie was gone by the time I arrived at the health food store. Considering the fact she had been inside just moments before, I found it easy to drop the line, "I could have sworn I just saw Kirstie Alley. Does she come in here often?"

My harmless conversation opener with the checkout clerk led me directly to Kirstie's personal shopping list. "Her diet isn't the best," he laughed. "Lately our store has been delivering food to the set of her show. It's mostly fried food like chicken nuggets and garlic potato wedges served with a dipping sauce."

In the amount of time it took to ring up a basket of groceries at *Globe*'s expense, I had learned of Kirstie's weight gain and her holiday binge of pies, cakes, and Russell Stover chocolates. With support from three outside sources, *Globe* was able to publish the story titled "Chubby Kirstie Alley Is Bursting Out of *Veronica's Closet.*"

Like most of the celebrities I covered, Kirstie's flaws led to my own success. In this case, her weight gain also contributed to stocking my fridge. That evening, I dined on smoked salmon, Ca Peachios vegetable biscuits, a bottle of Chardonnay, and Brie Isifrance that I had bought at

Gourmet Grub on *Globe*'s dime. As I smothered the creamy spread onto an herbed cracker, Kirstie Alley never once crossed my mind.

And why should she? Media attention is part of the package for actors. It simply comes with their job. As a tabloid journalist, exposing celebrities was simply part of my job. I felt I could justify writing what I did because of the situations that celebrities create for themselves. Hollywood breeds chaos, and often the stars themselves help feed the public's insatiable desire for more gossip. My latest assignment from Caelan was a perfect example.

"Marlise, you've to head toward Will Rogers Memorial Park. George Michael 'as been caught pleasuring himself inside the men's loo. 'E did it right in front of an officer, mind ya."

Presumably, average Americans would avoid such lewd behavior in public parks. Apparently leading an average life was much too blasé for George Michael, whose sexual preference was already being questioned by thousands of fans. For months, *Globe* had watched him move from park to park in search of gay men to seduce. The ritual could not have been any more impersonal. It consisted of eye contact with a stranger, five minutes in the bathroom, and then back to a shaded tree for a cigarette.

Globe had obtained photographs of everything from the singer's bag of condoms to the moment he returned home to his lover, Kenny Goss. No matter how solid the initial evidence, the tabloids would seldom publish reports of homosexuality or drug abuse, unless they could be confirmed by a police report or personal statement. Patiently, *Globe* had sat on those photographs, waiting for George Michael to come out of the closet.

Eight months after *Globe* received the pictures, an undercover cop named Marcelo Rodriguez arrested the singer for what was termed as "inappropriate sexual behavior." Only after interviewing Lieutenant Kreins of the Beverly Hills Police Department was I finally able to write the truth about George Michael's homosexuality. Editors argued about the appropriate headline, suggesting everything from "I Want Your Sex" to "Zip Me Up Before You Go-Go." They finally decided to title the article "Wham! Pop Star Confesses He's Gay." My George Michael cover story made CNN and international headline news.

"This is huge," my sister commented. "Don't you feel the least bit guilty?"

"You know what, Heidi," I answered, defensively, "I probably should, but I don't. I don't make the celebrities do what they do. I just report it."

Heidi's question was a valid one. As a writer, I had often wondered about the lasting implications of the facts that I was uncovering. George Michael's case should have been particularly troubling to me. Around the same time as he was outed by my article, he had lost his mother to cancer, lost his partner to AIDS, fought a legal battle with Sony, and now had suffered a humiliating blow on the pages of *Globe*.

A few days after our story ran, George Michael was invited to appear on *Oprah* to discuss his new life outside the closet. Feeling completely removed from the actor's emotions, I listened objectively like any other disassociated person who would be hearing his revelation for the first time. And then, I heard George Michael telling Oprah something completely unexpected. Apparently, our exposé forced him to make an admission he had wanted to make for a long time. Right there on national television, he thanked the tabloids for their role in helping him come clean. His reaction caught me completely off guard. Indirectly, he was thanking me, the little reporter nobody knew, for opening the door of his secret life.

Despite this, Heidi's question haunted me. Ultimately it was my frozen emotions that separated me from my sister. She had never approved of what I did for a living, and so I distanced myself from her righteous accountability. Now that my identity was completely absorbed by my profession, I felt that Heidi was rejecting me rather than my work. As a result, we talked less, knowing that whatever one of us said would be incorrectly interpreted by the other.

By now, my sister had bonded with Chantal, who had lost most of her East Coast accent but had fortunately retained her delightful spontaneity. Together, she and Heidi selected produce at the farmer's market and visited the tea gardens on Melrose. The sound of their laughter and late-night conversations made me jealous. Of course, I could not admit that. I refused to let my soul be thawed. Instead, I would simply close my door and pretend to be asleep.

Everyone close to me believed that Hollywood was having an effect on my personal identity. Everyone, that is, except me. It was becoming increasingly difficult to remember who I was. For my job I had masqueraded as everything from a law student to a cat owner, from a florist to a neighborhood jogger.

The final blow came during an argument with Heidi when she asked, "Who are you, Marlise?"

Rather than responding to her, I drove straight to work dressed in yet another disguise. I was about to play the role of a tennis player.

Globe had received photographs of Olivia Newton-John kissing an unknown man. In the background of the photo, we could make out an unidentified car parked in her driveway. Calling the DMV, I ran the license plate, which revealed that the car was registered to a certain Patrick McDermott. Whether or not he was Newton-John's new lover was yet to be determined. Using *Globe*'s database program Faces of the Nation, McDermott's name led me to an address in the Hollywood Hills. McDermott also matched a Yellow Pages listing under the category "Private Tennis Instructor."

Rather than calling his phone number, I decided to head out to the address and pay this mystery man a visit. Attired in my tennis outfit, I drove straight to McDermott's blue stucco house. No one was home. Fortunately, his chatty neighbor was.

"Sorry to bother you," I said, swinging my racquet over my shoulder. "I'm supposed to meet Patrick for tennis today. Do you know where he is?"

The man stood in the doorway, wearing nothing more than a white T-shirt and snug briefs. Taking a long swig of his Coke, he didn't seem at all embarrassed by his appearance. "Didn't he tell you? He's in Kansas on business."

Trying to keep the conversation going, I asked, "Do you have a number where I can reach Patrick? Maybe I can try and reschedule for later next week."

Looking behind him, the neighbor apologized in advance for the mess and invited me to come inside. The house was dark and had a musty smell, as if it were molded from ceramic clay set out to dry. "Can

I get you a Coke while I look for his number?"

Sitting on the edge of a La-Z-Boy recliner, I placed my racquet on the card table beside me. "Sure, that would be great. Oh, I'm Jasmine, by the way."

"Doug," he said, handing me the chilled can. "It's nice to meet you."

While Doug flipped through his address book, I began to fish for information. "Sorry about all this. I'm kind of surprised Patrick didn't call. He's probably so into his new girlfriend that he forgot to cancel."

Doug looked up from his address book. "Well, you know how Pat can be. He's shy about these sorts of things, especially because she's a movie star and all. What the hell is her name? You know the one. She's in that movie *Grease*."

I gave him a confused look.

"Olive something or other," he said, snapping his fingers. "Anyhow, they started dating about three months ago. I guess it's going pretty good."

I nodded. "Yeah, he told me a little bit about her right after they met at the . . . the . . . oh, my gosh! My mind has gone completely blank."

Doug shrugged his shoulders. "I don't know, either."

Dang it. Totally denied.

"So, did she go with him this weekend?" I was pushing the boundaries of casual conversation.

He nodded. "Yeah, I'm watching Pat's house while he shoots the Chiefs game. And then I guess they're going camping in Yosemite right after the trip."

"I didn't know Patrick had two jobs," I commented.

Doug was busy writing down the phone number on a scrap of paper. "Well, tennis is more of a hobby for him. But his full-time job is as a cameraman."

Taking a final swig of my soda, I grabbed the paper from his hand. "Well, sorry I took up so much of your time. Hopefully next time Pat will remember to call. I guess he's in love, huh?"

Silence . . . *Denied again.*

The neighbor just reached out his hand. "I'll tell him you stopped by."

"Oh, don't worry," I said. "I'll be getting in touch with him soon."

The neighbor's comments, combined with the revealing photos, provided sufficient sourcing for my story to run under the title "Olivia Newton-John Gets Mellow with New Lover." By the time it appeared on the newsstand, Madeline had returned from Florida and Caelan was no longer in charge. Surprisingly, she complimented my ability to blend into countless backdrops.

"Florida is currently reviewing the budget," she hinted. "It looks as if you might be next in line for a pay raise."

The thought had never crossed my mind.

"And, by the way," she added, "this week we had to take your name off of a few articles. You had five stories in this one issue. We wouldn't want you to get poached, now would we?"

"No, definitely not," I agreed. *Poached? What did she mean by poached?*

Karen later explained the term to me. She said that competing tabloids often target reporters who are efficient or over-productive. *Star* magazine had once offered Karen nearly twice the amount she was making at *Globe* for this very reason. Karen was able to use that offer as leverage to get the paycheck at *Globe* that she felt she deserved.

"Marlise," Sharmin said just then. "There's a 'Gretchen' on line two for you."

It was my mom, using her first name to save me the humiliation of getting a phone call from my mother. I was surprised that she had called me at work. Things had become so crazy lately that I barely had time to talk with my family. Our daily conversations had shrunk to weekly and now were semi-monthly.

"Mom," I whispered into the phone. "You know I'm not supposed to take personal calls here."

Her voice was firm, as if reciting a speech she had rehearsed just moments before. "Marlise, your grandfather just had a heart attack. If you want to say good-bye, you'll need to fly to Texas tomorrow."

Note:

Sharon Stone's marriage to her third husband, Phil Bronstein, ended on January 29, 2004. The couple has an adopted son.

In 2005, Kirstie Alley starred in her own show, *Fat Actress*. At the time of writing, she serves as the spokesperson for the Jenny Craig weight loss program.

Following their 2002 marriage, Jessica Simpson and Nick Lachey gained international fame through the 2003 television program, *Newlyweds: Nick and Jessica*. The couple divorced in June 2006.

Following his initial arrest in 1998, George Michael made a music video mocking the incident. On February 26, 2006, he was arrested for possession of Class C drugs and in May of that same year was reportedly found slumped over the wheel of his Range Rover. On October 1, 2006, George Michael was found, again unconscious, in his Mercedes-Benz. He was booked at the Colindale police station for possession of cannabis and released on bail.

On June 3, 2005, Patrick McDermott disappeared from a fishing vessel while at sea and was reported missing by his ex-wife in mid-August. At the time of writing, his whereabouts remain unknown.

CHAPTER 8

The Flight to Reality

News of my grandfather's condition didn't sit well with Madeline. "Well, he's not dead yet, is he? Can't you just wait and go to the funeral?"

The pain of losing a loved one was something she probably could not comprehend. Other than her husband, she had no friends or family that I knew of.

"I'll be back in a week," I promised. "And I can write articles from Dallas if necessary."

Disappointed, Madeline shook her head as if I had something to do with the health of my relatives.

"It's too bad, really," she taunted. "I was going to send you to Kauai for the taping of the *Live with Regis and Kathy Lee* show. We desperately need another Kathy Lee story and I figured you would be perfect for the job." She looked up at me, waiting for some sort of reaction. I remained silent. "I guess I'll just have to send Karen, then."

I felt cheated out of a golden opportunity to travel. "Yeah, I guess so." Handing her a stack of my stories in progress, I heard myself apologizing for my grandfather's illness.

"It's fine," she said. "You'll just have to work that much harder when you return."

Twenty-four hours later, I was in Texas, stuffing my face with battered foods and frosted desserts. Since moving to LA, my palate had learned to welcome the lighter California cuisine of fish tacos, roasted vegetables, and spinach salads. It was hard to imagine that twelve years earlier, I had been raised on chicken fried steak, buttery biscuits, and sweetened tea. Here I was, back in the Southern-fried environment of my childhood. My spotless arteries were now choking, not to mention the fact that I had abandoned my exercise regimen somewhere between LA and Dallas.

My grandparents lived in a small town outside Dallas called Grand Prairie, where the word "gym" was only a man's name. Even if there had been a place to exercise, I had no desire to leave an air-conditioned facility for a sweaty workout. So I hit the "what the hell, I've blown it already" wall where one contemplates devouring an entire cake before considering a simple fitness routine. By the second day, I was popping piña colada jelly beans five at a time as if they'd get lonely if I ate them one by one.

In the end, I blamed my trans-fatty diet on emotional stress and the decline of my personal life. Under normal circumstances, the idea of traveling back to Texas would probably have been a pleasant return to my forgotten childhood. I had even started referring to this trip as a family reunion rather than as a preparation for death.

The journey had started with our six a.m. flight out of Los Angeles. As usual, I awakened too late, which made Heidi panic. Nearly missing the plane after choosing Southwest's not-so-friendly skies, I began to wonder if lower fares were worth the extra hassle. Having to put her doctoral dissertation on hold had made Heidi begin to stress over the progress of her research. Being late to the airport only added to her tension. She ran around the terminal as if she were being chased in some B-movie that would only hit the industry on video. Chugging behind her, I dodged on-time passengers and hurdled luggage carts, stopping only when I reached security. The metal detector beeped as I passed through.

"Miss, please remove your belt," said a security officer, as she ran her hands up my thighs. Afraid of giving the impression of a striptease, I quickly yanked my belt through the loops. As the crowd of spectators began to form behind me, I became even more aware of the gigantic fever blister covering my mouth. My self-confidence was taking a beating.

Sprinting in clogs is never recommended, but I was willing to make an exception in light of our nearly missed flight. Throwing my boarding pass at the flight attendant, I ran down the jetway and grabbed the only open seats left on the plane. The flight offered first-come, first-served seating, meaning that Heidi and I ended up in the two front spaces facing backward. All one hundred and fifty passengers on board stared at us as if we were about to give the crash-landing safety speech.

"I just need to sleep," Heidi whined. For the next forty-five minutes she tried to rest on my upper arm, but her head kept sliding down and hitting my watch. I was aware of people staring at the drool running down her chin. "Okay, this is so embarrassing," I said, nudging her off. She sat up from her mental slur and gave me a look as if I had just stolen her candy.

Two hours later we landed in Albuquerque, New Mexico. There wasn't too much to do during our layover. Almost every shop seemed to be filled with the same Native American art work. There were terracotta pots filled with sprouting cacti, turquoise jewelry, eagle necklaces, and horse-shaped pewter belt buckles. As we walked around the stores, Heidi commented, "There are just way too many zigzags in this architecture."

Killing time, we peeled sour oranges and munched on tortilla chips, which had been pounded into crumbs by the turbulence. Neither of us mentioned the fact that our grandfather was dying. The flight to Dallas was brief, but there was absolutely no doubt we were in Texas. The moment we stepped off the plane, a woman passed us wearing a polka-dot dress and a white cowboy hat.

My parents had arrived earlier to help my frail grandmother. She hadn't eaten since my grandfather's heart attack. Even under these circumstances, it would be good to see my parents again. We hadn't been together since Easter and had arranged to meet at the hospital at the foot of my grandpa's bed. I had always made a point of avoiding medical facilities, where the smell of sickness is vainly masked by the scent of starched bedsheets and Pine Sol. I hardly recognized my grandpa. Like a stringed puppet, his thin body hung from tangled tubes attached to fluid bags and beeping monitors. His unshaven mouth kept opening to form unspoken words. This was coming from a man who had been an articulate missionary for more than forty years.

"Grandpa, you don't need to say anything," Heidi whispered. "We already know what you want to say. You've been preaching it your whole life."

Leaving his bedside, we said good-bye as if it would be the last time. No one was sure if he would even make it through the night. The realization that my grandfather's death was imminent was forcing my grandmother to readjust her life. Anything that we could do in this short span of time would help with her inevitable move.

The following day, Heidi and I "voluntarily" woke up and tackled my grandparents' garage. They had spent most of their lives in third world nations and, therefore, everything seemed precious to them and nothing had been discarded. Heidi and I found ourselves surrounded by dozens of boxes labeled "New stuff," "Old stuff," "Older stuff," and "New old stuff."

Noticing a rope dangling from the garage ceiling, I asked, "What's this string for?" That innocent-looking rope lowered a staircase that led to a disordered attic. In that hidden darkness we discovered even more mystery boxes. Like the others, they bore meaningless labels. We were suddenly overwhelmed by the prospect of having to open and unpack even more boxes.

Quietly folding the ladder back into place, Heidi whispered conspiratorially, "I won't tell if you won't." Blowing the dust off of her hands, she began whistling as she returned to her previous duties. Abandoned wasp nests, sticky cobwebs, and a millimeter of dust covered every crevice and corner of the garage.

"Send in the troops—we've got earwigs!" Heidi backpedaled across the garage, blasting a can of Raid as she ran. Twirling the can in her fingers like a cowboy's pistol, she tucked it into the pouch of her apron and walked away in silence.

Hidden beneath the dirt were steamer trunks, crinkled letters, Japanese rice trays, and faded photographs. We found an English tea set, games with cracked marbles, and puzzles with missing pieces. There were several boxes of recycled ribbons. My mother suggested that we toss anything we considered worthless. Confused by the term "worthless," and fearing how much fell under that definition, my sister and I looked at each other in silence. My mother went inside to order the largest Dumpster in Dallas County.

Things became even more awkward when my grandmother entered the scene. Although her tiny frame was bent nearly double by osteoporosis, she still seemed somehow regal. Her hearing was dull but her mind was sharp. She still devoured books and crosswords and eagerly embraced music and laughter. Despite the pain we were all feeling, she had managed to keep her humor intact.

"What's this perfectly good whiskbroom doing in the garbage?" she asked, carrying it past our disbelieving faces like crown jewels. "Can someone put it up there, in the attic, with those other things?" Waving the whiskbroom in the air as if she were swatting flies, my grandma reached for the dangling string to pull down the attic ladder.

"No," I screamed, grabbing the whiskbroom from her hand. "Uh . . . you are liable to injure yourself, Grandma." She had been collecting "keepsakes" for so long that she had absolutely no idea how much she had. We were all afraid she would find it impossible to part with any of her treasures if she knew what was really in the attic.

Heidi and I decided the only way to make progress was to take turns distracting our grandmother inside the house. At times we thought the day would never end. It was almost a relief to leave the garage long enough to head back to the hospital.

My grandfather's room was filled with relatives, several of whom I had never met. Many of them were in the ministry and all of them wanted to take us to dinner. With characteristic Texas hospitality, my Uncle Jimmy David drove us to a fast-food fish house. He corrected anyone who failed to use his full, three-part name, even if he wasn't your Uncle or Jimmy or even David, for that matter. For two hours, he carried on about his commitment to witnessing in restaurants. Apparently he had a talent for knocking people out with the power of God even before the waiter arrived with the check. His 24-karat bracelet dangling on the countertop made it somewhat difficult to swallow his evangelical energy. Digging into the communal checkered basket, I could hear myself saying, "Why yes, I'll take seconds on fried hush puppy balls." This was so not

Hollywood.

If nothing else, our visit was helping my grandma to relax a little. Back at the house she held out her tiny hands to show us her neglected fingernails. Despite my grandparents' simple lifestyle, my grandfather had habitually pampered my grandmother and she had come to enjoy and expect regular manicures.

"Do you want me to do your nails, Grandma?" I asked. She nodded, and waved me toward a beauty kit filled with bottles of dried-out nail polish with names like Summer Melon, Honeysuckle Hue, and Popsicle Pink.

Her spirits lightened as she shared the story of how she had first met my grandfather. "Male and female students weren't allowed to speak to each other in our Bible school you know. We were there to focus on God, and not on marriage. But we still communicated through love letters and little winks."

Seventy years later their relationship was back where it had started, their words imprisoned by illness, but freed through love. Once again, they were communicating their emotions through silent puckered lips and gently held hands.

Just then, the doorbell rang. I opened the door to discover even more relatives. "Oh, look," I announced loudly, hoping the senior citizens of the group could hear me. "It's Aunt Grace and Uncle Paul." Plopping into orange La-Z-Boy recliners, they began a conversation that had no end, let alone a point.

Although my grandmother cheerfully nodded in agreement, I knew that she could not actually hear what was being said. From time to time, the room would fall silent as everyone stared at her until she realized someone had asked her a question.

"Talk into my right ear," she would yell. "I can't hear in the left because when I was only seven . . ." Then she would repeat the story about her eardrum being ruptured by a firecracker when she was a child.

While Uncle Paul discussed cars and tools with my father, Aunt Grace began to tell us about her new cleaning lady. "She's Chinese or Japanese or something-or-other and I can barely understand a word she's sayin'. But my sweet Paul here can do pretty well. Can't ya, Paul?"

Rocking in his chair, Uncle Paul stared at her blankly.

Aunt Grace continued. "Anyhow, I just bow because I don't know what she's askin' or sayin' or what in the world she wants. The other day she cleaned the kitchen and then asked me to be the godmother of her baby. I just bowed, because what do you say really? I mean what could we say? After all, we can't hardly understand the woman! But that's okay. She sure can clean a toilet like you'd never believe."

From time to time, my grandmother would raise a subject completely unrelated to the topic being discussed and the cycle would start all over again.

"You know, I've worked for General Motors almost all my life," Uncle Paul was saying to no one in particular. "Then my boss asked me what I planned on doin' now that I'm retired. I told him I'm gonna buy me a Dodge."

There I sat, painting my grandmother's nails Flamingo Pink, and for the first time in my life, I began to understand something about why I was the way I was. Coming face to face with the raw reality of my roots was a jarring experience. Going from Hollywood to Grand Prairie was like visiting another planet. I couldn't tell what bothered me the most; seeing who I had been or realizing who I had become. Could I ever again feel at home in the Bible Belt? Or, could I, in fact, permanently blend into the glamour of Tinseltown? The biggest quandary of all was a question I couldn't answer: Who was I really?

After everybody left, I found myself rushing to the laptop computer that *Globe* had provided. As a link to my life back in LA, the computer had become my safe place. The laptop sat propped on a wobbly wooden tray table in a house full of history, tradition, and antiques. Here, in my grandparents' house, I was surrounded by countless memories of crawling around in footed pajamas that grew holes in the feet after too many runs through the garden. In the kitchen were cracked yellow countertops where I had tipped over blue Easter egg dye. There, in the dining room, was the table where I used to slide my grandma's macaroni noodles onto fork prongs before devouring the creamy bites whole. Outside in the prickly garden was the corner where we once spat watermelon seeds that somehow bloomed eight years later. Part of me wanted to stay and remember my innocence.

That night I had a lot of time to think. Even before this trip, I had started to feel tread-worn from life in the fast lane. I had become so deeply immersed in Fantasy Land that it was getting more and more difficult to separate illusion from reality. I had begun to feel like a human teeter-totter, my personality alternating between the callous reporter and the sympathetic me.

The next morning my sister, my mom, and I took my grandmother back to the hospital. These twice daily visits to her husband were the highlight of my grandma's day. In my grandfather's hospital room, I told him I wished I could take away his pain. He looked at me as if he really wanted out. I knew this would probably be the last time I would see him alive. He lay there, staring at me like a newborn baby, trying to understand the world from inside his barred crib. He lifted his hand as if grabbing at a dangling mobile and then valiantly gave a trembling thumbs-up sign. We cried, cried hard with spurts of uncontrollable heaving. No one pretended to be strong.

Just as we were leaving, my grandmother started to quote scripture but was too overcome by emotion to finish the verse. My mother picked up where she left off. "Yea, though I walk through the valley of the shadow of death, I will fear no evil: for Thou art with me; Thy rod and Thy staff, they comfort me. Thou preparest a table before me in the presence of mine enemies; Thou anointest my head with oil; my cup runs over. Surely goodness and mercy shall follow me all the days of my life; and I will dwell in the house of the Lord forever."

Although my grandfather was fully aware that his life was about to end, there was an authentic serenity about him that contrasted sharply with the superficiality of my life in Hollywood. For him, there was one way, one truth, and one life. In that hospital setting, I no longer fretted over bylines, leads, or cover stories. My priorities had become clear, at least for that moment. I stood there in awe, having started to see the truth of my life through the prism of death.

My mother was the only one who had not yet surrendered to tears. Instead, she looked straight into her father's dying eyes, and poured out her spirit as if Christ were speaking the words himself.

There was so much I wanted to say to my grandfather, but silence seemed to be the most appropriate. I was pacified with the mere idea of sitting beside someone so close to anticipated perfection. Like a sunbather soaking in a beaming ray of light, he closed his eyes. I said good-bye and walked away from his face forever.

This was the first time I had ever personally dealt with death. The open coffin made me uneasy. My grandfather looked pale and thin, yet completely at peace. It stirred me with a desire to grab back my righteousness and shove it into the darkest part of my soul. I became conscious of everything I wasn't. I wanted my grandfather to wake up and take me with him to a place where everything was safe and silent and still, a place without human judgment knocking at my head.

Together with my father I stood by the grave, sobbing and heaving. I knew that my dad was crying as much for the loss of my faith as for the departure of my grandfather's spirit. The coffin was lowered into the ground as I stood there and watched. A body sinking into the dirt rather than floating into the clouds didn't mesh with a sanitized vision of eternity. The crank turned. The chain unrolled. The wooden box was laid to rest, and I returned to my restlessness.

The flight from Dallas back to LA was not long enough to bridge my two worlds. Returning to *Globe*, I was somewhat disappointed to realize that the paper had "succeeded" so well without me. Everything seemed the same as when I had left. The only major change that had occurred while I was in Texas actually impacted the entire *Globe* team and not just me.

It involved Nick Royce, whom we fondly referred to as "Rent-a-Quote Man." Nick's abundant quotes had often provided the third-person sourcing that the editors required in order to validate our stories. Unfortunately, one of Nick's insider quotes had seriously backfired, ending in a libel suit against *Globe*. As it turned out, the legal blowup actually came as a result of the editorial policy that required three sources for every story. In CNN's report of the incident, *Globe* had allegedly received documentation indicating that Arnold Schwarzenegger had undergone surgery to replace a faulty aortic valve. Embellishing that lead story, *Globe*'s headline had read "Schwarzenegger Is a Ticking Time

Bomb."

Understandably infuriated, the former Mr. Universe retaliated by filing a $50 million libel suit against the tabloid. As usual, *Globe*'s Schwarzenegger story had been supported by three sources, two of which held up in court. When Nick was forced to take the stand, however, his sourcing proved to be inadequate to meet the legal standards. As a result, *Globe* was left with hefty legal fees and we were left having to scramble for our own third-person quotes.

As reporters, we were never told the whole Nick Royce story. All we knew was that we were never again to mention his name in the office. Overnight, Nick had gone from being an indispensable member of our team to an invisible part of the enemy camp. The whole event just made me realize how easily anyone at *Globe* could be replaced.

CHAPTER 9

Chasing Matt Lauer

"Marlise!" Instinctively I turned toward Madeline's voice. She was leaning through the doorway in her usual pose, with her head poking outside her office while the rest of her body remained hidden behind the door. Sharmin and Pete had an ongoing joke that Madeline was probably naked from the waist down. The fact that she hid behind her desk most of the time only fed into their theory.

"Can I see you for a moment, please?" Madeline held her office door ajar while I walked inside. As she shut the door, I plopped into the black leather chair opposite her desk. Clicking my pen in readiness, I flipped to a fresh page in my notepad and waited to learn the details of my next assignment. Leaning across her desk, my editor asked the one question all reporters long to hear: "Is your passport in order?"

"Yes," I replied, without asking why. Wherever she was sending me had to be a lot further than Hawaii.

"I know this is last-minute," Madeline said. "But you need to be on the next plane to Egypt."

I tried to contain my smile. Although I had traveled extensively my whole life, this would be my first trip to the Middle East. Madeline quickly explained that Matt Lauer, host of the *Today* show, was doing a special segment titled "Where in the World Is Matt Lauer?" My temporary mission would be to beat Lauer to Egypt and let the world know that *Globe* had discovered his "secret location" and had managed to get there first.

"We aren't quite sure what we want you to do there yet," she added. "But just get to Cairo as fast as you can, and we'll let you know what to do once you're there. I'll call Florida and see if they can have a car waiting for you on the other end. Arrangements have been made for your air tickets. You can pick them up at the ticket counter at LAX."

She slid the Matt Lauer file across her desk. "Take a look at these clippings during your flight. Pay extra attention to anything pertaining to women. You might be able to catch him cheating, if you're lucky."

Shutting down my computer, I waved good-bye to my envious colleagues, who were busily typing away at their Page Three columns.

"Hurry up, Marlise," Madeline barked from her office. "We don't know when he's arriving in Egypt. Just make sure you get there before Lauer does."

Rushing out the door, I calculated that I would have just enough time to stop at my condo to pack a bag en route to the airport. I ran down the hall and into the elevator. Suddenly a hand reached between the sliding doors.

"Goin' down?" It was *Globe*'s roving editor, Caelan Dunmore. Though still new to the LA office, he was fast becoming a welcome addition to the West Coast team.

"So, you've heard the news, huh?" I asked with a smile.

"Ye cheeky bitch," he joked in his thick Scottish accent. "That shoulda been my jaunt you know? Freezy is only sendin' you 'cause this assignment requires a lassie."

"Oh, no," I interjected. "If he thinks I'm going to pull some seduction stunt—"

"See 'ere, Marlise," Caelan interrupted. "No one knows yet what they want you to do in Egypt. But, here's what I heard in this mornin's meeting. They've been trying to get Lauer for quite a while now. Last year, 'e was staying at the Marriott in Monterey for a golf tournament. The editors sent in a blonde reporter as bait. Sad to say, the reporter walked straight up to Lauer and told 'im *Globe*'s plot. I suspect she might have thought that being so bonny and all, she could win him over. Instead, Lauer was furious with her, but not half as mad as ol' Freezy was. The blonde got herself sacked the very next day. Anyhow, everyone knows Lauer's a bit o' a ladies man. Tis just a matter o' catching him at it. All I'm saying is, take care of yerself, luv."

The elevator stopped at the ground floor. "Here's me stop," Caelan said, pulling a pack of cigarettes from his pocket as he stepped out.

Continuing down to the parking garage, I pressed the already lit P button and watched as the doors started to slide shut.

"Oh, wait," I said, throwing my foot into the closing gap. "Sorry I stole your assignment."

He flipped open the lid of his cigarette pack. "No worries, luv," he said confidently. "*Globe* is sendin' me to Poland in the mornin'."

"What?" I asked, in total surprise.

"'Tis true. We just bought a photo of David Duchovny cuddlin' a Polish masseuse," Caelan said, with a grin. "I 'ave to hunt her down and then produce a story titled 'The X-Rated Files.' When yer back, we'll have to go for a pint and exchange stories."

I nodded. As the elevator closed, he called, "Good luck, then."

Adrenaline and a waiting taxi somehow got me onto the next international flight. The plane was already airborne before I had time to think about the task I had undertaken. As it turned out, I had only thirty minutes to change planes in London. Locating a row of vacant seats, I stretched out and covered my head with a thin, staticky blanket, which kept slipping off my body and collecting cracker crumbs from the floor.

By the time we arrived in Cairo, it was after nine in the evening. I watched as the baggage carousel kept turning and spitting out luggage for all the passengers except for me. Apparently my bag had gone astray somewhere back at London's Heathrow, leaving me empty-handed in Cairo. Wearing jeans and a wife-beater tank top, I felt conspicuously out of place. Clearly, this was not the traditional dress of Arabian women.

After waiting a few minutes outside the Cairo airport, I realized that the anticipated "*Globe* car" was not going to pick me up after all. Forced to tackle the city alone, I took a deep breath and moved beyond the safety of the airport walls. Taxi drivers instantly surrounded me, grabbing for my carry-on bag and pulling me by the arm. It was already dark and there were no tourists, no women, and no security guards. Pushing away the eager drivers, I ignored them and walked directly toward a single cab waiting at the curb.

"Taxi?" I asked through the open window.

Jumping out from behind the steering wheel, the driver reached for my carry-on and opened the back door. "Yes," he nodded. "Would you like to see the pyramids?"

"Not at this hour," I said, in a panic. "Please, just get me out of here. I need to go to the Mena House Oberoi Hotel."

As we lurched away from the curb, the driver introduced himself as "Shariff" and assured me, "I give good price." Like the other Cairo drivers, he seemed to communicate through prolonged honks and bumper-to-bumper nudges rather than by signaling or stopping at streetlights. When he reached over to turn off the meter, I began to wonder what he actually meant by "good price."

Arriving at our destination, Shariff scribbled the illegible cab fare on a tissue. Much too exhausted to argue, I simply handed him the Egyptian currency and stepped from the taxi. It was a relief to finally reach the five-star hotel where Matt Lauer would be staying. When I inquired about the missing car, the Mena House receptionist was quick to explain that the staff had never received *Globe*'s message to have transportation waiting for me at the airport. That night, jet lag kept me awake as I OD'd on five hours of Egyptian MTV.

The phone rang precisely at seven the next morning. I figured the stateside editors were ready to bark orders. Instead, it turned out to be my tenacious taxi driver.

"How did you get this number?" I demanded.

"I ask at front desk." Shariff responded. "Now I give Cairo tour for good price."

It occurred to me that he must have been hanging around the hotel all night waiting for an appropriate hour to call me. It seemed a rather unusual business approach, but, out of guilt, I accepted his offer. My jet lag was only getting worse and I needed to explore the area anyway.

"You are one persistent taxi driver," I commented.

"Yes," he responded, unapologetically. "I wait you outside." He hung up.

Shariff's bloodshot eyes confirmed my suspicion that he had, indeed, spent the entire night in his car with the intention of showing me his city. His "tour" consisted of a trip to the pyramids, located just five minutes from my hotel room.

That afternoon I decided to try to start locating and buying hotel sources, beginning with the busboys. Generally speaking, employees with the lowest wages are the first who are willing to talk to reporters. On this occasion, one particular restaurant busboy seemed especially eager to strike up a conversation. As he cleared away my glass, I explained in present-tense English that a famous man was coming to the hotel.

"I pay if you give me room number of special guest," I promised.

"Yes," he agreed, perhaps a little too willingly. He nervously looked back at his boss, who was attempting to eavesdrop on our conversation. "You meet me on bottom floor of hotel. I give you all."

"Okay," I agreed. "I'll be there in five minutes."

After paying the bill, I made my way downstairs and waited for my first Egyptian source to arrive. It became immediately apparent that the restaurant staff had never been taught the tactics of tabloid journalism. Grabbing me by the arm, the busboy shoved me into a broom closet and closed the door.

"What the hell are you doing?" I screamed, throwing open the door. "You have me all wrong! I just want someone's room number!"

As he reached for the top button of my blouse, a stern voice interrupted from behind us. "What is going on here?" It was the bar manager, the same man who had been eyeing us earlier.

"I am sorry, but this is unacceptable behavior. We do not allow these sorts of activities to occur between our staff and the hotel guests."

Completely trapped, I could hardly place the blame on the busboy who barely spoke a word of English. Nor did I want him to lose his job over Matt Lauer's room number. On the other hand, to the casual observer, I clearly looked like a promiscuous woman.

"I'm sorry, sir," I apologized. "There's been some sort of mix-up in communication. I accept full responsibility."

With the manager following closely behind, I walked back to the lobby, feeling as if I had done something terribly wrong. The whole experience had left me a little shaken. Back in my room, I realized that I would need to try a different source-gathering approach in Egypt than I was accustomed to using in Hollywood.

That night I decided to try my luck at finding sources by working the hotel's entertainment bar. Cabaret dancers galloped around in glittery G-strings and feather boas.

"Is this seat taken?" It was the hotel director. "My name is Omar," he said.

He bought me a drink and within minutes went into a lengthy explanation of the marital laws of his culture. He launched into his well-rehearsed lecture with gusto. "I can sleep with other women, but my wife must remain faithful."

Although his ideas appalled me, it was clear that he saw nothing wrong with the terms of his belief system. At that point, my attempts to educate him on the feminist movement were pointless. He just stared at my boobs and smiled.

Abruptly leaving the bar, I headed for the hotel disco in search of a source. There I met an Egyptian girl named Ebtesam. She appeared to be in her early twenties and introduced me to her boyfriend, Sammy. In turn, I introduced her to the details of my assignment. Instantly the couple offered their assistance.

"As a matter of fact, I could use an interpreter," I said.

"Don't worry," they assured me, handing me Sammy's cellphone number. "We've seen this sort of thing in the movies. You'll have Mr. Lauer's underwear by the end of the week." I assumed this last statement was their quaint way of instilling confidence in their sleuthing abilities.

The following morning Ebtesam called from a pay phone.

"There is some good news and some bad news," she said. "I think my father will let me help you."

"Excellent," I said. "Come on over and we can get started. So, what's the bad news?"

"You first have to come to my village to get my family's approval." She hung up after giving me vague directions to a street with an unpronounceable name. One hour later, Shariff was dropping me in the center of a busy Egyptian village located just outside Cairo. He drove away even before I had a chance to reconsider my decision. Head down and eyes lowered, I briskly walked toward a dark alley in the general area where, supposedly, Ebtesam lived.

"Marlise!" I heard my voice being called in unison by several voices. "We're up here!"

Looking toward them, I saw Ebtesam and her family of ten staring down from a broken window. She met me in the alley and then led me to a musty stairwell for the five-flight climb to her family's apartment. Covering the concrete walls of their home were several wrinkled photographs that had become cracked and faded from filtered beams of sunlight.

In the center of the room was a tattered rug where her entire family sat in a perfect circle. In stark contrast to the threadbare surroundings, even the youngest girls were dressed in colorful bangles and lavish silks. I was still wearing my jeans and tank top. This would be my standard uniform for the next forty-eight hours until my missing bags finally caught up with me.

Occasionally a child would rise to empty the tin bucket in the corner that was collecting drops of water from a leaky faucet. Interpreting back and forth, Ebtesam introduced me to her family. Leaving us alone to get acquainted, she went to make tea.

Okay, how do we begin to cross this cultural bridge?

"So are you big fans of *Baywatch*?" I asked absent-mindedly.

They gave me blank stares.

"*Baywatch* country. That's where I live." Speaking more slowly, I continued, "I live in California." It sounded lame, even to my ears. We sat quietly, trying not to stare at each other.

The silence was killing me. "Ebtesam!" There was no response. *How long does it take to make tea?*

We sat there on the cold floor smiling awkwardly at each other. In desperation, one of the older girls silently slid a deck of cards toward me as if daring me to perform magic tricks. Playing for time, I began to shuffle the cards. Slowly. Very slowly.

In the middle of my act, a loud bell rang and the entire family unexpectedly fell to the floor. In a kneeling position with their heads pressed flat against the cold stone, they began chanting in unison. Apparently this was one of their five daily calls to Muslim prayer. Suddenly, they all sat up as if nothing had happened and watched me complete my card trick.

I noticed that they all had dirt-smudged circles on their foreheads. Later Ebtesam explained that the smudges were signs that God had blessed those who prayed faithfully. Reflecting on her comment, it seemed ironic that I had been ripped off by a taxi driver who was blessed with the darkest prayer blotch I had ever seen.

By late afternoon Ebtesam's family had taken a liking to me, or perhaps just to my card tricks. Whatever the case, Ebtesam was given permission to spend the week serving as my interpreter.

Her older brother, Ali, was assigned by their father to keep watch over us on the first day. I quickly adjusted to the feeling of being chaperoned. As we moved through the center of town, the faithful swarmed the mosque courtyard, periodically dropping to their knees whenever the prayer bell sounded. Each time this happened, I stood out like a giraffe in a snake pit.

We combed narrow alleyways in search of treasures, caressing replicas of stone pyramids and sculpted sphinx in the congested marketplace. We paused at a smoke shop filled with glass bongs and wooden pipes. With every breath, I inhaled another waft of Egypt. We sipped exotic fruit juices and sampled sweet milk potions sprinkled with nuts, raisins, and coconut shavings.

"Let's go see the movie *Titanic*," Ali suggested. I turned down his offer, dreading the prospect of three hours of Leonardo DiCaprio speaking Arabic.

Back at the hotel, a message was waiting from my assigned photographer, Randal Traub. I felt as if I already knew the famous paparazzo from everything James Churchill had told me about him when we were staking out Morgan Freeman. I dialed his room.

"Randal?" I said. "This is Marlise, the reporter from *Globe*."

"Sorry I didn't call you earlier today," he said, out of breath. "I pulled up to the hotel and the next thing I knew I was riding a camel in the desert."

"Well, I think we should get together and make a game plan," I suggested. "How about we meet at the hotel's Maleluke bar for a drink? I'll be the girl with hair down to my butt."

Half an hour later, a man approached me with the greeting, "So, you must be the one with the butt hair. Hi, I'm Randal."

We had an instant connection. He turned out to be a lot less intimidating than I had expected. We earmarked the following morning for research. For me, this meant preparation for the big story. For Randal, "research" meant sharing a desert adventure.

"It's time to get down to business," Randal ordered, dragging me to the stables. He bartered with the locals while I sank my clean-soled shoes into camel patties.

Mounting a double-humped camel, he patted the animal and announced, "You will be my beast of the desert."

Meanwhile I settled onto a rather unhealthy looking horse as we set off on a five-hour excursion to the Giza plateau. Galloping to the peak of a sand dune, I turned to soak in a panoramic view of the desert. Cradling the ancient ruins were rippled valleys, tattooed with traces of windstorms and animal tracks. Sand sprayed off the dusty mountains, as wind and time gnawed at their dwindling peaks.

"This is a Life Day," Randal said. "Each person is given only a few, maybe four or five. A Life Day is something to remember forever that can never be explained or captured in a photograph. And this," he declared, "this is a Life Day."

He was right. There I was with my horse kicking up sand behind us, his powerful hooves leaving prints in the virgin dunes against the backdrop of the Great Pyramid. Whipped-cream clouds stirred overhead as the blazing sun seeped into my bronzed skin like oil on a cotton ball. It was a perfect moment. I smiled and nodded in agreement, knowing that this was the first of my five yet-to-be-lived Life Days.

We were both still for a moment. Then Randal abruptly broke the reflective mood. Turning toward our toothless guide, he asked, "So, can you recommend a good dentist in the area?" The camel leader just flashed us his cave-like smile.

Sporting a white turban with a florescent headband, Randal sat cross-legged on his camel. Periodically he would lean down to feed an apple slice or half-eaten pear to his slave beast.

"Onward!" He pointed his staff toward the heavens and wobbled from side to side as we moved through the desert.

The Great Pyramid, oldest of the original Seven Wonders of the World, was a far cry from the image I had seen on the dollar bill. The sight was humbling. Randal and I briefly dismounted our animals to eavesdrop on the presentation of an English-speaking tour guide. Commenting on the fact that the Great Pyramid was made by the labor of man, Randal whispered, "I can't even make my own bed in the morning."

In addition to this famous landmark, we visited some of the lesser pyramids sprinkled across the Giza plateau. We stopped at one such half-ruined pyramid and paid the equivalent of $2 to enter the historical site.

"No photo," the guard said, pointing toward a sign that spelled out his command in four languages. After Randal slipped him a tip, however, the guard suddenly morphed into our personal photographer. Obviously experienced at this whole process, the guard told us exactly how and where to pose inside the pyramid. He even tousled my hair.

Randal belted, "Hey, stop with the hair. I'm the professional here."

Insisting we make a video inside the pyramid, Randal suggested I stage a mock resurrection from the tomb. "Oh, come on, Marlise. The mummy thing will be fun."

Getting into the spirit of the moment, I did the stiff-armed solider walk rather than the dragging-foot mummy walk he preferred.

"Stop it, Marlise. You are messing up our skit," Randal scolded. Sprawling flat on his back on the stone sarcophagus, Randal crossed his arms over his chest. His resurrection was much swifter than planned. Jumping up from the stone platform, he screamed, "Oh my gosh, my fruit!" Disgustedly removing two smashed apples from his safari jacket, he commented, "Now look what I've done. I've made myself a little applesauce."

Back at the hotel, we discovered that Matt Lauer and his entourage had just arrived. The security guards escorted him and his supermodel girlfriend, Annette Roque, to room 631, a little suite that I came to call "the love nest." Lauer's relationship with Roque was noticeably public, resolving the girlfriend portion of my Lauer assignment. There would be no need to "try to catch him cheating," as Madeline had instructed me.

Lauer's arrival marked the end of my Egyptian vacation. Every time he left the hotel, *Globe* was in hot pursuit. Less than an hour later, I actually heard myself directing Ebtesam, "Follow that car."

Behind the wheel, our Egyptian interpreter was weaving in and out of traffic at my command. Somewhere in the chaotic chase of jumping curbs and running red lights, we managed to lose sight of the NBC van.

"Remind me why we are doing this again?" Ebtesam asked.

"Because America wants to know what Matt Lauer eats for dinner," I responded curtly.

"Don't follow too closely," Randal chipped in. "They'll get suspicious. Great, now you've lost them."

Ebtesam poked her head out the window, calling sweetly to the still-invisible Lauer, "Here kitty, kitty, kitty. Where are you?" By the end of the week she had changed her tune, screaming, "Where is that bastard?"

After hitting every pricey restaurant in Cairo, we finally located the NBC van parked outside the Nile River Marriott. Grabbing a copy of the dinner menu to shield my face, I passed Lauer's table in order to catch a glimpse of his meal. Back at the car, I gave my team high fives and reported triumphantly, "He's a meat eater!"

By the next morning I had completely recovered from my jet lag. The day started bright and early—too bright and way too early. The phone rang at six o'clock. It was Cathy Tidwell calling from the editorial office in Florida.

"We know exactly what we want you to do now," Cathy announced on a conference call. "We want you to hold up *Globe* posters for the cameras when NBC shoots live from the Great Pyramids." It was a stupid idea, but I was willing to do just about anything in exchange for the privilege of international travel. "A roll of posters has been express-mailed to your hotel. Call us when you get the package."

Leaving the hotel, Randal and I went to great lengths to bribe local peasants to work with us. Finally, we convinced them to arrive for the shoot with herds of livestock adorned in *Globe* banners. In exchange for the money we were offering, the locals were only too willing to cooperate with our scheme. I have no idea what Ebtesam must have promised them, but each day they showed up with droves of camels and sheep.

Maybe their cooperation was the consequence of my little chat with the village chieftain during the preparation stage for our assignment. Through my interpreter, I had told him, "The more animals there are, the better. Do you have sheep? Camels? This is nothing illegal we are asking. All you have to do is tack posters on the saddles of your animals and then, when we give the signal, everyone must cry out, '*GLOBE* FOUND MATT LAUER IN EGYPT!'"

None of my Egyptian extras were quite sure what they were doing or why, but each day they dutifully showed up for the pittance that I offered. There was only one problem. None of us knew exactly when NBC was planning to shoot the live show. As a result, my Egyptian retinue showed up three days in a row dragging their tired animals, each of them wearing *Globe* banners.

After our countless trips to the ruins, the Egyptian Security Police started to become suspicious. Unfortunately, just when I needed her most, Ebtesam took a well-deserved day off. I found myself being interrogated alone after being picked up by the Security Police.

Closed in by several authority officers, I tried to explain, "I am not a terrorist." It was a waste of breath. Without the aid of my interrupter, I was completely lost. "I'm just a tabloid reporter with posters."

My explanation meant nothing to the police. Escorted at gunpoint, I was taken to an Egyptian prison. I should have been afraid, but I wasn't. During my years of travel, I had discovered a sort of international liberation free from the usual fear of consequences. For six hours, I struggled to define tabloid journalism and my reason for following the NBC film crew. Pointing to a copy of a recent issue of *Globe*, I tried to explain my latest article, titled "Cher's Lesbian Daughter in Bitter Love Triangle." My futile effort definitely lost something in the translation. Eventually Randal bailed me out. He considered my whole adventure rather amusing, which did nothing to improve my mood. "You weren't the one explaining lesbianism to the director of Foreign Affairs," I whined.

The success of our whole assignment was riding on the next few hours. Security officers had roped off the entire sandy area where the *Today* show would film. From that distance, even Randal's telephoto lens could not capture what we needed. We had to have a backup plan.

Marching toward the makeup tent, Randal announced casually, "I'm just going to ask our friend Matt to pose for *Globe*."

"No! Randal, that's not a good idea," I remonstrated. Pushing me away, Randal left me in his wake, holding an armload of his camera equipment.

"I'm from *Globe*, Mr. Lauer," Randal bubbled. "And we would love to get a picture of you holding a copy of our latest issue."

"You're from *Globe*?" Lauer said disgustedly as he rubbed sun lotion on his arms. "Best of luck, buddy." Dismissing Randal without a backward glance, Lauer walked into his tent and zipped the flap shut.

It was time for Plan B. Randal took out his telephoto lens and crawled behind a wall of fallen sandstone. Security police marched straight toward us and confiscated Randal's equipment. Obviously my tabloid-selling speech had not been sufficiently convincing. I was furious with the security guards.

"Do you honestly think we're going to kill the guy with a stupid telephoto lens?" I raged.

Randal covered my mouth with his hand. My options were running out. Hoping that at least one poster would make it onto live TV, I began shoving *Globe* posters and money into the hands of tourists and other members of the gathering audience.

"Just hold up these posters when the cameras start rolling," I yelled into the crowd. I felt like a cheerleader at a pep rally. Instead of doing as I had asked, one by one, people crushed the fliers into their pockets. Others used my precious posters as paper fans or bleacher mats. Already I was dreading having to submit my expense report to the editors back home. I found myself wondering how I was going to explain the entry, "Desperate bribes to uncooperative Lauer fans." The guards caught me in action. Grabbing me out of the crowd, they whisked me to their security tent, where I was frisked and accused of possessing a weapon.

"Aha!" chortled one officer knowingly, pulling a tampon from my purse. He sounded as if he had just discovered a bomb. "What do you call this?"

Another exercise in futility ensued as I tried to explain that it was my time of the month, thus requiring extra absorbent protection in the form of a cotton fiber tube. The police did not understand and kept my tampon for further investigation. I stood there in frustration and disbelief. How had things gotten so out of control? The clock was still ticking, and it was just moments before NBC was to go on the air. My idea tank had run dry. *Globe* would be furious when they learned that I had been arrested for "possession of a lethal tampon."

Just then, I heard a familiar voice in the distance, "Set that lady free!"

It was Randal, running with his retrieved camera in hand, "We're back in business, baby."

Somehow Randal had managed to convince the police commander that our photos could actually boost Egyptian tourism and benefit the local economy. Whatever the case, our names were cleared just in time.

"They mean no harm to our people," the commander was saying to the security guards. Then, pointing in my direction he ordered, "Release her immediately!"

By this time, Lauer's live programming had begun. Running directly toward the filming that was already in progress, I jumped in front of the NBC camera and waved a *Globe* poster high above my head. Only later did I learn that my antics had paid off. *Globe*'s poster was clearly visible in the crowd of fans cheering and waving as the live show was beamed back to America. Once the segment was over, Randal and I waited at the only possible spot where Lauer could exit the pyramids.

"What's going on?" It was Ebtesam. She had decided to forgo her day off to come to our aid. "Why aren't you taking pictures? *Globe* is going to kill you."

She grabbed a poster from my hand and started to duck under the security tape.

"Hold on, Ebtesam," I warned. "This is Matt Lauer's only way out. At some point, he has to exit here."

Pausing, Ebtesam smiled and started her usual routine. "Here kitty, kitty, kitty." Unwilling to surrender my reporter's anonymity, I suggested that Ebtesam pose beside Lauer. She loved the idea.

"Imagine me," she said ecstatically. "Imagine me on the cover of *Globe*. Do you think I'll become famous?" Her enthusiasm was adorable, especially considering she didn't know the first thing about our publication.

"Most likely," I assured her. Eventually the *Today* show host surfaced. Coming out of the mouth of the Great Pyramids, he walked straight into the belly of our trap.

"Smile, Mr. Lauer," Ebtesam gleamed. "*Globe* caught you in Egypt."

Clearly annoyed, he glanced over at Ebtesam and the poster that declared in bold letters, "*Globe* Finds *Today* Anchor in Egypt." Directly in front of him was Randal, holding down the trigger of his camera. As Randal jubilantly snapped picture after picture, it sounded like a model shoot for a fashion magazine.

"Brilliant," Randal declared, backing away from the approaching host. "Hold that pose, Lauer. I love it. Absolutely love it!"

Shaking his head in total disbelief, the only words Lauer could utter were, "You guys are unbelievable."

I jumped up and down beside Randal, clapping my hands together in complete excitement. Later that evening, the Egyptian team's farewell was an emotional one. I knew I would never see Ebtesam again, especially since there was no way of contacting her. She had no post box, no telephone number, and no e-mail address. As we hugged good-bye, I handed her an envelope that contained money, stamps, and my contact information. Ebtesam promised to open it after I left. That was my final communication with her.

Randal and I said our good-byes over one last drink in the Maleluke Bar. We didn't know when, where, or if we would meet again. Based in New York, Randal was debating whether or not he should get out of the business completely, thanks to several exclusives that had made him wealthy. Two weeks later, a package arrived at my Los Angeles home. Inside were two enlarged photographs encased in wooden frames. One was of the pyramids and the other of the sphinx. Taped to the back of the frame was a note that read, "Thanks for giving me a Life Day—Randal."

The next time I saw his face was six months later on E! The channel was interviewing Randal for a special on the world's leading paparazzi. When I called New York to congratulate him, I discovered the number he had given me had been disconnected.

Meanwhile, back in the States, *Globe* was thrilled with our work. As far as the editors were concerned, Randal and I were heroes. *Globe* loved the story and rewarded me with a three-day layover in England. After leaving Egypt, I flew to London and checked into a hotel near Piccadilly Square. A good portion of the first day was spent in my room as a consequence of having eaten carrot sticks at the Cairo airport bar.

Feeling a little better by the next evening, I began to walk aimlessly down the streets of London. Without any real destination, I stopped at the trendy Fashion Café. I had heard about this chain of model-themed restaurants but had never been inside one. It was obvious that something special must have been going on that night because security guards surrounded the London restaurant. Purposefully, I walked straight toward the entrance.

"Are you here for the Elite Model Show?" asked a woman who was holding a clipboard.

"Why yes, I am," I said, pointing vaguely toward the guest list.

She crossed off the name of an invited guest and then escorted me inside. The Fashion Café looked like a gathering for the National Society of Skinny People. It was a roomful of Gumby clay figures. Between pauses for three-peck-kisses, they nibbled on sandwich triangles and cherry stems. Free champagne kept me dancing until four in the morning before hailing a taxi and crashing out at my hotel.

Five hours later, it was time to catch my plane back to Los Angeles. Sleeping nearly the entire flight home, I again found myself fighting to keep the airplane blanket from falling to the floor. In between plane changes I kept thinking about everything I had experienced on *Globe*'s nickel. Two days after I returned, the magazine published my four-page cover story under the title, "Gotcha, Matt!"

Returning to the office, I learned that the celebrity television show *Hard Copy* had purchased exclusive rights to our Lauer story. *Globe* arranged for me to be interviewed for the show. Seated at Madeline's desk, I spoke on national television, sharing details of what I had witnessed in Egypt. It was excruciating to watch the program when it aired, especially when I heard myself saying, "There was definitely passion in the pyramids."

Hard Copy paid me $500 for the five-minute interview. It made me think that perhaps tabloid journalism had its privileges after all.

Note:

Matt Lauer married his second wife, Annette Roque, on October 3, 1998. The couple has three children.

CHAPTER 10

Dancing with Bobby Brown

Although I was still somewhere near the base of the tabloid totem pole, it appeared that I was inching my way to the top. Madeline kept me clinging to the pole by hinting that my dedication might result in an editorial position within a year. What really kept me motivated, however, was the fear of becoming desk-bound.

As our West Coast mother hen, Madeline gloated over her productive nest, priding herself on the fact that her handful of reporters produced seventy percent of *Globe*'s headlines. One by one, we hatched and grew.

I learned to lay low in the office, just as I did on the streets. I would grab my daily lead sheets and block out anything that might slow me down. This practice paid off. My Rolodex was bulging, my phone was ringing, and I was back on the road. One thing was certain, readership was on the rise. Either the celebrities were getting themselves into more trouble, or the tabloids were making a comeback. And I was a part of it.

Well, at least most of the time. Shortly after covering the wedding of Pamela Anderson to Tommy Lee, *Globe* employees got a private education on the couple's not-so-private life. It all began when pornographer Mack Ringley offered to sell *Globe* footage from the couple's infamous honeymoon video. He had reportedly obtained the tape from a construction worker who had been renovating Pamela's Malibu home. Acting as the middle man, Ringley was hoping to make a fortune by peddling the video to everyone from the tabloids to Hugh Hefner.

Ultimately, *Penthouse* magazine, together with the Internet Entertainment Group (IEG), slammed the world with images from the X-rated escapades. Both media companies faced legal battles with the newlyweds until IEG agreed to share its profits with the couple. As it turned out, Ringley and the construction worker walked away with mere pennies while the *Baywatch*-rocker couple pocketed a fortune. Coincidentally, the law firm involved in the case was owned by the father of my friend, Darin Leverett.

When Ringley initially contacted *Globe* with the video, our legal department rejected the offer, considering that the material was stolen property and overly graphic. Nevertheless, *Globe*'s West Coast staff had a chance to preview the stolen video before the images exploded onto the international scandal scene. When I entered the office on the day of the viewing, every desk was bare. Only Caelan was still at his computer, tucked into his private corner, typing away on a story about John Denver's plane crash.

"Hey Caelan, where is everybody?"

"Oh, mornin', luv." He smiled and pointed toward Madeline's closed door. "They're in there watching Pamela Anderson and Tommy Lee having a romp."

"What?" Peering below the glass barrier, I could see several sets of legs standing in front of Madeline's television screen. Sounds of muffled laughter came from the other side. "Since when did *Globe* start buying porn?"

"Well, it seems some bloke turned up this mornin' with the tape," Caelan explained. "Legal thinks it might have been stolen, so I doubt that we'll be buyin' it."

All of a sudden the door cracked open and Sharmin's head popped out. She looked both ways, as if surveying the scene. "Girlfriend, get your ass in here. You won't believe what we're watchin'."

Caelan looked at me, waiting for my response. "Well, what is it you're watching, exactly?" I asked hesitantly.

"Oh, don't go all innocent church girl on me now," she said, waving me into Madeline's office. "If it makes you feel any better, consider it as research."

Given the fact that Madeline was also watching the video, I wondered why Caelan was not in her office with the others. "Uh, no thanks," I answered. "I've got to finish my 'Brooke Shields's Love Diet' story by noon."

Sharmin shook her head. "Oh yeah, that reminds me. Brooke's dad returned your call this morning. His number is on your desk." The door slammed shut.

Caelan looked up from his computer. "I could edit that for ya, if you'd like."

I nodded. "Sure, that would be good."

"Oh, and 'bout that pint . . ." Caelan was clicking the cap of his pen. "What do you say we go for a drink at Barefoot Bar in Beverly Hills? Does nine o'clock work for you?"

I nodded again. "Sure, that would be good, too."

Spinning his chair toward his bulletin board, he ran his finger down the employee contact sheet. "Ah. Here you are, on Ohio Avenue. 'Tis on my way, really. Shall I pick you up, then?"

"Well, if it's not too much trouble," I responded.

"No trouble at all, luv."

Neither of us knew quite how to conclude the conversation, so I took it upon myself. "Okay, see you tonight then. And um . . . I'll get that Brooke Shields copy to you right away." I waved good-bye as if I were leaving the building and then sat down at my desk, just ten feet away from Caelan. It was an awkward moment.

As it turned out, what I had anticipated might become our first date was actually a bit of a fiasco. A group of photographers we knew ended up sharing our table at Barefoot, giving Caelan and me no opportunity to get better acquainted. Obviously, the evening had not gone as Caelan had expected either. When he dropped me off that night, he asked, "Shall we give it another go, then?" We agreed to see a movie and share a drink over the weekend.

At the office the next day, we both acted as if nothing had happened. And, in fact, nothing had. Taking my cue from Caelan, I realized that we would be compartmentalizing our lives into professional and private sectors. This segregation was reflected in his wardrobe, which was business-appropriate on the job and vintage casual outside.

At the office Caelan came across as neutral and reserved, like a tub of vanilla overshadowed by thirty-one flavors. Outside the office he spent several nights each week spinning records as an underground deejay at some of LA's finest clubs. These paradoxical contrasts even extended to his private life. When I was training for a charity marathon, my route took me right past his place in Venice Beach. Caelan used to sit on the balcony enjoying the sunset and it became a ritual for me to stop for by for a water break during my evening run. It was only after several visits that he showed me the hidden loft in his apartment, which he had converted into a deejay booth. Like many parts of his life, Caelan had tucked it away out of sight. Gradually, he began inviting me into the crawl spaces of his personality.

Caelan was even more chameleonic than I. It had taken several months for me to discover that he was a talented cellist, an experienced Web master, and a gifted artist. He often sketched charcoal images onto barren canvas for no one but himself to see. Years before, he had realized that it would take more than art to financially support himself and his widowed mother. Reluctantly, Caelan had surrendered his creativity in exchange for the regimen of a tabloid paycheck.

Just as Caelan struggled with the opposing sides of his career path, I continued to battle with moral schizophrenia. For both of us there was a disconnect between how we lived and how we viewed ourselves. It was our mutual disassociation that helped fuel our personal association.

We really began to know each other when we were both assigned to separate stories in Palm Springs. Madeline had sent me there to interview the singer and songwriter Carol Connors, who had coauthored the theme song from *Rocky*. Caelan was there to interview Jim Bakker following the televangelist's facelift. The Palm Springs setting gave us a chance to get better acquainted, despite the fact we were both working. Realizing that neither of us was mentally ready to make a romantic commitment, we avoided the topic of exclusive dating.

Back at the office, my influx of assignments had taken a change in focus, moving from weddings and births to divorces and deaths. For most people, these events would trigger images of pain, suffering, and remorse. In order to survive as a tabloid reporter, I felt I had to disassociate myself from such emotions. For me, the intensity of celebrity tragedy had to become "just another day at the office."

This was especially true in the nightclubs, where it was easiest for me to take on the role of someone else. Rarely would I use my real name, age, profession, phone number, or interests. When men asked for my telephone number, I would slip them a cocktail napkin on which I had scribbled 310-825-1492. This left them unknowingly holding the direct line to the UCLA Police Department.

This anonymity kept me invincible, or so I thought. The deeper I dove into the Hollywood pool, the more I realized it was no more than a shallow puddle. Night after night, I saw the same faces, in the same clubs, with the same people, telling the same stories.

This became even more apparent when *Globe* asked me to accompany Krystal Wynn, a novice reporter, on a few night assignments. She was making a test run to see if she could become a tabloid reporter covering the evening beat. Born and raised in Boca Raton, she had worked as a manicurist and was obsessed with the tabloids. As a devout rag mag reader, Krystal was on a constant hunt for gossip. Ultimately, the money she earned as a *Globe* source had surpassed her wages at the salon. After personally visiting Florida's head office, she was granted a one-week trial period in *Globe*'s Los Angeles office.

Admittedly, I felt threatened by her, especially considering that she possessed every physical trait I mocked: silicone breasts, colored contacts, platinum hair, and diamond-studded nails. She had them all. *Globe* gave the 25-year-old beautician a rental car, a hotel room, her meals, and $200 a day. After our exhausted staff reporters had missed a few late-night exclusives, the editors considered it a priority to have someone specifically assigned to cover the Hollywood night scene.

"I'm insulted," I complained to Madeline. "Why didn't Florida just ask me to do it, instead of sending Krystal?"

"Because, we need you available during the day," she explained.

"Have you seen those nails?" I blurted. "She can't even type with those things." As the youngest baby of the tabloid family, the last thing I wanted to do was share my crib.

Ignoring my comment, Madeline continued, "For the time being, I'm giving her a desk next to yours."

"Well, what am I supposed to do with her?"

"I don't know," Madeline answered. "It was Florida's idea to bring her out here and now we're stuck babysitting her."

"No," I corrected her. "I'm stuck babysitting her."

Madeline raised her eyebrows.

"Fine," I said, apologetically. "I'll show her the ropes. But there's no way I can be in the office at nine tomorrow if I'm expected to go clubbing with this girl tonight."

Madeline waved her hand in the air. "See you at ten."

That evening Krystal and I made arrangements to meet outside the Garden of Eden, a Hollywood nightclub where I often danced because of the hip-hop deejay. Contrary to its name, the place was cavernous and immoral. Red velvet seating, stone pillars, and glowing torches enticed curious Eves straight into the mouth of this Hollywood dungeon. The place was crawling with serpents offering much more than just a bite of the apple.

"Hey, baby," said the club bouncer, pushing aside the line of waiting clients. Unhooking the velvet rope, he ushered us toward the door. "I haven't seen you in a while. Where've you been hiding?"

"I've got finals," I lied. "But you'll be seeing a lot more of me now."

Taking two drink tickets from his pocket, he slipped them into my hand and opened the door.

"I'll put you on the guest list for tomorrow night, too," he said with a wink. Seldom did I take any compliments to heart, knowing that the majority of Hollywood men passed them out like business cards.

Once inside, Krystal asked, "Why didn't you introduce me?"

"Because I don't know his name," I answered. "You'll see. People don't really know each other in Hollywood."

As we walked through the door, Hugh Hefner was directly to our right. Dressed in his signature silk robe with a martini in hand, the *Playboy* icon was perched in the center of a red velvet booth. His harem of Bunnies encircled him like petals on a flower.

"Those women are perfect," Krystal said, eyeing the bouncing blondes.

"Perfect?" I responded, completely shocked. "They've got more plastic than a Tupperware party."

Krystal decided to take a look around the club while I ordered us a couple of drinks. Within five minutes, I caught a flash of light beaming into my eye from a distance. Looking around for the source of the flash, I realized that it led back to a security guard who was standing at the base of the VIP staircase. He was blinking his flashlight to get my attention. Standing beside him was Krystal.

"Come on," she said, pulling me through the crowd. "He's letting us into the VIP area." As a voluptuous blonde, she had successfully flirted her way into the zone reserved for exclusive guests.

"Nice work," I praised her. "How did you manage that?"

"Batting eyes, puckered lips, a bit of bouncing," she joked, taking one of the drinks I offered. "Men are so predictable."

We sat down on an empty couch and began to people watch. "There's Bobby Brown," I said, motioning across the room. "I'm sure he's here without Whitney."

". . . and is no doubt in desperate need of some attention," Krystal added.

Taking a sip from my straw, I continued. "I grew up listening to that guy—countless hours of lyric memorization and dance moves. I used to hide in my garage and choreograph routines to 'My Prerogative,' 'Don't Be Cruel,' 'Roni' . . ."

Looking a bit confused, Krystal lit a cigarette and scanned the room.

"I was always more of a Whitney fan myself," she explained. "I still think 'I Will Always Love You' is so romantic."

I took another sip and watched as Bobby Brown moved from the bar to a couch. Between puffs, Krystal sang the lyrics, "And I . . . will always love you . . ."

"Okay, I'm nauseous now," I joked. "I need to dance."

"No, don't leave the VIP area," she begged. "We may not get back in here."

"I'm not leaving," I explained. "I'm dancing right here, in front of Bobby. If he joins me, I want you to take a picture." I handed Krystal the small camera that I kept with me. "If you get a shot, we'll split the sales and will each come out with at least two grand."

"Are you joking?" she asked. "This is not going to work. No one else is dancing up here."

Waiting for the deejay to mix in some hip-hop, I stood up. "Do I look like I'm joking?" I asked, walking to the center of the room.

At first, I danced alone. Within five minutes, Bobby had moved away from the couch and was inching toward me. Slowly moving in, he wrapped his hands around my waist and pulled me closer toward his body. Using his signature dance moves I had witnessed in my youth, he grabbed my hands and began to grind. A small crowd of onlookers gathered around us.

Quickly gazing toward Krystal, I gave her a signal. Flash one. The picture was taken.

"What the fuck was that!" he screamed. Pushing me away, Bobby quickly scanned the crowd for the culprit. I had to admit, Krystal was quick. She was already engaged in conversation, taking long drags from her cigarette. I could see that her hands were shaking.

With no cameras in sight, Bobby pulled me back toward him and continued to dance just as he had moments before. No words were exchanged, only glances. This time he moved in closer, his face directly in front of mine. I couldn't believe what was happening. He was leaning in for a kiss.

Flash two.

"Who the fuck is taking pictures?" Picking up a glass from the table, he threw it across the room and screamed, "Lou, get over here!"

Suddenly three men who appeared to be his bodyguards responded to Bobby's call.

"Rip this shit up!" he ordered them. Charging the couch, they sent everyone screaming from the VIP area, including Krystal and me. Tables were overturned and pillows were flying until all that was left was a mound of velvet and cotton.

"You bitch!" Brown screamed as we bolted for the door. "Somebody stop them!"

Grabbing Krystal's hand, I pushed my way through the dance floor and out the front door. We looked back to see if they were following us.

"Quick," I said. "Give me the film. If they catch us, we'll just hand over the camera."

"I don't have it," she mumbled.

I stopped running. "What? What do you mean you don't have it?"

"Well," she said, still shaking. "I shoved it between the cushions. I figured it would be safe there."

Breathe, Marlise, breathe.

By now, Bobby's people would have found the camera and smashed it into pieces.

"That's all right," I lied. "Next time, hide the camera in your underwear if you have to."

The following day, I walked into Madeline's office. Without giving any explanation, I told her that I refused to work with Krystal ever again. I had walked away without a story. Krystal had walked away without a job. From then on, I decided to work alone.

The following evening I was driving to the Four Seasons Hotel to meet photographer James Churchill for a drink. As an aspiring paparazzo, he occasionally met me at posh bars to either gain sources or to catch exclusive photos. I made it as far as Beverly Hills when a black Ford Explorer pulled up beside me at an intersection. I felt dwarfed and exposed in my Karmen Ghia convertible.

"Hey, beautiful," asked a good-looking guy in the passenger seat, "want to meet us for drinks later tonight?"

"I would," I yelled over my roaring engine, "but I already have plans."

"Where are you going?" he asked.

Although I wasn't sure if I could manage it two nights in a row, I told him, "You can probably find me at the Garden of Eden."

"You're kidding me," he said. "That's where we're going. Why don't you just come with us? We'll get you in for free."

Oh, please. I never had to pay the $50 cover charge.

He continued as the light turned green. "Meet us at the Beverly Hills Hotel at nine o'clock tonight. We'll have a drink there first."

"I'll think about it," I called back, with a farewell honk.

Just as I was parking my car at the Four Seasons, my phone rang. It was James Churchill. "Marlise, I have to cancel tonight," James said.

"Radford and I just got shots of Keanu Reeves talking to a bum in an alley."

"So?" I asked, unimpressed.

"Keanu was completely drunk and peeing on a Dumpster," he explained. "It was hard to tell which man lives on the street. We're going to make a fortune off of these shots."

"No worries," I said, still somewhat disappointed. "I have a backup date anyhow."

"With whom?" he asked.

"Not too sure, really," I answered. "I just met him five minutes ago at a stoplight."

"I'm not even going to ask," James teased. "Call me tomorrow."

Fashionably late by fifteen minutes, I ran into the Beverly Hills Hotel to find the man from the Explorer waiting in the lobby.

"I never got to tell you my name," he said. "I'm Tyler Faben and this is Lou Jr."

My heart stopped the moment he said the name "Lou." I was shaking hands with the same man who had torn apart the couch at the VIP club the previous night.

"Nice to meet you," Lou said. Fortunately, we had not made contact in the darkened club the night before.

"I'm Jennifer," I said, holding out my hand.

"We're just waiting for our friend and then we can all head out," Tyler was saying. He was one of the most attractive guys I had seen in a long time. There was an innocence about him, a sort of carefree surfer look blended with a touch of *GQ* style.

"I wasn't sure we were going to see you," he said. "Generally, I don't make a habit of speaking to women at intersections."

"Generally, I don't make a habit of responding," I replied.

"Damn, he's taking forever," Lou said, dialing his cell phone. Turning away from us, he spoke into the phone, "We'll wait for you in the bar . . . sure, by the piano."

For such a lavish hotel, the lounge bar looked rather tacky. The baby blue velvet booths and curtains were in desperate need of an upgrade. Within seconds, the waiter had arrived.

"Jack and Coke," I told him.

"Make that three," Lou added. "No, four. Our friend is on his way."

Their friend? Oh no. It can't be! What if it turns out to be Bobby Brown? Think ahead, Marlise. Think ahead!

There was dead silence. "So, what do you do?" Tyler asked.

"I'm a student at UCLA," I lied. "Art major." Normally I tended to take on subjects I knew something about, but the word "art" had come out of my mouth before I had given it any thought.

"Really?" Lou seemed impressed. "So you actually draw?"

"No," I answered. "I paint."

"Damn, girl," he said. "I don't know too many artists. What type of work do you do?"

"I imitate the impressionists." I couldn't believe what I was saying. "Renoir, Monet, Degas—"

Tyler interrupted, "So, you paint the soft stuff?"

"I guess you can say that," I added. "Right now I'm trying to imitate the work of Degas. You know, the ballet paintings? Except, I'm replacing his dancers with contemporary break dancers."

"I bet that's hard to blend the classic with the modern," Tyler commented.

This was one of the most bizarre conversations I had ever had. I was running out of material. I had to change the subject fast. "So, what do you guys do?"

"Lou Jr. here is the son of Lou Rawls," Tyler said. Lou briefly looked up and then began dialing a number on his cell phone. The waiter arrived with our drinks.

"Charge it to our room," Lou ordered.

Tyler continued. "And our friend Bob is—"

Just then a familiar voice called out behind us. "Didja order a drink for me?"

I turned around and there he was. For the second time in two days, Bobby Brown was standing right in front of me. My heart missed a beat. Grabbing my drink, I tried to hide myself behind my glass, and then quickly grabbed a cocktail napkin and pretended to blow my nose.

"Holy shit!" he said, looking straight at me. "Weren't you with the girl who tried to take my picture last night?"

"No," I told him, nervously shifting over in the velvet booth. "I've been out of town. I just flew in from Chicago today. I've never met you in my life."

Buying my story, Bobby instantly apologized and reached over to properly introduce himself. "Sorry, girl," he said. "I thought you were someone else."

With only minimal conversation, all of us slammed our drinks and headed toward the lobby.

"So you ridin' wit' us, girl?" Bobby asked, motioning me toward his gold Mercedes. Without knowing where the evening would take me, I nervously agreed. Sinking into the leather seat, I sat in the back with Tyler, thinking about how many hours of my childhood had been spent listening to Bobby's music. At one point, I could have been labeled one of Bobby Brown's biggest fans. The car was silent until he turned on the radio to LA's rap station, 92.3, The Beat.

"Hey, Bobby," Tyler said over a Sprint advertisement. "Can you turn it up? This is my favorite commercial." I laughed at his dry humor.

Missing Tyler's joke entirely, Bobby adjusted the volume and asked if it was loud enough. As an advertiser's voice bumped through the bass, Tyler yelled, "Actually that was just a joke. I was kidding."

I could tell our group didn't really mesh. It was only the LA nightlife that had brought us together. Sunset Boulevard was packed and cars were cruising along the strip for miles. Completely oblivious to our identity, a cop car pulled up beside us.

"Fucking pigs," Bobby said, stretching out almost horizontally in the driver's seat. His hand, adorned with a gold watch and bulky rings, hung limply over the steering wheel. Turning to Lou beside him, Bobby added, "Those niggas are always on my ass."

Tyler and I looked over at the cops, who were staring straight ahead. With a discreet nudge on the leg, Tyler rolled his eyes and grinned.

"These two are so full of it," Tyler whispered in my ear. Bobby turned up the bass in an effort to irritate the police. They failed to notice his act of rebellion.

"I thought you guys were friends," I mumbled back.

Tyler repressed a laugh. "Are you kidding me? I hang out with them because, well, how cool is it to hang out with Bobby Brown? I'm experiencing the high life without all the hassle."

He was right. When we arrived at the Garden of Eden, we were given free parking and were immediately escorted to the VIP area through a private entrance. Once inside, we were seated at a back table and served free drinks throughout the entire evening.

"I want to dance with you," Tyler said.

Flashbacks from the night before played in my head. "Sure," I agreed. "But would you mind if we went downstairs to the dance floor?"

Grabbing my hand, he walked me down the flight of stairs and through the crowd. I liked him. I didn't know why exactly. In reality, he was using celebrities to get what he wanted just as I was. Perhaps we weren't so different after all.

"Bobby is dating Lou's sister," Tyler told me on the dance floor.

Knowing I was stepping into headline territory, I asked, "What about Whitney?"

"She's too messed up on drugs to even care," he answered.

Unbeknownst to Tyler, the entire evening was a shameless interview. Each time he opened his mouth, countless articles developed in my mind. Ultimately, I published six stories pertaining to the life of Bobby Brown. Tyler had unknowingly become my newest source.

"You're cute, Jennifer," Tyler said. "I'd like to see you again."

For a moment, I wished he knew me for who I really was.

"Can I call you?" he persisted.

Just as I always did, I slipped him a cocktail napkin with a phone number. This time, the digits were mine.

Knowing I had to work early the following morning, I caught a taxi back to the hotel where I had left my car. I drove home thinking about Tyler and how I wanted to see him again, knowing that I would never be able to do so because of my job. Tyler called me five times the following day. I refused to pick up the phone.

"Jennifer," one message said. "I think you're hot and I like your teeth . . . and I want to take you to dinner."

I saved Tyler's message for a week but never returned his calls. I wanted to phone him but I couldn't, because I was already living a lie. Chances were, I would never be able to gain his trust, nor he mine. That's the price I was willing to pay to stay with the tabloids.

As much as I would have liked to see Tyler again, it was actually Bobby Brown that I kept running into. Our third encounter occurred when I was attending the Emmys® with producer John Ritz. While Whitney was conducting an interview on the red carpet, Bobby Brown turned, caught my eye, and waved just before stepping into his limousine. I was beginning to feel that Hollywood was shrinking by the day.

Those within the tabloid family always said that the best way to capture a story is to pretend that you belong. In order to do so, I spontaneously assembled a wardrobe of disguises. It was during this time that I was handed a lead sheet stating, "Regis Philbin's daughter Amy arrested for DUI? Check it out."

Standing in the center of the office, I called out to my colleagues, "Does anyone here have any Regis sources?" A few reporters offered to share their Kathy Lee contacts, but the sourcing was too far removed to provide the information I needed. Contacting the Florida office, I asked them to run a Faces of the Nation on Philbin's daughter. The only info I got right away was that her last name is Philbin-Ferguson.

"Sorry, Marlise," said Marsha Powell, who handled Florida's research department. "We're slammed over here. I'll call you with her home address in an hour."

If the story was going to run in the upcoming issue, it had to be done that same day. Otherwise, it would be killed. Looking down at the phone lines, I could tell that Madeline was on another call. Crumpling a ball of paper, I tossed it at Sharmin, who was fast asleep at her desk. "Sharmin, wake up," I said.

Startled, she raised her head. "Thanks for calling *Globe*—"

"Do me a favor," I said, grabbing my bag. "Tell Madeline I'm working on the Regis story. I'll be back in an hour."

"Where're you going?" she asked, rubbing her eyes.

"To jail," I answered literally.

She laid her head back down on the keyboard. "Just don't go expecting me to bail out your white ass."

Based on information *Globe* had gained from a police scanner, it appeared that Amy Philbin had been arrested for drunk driving near Van Nuys. I had to prove it. Without much to go on, I headed straight for the police station. Obviously, bribery was out of the question. Unlike the movie version of investigative journalism, there was no chance of sneaking into the file room to steal a copy of the report.

Throwing my bag over my shoulder, I walked through the front door of the police station with enough confidence to leave the impression that I was part of the LAPD. My only disguise was a little plastic card hanging around my neck, a press pass. Issued by the LAPD, every legitimate Hollywood reporter was entitled to own one. From airports to hospitals, I had learned how to maximize the usefulness of the press pass by covering the word *Globe* with my thumb and exposing the letters "LAPD."

In this particular instance, I pressed my ID up to the window and said, "Afternoon. I'm Officer Kast, here to pick up the Philbin-Ferguson report."

The station was quiet and the woman behind the counter was working alone. She stopped typing. "Excuse me?"

"I understand a female by the name of Amy Philbin-Ferguson was charged with a DUI recently. There was a prior warrant out for her arrest for breaching a three-year probation sentence. I've been assigned to investigate the current status on the case. I'll need copies of those records."

"Well," she said, sliding a clipboard under the glass. "I can't give you copies of anything without approval from my sergeant. But here is our evening log from last night. It shows the name of every person booked and released over the past twenty-four hours. Will that help?"

Flipping through the pages, I found a dated log with the entry, "Amy Philbin-Ferguson, DUI." Now I had all the proof I needed.

Moments after I left the police station, Marsha called my cell phone from our Florida office to give me Amy Philbin's home address. The fact that Amy lived outside of Beverly Hills saved me the usual hassle of security guards and private gates, to which I had become accustomed. The moment I pulled into her driveway, I noticed someone peeking through the blinds.

Things didn't go as smoothly as I had hoped, however. I rang, and knocked, and waited on her doorstep. Assuming she knew I was a reporter, I blurted, "Amy, we're running the piece with or without your help. Don't you want to at least tell your side of the story?"

"Get off my property, please," she cried through the blinds.

Moving closer toward the window, I continued, "Amy, I promise I'll include your quote if you'll just talk to me." There was silence. "I'll even pay you for your time."

The blinds turned slightly as she spoke through the screen. "What do you want me to say? That my life is out of control? That I screwed up? It doesn't matter, does it? You people will just write what you want anyway."

"Amy," I said. "I give you my word to include everything you tell me."

She pulled the blinds up all the way. "Look, I really can't talk now. I've got my little boy in the house." Glancing back over her shoulder, she continued. "Just write that 'I'm sorry that this had to happen, but that it taught me a good lesson.' If that quote gets in your paper, then maybe we can talk about a doing an interview. Okay?"

I nodded, smiling back at Amy, who looked exhausted, ashamed, and emotionally beaten. "This is all going to pass," I told her. "Everything is going to be fine."

Returning to the *Globe* office, I quickly banged out the cover story, titled "Regis Battles to Save Drunk Daughter," and faxed it to Florida to beat their morning deadline. By the time I had finished, the office was empty. As I locked the door and walked into the darkness, I felt rather pleased with a day well done.

I had just crawled into bed when the phone rang. It was Madeline. "I know it's midnight, but Frankie just died. You've got to find his body."

The entire staff had known that Frank Sinatra was approaching death. The call came as no surprise. "I would ask someone else," she added, "but they are all asleep and—"

"What do I have to work with at this point?" I interrupted.

"Well," Madeline explained, "we were told he has a burial plot in Palm Springs, but now we think it might have been a false tip to throw us off track."

"Where is this information coming from?" I asked. "Where is the funeral going to be?" I felt somewhat foolish asking so many questions, but Pete was usually in charge of all Sinatra leads.

"Beverly Hills," she answered. "At the Good Shepherd Catholic Church. Just leave the local stuff to me." Madeline sounded out of breath. "We got a tip that he might be buried somewhere near Los Angeles closer to the funeral site. You just handle Palm Springs and find out if, in fact, Frank is going to be buried there."

Mid hang-up, I heard Madeline say, "Keep your phone on."

By three a.m. I had driven to Palm Springs and checked out the alleged gravesite in Cathedral City. Sure enough, there was just enough space for Frank to rest between his parents, Anthony and Natalie. However, since a barren plot of earth does not confirm or deny anything, I needed more information. From the cemetery I drove straight to the mortuary parking lot. I was planning to sleep in my car until the funeral home opened at nine. At seven, my phone rang.

"You know, when I sent you to Palm Springs in the middle of the night, I didn't really think about the fact the mortuary would be closed."

"Good morning, Madeline," I answered, somewhat dazed.

"Any news?" she asked.

"Well, the dirt is here," I answered. "But I'm not sure if Frankie will be lying under it. I'll call you after I get into the mortuary."

Dozing in and out of sleep, I instantly awoke the moment a car pulled into the parking lot. It was nine o'clock sharp. Ten minutes later, I entered the building and was approached by the funeral director. Uncertain of how the scene would unfold, I decided to play it safe and use a fictitious name.

"Hi, I'm Jade Rock," I said reaching out my hand. "I was wondering if you could tell me a bit about your mortuary. My grandfather is in the hospital right now and I want to make sure all the funeral arrangements are in order." After having so recently lost my own grandfather, playing this role was hardly a stretch.

"Of course," answered the funeral director. "Why don't we start with a tour of our facilities?" Within an hour, I had flipped though a stack of tombstone catalogs, chosen a style of casket, and conjured enough tears to gain the director's trust.

"Grandpa's final wish is to be buried next to Ol' Blue Eyes," I sobbed. "I know it's silly of me, but I heard this is where it's all happening." I blew my nose into a tissue. "Is that true?"

Handing me another tissue, the funeral director assured me that my grandfather would indeed be able to rest in peace as Frankie's neighbor-in-death. Wiping my tears, I drove back toward the office with a solid confirmation under my belt.

Just as I reached the outskirts of LA, my cell phone rang. "Turn around, Marlise, and head back." It was Madeline again. "You have to drive to Covina."

"Why? What's in Covina?" I asked, hesitantly. Madeline's request surprised me, given the fact that Covina was a small community halfway between Palm Springs and LA.

"We just got a call from a janitor at a mortuary there," she answered. "He says that last night when he was cleaning, a body was wheeled in. I know it sounds ridiculous, but he swears the death tag has Frank Sinatra's name written on it."

The other line clicked. "Madeline, I have to go," I said. "I'll check it out and call you back." I clicked over. "Hello?"

"Marlise—are you going to try to make it to church on Sunday?" It was my mother. "I'm a bit worried about you."

"Mom, I can't talk now," I said. "I have to check out Frank Sinatra's toes."

She didn't bother to ask me why.

Immediately my phone rang again. Madeline was on the line, calling back to give me the location of the Covina mortuary. When I arrived, the janitor met me at the back door, as he had arranged with Madeline. Immediately I recognized him as the type of source we are trained to avoid. The fact that he dusted corpses for a living only added to my suspicions.

"Shhh," he said, holding his finger to his mouth. "Be very quiet."

This struck me as odd, considering we were the only conscious bodies in the building.

"Okay," I said, already sensing that this tip might be a waste of time.

"Where's Frank Sinatra's body?"

"Follow me," he whispered, holding a set of keys in one hand and a mop in the other. We walked through a long corridor, neither of us saying a word. Suddenly my phone rang, startling both of us as it broke the silence.

"Get out," Madeline ordered. "He's a wacko. We just found Frank's body in Beverly Hills."

I hung up before she had a chance to explain. Sliding the phone into my purse, I turned toward the janitor, who was now unlocking a side door.

"Oh, I almost forgot your money," I said, my voice now trembling. "I'll go get it. . . . It's in the car."

"You mean you pay me now?" he asked enthusiastically.

"Of course," I replied, slowly backing away. "You wouldn't want to give me all your valuable information unless you were paid, right?"

He nodded.

"Give me two minutes and I'll be right back," I assured him.

He began walking toward me. "I'll come with you."

"No," I said, pushing my hand on his chest. "It's better if you keep an eye on Frank's body. When I come back, I'll knock three times on the door so you'll know it's me."

Trying to hide my nervousness, I forced my body to move slowly until I was past the door. Once outside, I ran toward my car as fast as I could. Driving back to LA, I phoned Madeline and told her that I needed a break. By that time I had gone without sleep for seventy-two hours straight.

Somehow I had gotten caught in a vortex of celebrity deaths. Shortly after Frank Sinatra's funeral, an even more tragic incident had occurred involving the murder of comedian Phil Hartman. Under the influence of cocaine, alcohol, and Zoloft, his wife, Brynn, had shot the *Saturday Night Live* alum twice in the head and once in the chest. Brynn then locked herself in the bedroom and shot herself.

The Hartman assignment had led me to the Hall of the Crucifixion-Resurrection at Glendale's Forest Lawn Cemetery. With only twenty relatives invited to the stone chapel, my chances of getting inside were virtually impossible. To protect their privacy, the Hartman relatives had hired Calvin Defoe, the infamous bodyguard of the stars. Rumor had it that Calvin was merciless when it came to protecting his clients. Although I had never come face-to-face with this security legend, tales of Defoe's torment had spread throughout the office, leaving warnings of danger across my impressionable mind. Years later, I heard whispers that Defoe used his celebrity proximity to sell information to the tabloids. Had I realized he was playing both sides of the game, I probably would not have been so intimidated.

Outside the crematorium, I waited in my car for the mourners to exit. Parked behind me was Edward Townsend, my assigned photographer. He was one of the youngest and most aggressive paparazzi in the business. Always clad in two-toned denim and wearing a leather fanny pack, the British native somehow managed to mingle in social circles with the likes of Anna Nicole Smith and B-movie stars. We worked well together, especially during out-of-town assignments that required us to masquerade as a couple. He loved his cell phone and had a habit of over-using it during stakeouts.

"Guess who?" It was Edward, his car bumper touching mine. "So, how exactly are things up there, mate?"

I looked in my rearview mirror to find him peering at me through a pair of binoculars. I waved. "I'm bored and hungry and I want to go home. Why is this funeral taking so long?"

He put down the binoculars and continued in his strong British accent. "Mind you, this is rather better than the office, isn't it?"

"Sure," I said. "I guess so. . . . Hey," I asked, turning up the volume on the radio, "what do you think of this song?"

"I'm British, you know," he said. "Hip-hop insults our cultural refinement. . . . By the way, d'you fancy meeting me later for a drink?"

"Sorry," I answered. "I'm busy. There's a major cockroach situation going on in my kitchen cupboards. I promised my sister we would bomb the house tonight."

"Oh, that's such a nasty business," he said. "Don't you suppose you could just hire it done?"

"Well," I said. "That would take all the joy out of family bonding, now wouldn't it?"

Aiming the binoculars toward the crematorium, Edward said, "Ladies and gentlemen, start your engines. We've got movement in the funeral home."

"That's an oxymoron if ever I've heard one," I replied.

I rarely allowed myself to feel much emotion during the assignments I covered, but this story was different because it included two newly orphaned children. Just at that moment, the children existed the building.

"Oh, splendid," Edward said, aiming his camera toward the subjects. "I hadn't expected to see Hartman's children here. I believe they witnessed the entire scene, actually. The editors will be quite pleased with these photographs. . . . Oh bloody hell. My lens won't reach that far. We must give chase."

"*Globe* is not paying me enough for this job," I said disgustedly as I started my engine. Car chases were so paparazzi and I had always managed to avoid them.

"Oh, do come on, luv," he snapped. "Where's your spirit of adventure? This is going to be such fun. But do be careful. Remember, Defoe's on this assignment."

To preserve our anonymity, we circled the crematorium, heading toward the exit from opposite directions. Keeping a respectful distance from the black SUVs, we followed the mourners to the Hilton Hotel in Canoga Park. We were confident that we had not been discovered. Sitting in my car in visitors parking, I killed time by chatting with Edward on the phone. He was waiting in his car at the front of the hotel.

Picking up our conversation where we had left off, I asked, "So, are you telling me that Raid is actually toxic to humans?" Suddenly my cockroach conversation was cut short as I stared through the windshield to see Calvin Defoe approaching my car. "You have got to be kidding me!"

"No, not at all," Edward replied, unaware that I had changed the subject. "Raid is actually quite toxic if used improperly—"

"No!" I whispered into the phone. "Defoe's right in front of me! He's writing down my license plate number. What should I do?"

Before Edward had a chance to answer, Defoe knocked on my windshield.

"Yes?" I said nonchalantly, rolling down the window.

"You need to leave now," he threatened.

Ignoring his demand, I pointed at the For Sale sign in the back window of my sister's car. I had known that her Honda would be less conspicuous at the funeral than my Karmen Ghia, which had a tendency to backfire. Reacting solely to Defoe's reputation for intimidation, I faked a bravado I didn't really possess. "Go ahead. You might as well write down my phone number while you're at it. The plate number won't do you much good after I sell this car."

Even after he walked away, I still felt that he was controlling the situation. My hand shaking, I grabbed the phone off the passenger seat. "Did you hear that, Edward? Quick! We need to do something. They're leaving the hotel."

Accustomed to chases like this, Edward agreed to take the lead. For twenty minutes, we played a dangerous game of cat and mouse on the streets of LA. Occasionally Defoe would stop at a green light, waiting for it to turn yellow before he moved forward, knowingly leaving us trapped by the red light. At one point, Edward maneuvered in front of Defoe, sandwiching Calvin's vehicle between our two cars.

As we turned onto Malibu's Pacific Coast Highway, Defoe pushed me out of the game. Slamming on his brakes, he peeled out in an effort to overtake Edward. To avoid hitting Defoe's car, I swerved onto the shoulder and abruptly stopped just inches before falling over the embankment.

At that point, I called Edward and told him to count me out. Undaunted, Edward followed the mourners to Catalina, where he captured pictures of the family scattering the actor's ashes into Emerald Bay.

For me, the story had literally come to a screeching halt.

Note:

Pamela Anderson divorced Tommy Lee in 1998. She and Kid Rock were married on August 3, 2006, and filed for divorce in November 2006.

After fourteen years of marriage, Bobby Brown and Whitney Houston filed for divorce in October 2006. They have one daughter, Bobbi Kristina.

CHAPTER 11

Becoming Leo's Neighbor

The risks I was willing to take were usually self-inflicted. The editors seldom knew what I had gone through to deliver their stories. During my first few months at *Globe*, I had been held in an Egyptian prison, locked in a mortuary, and run off the road by a bodyguard. The editors knew none of that. These events should have clearly signaled me to get out of the business. Instead, I began to feel almost indestructible. As an adrenaline junkie, I was unable to see that the negatives of my job were outweighing the positives. I felt that every assignment would take me one step closer to an echelon of invincibility. Each new day equaled another new adventure. Only God knew how it all would end.

Any break in celebrity gossip made me restless. These lulls bored me and made me feel as if I were working a predictable nine-to-five job. Such career flatlines could often be elevated through my own desire for the hunt. Madeline praised my motivated mentality and rewarded me with the added role as *Globe*'s night beat reporter. This meant that I would see even less of my sister, Heidi, who was increasingly entombed in the UCLA lab as she completed her doctorate. Knowing she disapproved of the risks I was taking, I made a point of telling her less and less about my job.

After Manuela returned to Peru, Chantal and Sharmin started to take turns accompanying me on my night beat adventures. What started out as a few hours of dancing on the weekend quickly turned into mandatory socializing on a nightly basis. Together we attended everything from award banquets to private house parties. We mingled with the Hollywood scene chasers and gained access to nearly every VIP guest list and red carpet event on Sunset Boulevard. Somehow my home phone number ended up in the database of several club promoters, all of whom I knew only by their first names. This handful of acquainted strangers, with names like "Awk" and "Enzo," would unhook the velvet ropes, stamp our hands, and exempt us from paying the cover charge. We knew the system well. The promoters brought in the women, the women lured in the men, and the men spent the money.

Apparently, these club promoters swapped contacts with those who organized after-hour parties. One promoter, whom I never met face to face, had the unforgettable name DJ Jailbird. He had taken to calling me every week regarding private events within the black community. One of his invitations landed us at a party thrown by Dr. Dre. The rap legend had rented a Hollywood mansion that was otherwise reserved for porn films and photo shoots. The place was decorated with black leather couches, marble floors, brass banisters, and leopard print curtains. During the party, I hesitated to sit down or lean on any furniture. For the women, the dress code was short and tight, and for the men, loose and baggy. Nearly everyone was wearing gold either around their necks or in their mouths.

Chantal and I clearly stood out. Sharmin came along to dilute our white-girl image, but even she had trouble blending in with the thuggish crowd. Her body was engulfed by the floor-length trench coat that she insisted on wearing to private parties and celebrity events. She would habitually sneak souvenirs into the deep pockets of the coat's lining, priding herself on her exploits as a modern-day Robin Hood. "Steal from the rich and give to the poor," she would say. We were always amazed at how many items she could stash away during the course of a night. One of her most unbelievable prizes was the eighteen-inch pepper mill she managed to sneak out of Spago's.

In Dr. Dre's rented mansion, the drawers and cabinets were barren, making Sharmin's hobby more of a challenge than usual. She did, however, manage to filch some bottles of Alaze? from the ice-filled bathtub. The marble tub with its gold plated fixtures was now loaded with forty-ounce beers, malt liquor, and bottles of Cisco. Every table and countertop in the kitchen was covered with disposable aluminum trays filled with collared greens and ham hocks, macaroni and cheese, and fried chicken wings.

Sharmin bit into a flaky biscuit and whispered, "You can take the gangsta out of the ghetto, but you can't take the ghetto out of the gangsta."

Sharmin's biscuit left behind flour remnants that caked the corners of her mouth. Licking my thumb, I wiped them away and said, "People are going to think you're snorting coke."

She shook her head at my ignorance. "Girlfriend, this crew smokes the chronic and nothing but the chronic. No seeds, no stems, one hundred percent, grade-A quality bud." Pointing toward the living room, she told me to go in there and take a whiff. Sure enough, the distinct smell of marijuana funneled through my nose and into my brain.

Secondhand smoke . . . Contact high . . . I'm feeling relaxed. . . .

Dotting the room were intimidating guests holding brown-bagged forties and paper plates of chitlins. Diamond-studded teeth flashed with every bite. At some stage, Chantal had wandered off, landing herself in the pit of the gangsta-rap family. I watched as she innocently sauntered into the center of the ring, introducing herself around the circle. "Hi, everybody," she said, in a series of firm handshakes. "The name's Chantal. Who ah ya?"

One by one with a single nod, they mumbled two-part names like "Chill-Z," "Puff 420," and "Big Bling." Several of them simply pulled their hats down over their eyes and remained silent. Turning to one of them, she insisted, "Ya do have a name, doncha?"

Realizing Chantal desperately needed to be rescued, I ran over to her. "So, this must be your party," I said, stepping between her and our host. "You're Dr. Dre, right?"

Before he had a chance to respond, Chantal turned toward the famous rapper and said enthusiastically, "Oh, you're a doctor! So, what's ya specialty?"

Through hints of gold-plated teeth, it was obvious that the entire circle was attempting to stifle resistant grins. Slowly lifting the brim of his hat, Dr. Dre looked directly at Chantal and answered earnestly, "I'm a heart surgeon."

Grabbing her hand, I pulled Chantal away from the group before the conversation could deteriorate any further. "Nice to meet ya," she waved back.

Suddenly Sharmin came running down the spiral staircase toward us, glass bottles clanging inside the walls of her jacket. Leaning in closely, she unknowingly poked my leg with the neck of a stolen champagne bottle. "We've got to get the hell outta here," she demanded.

"Why?" I asked, pulling the bottle out of her coat by its foiled cork. "Is your wine collection getting warm?"

Chantal glanced back at the circle of men who were still laughing at her amusing introduction. She muttered, "I gotta say, I'm with Sharmin on this one. I don't have a good feelin' about tha place."

Behind us was a group of women who looked like they were straight out of a rap video. "Don't you two get it?" Sharmin whispered. "It's a hoochie party. And we ain't hoochies."

Chantal eyed the scantily-clad women. "Wait just a second. Whaddya mean, hoochie?"

"I mean, pimps up, ho's down! These ladies are gettin' *paid.*"

"You're kidding me," I said in disbelief. "How do you know?"

Sharmin gave me the look of shame. "Girlfriend, I'm from Compton. Trust me, I know what a ho looks like." She threw her arms over our shoulders and formed a huddle. "Let's get outta here before they think we're part of the bootie crew."

During the drive home, Chantal finally figured out the true identity of Dr. Dre. On the local radio station 92.3, The Beat, it was his voice we heard rapping the familiar club song "California Love."

That was the beginning of many escapades to come for the three of us. It often took a great deal of convincing to get them to come along with me. In the end, they usually did, with only minor regrets the following day. Pete and Caelan occasionally joined our close-knit clique, meeting us at odd hours and in dodgy locations for all-you-can-eat buffets. Outside of the office, we formed a secret bond, making our work environment bearable.

Despite Sharmin's initial prediction that I wouldn't "last a week at *Globe*," she and I eventually became as close as sisters. Sharmin liked me because I could dance or, as she put it, I had "rhythm, for a white girl." I stored her compliment and let it all out on the dance floor. Time and time again, I would wake up in her Compton apartment. Gunshots, thumping bass, screaming children, and screeching tires were common sounds in her neighborhood. The fact that she had a three-year-old daughter seemed to make all those nights more bearable.

With cornrow braids and twin dimpled cheeks, little Ryann had more personality and dramatic flair than any child I had ever met. Her lips quivered when she cried, she talked with her hands on her hips, loved to dance hip-hop, and would hug me with her entire body. Sharmin refused to let Ryann know that her biological father was a gang member. Instead, she had convinced Ryann that the late rapper Tupac Shakur was her daddy. After years of fighting for child support, Sharmin took out a $100,000 life insurance policy on her ex in the event that he might ultimately die in crossfire.

I knew their story well, which only made me love Ryann that much more. Occasionally I would babysit on weekends or holidays, and I often attended Sharmin's all-black church. Even Madeline's heart defrosted when Ryann entered the office, showing us that there was, in fact, a soft side to our boss. Perhaps the greatest joy during my years at *Globe* was the honor of becoming Ryann's godmother.

This link brought me even closer to Sharmin, making her a fixed figure within my unstable private life. The only secret I kept hidden from her was the fact that I was falling for Caelan. No one knew how I felt, not even Caelan. I resisted those feelings, knowing that giving myself to someone would only lead to a further loss of my identity.

Instead, I took on the kind of assignments that required total submersion, knowing that in the end, there would be nothing left to give away. After one year at *Globe*, I stumbled across a story that nearly cost me my reputation. It began with a photograph of Leonardo DiCaprio that had found its way to the editors of *Globe*. A paparazzo had snapped Leo allegedly "fondling" a male friend in the swimming pool of the famous Chateau Marmont Hotel. At the time, *Titanic* was still showing in the theaters. This made anything associated with Leonardo worth a fortune. Although the photos were too risqué for *Globe* to publish, the editors felt that the pictures were suspicious enough to suggest that Leonardo was living a double life.

That's where I came in.

In typical *Globe* fashion, the editors assigned me to the story with little to go on. The entire lead was based on one simple assumption taken from those photographs. I had nothing else from the editors—no direction, no contacts, no supervision, and nowhere to start. Our files showed that Leonardo had been living at the castle-like Chateau Marmont for the past six months. It was my plan to become his neighbor. Given the fact that the photographs of Leonardo had been taken in the hotel's pool, I could only hope I would spot him there again. On that basis alone, I checked into a poolside bungalow. Sadly, it was the same suite where John Belushi had overdosed on heroin in 1982.

That whole next week, I detached myself from everybody I knew to take on the role of "Molli Baker." Supposedly, Molli was a bridesmaid visiting Los Angeles for her cousin's wedding. Using this persona, I intended to gain the trust of potential informants and to isolate and use those who seemed the most vulnerable.

Room service seemed a logical place to start. In general, nightshift waiters had the best idea of what went on behind closed doors. Despite the fact I wasn't hungry, I ordered a meal soon after checking into my bungalow. It was delivered by hotel employee Matt Shelton. An aspiring actor, he was pale, lanky, and in his mid-twenties. Playing the role of Molli, I asked, "So do you ever see anyone famous around here?"

"Nearly every day," Matt boasted. I knew he was telling the truth. In the short time I had been at the hotel, I had already seen Natalie Portman and Adam Goldberg. Rattling off the names of everyone from Johnny Depp to Sandra Bullock, Matt's list of well-known guests seemed to build to the final name, Leonardo DiCaprio.

"You're kidding me," I said, pretending to be surprised. "I absolutely love Leonardo. In fact, *Titanic* is my favorite movie." At that point, I had yet to see the film.

Matt lifted the silver dome off the dinner plate to reveal triangle toast and Norwegian lox. "You'd be surprised. Leo's not the same guy he is in his movies. He's been kicked out of the hotel twice because of all the problems he's caused. Recently Leo moved into the main tower with a bunch of his friends," he said, referring to the hotel center that was surrounded by several bungalows.

"Is he in the main tower now?" I prodded.

"No. Last I heard, he's in Thailand filming a movie. But I think his brother Adam is living up there with a group of guys while he's gone."

For a tabloid journalist, this was the ideal situation. Leo's absence would give me an opportunity to probe those around him without raising suspicion. Suddenly our conversation was cut short by the sound of Matt's pager.

"Sorry, I have to get back to work." Taking a pen from his pocket, he handed me a room service bill sandwiched inside a leather folder. I paid cash to avoid signing a false name. Eyeing the crisp bills, he told me he would be right back with the change. "Keep it," I told him, knowing very well the generous tip would work to my advantage.

Only two hours later, I called in another room service order in an effort to gain more information. And I did. Over time, Matt fed me details about Leo's alleged obsession with prostitutes and the mystery man who lived in his room. "Everyone at the hotel calls him 'Leo's Bitch,'" Matt explained. "You can't miss the guy—he's a little wimp with an enormous Afro."

The conversations with Matt continued all afternoon. Given the amount of food I ordered, he must have thought I either had a tapeworm or the munchies. By his final visit, Matt suggested we meet at the nearby Bar Marmont following his shift. It was midnight by the time he finally arrived, still wearing his black and white uniform minus the name tag.

Leading the way, Matt settled into a red vinyl booth under warm lights. Scooting in beside him, I knew very well that we had different agendas in mind. By now, I had developed almost a sixth sense about which sources could be bought. I was beginning to wonder if I could fully trust Matt with my true identity without him blowing my cover. If I told him why I was at the hotel and he revealed who I really was, I would get kicked out of the Chateau Marmont and lose the entire Leonardo story. Taking a deep breath, I decided to go for it.

"Here's the deal," I said, honestly. "My name's not Molli and I'm not a bridesmaid. I'm a reporter working on a story for *Globe* magazine."

Shifting in his seat, Matt looked over his shoulder as if we were being followed. I continued, knowing I only had a few seconds before I lost him. "I'm prepared to offer you five thousand dollars for signing a statement confirming what you already told me in the room. That includes everything about the women, the parties, the complaints, the roommates—anything you can think of that might contribute to my story."

He lit a cigarette and inhaled deeply. "Can I see some ID?" As I showed him my press pass, he asked, "What's your story exactly?"

Pulling the swimming pool photo from my purse, I pointed toward Leo's friend that I was trying to identify. "Well, it started with this," I explained. "And now, I'm not quite sure where the story's headed. It looks like there's much more going on in this hotel than we realized. Who else knows about this stuff?"

Matt blew smoke directly into my eyes, instantly drying out my contact lenses. I coughed, hoping he would get the hint. He pressed his half-smoked cigarette into an ashtray and continued. "Nightshift security knows Leo pretty well. Probably the cleaning staff, too. You know, I'm hoping to be an actor myself someday. I'm just not sure how comfortable I am about getting involved. When I become famous, I would hate for this to happen to me. Maybe if you could get me ten thousand dollars, I might be willing to sign."

The following day Madeline suggested I push Matt out of the story altogether and approach the security guards as firsthand sources instead. My room service ended abruptly. Targeting the security post outside my door, I sat on my bungalow porch and stared at books I wasn't reading. That's how I spotted Ramon Harper. Like a shadow, Ramon seemed to hang over the entire hotel. He had a shaved head and enormous arms that never laid flush to his body. His face was rough, as if he had been shaving with a dull blade. It was like looking at a Nestlé Crunch bar.

I struck up casual conversation about his life in LA. As usual, our talk led straight to celebrities in general and, of course, Leonardo in particular. Ramon was the second person to confirm that Leonardo shared his apartment with a "big-haired male." He also gave more specifics, including Leo's room number and the pseudonym he often used when he wanted to avoid fans. In and of itself, this information proved nothing, but it gave me a starting point. Before long, I was convinced that I could "buy" Ramon. Even before I told him the amount I was offering, he was willing to sign *Globe*'s contract as long as his name wasn't mentioned in the article.

Naturally Madeline was thrilled with my progress, knowing we were wading into headline waters. "You still need to get two more firsthand sources," Madeline explained. "Florida wants this story wrapped up in seventy-two hours."

Madeline had just restated the golden rule of tabloid reporting. At *Globe*, all high-risk stories required three firsthand sources in order to get published. Although Matt was not a paid source, his comments would still corroborate the other information I had already obtained. Unfortunately, I still did not have sufficient proof to print anything.

Early the following morning, I met with Ramon and a second security guard named Carlos Cortez. To avoid being seen, they had selected the unearthly hour of three a.m. and had chosen a deserted bungalow for our meeting. I began to feel nervous, realizing I had not told anyone what I was doing or where to find me if something went wrong.

Carlos was quiet, responding only when questioned directly. Short and stocky, he was Hispanic, with gelled hair and a thick goatee. Prior to our meeting, Ramon had briefed Carlos on the purpose of my visit. Neither Ramon nor Carlos could identify the man in the pool photograph, claiming Leonardo had countless friends coming and going every day. Carlos was the first to suggest that something unusual might be going on between Leonardo and the "big haired" friend.

"Doesn't anyone know this guy's name?" I asked. "If he's been living here for six months, someone has to know something."

Ramon was clearly getting into the tabloid spirit. "Wait here," he said. "Leonardo's brother, Adam, is staying in the room. We'll just ask him."

"No, wait," I begged. "It'll be too obvious. What would you say? It's the middle of the night, for heaven's sake. Come back."

Waving me away, Ramon told me to calm down and relax. For the next thirty minutes I paced the musty bungalow, waiting for my latest sources to return empty-handed. Instead, they came back with the name, Jerry Swindall. He was also in Thailand with Leo at the time, having been given a cameo role as a pothead in the movie, *The Beach*.

Ramon and Carlos turned out to be my prize sources, sharing dirty details related to the private life of *Titanic*'s hero. Every claim they made could be verified, right down to the security log that stated the dates that Leonardo had requested call girls and condoms. Although this was not a service provided by the hotel, the security guards were willing to accommodate Leo's request for the right price. Matters only became more complicated once Carlos revealed that Leonardo had a collection of pornographic photographs the actor had taken during his midnight escapades.

Given this latest information about the influx of call girls into Leo's room, I was certain that the editors would kill the storyline that had originated with the swimming pool photographs. Disregarding my misgivings, the editors interpreted the combined information to mean that Leo was presumably bisexual.

Now into day four, the editors extended my assignment another day, provided that I could obtain a copy of the security log and the photographs. They also required that every paid source undergo a lie detector test. Ramon and Carlos were willing to do anything, as long as money was involved. As expected, my sources passed their test and delivered the evidence needed for publication.

"We need to know more on this Jerry Swindall," Madeline said. "Florida wants to find out if Leonardo is bisexual or just kinky."

These demands pushed me into a whole new realm of exhaustion. By night, I was entertaining, spying, and manipulating at the hotel. By day, I was rushing back to the office to report the same dark secrets I had uncovered. Still a guest of the Chateau Marmont, I slipped generous tips to the cleaning lady and praised the pool boy for the way he waved his net like a magic wand.

The editors believed that if Leonardo was in fact bisexual, perhaps he had a former lover who would be willing to talk. After searching *Globe*'s photo archives, one man's face kept reappearing in countless shots with Leonardo. At that time, no one knew the identity of this unknown friend.

That meant I would have to find yet another contact that could recognize the face in the picture. I decided to go directly to Leo's publicists, telling them I needed to know the name of Leo's unidentified friend for photo caption purposes. They declined to cooperate with my request, knowing there had to be a hidden agenda. This left me blindly searching the Internet for any other clues I could find. In order to locate sources, I decided to trace other work that Leonardo had done. Although I had not previously heard of it, the name of one of his unreleased films kept popping up. It was *Don's Plum*.

Around that time, a $10 million lawsuit was being filed against Leonardo and Tobey Maguire by a co-producer named David Stutman. This was long before Tobey's *Spider-Man* days. At the time, he was still a struggling actor landing bit parts on sitcoms. Allegedly, he and Leo were blocking the release of Stutman's film, *Don's Plum*. Although the two actors had agreed to appear in the film, they had never expected that it would be released in theaters. They claimed that their improvised dialogue contained personally revealing lines that could tarnish their clean images. With Leo's recent rise to fame, the *Don's Plum* crew was hoping that the release of their movie could finally land them some recognition. Clearly, a rift had formed between the two sides.

Now all I had to do was find out who Leo's enemies were. Starting with the cast list of *Don's Plum*, I located the home address of a Kevin Connolly. At that time, he was a struggling actor who didn't seem to have any negativity toward anyone in the industry. I told him I was a freelance reporter writing a lifestyle piece on Leonardo DiCaprio. He offered some harmless information, admitting that he didn't know the actor all that well. Handing him my stack of photographs, he took one look and said, "Oh, that's Tobey. Tobey Maguire."

Back at the office, I told Madeline I had identified Leonardo's mystery friend, who happened to be involved with him in the *Don's Plum* lawsuit.

"Run Faces," she said, referring to Florida's database program on celebrity information. "Call him and then just ask the guy if he's Leo's lover."

It seemed a ridiculous request, but I was willing to go through anything if it would bring closure to my story. The telephone number provided by our research department actually led me to Tobey's mother, Wendy. At the time, she lived in the Northwest and was working as a secretary. Immediately, I told her that I was working on an article for a gay pride magazine about sexual expression among Hollywood stars. I asked if she would be willing to share any thoughts about her son's close bond with Leonardo.

"I figured this subject would come up sooner or later," she explained, casually. "Those two are just free-spirited guys. Most of the friends they hang around with are gay. They're comfortable with it. But I think Leo and Tobey are the crossover between men and women. They have feminine traits that they are willing to accept. They aren't ashamed to have any sort of title, even if that means someone calling them gay."

For the next thirty minutes, Wendy continued to recount her liberal views, divulging details of how the two friends "shared a bed and wore ribbons in their hair." I still did not have enough proof to specify that either Leo or Tobey were gay. However, Wendy had provided exactly what the editors wanted—insinuations. After I ended my call with Wendy from the LA office, I headed back to the Chateau Marmont to try and find yet another source.

By now, Pete was also involved in the story, tracking down prostitutes and strippers who had allegedly spent nights in room 69. With the help of Pete's knowledge of Spanish, we managed to find a cleaning lady who, for $10,000, was willing to support our headline, "Leo's Kinky Secret Life."

It was a relief to check out of the hotel. The story was finally closed, or so I thought. Minutes after I left the Chateau Marmont, Madeline phoned. "I'm sorry to do this to you," she said. "But Florida has asked that you get on the next plane to Portland. They think you might be able to get a photograph from Tobey's mother."

Over the past five days, I had averaged three hours of sleep per night. Exhaustion had set in and I wasn't sure if I could physically handle another day. "Madeline . . ." My voice started to crack. "I'm trying my best here, but I honestly need some sleep. Can't you send someone else?"

"I'm sorry, Marlise," she explained. "I tried to talk them out of it, but the orders are coming straight from the top. Just do this one last thing, and I promise I'll give you a break."

Madeline sounded sincere. I took a deep breath. "When do I leave?"

"Be at LAX in three hours," she said.

As I had anticipated, Wendy refused to give me a photograph when I showed up to her door. Instead, all I got was a verbal retraction of everything she had shared over the phone. "Tobey is so upset with me for talking to you," she explained. "You know this whole Hollywood thing is still really new to me. I guess I have a lot to learn."

Although I was in the Northwest less than twenty-four hours, it was just long enough to meet my old friend Darin Leverett for a drink. This time, there were no shared Pringles or chocolate chip cookies. The only thing he shared was the time and date of his upcoming wedding.

Back in my Portland hotel, matters only turned from bad to worse. After I had left LA, Madeline had placed a "comment call" to Leonardo's representatives, informing them of our upcoming story. *Globe* stated that if no response were obtained within a specified time frame, the story would run "as is." When Leo's representatives failed to respond to Madeline's comment call by the deadline, *Globe* proceeded to run my article as a cover story.

On the day of publication, Leo's legal team responded by threatening to sue our magazine. Leo's attorney John Lavely had sent twenty-six pages of defensive documentation to our lawyers. Lavely demanded that *Globe* publish a retraction and apologize for false and defamatory statements. An investigation of Chateau Marmont was well under way to determine who had sold the information to *Globe*. Nearly all of my sources cracked under pressure. Ultimately, this resulted in Carlos Cortez, Ramon Harper, and Matt Shelton losing their jobs.

That evening, *Globe*'s head lawyer, Mitchell Cain, called my Portland hotel, asking that I prepare a detailed rebuttal to defend myself and my story. Sixteen pages and two hours of sleep later, I faxed Cain every bit of substantiating proof that I had collected. To back up my statements, I included copies of the security log, signed statements from sources, and transcriptions of my taped interviews. Returning my call, Cain informed me that I had successfully provided the most detailed report he had ever seen from any *Globe* employee.

Despite the praise, by the end of our conversation I was in tears. I was devastated because people had lost their jobs while helping me do mine. "I want out of this business," I told Cain. "I just don't want to spend the rest of my life justifying who I am or what I do." The attorney advised me to keep my sources and my friends separate.

"Sometimes relationships develop against our will," I told him.

He assured me that my guilt would pass. Apparently my written statements were enough to convince Leo's attorneys to drop their suit. They never took any legal action, nor did *Globe* ever print a retraction. The editors got the story they wanted and I landed a $1,500 bonus. I was just glad to have the whole episode behind me.

It had been weeks since I had slept in my own bed. Chantal knew I was upset and suggested that we try to get my life back to normal. We decided to go dancing at the Garden of Eden just like old times. It had been exactly two days since my article on Leo had been published.

Of all the people in Hollywood that night, I ran into Leo's same friends, whom I had been following at the Chateau Marmont for several days. Every character that had appeared in my eight-page article was at the club that night except for Leo himself, who was still in Thailand. I couldn't seem to get away from the Leo story. Although we had lived in the same hotel, I had maintained my secrecy so well that Leo's friends had never seen me.

And so, I danced close enough to the group to get the attention of Leonardo's step-brother, Adam Farrar. In his mid-twenties, Adam had short, brown hair and a toned physique that was clearly visible beneath his fitted T-shirt. In contrast to those around him, he wore faded jeans and skate shoes and danced as if no one were watching.

It didn't take long for him to notice that Chantal and I were also dancing alone. Oblivious to my identity, he invited us back to his brother's new home and asked if he could ride with Chantal and me. I was unsure how I would handle things once we reached the Chateau Marmont. Fortunately, instead of driving to the place I had come to know as Leo's home, Adam directed me to drive further down Sunset Strip to the Mondrian Hotel.

"Hey, don't tell anyone this is Leo's pad," Adam warned me. "We just moved out of the Chateau Marmont because some bitch printed his room number in the tabloids. Fans were calling our room nonstop." During the drive, we continued to speak about me in the third person, discussing how that "bitch reporter" could live with herself after exposing someone who only longed to act.

Once we arrived at the hotel, Adam told me to pull my Ghia into the no parking zone. We were instantly approached by an angry valet attendant. "Hey, this is reserved for VIP only."

Adam didn't respond well to the man's tone. "Listen, you son of a bitch," he yelled. "I'm Leo's brother!"

The idea of name-dropping for the sake of a parking space seemed ridiculous, but it did the job. The valet attendant came rushing around to my door. It was stuck.

"Stand back," I said, thrusting the door open with my shoulder.

"I'm very sorry," the valet attendant said. "Please forgive me. Your car will be waiting at the front when you return."

There was no question we were in Hollywood. As we entered the lobby, LL Cool J passed by, again reminding me just how small this city truly was. Leonardo was now living in room 1225 of the Mondrian Hotel.

Adam pushed the elevator button and asked, "So, what's your name?" It was strange that we had made it this far without introducing ourselves.

"I'm Molli," I lied. "With an i."

He shook my hand and said, "Well, Molli with an i, it's very nice to meet you." After introducing herself, Chantal stared at me, wondering what we had gotten ourselves into. By this stage in our friendship, she had learned to go along with my improvisations. In this case, we were UCLA undergrads.

Adam unlocked the door to the suite and kicked it open with his foot. Other than being overly modern, the room looked fairly average for any 22-year-old guy. The floor was littered with Sega cartridges, Pepsi cans, and Doritos bags. Even Jerry Swindall was there, passed out on the white leather couch with a full beer bottle still in his hand. There was only one surprise. Spread out on the armrest of a chair was the C.S. Lewis book *The Great Divorce*.

"Who's reading this?" I asked, impressed.

Adam grabbed it from my hand and returned it back to its place, just as it had been. "Oh, that's Leo's. Don't move it. He hates it when we lose his page. When he gets back from Thailand, he'll want to find everything just the way he left it."

That evening Adam and I sat on the balcony, talking about his view of Christianity versus new age philosophies. Sharing my true family background, I explained that I came from a long line of missionaries who had deep roots in South Africa.

"Leo wants to do that too, you know," Adam said, lighting up a cigarette. "Just run away from everything and live in a village where nobody knows who he is. I don't blame him. He can't go anywhere without getting mauled—it's a pain in the ass if you ask me. Last week a chick fainted in the airport. Can you believe it? Leo picked her up and told her how ridiculous she was acting. These fans are in love with his characters and not him. I swear, he'll never forgive himself for doing *Titanic*. It was the worst mistake of his life." Adam crushed his cigarette into the table and took a swig of his beer.

"Are you okay?" he asked, gazing at me. "You look sort of confused."

I took a look at my watch and told him I had to get going. The idea of building a friendship with someone I had just exposed made me feel nauseous. "Sorry to drink and run," I said, setting down my bottle. "It was nice talking to you. Maybe we'll meet again someday."

He nodded, without getting up. "Yeah, who knows? Maybe we will."

On the drive home with Chantal, I thought about everything that had happened over the past few weeks: the sources I had come to know, the jobs they had lost, the legal ramifications, the editorial demands, the lack of sleep, and now, the bizarre evening at Leonardo's new home. I regretted having wanted to get to know Leo or his friends. Now their faces were no longer just subjects for an article. They were real people, and I had negatively impacted their lives.

Distraught, I shared my feelings with Caelan. He said there comes a time in the tabloid world when you lose your conscience and just keep on doing what you do. He seemed to think that I took my job too seriously, allowing my emotions to get twisted inside the tabloid printing press.

Generally I could dispel these guilt-ridden moments with a long run on the beach. Even if I didn't have enough time to get as far as the beach, I had to run somewhere every day. During one of my lunch-break runs, Madeline spotted me jogging and suggested I join a celebrity gym. "Think of all the story leads you could get," she said.

Globe forked out the $2,500 initiation fee, which allowed me to join The Sports Club/LA. The gym was equipped with valet parking, a hair salon, and my own personal trainer. Suddenly my tangerine sunsets along the beach had been replaced with barbells, stationary bikes, and StairMasters. Crashing waves were now silenced by blaring TVs, grunting men, and the sound of metal on metal. Women "worked out" in thong leotards and lavish jewelry, and often touched up their makeup right before hitting the machines. For the sake of *Globe*, I jogged on treadmills alongside Brooke Shields, Katie Holmes, and Sarah Michelle Gellar. I realized that what had once been my only means of mental detachment from the office had now become another extension of my tabloid career.

Even my social life had become work-related. It was virtually impossible to enjoy a night out without hunting for a headline. Sharmin had also realized that there was financial gain to be made from gathering gossip. Except for staff reporters, any *Globe* employee could earn $200 for celebrity contributions. Suddenly Sharmin and I were attending everything from rap concerts to the Black Music Awards.

We always seemed to be invited by the friend of someone famous, but never by the celebrities themselves. Our wardrobes were black, our lips were glossed, and our cell phones were charged. Weekdays had blended with weekends and work had blended with play. Sharmin and I hummed "Ebony and Ivory" under our breath whenever we entered private events. We were like Batman and Robin, Starsky and Hutch, Bonnie and Clyde—bailing each other out in times of need. That was always our practice, unless of course one of us went missing. Shamefully, right at the height of my tabloid career, my actions warranted a search party on the streets of Hollywood.

It had all begun at a Fugees album-release party. With Jackie Brown boldness, Sharmin wore a plum velour bodysuit, leaving spectators with a taste of Pam Grier. As usual, she carried her customary trench coat. Still unwilling to abandon my "frosted" look, I wore black pants with an ice blue top, accessorized with platinum lipstick and powder-blue eye shadow. My black leather boots provided both height and comfort, just in case dancing might be involved.

Of all the locations LA had to offer, the Fugees party was held at the Mondrian Hotel, unbelievably in suite 1225. Shortly after returning from Thailand, Leonardo DiCaprio had moved out of the suite and eventually bought his own home. Now I would walk into that very same room for the second time in six months.

The first thing I noticed upon entering the familiar suite was that I was the only white person at the party. The second thing I noticed was the bar. Having grown up in a conservative home, I had not been exposed to the taste or effects of alcohol. It wasn't until my twenty-first birthday that I had first experienced the sweet lime florescence of Midori Sour. It looked as harmless as a Slurpee but had the traits of a whisky shot. The tingle, the legality, and the fact there were a thousand other drinks to choose from, made me okay with my decision to drink. Pacing myself, however, was a skill yet to be mastered.

Making my way to the bar, I ordered my usual party drink of Jack and Coke. The place was packed with tailored guests, the type who dressed in custom-made outfits rather than in pieces sold separately. Within five minutes, Sharmin and I had already gotten separated. While I was ordering my cocktail, she had moved toward the food table and was grabbing a slice of a cake. Shoveling a bite of pink frosting into her mouth, she motioned to me with her fork to join her.

"I'll be right there," I shouted over the music.

The bartender tossed a maraschino cherry into my glass and handed it over with a cocktail napkin. "I made it extra strong for you, baby," he said. Digging into my pockets, I realized I didn't have enough bills to leave a tip. Setting my drink on the bar, I motioned that I would be right back. Sharmin reluctantly handed over a few dollar bills. By the time I pushed my way back to leave the tip, several other drinks were lined up on the bar. Neither I nor the bartender knew for sure which one was mine. "I'll make you another," he offered.

Checking for lipstick stains, I held one glass up to the light. "No, don't worry about it," I said, taking a sip. "I think this one with the cherry is mine."

It seemed to take forever for me to finally reach the food table. Sharmin had since left the area and was busy introducing herself to supermodel Tyson Beckford. As Ralph Lauren's leading icon, he had been featured on countless billboards with his chiseled cheekbones, feline eyes, and plump lips. Even Michelangelo would have struggled to reconstruct such a flawless creation. Contrasting with his white three-piece suit was the darkness of his skin. I had to meet this exotic-looking man.

Just as I gained enough courage to make a move, my equilibrium reminded me of why I had flunked out of ballet school. Suddenly the room tilted forty-five degrees and I felt myself sliding down the picture. Clutching onto the base of a tablecloth, I somehow pulled the entire buffet toward me, including the pillow-sized cake. Mere seconds before the sponge block toppled onto my head, I grabbed the cake's edge and pushed it back onto the table. The tips of my fingers were now buried in a row of sugar roses.

My body had far surpassed the tingling phase. *I probably looked like Gumby on crack.* Pulling myself off the floor, I tried to regain my balance but fell yet again, this time onto a woman the size of a Mini Cooper. Whatever had still been left in my glass was now adorning the front of her tan suede jacket.

"Oh no, you didn't!" she screamed.

Reaching for a stack of fanned napkins, I tried to pat her chest dry, slurring, "I'm sooo sorry."

Her long nails curved downward, each one decorated with diamond studs and flakes of gold. She waved one manicured finger back and forth in front of my face while her head simultaneously followed its angry path. "Bitch, you better get the hell out of my face before I fucking rearrange it!"

Bathroom. I need a bathroom.

Faces blurred into one gigantic stream, as if I had been watching the party from a twirling carousel. With my motor skills left somewhere back at the bar, my only goal was to make it to the bathroom without vomiting. I successfully made it there, only bumping into inanimate objects along the way. Locking the door behind me, I began to verbally guide myself through basic steps.

Turn on the faucet. Put hands under water. Splash face.

I needed an instruction manual to function. Looking into the mirror, I focused on my dilated pupils, wondering how on earth they had gotten so big. Suddenly, I realized I wasn't alone in the bathroom. Three other faces were staring back at me.

"Hey, Baby-Boo," said one voice. "You wanna smoke some bud?"

I turned around to make sure the faces were real and not just hallucinations in the glass. There, sitting on the rim of the bathtub were two guys and a girl smoking marijuana. In a curtain of drifting smoke, the girl lifted the joint in the air and offered it to me.

"Uh, no thanks," I mumbled. "I need to get out of here. I need some air."

Standing up from the tub, she walked toward me while the two men remained seated. "Oh come on . . . I've never smoked bud with a white girl before." Inhaling deeply, she blew a cloud directly into my pale face. The fact that I coughed uncontrollably made them laugh. Slowly, I backed toward the bathroom door. The girl passed the joint to the men behind her and started moving closer toward me.

"There's nothing to be afraid of, girl." Caressing the side of my cheek, she ran her hand down my shoulder, to my arm, stopping at my wrist. "I like your watch," she said, fingering the circular face. "You think I can take a look?"

My mouth couldn't seem to form any words. I just shook my head, banging it against the bathroom door to try to get someone's attention. She forcefully flipped my wrist as if ready to take blood, unhooking the clasp with a flick of her finger. Fumbling with my free hand, I reached behind me to turn the doorknob. Pushing her off me, I stumbled to the other side of the door, just as my watch dangled loose at my wrist. Instinctively, I spread my fingers to keep the watch from falling off.

The door had opened into an opulent bedroom. There, lying alone on a queen-sized bed was my partner in crime, Sharmin. Gripping a $350 bottle of Cristal, she was guzzling it down like it was thirst-quenching Evian. Clearly, she was as surprised to see me as I was to see her. The bedroom had been empty when I had stumbled through it earlier on my way to the bathroom. Popping up, Sharmin hid the Champagne behind her back and tried to act natural.

"Girlfriend, where the hell you been? I've been looking all over for you."

I glanced behind me to make sure the others hadn't followed. "Sharmin, we have to get out of here—"

"Hell no," she interrupted. "This party's pumping. We've got Tyson Beckford doing coat check, Lauren Hill on the mic, and bathtubs full of Cristal. Your ass is going home alone."

I refastened the clasp of my watch. "Sharmin, I'm not kidding. I feel nauseous and I nearly got jumped in the bathroom."

"What?" Sharmin stood up from the bed. "Who tried to jump you?"

"A girl in the bathroom," I said, pointing toward the closed door. "She tried to take my watch."

Suddenly, as if on cue, the bathroom door flew open. Without looking toward us, the girl hurried through the bedroom and made her way toward the balcony.

"Is that the bitch who tried to take your watch?" Sharmin was angry now. It was the first time I had ever heard such a tone in her voice. I remained silent. "You better answer me," she demanded. "Now!"

I nodded hesitantly. "Please, Sharmin, don't start anything. I'm fine, really."

Before I knew what had happened, Sharmin ran straight toward the balcony and grabbed a handful of braids. "You bitch. Let me see you mess with the white girl now!" Stumbling toward the commotion, I tried to push my way through the crowd that had circled around the catfight. The two girls were swinging punches with closed fists.

"Sharmin, stop," I yelled. "Please." By now, the forty-five-degree room had shifted to a full ninety-degree angle. I have no recollection of what happened after that. What I know of the rest of the night, I heard only from Sharmin. According to her account, she was detained by bodyguards and thrown out of the party. Returning to the suite with hotel security, she demanded that the bodyguards allow her back inside to search for her "lost white friend." The bodyguards managed to convince hotel security that Sharmin was an embarrassment to the establishment. After they threw Sharmin out onto the street, she flagged down LAPD and then notified everyone, from my parents in Monterey to my sister. When Heidi got Sharmin's call, she figured that I might have contacted Caelan, whom I was now casually dating. That's how he, too, became involved in the mad search for my missing self.

Somehow in the midst of Sharmin's balcony brawl, I had managed to get out of suite 1225 and make my way downstairs to the bathroom in the hotel lobby. I was not found until eight o'clock the following morning. Hotel security discovered me locked inside a handicapped stall, passed out in a pool of vomit. According to a hotel manager, someone had heard me tapping the bathroom tiles with the face of my watch, presumably because I was unable to cry for help.

Needless to say, my sidewalk reunion with Sharmin was a tearful one, with anger and joy shed in every drop. "Don't ever do that again," she said, hugging me so tight it hurt. I could hear the unmistakable sound of glass clanging inside her trench coat pockets. Looking at her questioningly, Sharmin mouthed the words, "votive candles."

The entire drive home was nothing but one long lecture. The pain in my head was fifty times worse than her scolding. Sharmin told me my parents were already waiting at the Monterey airport, preparing to fly to LA to give me "the talk." She insisted on dialing their number when I got to her apartment.

"There's no need to come down," I told them. "I'm fine, really."

"Do you think the poison is still in your system?" my mother cried. "Should you get your stomach pumped? What if you were raped when you were unconscious?"

I realized the level of their concern when they suggested I join AA. In the end, we reached a compromise after I promised to rest and replenish my electrolytes with plenty of Gatorade. By now, it was time for Sharmin to start her workday. Meanwhile, I left Sharmin's place and headed home. I was forced to call in my first sick day since beginning to work for *Globe*.

During his lunch break, Caelan secretly dropped by my condo to deliver healing elixirs like vegetable soup and Arizona Green Tea. As he was leaving, Caelan said with a grin, "You know luv, if you canna take care of yerself, then I'll hafta dew it for ya."

The poor guy had no idea what he was getting himself into.

Note:

Leonardo DiCaprio was romantically linked to Brazilian model Gisele Bundchen from 2002 to 2005.

On March 21, 2006, *USA Today* reported that Tobey Maguire and Leonardo DiCaprio purchased property together at the Las Vegas Panorama Towers.

Kevin Connolly went on to star in HBO's *Entourage*.

CHAPTER 12

Bringing Hollywood
Out of the Closet

After the success of my stories on Jodie Foster, George Michael, and Leonardo DiCaprio, the editors began to assume that I should be the one to open the doors of closeted celebrities. *Globe* sent me on a mad hunt to investigate the sexual preferences of everyone from Tom Cruise and Brad Pitt to Hillary Clinton and Lisa Marie Presley.

In the midst of the *Titanic* craze, I had written an article about director James Cameron's split from his wife, Linda Hamilton. The mainstream media had focused on Cameron's alleged off-screen romance with *Titanic* actress Suzy Amis. Meanwhile, my article had covered the lesbian relationship between Cameron's wife, Linda, and Cindy Short, her movie stand-in.

Another assignment had me tracking down David Riva, the homosexual grandson of Marlene Dietrich. When initially approached, Riva was hesitant to cooperate. He loosened up after I promised him full copy approval and a $7,000 story payment. When Riva and I met in his living room, he told me of his grandmother's open bisexuality and how she had given him the courage to "come out of the closet." The notion of being able to discuss one's sexuality with a grandmother, let alone with Marlene Dietrich, gave the story a unique twist. My full-page spread ran under one of *Globe*'s more memorable headings: "Marlene Dietrich Made Me Gay."

These assignments kept taking me back to the homosexual haven of West Hollywood, where gorgeous men roamed the streets, holding the hands of other gorgeous men. This gay zone became my gossip library where I spoke openly to the locals, landing some of my most colorful and dedicated sources. One man in particular agreed to provide celebrity leads on the condition that his payments would be donated to AIDS research. He and I danced together at gay clubs and attended charity events, like the Splash Pool Party held in Bel Air. My $150 ticket included a live performance by Erin Hamilton, the daughter of comedienne Carol Burnett.

Before heading to Bel Air, I had conducted a background check, which showed that Erin had recently filed for divorce from her husband, Trae Carlson. Claiming to be a freelance writer, I had phoned Erin's publicist and requested a press packet. Inside was information about Erin's new singing career and the release of her techno single, "Dream Weaver." Void of expectations, I reached inside my armoire of disguises and pulled out my latest costume, that of a lesbian.

Set in the courtyard of a rented $20 million estate, the Splash Pool Party was packed with hundreds of Speedo-clad gay men. Sipping on umbrella-topped cocktails, guests were lounging by the pool and rubbing oil on their neighbors. Having grown up in the church, it was my first exposure to such open same-sex displays of affection. Included in the group were dozens of transvestites, several of whom looked strikingly beautiful. One man was dressed as a candy striper and wheeled around a cart filled with condoms, lollipops, cigarettes, and sunscreen. Apart from Erin and her backup dancers, I seemed to be the only biological female at the event. Moments after entering the party, my West Hollywood contact abandoned me. He claimed there were too many attractive men for him to be seen focusing on one woman. Needless to say, I was ignored by all the other guests, except by Erin herself.

Prior to her performance, Erin stayed hidden inside the mansion with her two-year-old son, Zachary, her sister Carrie, and her mom, Carol Burnett. While they were busy doing hair and makeup, I sat outside their door doing what I did best: eavesdropping. Extremely thin, Erin's bones protruded from her neck and pelvis, like those of a gaunt and fragile runway model. Sunshine tattoos covered her shoulders and back. Her body had taken on a painful hue due to a sunburn covering her wiry frame like a pink sheet. Her hair had been dyed an unnatural shade of charred cherry and her tinted sunglasses squared at the rim like those of Elton John.

The already wild crowd grew even louder as Erin stepped onstage. Considering that her repertoire consisted of only two songs, Erin's grand performance was rather brief. After gyrating with her female backup dancers, Erin blew a kiss to her mother, who was watching from a balcony above. Even if Erin turned out to be straight, I knew the photos captured by paparazzo Radford Thayer would go over well with *Globe*'s editors. Like me, he was posing as a gay person, and found himself awkwardly fending off unwanted advances throughout our assignment.

Following the show, Erin mingled in the crowd and took pictures with fans. Without much of a game plan, I simply grabbed a cocktail and waited until she was alone. And then, it was my turn to capture Erin's attention. Jumping directly in her path, I assumed a young and impressionable air. "Hi, Erin. I just wanted to tell you how much I loved your show."

"Thank you so much, sweetie," Erin said, somewhat distracted by the crowd. "What's your name?"

I fell back on a familiar pseudonym, assuming it might bring confidence to my deception. "Molli," I answered.

Brushing a wisp of hair from my face, Erin turned toward one of her backup dancers who was walking past. "Isn't this girl adorable?" she asked, pointing toward me. The dancer nodded and flashed me a plastic smile. Responding on their behalf, Erin continued, "You're adorable, Molli."

Taking a sip from my straw, I suddenly felt sixteen again. "Thanks . . . umm . . . Actually, I wanted to get your advice on something."

Losing her focus, Erin was looking past me now. "Sure, what is it?"

"You see Erin, I'm a lesbian. No one in my family knows the truth and I really want to tell them, but I'm afraid. I just thought maybe you had some advice about how to handle the situation."

Erin's eyes were no longer wandering. "Molli, you have to be honest with your parents. For me, it was difficult at first, especially because I hid it for so long. But when I told my mom, she understood that I'm going to love who I love. Now she's totally supportive of my lifestyle."

I took the conversation a step further. "Well, are you still a lesbian or was it kind of a phase?"

Erin laughed at my question. "I'm sure you know it's not something that can be switched on and off."

I nodded, as if I knew the feeling well.

"Actually," Erin continued. "I'm dating an amazing girl named Angie. We met in Miami last year."

My mind was writing pages of mental notes. "Well, I wish you two the best. And thanks so much, Erin, for your advice."

Leaning forward, she reached her boney arms around my neck and gave me a hug. "Just remember to tell the truth," she said. "I'm sure your family will appreciate your honesty."

Ironically, her statement about embracing honesty hit a nerve in my own life. Since starting to work for *Globe*, I had become a skilled liar and hypocrite, masquerading in identities that were not my own.

Back in my car, I scribbled down the words Erin had shared in confidence and then typed them up for the world to see. Since I was quoting Erin directly, I was not expected to provide the customary "three sources." The following week, *Globe* published my article, which was titled "Carol Burnett's Gay Daughter: Why I Was Scared to Tell Mom."

Along with editorial praise came a legal letter from Erin's representatives, accusing *Globe* of having printed lies and false accusations. "Add this one to your collection," Madeline said, handing me the letter from Erin's attorneys. Tacking it onto my bulletin board, I put it alongside my other legal threats and growing stack of hate mail. As it turned out, Erin's lawyers soon dropped their charges and I never had to defend my story. By now, *Globe*'s legal team realized they could trust my research.

When Erin told me about her new partner, Angie, it led to a follow-up story. In typical *Globe* fashion, Erin's comments triggered an exclusive interview with Angie's ex-girlfriend. The article, which featured a partially nude photograph of Erin and Angie, appeared under the headline "Carol Burnett's Daughter Stole My Lesbian Lover."

The only thing that seemed to interest readers more than the sexual preferences of celebrities was their divorces. *Globe* kept a careful watch on such Hollywood favorites as Bobby and Whitney, Bruce and Demi, and Kurt and Goldie. One of the most publicized splits was that of Tom Cruise and Nicole Kidman, who divorced after ten years of marriage. Their separation came as no shock to the editors. Three years before, *Globe* had published an article titled "Is Tom Cruise's Marriage Hanging by a Thread?" That article had been based on information provided by Eric Ford, a source who had tapped into the couple's cell phones. Although *Globe* had neither initiated nor participated in the wiretapping, there were still serious legal risks involved. This only served to make the story all the more intriguing.

After the tape was delivered, Madeline called us into her office to replay the recorded conversation. Pete typed up the argumentative dialogue on which the article was based. When it appeared on the newsstands, the Cruise-Kidman legal team was quick to threaten *Globe* with a lawsuit. After *Globe* identified Eric Ford as the source of the incriminating evidence, all charges against the magazine were dropped. After pleading guilty to wiretapping, Ford was convicted, fined, and sentenced to six months in a halfway house.

While this was going on in the LA office, I was sent to Farmington, New Mexico, to cover the divorce of Demi Moore and Bruce Willis. Since the couple had publicly announced their separation in June 1998, the media had been unable to find Demi. She had supposedly gone into hiding. Reporters were sent everywhere, from Hollywood to the couple's vacation home in Hailey, Idaho. Considering Demi's history with her mother, Virginia, no one expected to find her back in her home town of Farmington.

Eager to travel, I willingly accepted the Farmington assignment without realizing how isolated I would feel in such a pioneer settlement. All of *Globe*'s freelance photographers had rejected the lucrative offer, claiming that the remote New Mexican hamlet was too hot and desolate for shooting purposes. Not quite sure what that meant, I made personal phone calls to paparazzi Edward Townsend and James Churchill, begging them to join me on the adventure. They both turned me down.

Having exhausted every other possibility, *Globe* was forced to hire a Colorado newspaper photographer named Jake Quaden. From the moment we met at the airport, it was obvious that this family man was nothing like the aggressive paparazzi I had worked with in the past. Jake was quiet and reserved. Immediately I knew that having him as my partner would make the assignment a challenging one.

My first task was to determine if Demi Moore was even in town. In situations like this, my usual practice was to spend time where the locals gathered, hoping to pick up some information that would point me in the right direction. In Farmington, this left me with only three locations to explore: the airport, Denny's, and a coffee shop. The last of these turned out to be the most promising.

Behind the coffee shop counter was a man who appeared to be in his early twenties. Tattoos peered beneath the sleeves of the snug T-shirt that clung to his defined upper body. His blue jeans were faded and torn at the knee, and his back pocket bulged from the circular formation of a tobacco can. With trim brown hair, blue eyes, and small town appeal, he looked like a hardened version of Chris O'Donnell. Stretching the collar of his T-shirt, he pulled it up over his face and wiped away a trail of sweat.

Given the fact I was the only customer in the coffee shop, he seemed unnecessarily preoccupied as he steamed milk inside a chrome jug. Looking up, he asked, "Hi. What can I get you?"

"I'll have a blended frappuccino," I said. Glancing over at a glass display case, I peered at the baked goods, wondering how long they had been there.

Dipping a spoon into the thick cloud of foam, he dropped a dollop into a cappuccino mug. "You must be from out of town. We don't have those fancy drinks around here."

Squinting toward the chalkboard menu without actually reading it, I murmured, "Oh. I'll just have a vanilla latte then."

He wiped his fingers with a dirty towel before tossing it over his shoulder. "Sorry. No flavored syrups either."

I must have sounded so LA. "Okay. Let's keep it simple. Coffee with soy milk."

His grin had turned into a full-blown smile. "How 'bout a coffee with cream?"

My mind did a quick calorie count and then ignored it. "Sounds perfect. How much do I owe you?"

"It's on the house," he said, reaching for a Styrofoam cup, "on account you're from out of town. So, what brings you to Farmington?"

Popping a lid onto the cup, he slid the coffee toward me. Taking a sip of the bitter blend, I reached for two packets of sugar. "Just passing through, really."

Resting his elbows on the counter, he leaned forward as if placing an order. "No, you're not."

"Excuse me?" I questioned.

"You're not passing through," he repeated. "Dust storms and odors and marching bands pass through Farmington, but not people like you."

"Well, you can add Marlise to the end of that list," I said. "Marlise from California." It was the first time in a while I had used my real name with a stranger.

"Nice to meet you, Marlise from California. I'm Derrick Dalton."

As the door opened, the ringing of the bell interrupted our conversation. Two customers walked into the cafe. Raising my cup, I thanked him for the coffee and walked out the door, knowing without a doubt that I would return. Heading along the main street, it took me less than ten minutes to walk through the entire downtown area. There was a library, a family diner, and several boutiques selling everything from secondhand clothing to plastic garden gnomes. Looping the strip, I found myself back at the café. Glancing through the window, I could see that Derrick was alone again. On a whim, I decided to go in and tell him exactly why I was in Farmington.

"Okay, so I'm not passing through. I'm looking for Demi Moore, which is totally absurd because I know she's not here."

He held up his hand. "Wait, wait, wait! Start over from the top. Why are you looking for Demi Moore?"

I rolled my eyes, preparing to give the shortened version of my speech. "I'm a tabloid journalist. Demi and Bruce Willis just split up and the world wants to know why."

He shook his head. "I don't believe you. You're too young to be a reporter."

"No, I swear," I told him, fishing in my bag for my press pass. "Everyone's looking for Demi in California, but my editors sent me here because they thought she might be hiding at her mom's place."

He nodded. "Well, she is. At least I think she is. She's been in here the past two days to buy my bagels. She loves 'em."

I couldn't believe what I was hearing. "You're joking, right?"

Motioning for me to move in closer, he whispered, "Marlise, I never joke about my bagels."

Resisting a laugh, I tried to stay focused on the assignment and not on the man standing in front of me. "Was Demi alone? Do you know where she's staying? How did she look?"

"Don't stress," he interrupted. "I've lived in Farmington my whole life. We'll find her. It's a small town—she couldn't have gone too far."

"So does this mean you'll help me?"

Without answering, Derrick walked to the front door and flipped a sign which now read Closed.

Assuming that Demi would be staying at the town's leading hotel, I checked into the Ramada Inn. With Derrick in tow, I then phoned my assigned photographer, Jake. Although I hoped to see Demi, it was hard to imagine that this high-maintenance actress would be staying at two-star accommodations. While Jake settled into his room, Derrick and I headed to the hotel bar to devise a plan. We ordered two margaritas and carried them out to the sundeck, where a few children were splashing in the pool. Taking a long sip, I turned toward Derrick, who was now lounging on a lawn chair.

"Thanks so much for helping," I told him. "I honestly have no clue where to begin on this one." I was waiting for his suggestion when a beach ball came bouncing out of the pool and landed at the foot of his chair. "Don't get up," I told him. "You look way too comfortable. I'll get it." Carrying the ball to the pool's edge, I leaned down and handed it to a young girl.

"Throw the ball, Tallulah," a little voice yelled from behind her.

Instantly recognizing the unique name, my heart skipped a beat.

Suddenly, I realized I was looking directly into the face of Tallulah Belle Willis, Demi's youngest daughter. Scanning the water, I saw that Demi's two other children, Rumer and Scout, were also in the pool. Only Demi was missing.

Casually, I walked back to Derrick and whispered, "Tell Jake to start shooting pictures from his room."

While Derrick headed into the hotel, I stayed by the pool, hoping that Demi would show up for a sunset dip. Just minutes after Derrick left, a black man holding a cell phone stood up from a chair and walked toward the girls. He was obviously the family bodyguard.

"That was your mom on the phone," I overheard him say. "She wants to meet you girls for ice cream later. Come on. Everyone out of the pool."

As he bundled them in towels, I headed toward Jake's room to see how things were moving along. By the time I got there, he had already managed to shoot three rolls of film of the children. He was ecstatic over his accomplishment, but I knew the only person the editors wanted on film was Demi herself.

"So, where do people go for ice cream around here?" I asked Derrick.

He suggested we head for Baskin-Robbins. Unsure of the exact time that Demi was supposed to meet her children, the three of us piled into Jake's rental car and headed there. By now it was dark. This meant Jake would either have to rely on flash or else take the pictures inside the ice cream shop. That section of town was devoid of cars and trees, so there was no place for us to hide except in the backseat of Jake's car. There we were, all three of us crouched down, ready to take aim the moment Demi arrived. At 8:30 on the dot, the bodyguard showed up in a black Suburban with Demi's daughters. Ten minutes later, Demi herself arrived in a second black Suburban identical to the first. Derrick and I were beside ourselves, trying to silence our cries of joy and keep our high-fives to a minimum. The only person not overly thrilled was the photographer himself.

"Take the picture, Jake," I urged. "Look. Demi's licking her daughter's ice cream cone. This is cover shot material!"

Lowering his camera lens, Jake shook his head. "I'm not doing it. They'll see the flash and come running after us."

We were losing our window of opportunity. "So, we drive off," I said. "What's the big deal?"

"No . . . I don't want to chance it," he stammered. "Plus, my lens isn't strong enough. It's better that we shoot tomorrow during the day. I bet Demi will go to the pool then."

I couldn't believe what I was hearing. I reached for Jake's camera, "Give me that. I'll take the picture myself."

He pulled the camera back toward him. "Look, I'm the photographer. You're the writer. I'll let you do your job if you let me do mine."

"Hold on," Derrick interrupted. "Everyone calm down."

I tried to, but I couldn't. Even before Demi and the girls had finished their ice cream, Jake had climbed back into the driver's seat, started the car, and driven away. I had no choice but to report him to the editors. As long as he was on this assignment, I knew it would never work. To make matters worse, Madeline was in Florida and had put Caelan in charge of the story. It was the first time I had been under his direct leadership since we had started dating.

Needless to say, Caelan was furious. "You're telling me Demi 'as been there the whole day and you two 'aven't got a single picture? What's goin' on with you?"

"Well, we do have shots of Demi's kids," I mumbled, trying to justify the lack of material.

"Look Marlise, *Globe*'s not lookin' for the children. We want Demi. I'm pulling Jake straight off the story and I'm bringing in a new photographer. The issue's meant to close in twenty-four hours, ya know." Hanging up, I wondered what had happened to him calling me "luv."

The replacement photographer was the complete opposite of Jake. Just hours after his arrival, he was ticketed by local police for aggressively chasing Demi's car through the streets of Farmington. To maintain our anonymity, we both traded in our rental cars five times in eight hours. Derrick and I went out on our own, he on a bike and I in a car. We hoped to double our chances by splitting in two directions with disposable cameras in hand. Demi had spent the day at her mother's house and we knew there were only two ways out of that neighborhood.

By this point, Demi was well aware that she was being followed. As a result, she brought in a second bodyguard to drive yet a third black Suburban as a decoy. All three cars had dark, tinted windows, which kept us from knowing in which of the three Demi was hiding. Eventually, it turned into a cat-and-mouse game, none of us quite sure who was the cat and who was the mouse. At one point, while following one of the black Suburbans, I looked into my rearview mirror and saw Demi driving another one directly behind me. The moment I reached for my camera, she made an illegal U-turn and left me surrounded by local police. Like my photographer, I received a verbal warning and was asked to leave town immediately. Upon hearing this latest news, Caelan killed the story and demanded that I get on the next flight home.

"But there's nothing else I could have done," I told Caelan defensively. "It's not fair that I'm being blamed for the photographers' failure."

"You're right," he said, coldly. "Just like it ain't fair that I'm being blamed for your failure." He hung up, leaving me with a feeling of rage stemming from my own incompetence. I was angry at the photographers for ruining my reputation, angry at Caelan for his lack of sympathy, and angry at myself for my inability to take control.

And so, I did the only thing that I knew would bring me peace of mind. Deliberately missing my return flight, I waited for Demi to exit the hotel and then I took a picture of her myself. Having missed the deadline, the editors were no longer interested in the photograph. Nevertheless, I felt I had outsmarted both the tabloids and the celebrity. I had sought and found revenge—revenge on the paparazzi, on the editors, on the police, on the bodyguards, and even on Demi.

By the time I returned to the *Globe* office, no one seemed to care that the Demi story had turned into a fiasco. They had already moved on to the next week's issue, searching for headlines on the couple's custody battle and secret lovers. Deliberately stripped of anything related to Demi or Bruce, I was instead assigned to a story involving Farrah Fawcett.

Globe had obtained a 1992 police report stating that Farrah's current boyfriend, tennis pro Martin Barba, had once been charged with rape. At the time of the trial, Barba had been sentenced to 120 days in jail and three years' probation. I had been in the office less than one day when I was sent back on the road. This time, I was heading for San Diego in search of Barba's 1992 rape victim, "Donna." The editors' orders were clear: "Find the woman and pay her to warn Farrah about Martin."

Before leaving for San Diego, I had run Faces of the Nation to determine Donna's home address. Unfortunately, by this time all four of her known past residential locations were already occupied by new tenants. No one seemed to know where to find Donna. And so, I sat in my car and began calling every number in the local phone book that matched her last name. To my amazement, she had a listed number. From the start, I told her who I was and why I was calling. I suggested that we meet that evening to discuss matters face to face.

"This isn't something I want plastered in a tabloid," she said. "You have no idea what I've been through. It happened years ago, but I still relive it every day." Without realizing what she was doing, Donna naively shared the details of her living nightmare. She began to cry. "I don't know if I can give you the story you want."

She already had.

"Look," I explained. "I'm prepared to offer you twenty thousand dollars upon signing this contract. And don't worry. The article isn't about you, Donna. It's about Farrah Fawcett."

Suddenly, I heard Donna speaking my tagline. "Well, Farrah needs to drop him. If he did it once, he'll do it again." Donna said she would discuss the offer with her lawyer and get back to me within the hour. Meanwhile, I phoned Florida's managing editor, Cathy Tidwell, who was overseeing the assignment. I told her every detail Donna had shared with me about the rape.

"I doubt she'll sign, Cathy," I said. "She's been through a lot over this whole thing and doesn't think the money is worth it. The poor woman was in tears."

"Well, what are you waiting for?" Cathy asked. "You've already got the whole story right there."

I couldn't stand the idea of leaving Donna empty-handed. "But she's discussing the offer with her attorney as we speak. Plus, I gave her my word."

There was a long pause before Cathy spoke again. "You may have given her your word Marlise, but I didn't. Forget about Donna. Go back to your hotel room and file the copy this afternoon. I'll be waiting at my desk until it arrives."

I walked away with another *Globe* cover story. Donna walked away with nothing, having been violated once again.

Having turned the story in at no cost to *Globe* in less than twenty-four hours, I fully expected to receive a positive reaction when I got back to the office. Instead, Madeline was waiting with a reprimand. Her scolding stemmed from a non-work-related oversight on my part. Before going to San Diego, I had applied for a job with the television show *Extra*. My curiosity about that position began when I met Rick Schwartz, one of the show's producers. After learning about my world exclusives, Rick suggested that I make a break from print journalism to celebrity television.

On Rick's recommendation, I had written a cover letter to send with my resume to *Extra*'s human resources department. As much as I still welcomed the challenges of tabloid journalism, I had started to feel undervalued and underpaid. I was also curious to see what the world of television reporting had to offer.

While I was out of town on the Farrah assignment, Madeline had scanned my computer. She later claimed that she had done so to locate a story. Among the other computer files, Madeline had found my cover letter to *Extra*. The moment I returned from San Diego, she asked, "Can we talk?" Leading me into her office, Madeline closed the door and handed me a printout of my cover letter to *Extra*. My face turned as red as the coils on a stove. "I see you've been looking elsewhere," she continued, holding up my cover letter. "First of all, you should never use company equipment for your personal correspondence. Ever! Second, *Globe* is prepared to offer you a twenty-five percent increase, on the condition that you sign on for another two years."

I stared at her blankly, confused by the mixed messages she was sending. Her offer completely caught me off guard. I knew that locking myself into the commitment she was suggesting would rob me of life's spontaneity and freedom. "I'll think about the offer while I'm away," I told her, trying to buy time.

When she gave me *Globe*'s proposal, Madeline knew only three days remained until I would leave for a family vacation to South Africa. The fact that I would be gone for several days seemed to give her a license to work me to a level of mental exhaustion. Over the next three days, my tabloid-tainted brain generated five separate stories.

One of them included an interview with Monique Gavet, the lesbian lover of Joe Pesci's girlfriend, Christina Busin. Although Monique was a distant connection to the celebrity, she was a "reliable source."

Prior to my trip to Africa, Monique and I had met to discuss the anger she felt toward Pesci, whom she believed was trying to steal her girlfriend. Over lunch, Monique disclosed the details of her relationship with Christina and how she felt Pesci was coming between them. Monique even tipped me off to her dinner plans with Christina at Drai's eatery. Sitting in the restaurant, three tables away from them, I witnessed the entire romantic exchange between the two women. Monique ultimately betrayed her friendship for money and revenge. The details she had shared during our interviews appeared in two issues of *Globe*.

After observing Monique and Christina at Drai's, I drove directly to Spago's restaurant to meet with my ex-fling, Ahmed Ahmed. Almost a year had passed since we had last spoken. Calling him out of the blue, I explained, "Taking you to dinner is the least I can do for not returning your calls."

In reality, I wanted to meet with him to get information on his friend, Vince Vaughn. With the release of the movie *Psycho*, *Globe*'s editors were now looking for an article on Vaughn's personal life. Ahmed had never learned the truth about my tabloid profession. By the time dessert arrived, he had unknowingly leaked several details about Vince Vaughn's romance with actress Joey Lauren Adams. That information ran in my article, titled "Love Helped Vince Vaughn Conquer His Demons."

By three in the morning I had typed both articles. After only four hours of sleep, I woke up to write another article, this one about Annette Funicello's recovery from multiple sclerosis. My fourth article was a first-hand interview with actress Shirley Knight about her husband's pool drowning. The fifth was an interview with actress Angela Lansbury about the death of her dear friend, actor Hurd Hatfield.

Physically and mentally I was a wreck, too exhausted to even wonder why I was putting up with so much stress. At that pace, I wouldn't survive another day, let alone another two years. Finally I was cashing in my hard-earned vacation days to celebrate my grandmother's one-hundredth birthday in South Africa. All of my grandparents had served in Africa as missionaries, as had my parents, who had spent ten years volunteering in Lesotho.

My dad's side of the family was nothing like Mom's rocking-chair, southern-loving relatives, whom I had encountered in Texas. Visiting South Africa would involve monkeys at the breakfast table, snakes in the garden, and barbeque at every meal. Sometime during every family trip to that continent, we would always head to the villages to hear the beating of the drums and the melodious sound of African children singing. To my parents, this was home.

Getting there always seemed to be more of an adventure than the destination itself. I was ready to embrace Africa, but nothing was ever simple in my family. After having driven seven hours from Monterey, my parents slept at the condo that Heidi and I shared so that we could all fly together from LA. The night before our flight, I slept a total of two hours and still had not packed. Early on flight day, my mother waltzed through the bedroom singing, "Keep moving!" She seemed to think that stress in the form of praise songs would be an effective way to motivate me.

"Say, why don't we make this permanent and all just move in together?" I commented sarcastically. "You know, just for old time's sake?" My mother insisted on tossing change purses, fanny packs, and travel kits onto my bed, until eventually I had ten little purses inside one big purse. "Time to go . . ." she sang in an operatic voice. "Our ride is here!"

Waiting by his car was Nirajan, a Bengali doctor who worked in Heidi's biochemistry lab. He insisted on driving us to the airport simply because he was obsessed with her. As we loaded the car, Nirajan's 1978 Toyota Tercel immediately bottomed out from the weight of our luggage. During the drive to LAX, all I wanted was some peace and quiet, but my dad persisted in making small talk. "Play any sports, Nirajan?"

"No," Nirajan answered. "But I do like cricket." Resting my head on my mom's shoulder, I listened absentmindedly as my dad discussed the strategy of the game. "I love the sport," Nirajan said, now driving only 40 miles per hour on the freeway. "But I quit when my friend got hit in the jaw and fell into a coma."

Suddenly my mom piped up from the backseat. "That's what I call a real jawbreaker."

Heidi covered my mother's mouth halfway through the pun but unfortunately couldn't reach my dad, who said, "I quit cricket when I learned ya' hafta spend five days aiming at wickets."

By this time we had arrived at LAX and were relieved to see there was only minor weight damage to Nirajan's Tercel. "I'll miss you," he said, handing Heidi a plastic bag. She returned his gesture with distant pats on the back.

"Fifty bucks says it's a stuffed animal," Heidi mumbled, as we walked through the airport's sliding glass doors. Reaching into Nirajan's gift bag, she pulled out the stuffed toy and waved it in the air as if shaking a rattle. "Sure enough, a cuddly skunk to lug around Africa."

While I examined the toy's tag, which read, "Stinky needs a hug," my mom scratched its head, saying, "Oh, now that's cute."

We would be flying from LA to Hong Kong, then would change planes to Johannesburg and finally arrive in Durban thirty-six hours later. Racing up the escalator, we were congratulating ourselves for having arrived two hours early, when we heard my dad shouting from the ticket counter, "Hurry! Our flight has been changed. We're boarding in ten minutes."

During the chaotic security clearance process, I wondered if my new belly button piercing might set off the metal detector. Since childhood, our family policy had been to tell the truth in order to eliminate punishment. Banking on that policy, I had to confess.

"Mom," I said timidly. "I have something to tell you, as long as you promise you won't get upset."

"Oh no," she said, covering her mouth. "Don't tell me, you're engaged." In the eyes of my parents, I was neither old enough nor mature enough to become a bride.

"Mom, don't be ridiculous," I said, as I lifted the base of my shirt to flash her my belly button piercing.

"Oh that's wonderful, sweetheart," she echoed through the terminal. "Let's show Daddy."

Due to our last-minute arrival, our family was forced to sit in separate sections of the plane. Beside me in 35G was Heidi, who was halfway through *The Brothers Karamazov*. In the book's front panel, she had sketched a detailed family tree to keep track of all the characters. Her behavior struck me as far from normal, leaving me with no choice but to try to sleep away the fifteen-hour flight to Hong Kong. I didn't quite make it the whole way, however. When I awoke, Heidi was circling rings in her Blistex container with her pinky finger.

"Need a pat of lip balm?" she offered brightly. "How 'bout some lotion?" Without waiting for my response, she squirted cream from a tube onto my hand. "The air in these cabins tends to leave my skin feeling dry and cracked. Wouldn't you agree?"

Leaning over, I wiped the blob onto her cheek. "Heidi, I just woke up and your perkiness is so annoying."

Patting her face with the airplane blanket, she calmly screwed the cap back on the lotion tube. "Sorry," she explained. "You've been asleep for the past seven hours and the only person I can talk to is the flight attendant. The silence is killing me."

Getting up from her seat, Heidi told me she was going to do a few airplane laps in order to keep the blood flowing in her legs. Two steps down the aisle, however, she involuntarily returned to her seat, belatedly realizing the headphones she was wearing were still connected to the armrest.

My father and I seemed to be on the same sleeping pattern. This resulted in a family rotation with my dad now seated in 35G and Heidi two rows back with my mother. As she always did on these family trips, my mother soon raced to my row, waking my father and me for the highly anticipated in-flight meal. Our choices were either a Texas omelet or Chinese dim sum. Suddenly, I could hear Heidi calling from behind us, "Hey Lise, what'd you get?"

Standing up, I looked back over the sea of heads and answered, "Dim sum." My entire family threw our hands into the air as if we had just scored a goal. The man behind me made a face. I believe he had chosen the omelet.

Meeting us at the airport, my aunt drove us to her home, where the rest of our relatives awaited our arrival. Everyone was on hand for my grandmother's one-hundredth birthday. The lack of guest rooms left Heidi and me sleeping in a backyard camper. Flinging open the door to our trailer, Heidi pinched her nose and said, "Nothing quite like the stench of a septic tank."

In my last-minute packing frenzy, I had mistakenly forgotten about the contrasting seasons of the Southern hemisphere and had chosen only shorts, tank tops, and sandals. It had been snowing on the Drakensburg mountains not far away, leaving remnants of frost on blades of grass outside our door. On that first night, I put on Heidi's only sweater to keep warm while I slept.

"Take that off," she ordered, as I crawled beneath the covers. "You cannot wear my sweater to bed."

I begged for just one night with her cherished threads.

"Okay, you can wear it," she agreed. "But in return, you must warm my side of the bed for exactly twenty minutes prior to my arrival." As far as I was concerned, twenty minutes of suffering was worth a peaceful night of slumber. Upon her predicted return, I rolled over to my chilled side of the bed, begging her to spoon me. "No way," she said, turning to face me with her knees. "I'm a grown woman. I refuse to spoon my sister. Besides, it's unbiblical."

I swatted her with the pillow, triggering a brief gust of cool breeze that made us both shiver. That entire night was nothing but the knocking of kneecaps. We spent as little time as possible in that camper. By night we froze and by day we searched for the mystery toilet my aunt had told us was somewhere inside the camper. Its location remained a well-kept secret for our entire visit.

On the day of my grandmother's birthday, Heidi and I were awakened by the sound of my mother's singing commands. "Let's not forget why we're here—it's Grandmother's one-hundredth birthday celebration."

My dad's mother was the only woman I knew who could eat a bowl of prunes with elegance. Even after a century, she still amazed us with her vibrant wit and clever mind. She remembered odd details of life, such as my imaginary romance with Barry Gibson, the neighbor boy from Denver.

"Why didn't you marry that nice fellow?" she asked.

"Grandma," I replied. "I was only seven."

Her birthday gifts were ones of sentiment, like her journals that my mother had typed and bound into a book. After generations of missionary roots in Africa, Heidi and I were the first in the bloodline to choose our own paths. Other than my immediate family, no one else in the room quite understood what I did for a living.

Clapping her hands together silently, my frail grandmother cheered, "Oh, I must not die now. I must live and enjoy all my wonderful new things." Knowing that this would most likely be the last time I would see her, I tried to videotape the party without her noticing. It was clear she had yet to understand modern technology. Thinking that I was holding a still camera, she kept screaming into the video lens, "Take the picture already!"

During the party, my sister and I helped serve pastries and punch to more than a hundred guests. As part of the entertainment, my aunt had hired an interpretive dancer who wore leg warmers under her flowing chiffon skirt and carried a tambourine with trailing silk ribbons. Growing up, my sister had often mockingly imitated such dancers when my mom would play praise music throughout the house. Just as the dancer leapt past the buffet table, Heidi and I caught each other's eyes. Trying to suppress her laughter, my sister ran from the garden and slammed straight into the sliding glass door.

After days of socializing, my father insisted we go on a family sunset safari before we left. It was something we did every time we returned to his homeland. My dad snapped five rolls of photos of everything from rhinos and hippos to lions and giraffes, as if the animals had evolved since our last trip.

Chasing wild animals across the savannah with my father was a world away from chasing celebrities across the nation with the paparazzi. For nearly two years, I had embraced my profession and abandoned my family. Now, the last place I wanted to be was back in LA.

Our return flight from Johannesburg was delayed, giving me just enough time to skim the magazine racks at the airport gift shop. Directly in front of me was *People* magazine, no relation to North America's popular celebrity publication by that same name. South Africa's version of a tabloid, this paper featured the cover story "William Declares War on Camilla." I bought the issue, reading it only after I had boarded the plane. Sinking into my seat, I flipped through the pages. Immediately, I recognized three separate articles on Liz Taylor, Michael Douglas, and Will Smith. I knew those stories well because I had written them. My articles had been copied word for word. The only thing missing was my byline. Up until now, I had put *Globe* out of my mind for the entire trip. I had not discussed their offer with my parents and had no intention of addressing it until I felt ready.

Now, staring down at the magazine, I realized that the tabloid world had followed me around the globe. In my hands, I was holding evidence of either blatant plagiarism or proof of employee betrayal. At the time, I was still so naïve that it never occurred to me that I was being undermined from within *Globe*. I refused to believe that anyone inside the tabloid empire could have been selling my articles without my knowledge or my benefit.

Soon, however, I would become a believer.

Note:

During an interview with *The Advocate* in 2002, Erin Hamilton credited *Globe* for helping her to come to terms with her sexual preference.

Tom Cruise and Nicole Kidman were married from December 24, 1980, until August 8, 2001. They have two adopted children. Nicole Kidman married singer Keith Urban on June 25, 2006. Tom Cruise and Katie Holmes became the parents of a daughter in April 2006, and married in Italy in November 2006.

Demi Moore married Ashton Kutcher on September 24, 2005.

In October 2006, Farrah Fawcett's longtime friend Ryan O'Neal announced that she had been diagnosed with intestinal cancer and vowed to help her regain her health.

CHAPTER 13

The Commitment

By the time I returned from Africa, I had been out of the office for only a few days, yet I felt unnecessarily apologetic for my absence. The concept of personal vacation time was foreign to those in the upper echelon. We admitted our need to take a break only under extreme circumstances. As reporters, we were viewed as expendable and realized we could easily be replaced, so we never strayed too far.

Immediately after returning from my vacation, I felt an urgency to get back to my desk to safeguard my position. Above all, I wanted to demonstrate my loyalty to *Globe* by showing Madeline the South African magazine that proved someone was stealing our articles.

"Welcome back. Have you had a chance to think over *Globe*'s offer?" Madeline said, getting straight to the point.

"Actually," I lied, "I haven't given it much thought. I was hoping you might be able to give me another week to reach a decision."

Removing her glasses, Madeline began to rub her temples in a circular motion. "Marlise, I think you should be aware that these types of offers are extremely rare within the company. When we hired you at *Globe*, we didn't see you as a temporary employee. We saw you as a dedicated editor. There's no reason why you couldn't be sitting at my desk two years from now."

Me? An editor?

The idea of managing my own team of writers had never entered my mind. "Well, I'll think about that," I told her. "I just need a bit more time. You know, to kind of think about what I want to do with my life."

Madeline nodded patronizingly, as if she did not really agree with what I was saying.

Throwing the South African *People* magazine onto her desk, I tried to sound casual. "Oh, I almost forgot. Someone's selling us out."

As she scanned the cover I felt like a hero, displaying my allegiance by trying to protect *Globe*'s integrity. Flipping through the pages, Madeline closed the magazine and tossed it into her file tray dismissively. "Well, unfortunately, that's how the industry works. There's a lot of money to be made from the tabloids, but ninety percent of the time, it involves stabbing someone in the back to get the top dollar."

"But those are my articles," I protested. "Word for word."

"No," she corrected. "Those are *Globe*'s articles. You wrote them. We own them."

Never before had I felt such a strong division between "them" and "us." Madeline could tell I was stunned by her response.

Belatedly trying to pacify me, she continued, "If it makes you feel any better, I'll check it out with the Florida office." As I reached over to retrieve the publication, she stopped me with her hand. "In the meantime, why don't you leave the magazine with me?"

As I slowly walked back to my desk, I struggled to make sense of our exchange. Why had Madeline not seemed surprised to see my articles in the South African publication? Why had she remained completely unimpressed by my efforts to defend *Globe*? She and I never again discussed the subject of my stolen stories and my magazine was never returned to me.

That first week back at work, I was thrown into an O.J. Simpson story. Despite the fact that considerable time had passed since the 1994 murder of his ex-wife, Nicole Brown, the editors seemed determined to feature at least one follow-up O.J. article per month. O.J. detested the tabloids, especially since they had been indirectly involved in his trial. During the proceedings, the tabloids had revealed a photo of O.J. wearing a pair of Bruno Magli shoes similar to those that had been identified at the crime scene.

It seemed that every time O.J. stepped out in public, we ran another headline. One such story came about after *Globe*'s London correspondent, Geoffrey Bingham, informed me that O.J. had appeared on a British talk show. During the interview, O.J. had mockingly stabbed the host,

Ruby Wax, with a banana while humming the theme music from *Psycho*. Clearly, it was a tasteless move in the wake of his wife's death.

Featuring still photographs taken during the taping of the show, my article was titled "Sicko O.J. Mocks Nicole's Murder." The story also included my interview with detective Mark Fuhrman and former LAPD officer Ron Shipp. As with the majority of my tabloid stories, I was not necessarily expected to have direct contact with celebrities themselves. Instead, I might speak with their relatives or co-workers to get the information I needed. In O.J.'s case, I interviewed his neighbors.

On this assignment, however, I was expected to follow O.J. himself. "Marlise," Madeline called. "You need to head to the Dungarees clothing store in Santa Monica. O.J. is there shopping with a woman who looks just like Nicole. Watch what they do, see where they go, study their interaction. And keep your phone on."

Located just minutes from *Globe*'s LA office, the store featured casual clothing at unreasonable prices. I was unaccustomed to paying hundreds of dollars for ripped blue jeans, unless, of course, *Globe* was footing the bill. With a second-story loft, the store was high and narrow and had wooden floorboards that creaked with every step. When I entered, it appeared that O.J. and I were the only customers there. As a female shopper, it was easy to go unnoticed in that setting. By the time I approached the first clothing rack, O.J. was already at the register, digging into his back pocket for his wallet.

Despite the fact that he had played for the NFL and was implicated for the murder of his wife, I could not mentally separate O.J. from the comedic role he had played in *Naked Gun*. At that exact moment, a tall blonde pushed her way through the swinging saloon-style doors of the dressing rooms. Her eerie resemblance to the late Nicole Brown was unmistakable. Not only were her features and general appearance and style the same as Nicole's, but she even seemed to have the same mannerisms. Walking toward O.J., the woman twirled around in a circle, stopping midway to examine her backside in the mirror. She was modeling a two-piece mint-green workout ensemble.

"Are you sure this outfit doesn't make me look too fat?" she asked.

O.J. studied her carefully from top to bottom. "Christie, I already told you, it looks good." Throwing his credit card down on the counter, O.J. motioned to the salesman, "We'll also take the outfit she's wearing."

"I'll just keep it on," the girl added. She balled up her other clothes and shoved them into a shopping bag on the counter. O.J. quickly signed the receipt as they prepared to leave the store. Knowing I had only a moment to catch up with them, I grabbed the closest item within reach and stood directly beside the couple.

"Excuse me, is this shirt on sale?" I said, tossing it onto the counter. While the employee studied the tag, I glanced at O.J.'s receipt, which totaled $235 for the jogging outfit and some underwear. My sense of urgency seemed odd, even to me. Before the employee could answer my question, I had already handed him cash for the $85 pajama top. With Christie leading the way, O.J. grabbed the plastic bag, waved good-bye, and made his way to the door.

Carefully wrapping up my item, the salesclerk asked, "Would you like us to inform you of our monthly promotions?"

Snatching my bag off the counter, I ran toward the door, calling back, "Maybe another time."

Operating out of habit, I rushed to my car. I wasn't exactly sure why I was following O.J. and the mystery woman. It wasn't as if I were going to talk to either of them. It was somewhat unsettling to be trailing someone who had been tried for murder. After the couple's shopping spree, they drove back to O.J.'s house. While I sat across the street in my car, I dialed Madeline, trying to convince her that I had already done everything possible to complete the story. I even provided her with a license plate number of the vehicle that was parked in O.J.'s driveway.

As I was concluding my conversation with Madeline, she asked, "Did they see you following them?"

"Of course not," I answered proudly. "Does anyone ever see me?" Grabbing binoculars from my glove compartment, I focused on the house. Just then, a curtain in the front window was pulled aside and there, staring back at me, was the face of O.J. Simpson.

"You won't believe this, Madeline," I whispered instinctively. "I guess they must have seen me because O.J. just blew me a kiss from his living room window."

Back at the office, we ran the license plate number of the car I had seen parked in O.J.'s driveway. We determined that the car was registered to a Christie Prody. This information enabled us to track down the relatives and a former roommate of O.J.'s new girlfriend. Interviews with them, combined with *Globe*'s look-alike photographs of Christie and Nicole, gave us exactly what we needed for the O.J. cover story. All that was left was to make the routine comment call.

Whenever possible, it was company policy to contact celebrities themselves. When this was not feasible, we would contact their representatives, such as their publicists, agents, or legal advisers. Since we had O.J.'s home number, Madeline suggested we call him personally to inform him of the upcoming story.

"Don't look at me," I told her. "I'm terrified of the guy."

Walking out of her office, Madeline handed O.J.'s home number to Sharmin and told her to call him, using her best telephone voice. After giving Sharmin a quick pep talk, the entire staff surrounded her desk in anticipation of the comment call she was about to make.

"Hello Mr. Simpson, this is Sharmin calling from *Globe*. . . . Yes, that's right, as in the tabloid. . . . Sharmin . . . Yes, as in the toilet paper. . . . I don't see why my last name is relevant to this conversation. . . . Actually, I'm calling in regards to your relationship with a Ms. Christie Prody. . . . Okay, Mr. Simpson, shall I take that as a 'no comment'?"

Suddenly Sharmin's eyes bulged from their sockets as she slammed down the phone. "Oh sweet Jesus, save me from my enemies," Sharmin said, fanning herself. "O.J.'s real mad at me."

Pete made matters even worse by chiding Sharmin, "Uh, oh . . . O.J.'s gonna kill you."

Despite Sharmin's fear of O.J.'s anger, *Globe* ran the piece as a cover story titled "Nicole Look-Alike Is Raising O.J.'s Kids."

There was never a dull moment at *Globe*. Even the most predictable stories contained odd twists. Such was the case at the wedding of Sylvester Stallone's mother. It was rumored that several years earlier, Stallone had made a deal with *Globe* to keep his family on the tabloid's "safe list." Consequently, as reporters, we were urged to only submit leads that showed the *Rocky* star in a positive light. This cooperative relationship between the hunter and the hunted gave *Globe* exclusive coverage of family events like Jackie Stallone's wedding.

This whole concept messed with my mind. As an investigative reporter, it now felt almost unethical for me to cover a celebrity wedding without having to sneak in or use a disguise. At this wedding, I would be treated as a legitimate journalist, without the challenge of my usual assignments. Jackie Stallone was marrying a brain surgeon named Steven Marcus Levine.

Held in a garden of the Beverly Hills Hotel, the wedding was small, with only a few recognizable guests. I sat in the third row between Al Pacino's father, Salvatore, and O.J. Simpson's previous house sitter, Kato Kaelin. As far as I could tell, these two, along with Sly, made up the entire celebrity guest list. The majority of guests were seated on the groom's side of the lawn. Considering it was Jackie's third trip down the aisle, I expected that the ceremony would be flawless. I was wrong.

"Hello. Do you know my son, Al?" It was Salvatore Pacino. As he shook my hand, I looked beside him, wondering if he was trying to introduce me to Al himself. The seat next to him was empty. Clearly this was just his standard introductory line.

"Um . . . no, not personally," I replied, somewhat confused.

Kato Kaelin leaned toward me and whispered, "Go with it."

"But I do love his movies," I continued. "I thought Al was brilliant in *The Godfather.*"

Salvatore gave a nod of approval. "Did you see him in *Scarface?*"

I felt I was being tested. "Well, it was only the greatest Al Pacino movie of all-time."

"Very smooth," Kato whispered again.

Turning toward the infamously recognizable Kato, I asked sarcastically, "So, what makes you famous?" Just then, wedding guests began standing, one by one. Turning to Kato, I asked, "What's this all about?"

Also rising from his seat, Kato motioned for me to be quiet.

"Did you just shhh me?" I joked. Suddenly, the soft voice of the priest requested that everyone be seated. I was confused. Somehow the bride, dressed in an olive green pantsuit, had managed to make it all the way down the aisle without anyone noticing. There was no wedding party, no music, and no warning. The bride's entrance consisted of her famous son dropping her off near a tree toward the front of the lawn.

Growing up, I had seen my father conduct countless wedding ceremonies, most of which were emotional for both the couple and the guests. This ten-minute exchange, on the other hand, was over before my tear ducts had a chance to warm up. From where I was seated, I had a perfect side view of Jackie's mouth. It seemed to be pulled taut for the occasion. Bubble-gum-pink lipstick lined the corners of her lips, which appeared to be slightly parted, creating a fixed smile. Uncertain if she was, in fact, smiling at me, I just kept smiling back. I didn't want to appear insensitive on her wedding day. This same thought must have crossed the minds of many guests. Like a crowd of mannequins, the entire audience sat there wearing plastered grins.

"Let's see if the couple can actually kiss," Kato mumbled.

Jackie turned her head back and forth several times, like a baby resisting a spoonful of peas. A little voice inside of me wanted to start chanting, "Puck-er! Puck-er! Puck-er!" The groom eventually grabbed Jackie by the jowls, forcing on her the most unromantic kiss I had ever seen. The sound of single, delayed claps could be heard from several rows behind us. And then, just as quickly as Jackie had come down the aisle, she once again vanished. Uncertain of what to do next, guests started to trickle slowly into the reception hall. Kato and I parted as we moved toward our assigned seats.

Before we separated, he turned back and mumbled, "That ceremony was so brief, we should have thrown Minute Rice."

Passing the cake table, I paused briefly to congratulate the newlyweds. Jackie's new husband was already scolding her for downing one too many glasses of champagne.

"You did great," I said, smiling back at Jackie's permanent grin. "I'm sure it's not easy to stand up there in front of all those people."

Her hands were shaking as she reached toward a miniature rose that trimmed the edge of a three-tiered chocolate cake. "Thank God I drank before the wedding," she said. "I'm a complete wreck." Popping the flower between her parted lips, she added. "Ohhh . . . I just love frosting, don't you?"

Clearly the woman was under stress. I didn't have the heart to tell her she had just devoured an actual fresh rosebud. In the next moment, her eyes widened as she pulled soggy petals off her tongue. "That didn't taste like frosting at all," she said, spitting into a cocktail napkin. "I'll have to speak to the chef about that."

Not quite sure how to respond, I simply backed away and said, "I should probably find my seat before my food gets cold." As the only wedding guest who was being paid to attend, I had been assigned to a round table beside people I had never before met or seen. Grabbing the menu off my plate, I shoved it into my purse and waited impatiently for Sly to offer a toast.

"Is the menu really worth stealing?" a man beside me joked.

I hadn't realized I was being watched. "Oh, I'm actually a reporter covering the wedding." It was one of the few times in my career that I could openly state my identity. "What brings you here? The bride or the groom?"

"The bride," he answered. He then lowered his voice to a whisper. "Jackie says I'm the son she always wanted Sly to be. I've known Jackie for years. In fact, she recently gave me this." Pulling back the sleeve of his jacket, he flashed a golden bracelet that had supposedly been a Stallone family heirloom.

Suddenly, our heads were separated as the angry face of Rambo came between us. Forcefully grabbing the man behind the neck, Sly spoke in a low yet demanding tone. "You son of a bitch, that bracelet should have been mine. I swear to God, I will kill you before I let you take my place."

I couldn't believe what I was hearing. Headlines flashed in my head like lights on Broadway.

"Sly," a voice called from the front. "We need to get some pictures of you with the bride." Straightening his jacket, Sly walked toward the photographer, who was now motioning for me to join him.

"Me?" I asked silently, pointing toward myself.

The photographer waved me over impatiently. Keeping my distance, I waited for the two men to finish their brief conversation. "Hi," I said, reaching my hand toward the photographer. "I guess we've been assigned to work this story together, huh?"

"Stop with the bullshit," the photographer said. "I know what just happened at that table. Obviously Sly didn't realize you were a reporter. I've talked to him about everything and he seems to have calmed down.

So, we both want you to erase that scene from your pretty little head and go on eating your shrimp and caviar. Have I made myself clear?"

It was my first encounter with such an empowered paparazzo. Nodding agreeably, I fed into his game, "What little scene are you referring to exactly?"

Patting my face, he smiled and said, "That's my girl. I think we could make a good team. What's your name?"

"Marlise," I told him. "And yours?"

Taking out his business card, he slipped it into my hand. Then, ignoring me, he looked toward Sly, who was now proposing a toast. I was left standing alone, holding his business card. Glancing down, I read the name of the world's most famous paparazzo, Paul Radley.

Discounting Radley's threat, I submitted a lead sheet on Monday morning that read, "Sly threatens to kill a guest at his mother's wedding." Calling me into her office, Madeline closed the door and asked me about the details surrounding my latest adventure.

Before I could finish my pitch, Madeline interrupted, "As you know, Sly has a deal with *Globe*. That deal includes everyone from the owner to the photographer. Don't even think about a Stallone story unless it has a positive spin." Looking directly at me, Madeline ripped up my lead sheet and threw the tiny pieces into her wastebasket.

In the end, my dull wedding exclusive ran as a two-page spread titled "Sly Gives His Mom Away to Hubby #3."

Between celebrity weddings and last-minute assignments, my weekends were becoming as demanding as my workdays. *Globe*'s newest editor, Caelan, was now also overcommitted, often dedicating nonstop weeks to his job. Finally, it was his turn to take a break. Two days after I returned from South Africa, Caelan headed to Paris for the soccer World Cup. Rather than exploring the treasures of the Louvre or climbing the Eiffel Tower, he spent $4,000 to watch a soccer match featuring Scotland versus Brazil. Caelan claimed that soccer was culture, religion, pride, and politics, all wrapped into one glorious sport.

While I typed away at my desk, jealousy-induced visions began to fester and boil in my head. I pictured Caelan and his Scottish comrades downing bottles of whisky. I envisioned French women flirting with their puckered lips and subtle winks, luring him into endless nights of drunken debauchery. Caelan had left me alone for soccer, without a single phone call, postcard, or e-mail. The idea that Caelan was, in fact, in Paris to watch the game never crossed my mind. The idea that I could have been overreacting also never occurred to me. My head was too jumbled for sensibility. Just when I least expected, it seemed I was falling for him.

This foreign feeling was quite a nuisance, really. I thought about Caelan when he wasn't around and even more so when he was. In an effort to hold onto my independence, I ignored his calls when he was in town and pretended not to care. In reality, I was falling in love.

Refusing to play my mind games, Caelan simply called me on my actions. He was forcing the relationship to either bloom or die. And so I surrendered, giving my emotions the freedom to move toward a predictable outcome: a committed relationship and all that entailed. Little by little I knew I was losing my identity by falling in love, but I didn't care. For years, I had been ruled by guilt and pride and religion, something which I could neither explain nor justify to those on the outside.

"Live for yerself a bit, luv," Caelan told me. Little by little, he chipped away at the shell I had built around myself. I was discovering who I was and who I was not. In the midst of my self-realization, Caelan was somewhere in Paris, cheering on his favorite team. It seemed the only way I could keep him out of my head was to fill it with other things.

With Caelan out of town, it was the ideal time to reconnect with my girlfriend Janine. We had arranged to spend the weekend in Santa Barbara, where we had both attended college. Thirty minutes into the drive, I received a call from Madeline wanting to know where I was. After I told her, she said, "You need to drive two hours north to Ojai Valley Inn and Spa. Roseanne is there with ten of her girlfriends for the weekend."

This was the third time I would have had to cancel plans with Janine because of my work. "Why don't you just come with me?" I suggested. As an avid tabloid reader, Janine welcomed the opportunity to assist me on a *Globe* assignment. It was Saturday morning and the only vacant room at the Ojai Valley Inn was a suite that cost $1,200 a night. "We'll take it," I said, handing over my company credit card.

The Roseanne story was expected to be written and sent to Florida within twenty-four hours. Fortunately, my mission was to simply follow

Roseanne and her entourage around the spa. Our afternoon was spent tracing Roseanne's beauty treatments through manicures, pedicures, and massages. Hidden beneath cucumber masks and terrycloth robes, Janine and I sat poolside while Roseanne discussed plastic surgery, stretch marks, and the Super Bowl. Masquerading as members of her pampered crew, Janine and I shadowed her every move, and even took a picture of Roseanne walking out of the spa. While she was at dinner, I bribed a bellman to let me into her private cottage.

After he left, I directed Janine to keep a lookout while I explored Roseanne's room. As if she had suddenly had an epiphany, Janine whispered. "This is wrong. I don't think we should be doing this."

I couldn't believe my ears. These words were coming from the same girl who had just begged me for a yearly subscription to *Globe*. It was hard to imagine that just a few years before, Janine and I had been very much alike.

How did she suddenly become the voice of reason?

"Janine, this is neither the time nor the place to be discussing the ethics of my profession. Are you going to help me or not?"

"No," she said, stepping away. "I just can't imagine that this type of work is pleasing to the Lord."

What did she just say?

"Who the hell do you think you are?" I asked. "How dare you pull some self-righteous act on me right now? Why didn't you speak up when you were getting the massage or manicure? Were those things displeasing to the Lord, too?"

"That's different," Janine explained. "No one was getting hurt."

"Right," I said. "Only pampered."

Throwing her hands in the air, Janine was already walking back toward our suite. "I didn't come all this way to fight with you," she said, looking back. "But if this is the way you're going to live your life, then I don't want to be any part of it."

I was halfway into Roseanne's room by now. "Fine. But next time, I suggest you leave the judging to God."

Ignoring Janine, I stayed on track and made my way into Roseanne's room. It took only three minutes to make enough mental notes of the surroundings to complete my article. The room was strewn with damp towels, empty soda cans, and Champagne buckets filled with melted ice. Discarded candy wrappers peered from beneath Roseanne's pillow. Finding no other hard evidence to add to my story, I left the room and returned to our suite. By the time I got there, Janine had already packed her bags and left the resort. The only sign that our friendship had ever existed was a farewell note telling me it had ended.

That weekend, I gained another byline and lost another friend.

On Monday, Madeline sent me directly to Utah rather than having me return to the office. According to a tip from a source, President Clinton had been staying at the home of DreamWorks mogul Jeffrey Katzenberg in Deer Valley. *Globe* wanted to build a story surrounding the real purpose of Clinton's trip. It took me less than twenty-four hours to bribe my way into the gated property and take photographs of the Katzenberg estate. After quickly locating seven sources to support my article, I typed it up but did not send it to Florida.

Without feeling a single moment of guilt, I stalled the editors, turned off my phone, and spent the next two days on the slopes. On my last day in Deer Valley, I filed the story, which *Globe* ran under the headline "Clinton in Marriage Crisis."

When I returned to the LA office, Madeline noticed the signature tan of a sun-baked snowboarder. Capitalizing on my guilt, Madeline took advantage of the moment and asked with a smile, "So, tell me Marlise, are you going to accept *Globe*'s offer?"

Her timing was impeccable. Madeline had caught me right after a highly rewarding assignment. Mentally recapping my time in the tabloid industry, I thought about the new friends I had gained at *Globe*, the places I had been, the adventures I had experienced, and now, the chance of a twenty-five percent increase.

"Okay," I told her offhandedly as I walked out of her office. "Sign me on for another two years."

Note:
After seven years of marriage, Roseanne Barr divorced her third husband, Ben Thomas, in October 2002. They have one child.

CHAPTER 14

Two Hundred Reflections of Me

lthough it was a spur-of-the-moment decision, accepting *Globe*'s offer seemed like the right thing to do. Yet for some reason, I was hesitant to tell others about the commitment I had made. Caelan was the last to find out. He had just returned from Paris and said he wanted to discuss some things that were on his mind. I was convinced he had somehow found out about his new fish. I had bought it to replace the one that I had forgotten to feed while he was away. He never mentioned the fish.

When he picked me up, Caelan seemed nervous, kissing me on the cheek as if too much time had passed for anything more. He took me to a 1920s Italian restaurant called Cicada, where rows of oak columns supported extravagant thirty-foot gold-leafed ceilings.

"I thought a wee bit about us while I was in Paris," Caelan said. "To be frank, 'twas more than a bit. 'Twas a lot. I think we should be getting more committed to one another."

What does that mean?

"I thought we were committed," I responded. "Do you want us to exchange promise rings or something?"

Caelan laughed. "I'm not quite sure what those are. But I doubt I want to discuss anything associated with rings at the moment. I just feel that we should be thinking about this as more long-term. Exclusive-like, ya know?"

Permanency scared me. My love life never seemed to exist beyond dinner. "Okay," I agreed. "I'm just not happy with us sneaking around the office. We aren't doing anything wrong, really. Sometimes I think Madeline already knows about the relationship."

He pointed at me with his fork. "Perhaps she does. And perhaps you should stop pinching me bum in the file room, eh?"

Just then, Val Kilmer and his ex-wife, Joanne Whalley, walked past our table. "Quick, Caelan. Give me your camera."

Caelan leaned toward me. "Eh luv, what's the matter with ya? Can you not stop workin' for a second? I haven't seen you in two whole weeks and all you can think about is *Globe*."

He had a point. "Sorry," I said. "Forget the camera. So, I guess now isn't the best time to tell you about my new contract, huh?"

Caelan took a sip of wine. "So, 'ow long are you committed for?"

"Two years," I mumbled. "The raise already kicked in, but I haven't actually signed the papers yet. Madeline says it takes a while before everything is approved."

Caelan shook his head. "'Tis yer life, luv. Just be careful what you do with it."

I should have heard the warning in his advice. Instead, I pushed myself harder at *Globe* than I ever had before. Consistently bringing in a minimum of two published articles per week, I was no longer driven by fear of termination, but rather by the promise of financial security. I felt that *Globe*'s offer might lead to upward mobility within the company.

Heidi and my mother shared Caelan's views of my decision. They all thought a binding contract with the tabloids would be detrimental to my journalistic future. Ironically, it was my dad who seemed to be the most supportive of my decision. After preaching at a seminar in Los Angeles, he joined me for a workout at The Sports Club/LA. He was enthralled by the luxurious facility. I thought we'd never make it past the juice bar.

"Don't ever quit this job," my dad begged, reaching for a blended smoothie. "You're living the life everyone dreams about." I realized then that he understood very little about the stress that I was experiencing at *Globe*. As we walked into the fitness studio, I spotted Sarah Michelle Gellar riding an exercise bike.

"Dad," I whispered under my breath. "That's Buffy."

Oblivious to her television show or her identity, he glanced at her and said, "She's not that buff."

Later, over dinner at The Cheesecake Factory, my father and I managed to blow the benefits of our entire workout. "Order whatever you want," I said, flashing my company credit card. "It's on *Globe*."

We ordered appetizers, entrées, drinks, and desserts, an act of overindulgence seldom practiced by our family. I looked over at my dad, who was busy twirling a greasy bone in his hand. "These are the best baby back ribs I've ever had," he raved. "Look, there's no fat on these things." Between sauce-glazed lips, he smiled contentedly. Somehow, I interpreted his pleasure as confirmation that I had made the right decision about staying on at *Globe*.

While I pushed forward in my career, Caelan backed away from the tabloids, spending less time at his desk and more time in the deejay booth. He began to focus on his weekly gigs at Chasen's and Barfly, perched high above the crowd spinning hip-hop and house music. As his newly committed "girlfriend," I cheered him on from below his booth, sometimes waiting for him until three in the morning before his records were packed. Caelan was never the jealous type. He knew he could desert me for five hours and still find me dancing in the same spot when he returned. My abnormal routine was eventually noticed by Barfly's owner, Franck Fortet.

"You're like one of those wind-up dolls that never stop," he said. "Why don't you take a break and join me for a glass of wine?"

Motioning toward Caelan, I gave him the universal drinking sign before following Franck toward a plush booth in the corner. Abandoned cocktails and plates of sushi covered the table, where Franck's guests periodically stopped to see and be seen. Introducing myself as Jade Rock, I told him I was a UCLA student and a loyal fan of the deejay. By now, using a fake name and background was becoming my habit.

"If you like hip-hop, you should come tomorrow," he suggested. "No, wait. Not tomorrow. I almost forgot. Tomorrow's reserved for a private party."

My tabloid ears perked. "Are you telling me that the owner of Barfly doesn't have the power to get me in?"

Franck nodded. "Not this time, I'm afraid. Brad Pitt is throwing a surprise party for Jennifer Aniston. The guest list is extremely tight."

For months, the paparazzi had been trying to get a photograph of the two together. Despite the fact that the media claimed Brad and Jennifer were romantically linked, their representatives were still denying that a relationship existed between them. A photograph of the couple together would be worth a fortune. Excusing myself from Franck's table, I made my way to the outdoor patio facing Sunset Boulevard. My cell phone showed that I had two missed calls, one from the British paparazzo Edward Townsend and the other from Madeline.

Considering the success record of Edward's recent work, he seemed to be the ideal candidate for the Pitt-Aniston job. When I returned Edward's call, he was even more excited than I was about the idea of capturing such a shot.

"Have you informed anyone else about the bash tomorrow night?"

"No one," I told him. "But I'm just about to phone Madeline and have her assign you to the story."

"No, wait," he pleaded. "Don't call Madeline. Have you any idea of how much money we could make by selling the picture back to *Globe?*"

"What are you talking about?" I asked. "I'm staff. They don't pay me extra if I bring in photographs. It's considered part of my job."

"Aren't you being a bit rash?" he asked. "After all, is it really necessary to inform Madeline about all this? If you do, I'll only earn the paltry day's wages. In that event, the bloody copyright will belong to *Globe.* On the other hand, we could keep this as our little secret now, couldn't we? If I were to independently take the photograph, I would have full international rights. That's where the real money is, you know. I could easily make one hundred and fifty thousand dollars off of these pictures. We could split the profit fifty-fifty."

What Edward was suggesting certainly had its appeal. An extra $75,000 would definitely change my lifestyle. Oddly enough, I didn't give his suggestion any serious consideration. Perhaps it was my principled upbringing or maybe it was just an effort to preserve my reputation as a dedicated *Globe* employee. In retrospect, it strikes me as odd that I felt such a deep allegiance to such a corrupt industry.

Ignoring the financial carrot that Edward was dangling, I immediately returned Madeline's call. Dialing her number, I was confident she would praise my latest scoop. Instead, she reprimanded me for calling her after midnight. My first instinct was to remind her of her countless "urgent" calls that had awakened me on so many pre-dawn occasions. I never got the opportunity to act on my instinct, however, because she immediately began explaining my next assignment.

The following night, while I was off chasing a false lead, Edward was standing curbside at Barfly when Brad and Jennifer emerged. My tip had given Edward the opportunity to capture the now-famous first shot of the couple together. Edward earned *Globe*'s $250 day rate, the tabloid made a fortune in sales, and I got nothing.

It seemed that the more I gave, the more the editors demanded. There were times I was sent to the airport without knowing what my actual destination would be. It had been several weeks since *Globe* had featured an Oprah headline. Although they had no storyline per se, the editors felt it was worth sending me to San Francisco, where Oprah would be taping her next show. Just moments before boarding my flight, however, I was redirected to Las Vegas for the wedding of Michael Fishman.

My first question was, "Michael who?"

Madeline told me that he had played the son, D.J., on TV's *Roseanne*. For whatever reason, the editors had decided to give the former child star priority over the queen of talk shows. *Globe* had learned that Michael Fishman had gone to Las Vegas to marry his pregnant girlfriend, Jennifer Briner. My task was to search every wedding chapel in Vegas until I found them. At chapel after chapel, my taxi driver would wait curbside long enough for me to run questions past the presiding minister. Three hours later, I phoned Madeline with bad news.

"Michael and Jennifer have already left Vegas," I told her. "They were married at Wedding Bells Chapel several days ago."

After phoning *Globe*'s research department, Madeline gave me Michael Fishman's home number. From my Las Vegas hotel room, I interviewed Michael, who by now was back in Los Angeles. He gave me full details of the wedding for my article, which appeared under the heading "Roseanne's TV Son Ties Knot with His Pregnant Gal Pal." He later provided me with photos and exclusive rights to a follow-up story, titled "Roseanne's TV Son Has Bouncing Bundle of Joy."

Fishman's cooperation allowed me to take a short nap before catching an early flight back to LA. It was five o'clock in the afternoon when I fell asleep in my Vegas hotel room. When I awoke, it was eight o'clock. Only after opening the curtains did I realize that it was actually the following morning. I had been asleep for fifteen hours straight. Of all the places to recuperate, Las Vegas would have been last on my list. Ironically, the city that never sleeps had gifted me with a peaceful slumber.

Later that day, I flew back to LA and drove straight to Caelan's apartment. I was looking forward to spending some time alone with him. Lounging on his couch, he had spent the morning watching soccer. I was hurt when Caelan said that he had made plans for us to go clubbing that night with his friends. Resentful that I would have to share his time with others, I retorted that I couldn't go clubbing with them because I would be running in a 10K charity race the following morning.

"Canna you just relax for once?" Caelan asked.

Slamming the door on my way out, I screamed back, "I am relaxed!"

The next morning, I was still pinning on my contestant number when the starting gun sounded. This was typical of my life. I was late to the race, but I caught up and managed to keep a steady pace with those around me. Near the finish line stood an attractive man who was cheering me on. He must have noticed that I was running alone and that I was running to no one in particular.

"Come on, beautiful," he yelled, jogging alongside me. "Don't give up."

He was holding a basketball under his arm, most likely waiting for the court that had been occupied by the morning race. We caught eyes and smiled. Flirting seemed justifiable considering how badly things had gone with Caelan the previous day. Later, as I walked back toward Caelan's apartment, the mystery man came running after me, offering a Dixie cup of water. "Hey, champ. You've got any energy left for a game of basketball?"

Glancing at Caelan's balcony, I reluctantly told him I already had plans. His offer made me wish I were single, and only more so when I arrived at Caelan's apartment. He was still passed out from the previous night's binge. The floor was littered with bottles and unconscious friends whom I had never met. Stepping over unfamiliar bodies, I opened the curtains and nudged Caelan with my knee. "How can you still be asleep? It's nearly one o'clock."

Caelan covered his head with a pillow and mumbled, "Will ya stop acting so self-righteous?"

I walked out of his apartment and slammed the door. We liked to slam doors in our relationship. I thought about the guy back at the basketball court, wondering why I was dating someone whose ideals were so different from mine.

I rode my bike back to my condo and found two messages on my voicemail. One was from Caelan, saying he was sorry for allowing his hangover to take control. The other was from Madeline, telling me to return to Las Vegas. *Globe* had received a last-minute tip that Evel Knievel was planning to marry Krystal Kennedy, a woman thirty years his junior.

Fortunately, my bags were still packed from my last trip. Knowing the territory well, I flew back to Vegas and headed straight for Caesar's Palace. In 1968, Knievel tried to jump the fountain at the famous hotel. Instead, he had landed in a coma with a fractured hip, shattered pelvis, and broken femur. Considering his history there, Caesar's Palace seemed to be the most likely place for Knievel to hold his wedding ceremony. When I tried to reserve a room there, I discovered that the hotel was fully booked due to a Tyson fight scheduled for that same weekend. The only available room in town was the honeymoon suite at Circus Circus.

Leopard-print velour covered the walls of my suite, making it look like something straight out of the Discovery Channel. Granite pillars emerged from the marble floor like Pepperidge Farm Pirouette cookies in a bowl of swirled ice cream. An elevated Jacuzzi was oddly located in the center of my room. Every button, knob, dial, and fixture was gold-plated, including the lion heads that spouted water from their mouths into the twin sinks. There were mirrors everywhere, above the bed and lining all four sides of the shower. This made it virtually impossible to escape the two hundred Marlise clones staring back at me.

By mid-afternoon, I was prepared to return to Caesar's Palace to begin my Knievel hunt. *Globe*'s editors were convinced that Evel Knievel was a tabloid name still worthy of centerfold placement. Knowing their demands, I planned to bribe hotel security for information regarding the ceremony's location. Fortunately, I didn't have to search for the wedding, because the wedding came to me.

As I was nearing Caesar's, I heard the rumble of a motorcycle approaching from behind. Heading straight toward me was the legendary stuntman, perched on his famous red, white, and blue bike. He was tall, thin, and pale with fuzzy white hair circling the top of his head like the tip of a cotton swab. Pinned to the lapel of his dark blue suit was a red rose that matched the shade of his tinted sunglasses. He sped right past me, leaving me no choice but to follow him.

My casual stroll quickly turned into a brisk walk, then a light jog, and finally a sprint. He was heading straight for the hotel gardens. Catching up to his roaring bike, I stayed close behind him, waving at confused gamblers and tourists who cheered in our wake. I felt as if we were in a parade. Ushers dressed as gladiators raised their golden swords as we approached the center aisle. From the corner of my eye, I caught the blurred image of staff members dressed as Cleopatra and Caesar. Knievel drove down the turquoise carpet that divided the two sections of white folding chairs.

Similar to many of Knievel's previous stunts, this flamboyant wedding was clearly a publicity event. Sliding into an empty seat, I remained unnoticed throughout the entire wedding ceremony. There was no need for bribery and no need to hide. My published article was titled "Evel Knievel Takes the Leap of His Life."

By this time, *Globe* had become much more computer-savvy. Though still limited to dial-up connection, I was able to send most of my copy to Florida by e-mail. This was not always possible on the road, however, which often forced me to fax stories from hotel business centers. Such was the case at Circus Circus. By early evening I had faxed the copy to Florida, after inserting such formulaic tabloid language as "blushing bride," "wedding bliss," and "tears of joy."

By the time I was finished, it was still only six o'clock in the evening. Unable to change my return flight, I was stuck in Las Vegas for the night.

For the first time in my *Globe* career, I was utterly bored. Picking up the phone, I dialed Sharmin and then Chantal, begging each of them to join me in Sin City. Both bowed out because of their jobs.

Even my sister was too busy to take a break. She was writing her doctoral dissertation. "But we haven't bonded in ages," I pleaded. "Come on Heidi, I promise you won't have to spend a cent."

"I just don't have the time," she explained. "By the way, what's that sound in the background?"

I glanced around the room. "Oh, that's just the power jet on my Jacuzzi."

Hanging up the phone, I had never felt so alone. Next door a group of teenagers kept dialing my room, pretending to be everything from room service to sex service.

"I can hear you through the walls," I yelled into the phone. Out of pure loneliness, I almost went next door to introduce myself. I missed the innocence of being a child. I headed out for something to eat, but nothing seemed to satisfy my appetite. Lining the Strip were fast-food restaurants like McDonald's, Bob's Chicken, and Pizza Hut. Some of the hotel restaurants advertised all-you-can-eat meals for $3.99, which sounded even more unappealing. Tourists lined up at the buffets like animals at a trough, digging into bins of beef and mountains of soggy pancakes, piling mismatched cuisine onto oval platters. Despondent, I finally stopped at the Bellagio hotel for a meal. All I really wanted was someone to talk to. I'm not sure why I expected to find deep conversation in this shallow city.

On my way out of the Bellagio, I dropped a coin into the hungry belly of a slot machine. It swallowed my money and, in return, showed me three pictures of mismatched fruit. Suddenly, my head began to throb at the sound of clanging coins, spinning wheels, and screaming sirens. In the casino, void of light and direction, I watched as dealers shuffled stiff cards before raking towers of chips across fields of felt. Lifeless bodies parked themselves in front of slot machines, popping in coins and pulling down levers. They looked more like machines than the slots themselves. Aimlessly, I walked through the air-conditioned labyrinth of flashing lights and patterned carpet.

By the time I returned to my room, it was past midnight. Climbing up the steps of my elevated Jacuzzi, I felt like the plastic bride atop a three-tiered wedding cake. Sinking into the gurgling water, I pushed buttons on the remote control, empowered by the fact I could operate the stereo, lights, television, and curtains all by touch. Unveiled behind me was the bustling city below. Brake lights and headlamps lined up like beaded strands of diamonds and rubies. The Strip was alive, awake, and ready for another night of pleasure. It was all so intriguing, but strangely enough, the only place I wanted to be was home.

Submerging deeper into the water, I scraped my fingers across a layer of suds and propped my feet onto the tub's edge. Inhaling deeply, I blew foam bubbles into the air. And then, I began to cry.

I wasn't exactly sure why I was so sad. Maybe it was exhaustion, or maybe it was the fact I had invested myself in a career that was not fulfilling. During these out-of-town assignments, I had too much time to think. Too much self-reflection can be a dangerous thing for a woman seeking contentment.

Each week, the sorrow grew. I had the money, I had the career, I had the boyfriend. But I didn't have me. Somewhere during the search for success, I had lost myself. Challenging assignments had become no more to me than the next paycheck. Worst of all, I had trapped myself inside this exit-less industry for another two years.

Although the flight back to LAX was brief, it was long enough for me to realize I was losing my tabloid passion. In the seat next to me was actress Alfre Woodard, reading a movie script. Under normal circumstances, I would have tried to strike up a conversation to get a story. But nothing seemed normal anymore and I just didn't care. I wondered what I was doing signing on for two more years with the tabloids. My raise had already kicked in, but the contract was still being reviewed.

What is taking Globe *so long?*

Back at the office, my latest assignment only made matters worse. Florida editor Cathy Tidwell had asked that I meet with Nicole Brown's sister, Denise. The lead sheet simply read, "Denise Brown Special." Without knowing the real purpose of our meeting, I drove one hour south to Islands Restaurant in Irvine. Denise was easy to spot in the

crowd with her silken brown hair and dark eyes. She had become a leading figure on television during the O.J. Simpson trial and now was
immersed in a campaign against domestic violence.

Apparently, she had a story to sell to the tabloids, and I was there to
listen. Denise had already been informed that in order for the editors to
make a financial offer, they needed to know what her story was worth.

"I'm telling you from the start that I won't take less than one million
dollars for this story," Denise said.

I told her that such an amount had never been paid by a tabloid. She
smiled and said, "This will be a first."

I knew then that the story I was about to hear would be scandalous.
Pulling out a large folder, she handed me a stack of letters, plane tickets,
receipts, and photographs. "I've been having a three-year affair with
Geraldo Rivera."

I tried not to wince. The thought of such a mismatched union reminded me of Beauty and the Beast. "How did you two meet?" I asked.

Taking her story from the top, Denise explained that just weeks after
her sister's murder, she had been approached by Geraldo. Before her
public speeches and TV appearances, he provided moral support.
According to Denise, their friendship turned into a romance, which then
led to three years of lies. She claimed that during the affair, Geraldo
would send his helicopter to fly her to secret locations.

"He promised to leave his wife so we could be together," she said.
"He even told me he loved me. But later, I realized he was just using me
to boost his own career. Geraldo had horrible ratings until the O.J. case.
He knew I was in the middle of it all and had connections. I got hurt, but
it was my own fault for loving him."

For the next two hours, Denise shared specific details about their romance. She showed me pictures of the two during a sailing trip and a
winter vacation to South Carolina. Unfolding one of Geraldo's letters,
her eyes began to water as she spoke in a cracked voice. "He signed his
letters 'Love, Gino' so his wife would never find out."

"Do you still love him?" I asked, somewhat puzzled by her emotion.

She nodded, claiming that he had cut off all contact with her just
one month before our meeting. "Everything I have been fighting for, all

the causes I stand for like women against verbal and physical abuse, have now become part of my own life. I have become a victim of that same type of relationship. Geraldo sucked me in and mentally abused me. I feel so used."

Clearly the money was an incentive to sell her story to the tabloids. Still, the idea of tarnishing her name for financial gain didn't seem to mesh with her public persona. "Why *Globe*?" I asked.

Denise reached for a tissue. "You mean you don't know? I was *Globe*'s main source during the O.J. trial. I've had a very profitable relationship with your magazine."

"You're kidding me," I said, probing for more information. "So, you must know the editor-in-chief, Trenton Freeze?"

"Know him?" she laughed. "I've slept with him."

Later that day, I typed up the recording of my meeting with Denise. I then sent a copy of the transcript to Cathy in Florida, purposely omitting the Trenton Freeze reference. Later, over the phone, I explained the situation to Cathy, who didn't sound at all surprised.

The following day, I contacted Denise regarding Trenton's financial offer. "I'm sorry Denise. Twenty thousand is as high as he'll go."

There was a long pause. "Tell Trenton to go fuck himself." Denise slammed down the phone, as if I had something to do with her affair or with our magazine's budget limitations. Her story was never told in *Globe*. As it turned out, the only time the affair was ever addressed by the media was during a CBS interview. Denise told me that she had been completely caught off guard when Geraldo himself asked her, on air, about their rumored relationship. Although furious with Geraldo, Denise tried to laugh off the question by responding that the rumors were ridiculous.

The next time Denise and I spoke was six weeks later regarding an unrelated story. This latest assignment focused on assertions that Denise had stolen funds from the Nicole Brown Simpson Foundation. *Globe* had asked me to contact Denise for her comment on those allegations. I hated making the call, but the editors felt Denise would talk to me more easily than she would to anyone else on staff.

"I'm not a thief," Denise told me. "The IRS searched the Foundation from top to bottom and everything was accounted for." Despite all of our hours of communication, this led to the only article I ever actually wrote on Denise. It was titled "Denise Brown Cleared by IRS in Charity $$ Probe."

In every situation, the tabloids seemed to win. *Globe* always came out ahead, whether it was celebrities willing to expose their secrets or reporters willing to sacrifice for a headline. After nearly two years with the tabloid, this pattern had started to take its toll on me. Caelan recognized that something in me had changed. I laughed less and my smile had nearly vanished.

No matter what was happening to our relationship outside the office, we were forced to remain a team inside the office. There were days I nearly walked out, claiming that his editorial demands were unreasonable. He would then pull me aside and quietly, but firmly, reinforce the fact that he was still my superior at *Globe.*

With that in mind, he handed me a new lead sheet stating, "Brad and Jennifer getting married? She was spotted trying on wedding dresses at Vera Wang. Check it out." This was a cruel assignment. Forcing any woman to try on bridal gowns before she has even discussed the subject of marriage should be outlawed. The only way I could go undercover at a bridal shop was to pretend to be a bride. With no other option, I borrowed Sharmin's cubic zirconia ring and headed for Barneys of Beverly Hills.

I had never primped so much for a day of shopping. Despite my best efforts, I still looked out of place. In an effort to appear poetically French, I wore linen capris, ankle-high boots, and a mock turtleneck. Climbing my way to the second floor of Barneys, I walked into their Vera Wang Bridal Salon and came face to face with a mirror. Suddenly I realized how ridiculous I looked.

Why didn't anyone tell me ribbed was out?

To make matters worse, I was under-accessorized. Everywhere I looked were stunning women dressed in strings of pearls with cashmere pashminas draping their bodies like cloaks of superiority. Fortunately, I had left my beret in the car.

I must have looked completely lost, because it took less than thirty seconds before I was approached. "May I help you?" In front of me stood a blonde wearing cropped cuff pants and a peach cardigan with abalone buttons down the front.

"Yes," I said. "I'm getting married." I had no idea what I was talking about. After all, trying on wedding dresses was supposed to be a sacred moment shared between mothers and daughters and bridesmaids. It was supposed to a day of emotion, filled with tears and laughter and ohhs and ahhs. Here I was, dressed in my French ensemble, totally alone. "I'm looking for a dress," I continued. "A few dresses, actually, for me and my bridesmaids."

She nodded. "Do you have an idea what you're looking for?"

I glanced at the displays around the salon and began to improvise. "Something simple, yet elegant. Nothing too frilly. Easy on the beadwork and definitely no bows or ruffles."

The woman seemed to be taking mental notes. "What about a train?"

"Yes!" I cheered, getting into the bridal spirit. "I love trains. I mean, I don't need to go Princess Diana-style or anything, but a satin five-footer would be nice."

I could see her studying my fake diamond. "Where are you getting married, exactly?" she asked. "Maybe we can try and match the style of your dress with the overall feel of the chapel."

Panic set in as I realized that I could not recall the name of a single church in LA County. "I'm getting married at the Monterey Bay Aquarium," I blurted. In high school, I had worked there as a presenter for aquatic shows with sea otters. On occasion, the aquarium would rent out its facilities for private events and weddings. I was prepared for any question she was about to ask.

"The aquarium? As in, a place for fish?" She sounded doubtful.

I crossed my arms, with an air of confidence. "Yep, right in front of the kelp forest exhibit."

"Wow," she said, clearly unenthused. "I've never heard of that before. Maybe your bridesmaids can wear aqua blue or even a marine green to match the plants."

Is she mocking me? How dare she belittle my wedding venue?

"Actually, when the light shines onto the kelp's amber fronds, they tend to appear almost iridescent."

"Okay," she said, taking a step back. "Well, then. Why don't we just start with the wedding gown?"

After she took my measurements, we looked through several catalogs to get an idea of what I wanted. I desperately needed to probe about Jennifer Aniston before the episode went any further. "So, you must love working at Barneys, especially with all the celebrities coming in to look at your Vera Wang gowns."

She looked up from her catalog. "Oh, I'm not all that starstruck. To me, a celebrity is just like any other customer."

"I'm exactly the opposite," I lied. "I'm such a sucker for celebrity fashion trends. It's embarrassing to admit it, but I'm actually here because I heard that Jennifer Aniston was buying a Vera Wang."

"Oh, I wish she was," she said, draping a garment bag over her arm. "Could you imagine what that would do for our business? Unfortunately, I haven't seen her step foot in the door since I started working here." So there I had it: a lead killed on the spot.

Clearly, *Globe* had been given yet another of the many false tips that were continually funneled into the tabloids. Sometimes such tips were deliberately planted to send reporters in the wrong direction. Occasionally, these misleading tips were suggested by publicists to protect the privacy of their clients. I was surprised to learn that some of these tips even came from our competitors. By throwing us off track, other magazines could then follow the real story and scoop exclusives.

Whether or not the Aniston lead was true or false, there was no way I could instantly drop my masquerade as an undercover bride. By this time, assistants were already pulling my selection of dresses off the racks. Trapped, I followed the bridal consultant into the dressing room. I was stunned by the irony of my situation. My relationship with Caelan now seemed years away from any sort of permanent commitment. We had never discussed marriage, nor had the thought crossed my mind. After months together, our relationship seemed to have flatlined.

How long should it take until a woman knows that she's found "the one"? Are men like wine and cheese? Do they improve with time?

Unlocking the dressing room door, the consultant carefully hung the selected gowns and unzipped the garment bags. "Just call if you need me," she said, closing the door behind her.

I had no intention of trying on the dresses. It seemed almost sacrilegious, especially considering I was falling out of love. After the door closed, I dropped onto the white satin bench and felt a lump beginning to form in my throat. My eyes welled up.

Why am I crying so much lately?

My emotions were spared by two faint knocks on the dressing room door. "Are you okay in there?"

Stepping out of the room, I surrendered the gown to the waiting saleswoman. "I'm sorry to have wasted your time. But I just can't go through with this."

Suddenly, this one-hour acquaintance reached out her arms and gave me a hug. Patting my back, she said softly, "It's perfectly normal to have doubts before the wedding. This sort of thing happens all the time."

I let her believe whatever she wanted to believe. It was virtually impossible to explain my sadness, even if I had tried. I might as well accept the truth. I would forever remain a bride-stalker and never a bride.

Note:

After dating for two years, Jennifer Aniston and Brad Pitt were married on July 29, 2000. Their divorce was finalized on October 2, 2005. Shiloh, his daughter with Angelina Jolie, was born in 2006.

In 2002, Geraldo Rivera married his fifth wife, Erica Levy, with whom he has one daughter.

CHAPTER 15

Seven Pounds of Trail Mix

B y this time, I had started to dread coming into the office. More and more I was being assigned prearranged interviews that required minimal investigative effort. Even before giving me the lead sheets for such assignments, the editors would have predetermined which direction they wanted the stories to take. This completely sucked the journalistic challenge out of my job, and I wanted it back. I was sure I was being sent on another one of those unwelcome assignments when Caelan called me over to his desk.

"Marlise," Caelan said. "Yer being sent to Portland to interview Tonya Harding." The figure skater had just been charged with fourth-degree domestic violence against her boyfriend, Darren Silver. "It'll be an easy one," Caelan assured me. "You'll be back before the weekend."

His confidence came from *Globe*'s long-established relationship with Tonya, who had sold us stories in the past. Facing a publication time crunch, Caelan sent me straight to LAX while he tried to set up an interview with the figure skater by phone. Moments after my plane touched down in Oregon, my cell phone rang.

"So, how's the story coming?" Caelan had a tendency to seem overeager when he was in charge of an assignment.

Pulling the handle out of my portable luggage, I wheeled toward the Dollar Rent A Car counter. "Fine, considering that I'm still at baggage claim."

"Oh." There was a long pause before he continued. "Well, I have an address for you. 'Tis Tonya and Darren's place where the brawl occurred."

Grabbing a pen, I jotted down the Camas, Washington, address.

"The drive'll be 'bout half an hour for you," Caelan explained. "Hopefully, by the time you get there, I'll have arranged a deal with Tonya."

"You mean she still doesn't know I'm here?" I asked.

"Not quite," Caelan said. "She just got arrested so it ain't so simple to reach 'er. No one's answerin' the phone at her house neither, but I'll keep trying."

I was becoming increasingly annoyed at the disorganization of this assignment.

"And another thin' . . ." Caelan's voice dropped into a low whisper. "I miss you."

His comment unexpectedly threw me from my one world into the other, reminding me that we were, in fact, a couple. "I miss you, too," I mumbled.

It wasn't easy bouncing back and forth between all my identities. I had learned to accept it as just another part of the job. "Gimme a ring when you get to their place," Caelan added, returning to his editor's tone before hanging up the phone.

The moment I reached the address Caelan had given me, I was sure there had to have been some sort of mistake. At the end of a dusty road sat a small frame house stuck between an open garage and a dilapidated barn. Although this was a farmhouse, there was no sign of animals other than a barking dog. Scattered motorbikes and rusty pickups were perched on top of cement blocks. Overgrown weeds, patches of dandelions, and sun-faded beer cans indicated neglect. Stepping from the rental car, I headed toward the wooden porch that was peeling and splintered from one too many harsh winters. Just as I reached for the screen door, I heard the sound of tires on gravel approaching from the driveway. The car abruptly stopped in a cloud of dust. Inside the car was Tonya Harding, accompanied by an older couple.

Waving at them from the porch, I waited for the trio to get out of the car before I approached. "Hello," I said, handing the man my card. "My name is Marlise. I'm not sure if my associate, Caelan Dunmore, has been in touch with Tonya, but I was hoping to discuss Tuesday night's event for our publication."

Acting as if I did not exist, Tonya walked right past me toward the house. She was wearing a flannel shirt over snug acid-washed jeans that tapered at the ankles. Her blond perm and straight bangs hadn't changed much since her days as a skater at the 1992 Winter Olympics. Stepping onto the porch, Tonya slammed the door behind her as her tight pony-tail swung back and forth like a horse's tail.

"I'll handle this, Linda," the man said to the older woman who was still sitting in the car.

Before he had a chance to continue, I explained, "I realize the timing of my arrival is not ideal, but unfortunately I'm under a tight deadline. We've worked with Tonya in the past and I promise to make this as painless and profitable as possible."

The man looked down at my card. "Actually, we're only here to pick up a few of Tonya's things. I'm afraid you'll have to wait until after the trial. Otherwise, you may want to talk to her lawyer, Steven Thayer."

"Are you Tonya's father?" I asked.

His answer was interrupted by yet another slam of the screen door. Invisible once more, I was again ignored by Tonya, who tossed two black trash bags into the trunk.

"Greg, let's go," Tonya demanded.

With all three passengers now in the car, I talked to them through the window as the engine started. "Just give me a call if you get a chance."

They drove away, leaving me coughing in their dusty wake. Calling Caelan, I explained that his name had carried very little weight during my pitch to Tonya. Based on my description, he informed me that I had just spoken with Tonya's godparents, Greg and Linda Lewis. Their rejection didn't matter, however, because the editors no longer wanted an interview with Tonya. Now, they wanted a tell-all from the "beaten and bloodied" boyfriend. The only problem was that no one could find him. While Caelan worked his tabloid magic from LA, I called every matched listing in the Camas Yellow Pages. After an afternoon of unsuccessful hits, I started to knock on doors. Finally I was getting warmer.

"Sorry to bother you, sir," I said when the door opened. "But I'm looking for a Darren Silver."

"Oh Darren's staying at a friend's house right now," the man said. "At least for a while, anyhow."

"So you know him?" I asked.

The man laughed. "I should hope so. Darren's my son."

Houston, we've made contact.

"Do you know how I can reach Darren? I'm trying to get in touch with him regarding the fight with Tonya. It's for an article I'm working on."

"I might have that number here somewhere," he said, leaving me on the front doorstep. When he returned, he offered a phone number, along with photographs of Darren and the skater. He also shared stories of Tonya, who often visited their home, always trying to be the center of attention. He told me of the couple's fight that had started with dinner at Sidelines Sports Bar and had ended at their home, when the police were called. By the time I drove away, I knew that if nothing else, I could write the article from the father's point of view.

With the contact information I had provided from Darren's father, Caelan arranged for Darren and me to discuss *Globe*'s offer. Darren would agree to meet with me himself only on the condition his lawyer would be present. With *Globe*'s contract in hand, I headed to the attorney's office, where Darren and his lawyer were waiting inside a conference room. Before the meeting, Caelan had told me to offer no more than $10,000 for an exclusive tell-all including photographs. As I entered the conference room, only the lawyer stood to shake my hand. Darren, dressed in a plaid button-down shirt and black baseball cap, remained seated at the far end of a long wooden table. The only proof that Tonya had attacked him was a small scratch above his upper lip.

Looking around the room, I noticed that the only available chair was at the complete opposite end of the long table. "Thanks for meeting me on such short notice," I shouted across the room.

"I'm not taking a penny less than twenty thousand," Darren hollered. "I know how you tabloids work and I know what my story's worth."

Ignoring Darren's bark, I pulled out the contract and slid it across the table for the lawyer to review. "This is our standard source agreement.

We are prepared to pay five thousand dollars for the exclusive rights to Darren's story."

Throwing his hat onto the table, Darren stood up from his chair and headed toward the door. Clearly there were some anger management issues going on.

"Calm down, Darren," the lawyer urged in a soothing voice. "This is a customary financial negotiation. You need to sit down and relax."

I was totally confused. "Am I missing something here? I thought Darren had agreed to sell his story to us."

"Only for the right price," Darren interrupted. He then pointed toward his attorney. "And don't try and make me settle for anything less. I know I can sell this story for a whole lot more."

"Here's the deal," I explained. "I'm going to step outside for about five minutes and let you two get onto the same page. Try and settle on a dollar amount and I'll see what we can do. Clearly, we're not going to give you twenty thousand dollars for this story, because frankly, it's not worth anything close to that. If you feel you can sell it elsewhere for that amount, by all means, be my guest. But if we do come to a financial agreement, I will need Darren's cooperation and honesty on everything I ask."

There was silence as I walked away. When I returned to the room, Darren's hands were folded on the table in front of him. He looked toward his lawyer as if giving him the cue to speak. The lawyer gave him a single nod in return.

"My client is prepared to sign the contract for ten thousand dollars, on the condition that he receives final copy approval of the article."

It seemed fair enough to me, yet as reporters, we were expected to barter as low as possible. "If you agree to nine thousand dollars, I'll guarantee copy approval and an early story payment."

Darren, who seemed much calmer now, gave his lawyer a single nod. He, in turn, passed the nod onto me. It was a like silent version of the telephone game. After Darren signed the contract, the lawyer stepped out of the room so that I could conduct the interview with Darren alone.

"So it all got started when I was eating my pork chop dinner while Tonya was slamming beers at the poker machine," Darren explained. "We go there about three times a week because Tonya loves to gamble with my money. She was up six hundred dollars but then just kept playing and lost it all."

According to Darren, Tonya refused to leave the bar, claiming she was on the verge of hitting the jackpot. Once they got inside Darren's Jeep, he said Tonya kept screaming, "I'm not drunk. I'm not slurring. I don't need you anymore because I'm gonna be in the Ice Capades."

The rendering of Darren's two-hour story fit every redneck stereotype the editors had hoped for, from the drunken ice princess to the chrome hubcap she threw at his head. "She was beating the hell out of me and I kept backpedaling because I had nowhere else to go," Darren said. "I was afraid she was going to either kill me or end up hurting herself to make it look like I beat her."

His story continued. After the police arrived, they took statements from witnesses, checked Tonya's body for injuries, and charged her with fourth-degree domestic violence assault. So far his report sounded quite predictable. The story needed at least one tabloid shocker. In March 1994, Tonya Harding had pleaded guilty to obstructing the investigation of Nancy Kerrigan's attack. Tonya subsequently maintained that she was innocent of any involvement. It was, however, a topic that would not die.

Now, throwing out the bait, I asked Darren, "So do you think Tonya was capable of planning the 1994 attack on Nancy Kerrigan?"

Without hesitation, Darren answered, "I know that Tonya was involved in the whacking. We've talked about it several times and she keeps slipping up and can never keep her story straight. I know she's guilty and there's not a doubt in my mind that she has it in her. Tonya's vindictive, possessed, and has a devil living inside her. There's no telling what will make her snap. During the 1999 ESPN Championship, her emotions were so up and down because of all the steroids and pills she was popping to help her cope with her diagnosed manic depression. I'm just relieved to have Tonya out of my life now."

Following the interview, I phoned Caelan to tell him how well things had turned out. Unsure of exactly what the editors wanted, Caelan asked that I type up the entire interview and fax it directly from my hotel to Florida. In the meantime, *Globe*'s freelance photographer would independently meet with Darren to take pictures of his scratched lip.

Despite the fact Darren was a first-hand source, I also interviewed neighbors and employees at Sidelines Sports Bar, where the argument had started. Everyone in town was more than cooperative, professing their hatred for Tonya and their love for the tabloids. It was the only time I had ever been asked for my autograph in connection with my profession as a tabloid reporter. Deadlines were met, editors were happy, and I was going back to LA just in time for Saturday night. It seemed to be a win-win situation for everyone except Tonya.

"Welcome back to hell," Sharmin said, handing me my stack of messages.

"I never left," I told her. "I was in Camas, remember?"

"Well apparently they love you there," she said. "This Darren Silver guy has phoned you five times in the last hour."

Dialing his number, I fully expected Darren to thank me for the rush payment on his $9,000 check. Instead, he demanded that *Globe* run a retraction of the story. "How dare you print a photograph of me looking completely beaten up? You know I didn't look like that. No matter how much I hate Tonya, it's just not right to publish a doctored photograph that can affect someone's future."

I had no clue what he was talking about. "Look Darren, I just walked in the door and I haven't even seen the article yet."

"The article's fine," he interjected. "It's the photo that I have a problem with."

There had to be some explanation. As long as I had worked for *Globe*, I had never known them to tamper with a photograph in a way that could lead to legal action. "Give me an hour and I'll get back to you," I told him.

I asked Sharmin for the latest issue of the magazine. Turning to the cover story, I hardly recognized the man in the photograph. In *Globe*'s picture, the entire left side of Darren's face was bruised and his eye was nearly swollen shut. There were also two cuts on his lip that split all the way up to the base of his nose. Throwing the magazine on Caelan's desk, I demanded an explanation. "What the hell is this?"

He looked down at my story. "I think the article turned out rather well, don't you?"

"No, Caelan, I'm talking about the photograph, not the article. Darren looked nothing like this when I saw him shortly after his fight with Tonya."

Caelan's expression remained neutral. "You know the editorial department has nothing to do with photo layout. Perhaps, Madeline knows something 'bout it."

Madeline gave me more or less the same explanation as Caelan, adding, "Well, it's too late to do anything about it now. If it bothers you that much, ask Richard Hughes in the photo department."

Like most of the other Florida-based employees, Richard Hughes existed only as a faceless voice on the other end of the line. When I asked Richard about the photo, he explained, "We wanted to recreate what Darren would have looked like right after the beating. This is entirely justifiable. Plus, we had Darren write a written statement approving the alteration to the picture."

After Darren's complaints, I knew there was no way he had agreed to publication of that photo as it appeared. Richard continued, "If you have a serious problem with the way the story turned out, then you can take it up with Freeze."

Taking it to the top would only move me one step closer to the tabloid guillotine. Realizing that I had hit the proverbial wall, I explained to Darren it was futile to retaliate. Furious, he hung up on me and I never heard from him again.

Four months later, Tonya appeared on CNN's *Larry King Live* holding a copy of my *Globe* article. On air, she blamed the loss of her Ice Capades contract on the fraudulent picture that had been published in our magazine. Her comment made me regret that I had not pursued the issue further. I had allowed myself to be intimidated by my superiors in order to protect my job. In the process, Tonya had lost hers.

There was barely time to let the reality of my work situation digest before I was sent off on my next adventure. That same week, more than 22 million viewers had tuned in to watch TV's first reality game show, *Who Wants to Marry a Millionaire?* Darva Conger and Rick Rockwell had become a leading topic of conversation following their impromptu marriage on national television. Knowing that the now-familiar faces of the couple could lead to increased sales for *Globe*, Trenton Freeze was ecstatic over the story possibilities.

While Darva and Rick were still honeymooning in the Caribbean, I was handed a lead sheet titled "Millionaire Bride's Own Story." Only through investigation could we find enough information to write an article based on the premise of the lead sheet. Unfortunately, the issue was closing that evening and there was no time for travel or meeting with sources. Within hours, I was able to locate legal documents pertaining to a 1991 restraining order against Rick. The order had been filed by Rick's ex-fiancée, Debbie Goyne, after she had reportedly called off their engagement. Barely meeting *Globe*'s editorial deadline, the final story was titled "TV's Millionaire Bride: I Want Out!"

Everyone from Larry King to Matt Lauer had arranged to interview the highly publicized bride and groom, who were just returning from their honeymoon. *Globe*'s editors were determined to stay inside the media loop. The following day, I submitted a lead stating, "Is TV's *Millionaire* couple really in love? Let's follow the newlyweds and see if they live in separate homes. Do they have other lovers? Is she buying gifts with his cash? Is the whole thing a scam?"

The lead sheet came back approved from Florida and sat untouched on my desk. I could begin working on it only after Madeline moved the assignment up on the priority list. During this two-week waiting period, the newlyweds annulled their TV marriage. This only served to spark increased interest in the noncelebrity celebrities.

"I realize you are supposed to have the weekend off," Madeline acknowledged. "But your *Millionaire* lead has been slightly reworked." Handing me a new lead sheet, I read the words, "My Dinner with Rick Rockwell—*Globe* reporter goes on a date with *Millionaire* groom."

I looked up from the page. "I assume that I'm the '*Globe* reporter' . . . ?"

Madeline was smirking now, fighting back a grin between tight lips. "I'm sure Rick's not as bad as he sounds. He lives in San Diego, so at least you can enjoy the city while you're there. Plus, I've assigned Edward Townsend on photos. You two are friends, right?"

I nodded hesitantly, thinking back to the $75,000 business proposition he had offered me on the Brad and Jennifer photos.

"Yeah, we're friends. So, what do I have to do, exactly?" I asked. "You don't expect me to seduce this guy for a story, do you?"

"Don't be ridiculous, Marlise. Just go to his home and invite him to dinner or something. Play it by ear. Do whatever you think works best for a headline. Trust me, this guy loves publicity and he'll be grateful for a chance to appear in *Globe*."

That evening I met Edward in the lobby of La Jolla's Grande Colonial Hotel as arranged. "Fancy meeting you here, luv. So, have you already registered at the night desk?" Edward jangled his room key and glanced at the reception counter.

"I can't stay at this hotel," I said, scanning the room rates. "I don't have pre-approval from the expense department and it's over my regular per diem."

Edward shook his head. "Oh, do come on Marlise. Are you still so young and naïve? You've only to tell the editors that all the other lodging was booked. They'll buy your story, you know. After all, this is the peak of tourist season. No one will ever question your expense report. But do hurry along, dear. I'm quite famished."

It only took me a second to realize Edward was right. Besides, this was the least the editors could do for taking away yet another weekend. After checking into the hotel, I met Edward at a nearby Thai restaurant.

"So what's tomorrow's schedule, then?" Edward asked.

"I wish I had one," I responded. "I may just go alone to Rick's house and then give you a call once I have a plan."

Considering that a woman had once filed a restraining order against Rick, I decided it was probably best to notify him prior to my arrival. Our phone conversation was brief, but Rick seemed to be open to an impromptu date with a tabloid reporter. Locating his contact information had been something of a challenge for *Globe*'s research department. Contrary to media reports, Rick was actually a stand-up comedian rather than a real estate developer. The name "Rockwell" was, in fact, a stage name that he had chosen out of the phone book. His birth name was Richard Scott Balkey. I was beginning to believe that there was more, or perhaps less, to the 43-year-old groom than the public realized.

Arriving at his modest home in San Diego County, I was greeted by

Rick, who was dressed in grey sweatpants and a white T-shirt. Holding a cordless phone in one hand, he shook my hand with the other. Opening the door wide enough for me to enter, he mouthed the words, "I'll be just a second."

The living room was bare, with blank walls and one faded white couch facing the front door. I wondered if he had just moved in. As far as I could see, however, there were no signs of unpacked boxes. There was a '70s feel about the place, with its gold curtains, cottage cheese ceilings, white brick fireplace, and shag carpet.

"Sorry about that," Rick said, coming back into the room. "I've been on the phone literally all day. I've got interviews and book deals and movie deals . . . maybe I should get married more often."

He waited for me to laugh and then he laughed even louder than I had. Staring at him, I honestly had no idea how this man's face had ended up on every magazine cover and news channel in America. "I bet your life has changed quite a bit," I said.

Rick nodded slowly with his eyes closed. "You have no idea, Marlise, no idea. . . . Hey, can I get you something to drink?"

"Sure, what do you have?"

He walked toward the kitchen. "Unfortunately, I've been too busy to shop. All I can offer you is water."

"Water is fine," I called back.

"Sorry about my appearance," Rick said, fanning out his baggy sweatpants like bat wings. "I wanted to go to the gym today, but never got around to it because of all the phone calls."

I could taste the chlorinated water running down my throat. "Don't worry about it. I'll be in San Diego the whole weekend. If you aren't too exhausted tomorrow, then maybe we can work out together. I can even take you grocery shopping if you have the time. You know, sort of kill a flock of birds with one stone."

Rick took a long swig of his water. "That would be excellent. Ever since the show aired, I've been slammed with e-mails and letters and calls for public appearances. It's gotten even worse since the annulment. Come check this out."

I followed him into his office, where a computer showed that he had one hundred and twenty-nine new messages. "Can you believe it? Look at all this fan mail. I have hundreds of photos from women who want to meet me. Most of the girls encourage me to stay strong and consider the failed marriage a learning experience. Other women send me nude pictures and ask if I want to marry them."

While Rick continued to download his messages, I jumped onto his NordicTrack machine. It was just like the ones I had seen countless times on infomercials. "Do these things really work?" I asked, awkwardly moving my legs like a cross-country skier.

Rick answered without looking up from his computer. "Sure they do. I usually work out a few hours before I start my sit-ups and push-ups."

The ungraceful sound of my tempo-less strides must have caught Rick's attention. Quickly leaving his computer, he placed his hand on the small of my back and helped me regain my balance. Letting out a nervous giggle, I jumped off the machine and said, "Why don't you show me how it's done?"

Grabbing hold of the cables, Rick slid his shoes onto the wooden platforms and began to glide his legs back and forth. "See, just like that, nice and smooth. I've been thinking about turning this room into a fitness studio, but I'm not quite sure yet. Perhaps I'll invest in a few free weights, maybe some barbells."

Rick seemed to be talking to himself as I looked around the threadbare room. "So, did you just move in?" I asked.

"No. I've been here about a year now," he explained. "I just didn't want to buy any furniture because I had planned on decorating the place with my new wife. Come on, I'll give you a tour." It took thirty seconds to walk through the two-bedroom house. We even peeked into the speckle-tiled bathroom and examined a basketful of hotel soap. "See there," Rick said, pointing to one label. "That one's from my honeymoon in Barbados."

Just then, the phone rang. It was Rick's manager reminding him of a speaking engagement later that night. Hanging up the phone, Rick apologized and asked if we could reschedule for another time.

I had no intention of sacrificing another weekend on account of Rick

Rockwell. "Why don't we just meet up after your event?"

Rick looked at his scratched Timex watch. "I probably won't be done until around ten o'clock. Is that too late?"

"No, that's fine. Just tell me where you want to meet."

"How about at the Belly Up Tavern in Solana Beach?" he suggested. "Say, around ten thirty?"

"Perfect. I'll see you then."

When I arrived at the club, Rick was standing at the curb waiting to open my car door. "Well, hello, beautiful." Apparently Rick had already thrown back a few drinks during his previous event. He seemed revived and much more energized. "I've heard this is a good place to dance all night if you're in the mood."

While he made small talk with the doorman, I paid our $35 cover charge for a band called Tainted Love. Walking inside, Rick nervously eyed the crowd. "This is the first time I've really been out in public since the wedding. I'm not exactly sure what to expect tonight."

It was an untailored crowd, with thirty-something locals dressed in jeans and casual tops. As we entered, nearly every head turned toward Rick, who was wearing a dark blue suit and rainbow tie. Women moved in closer to take a look at the man of the hour. Several even asked for his autograph.

"Oh my gosh!" One woman pointed back and forth between Rick and me. "Are you cheating on Darva with this girl?"

Shaking my head violently, I tried to diminish the accusation, but Rick only fed into the rumor by putting his arm around my waist. Spinning loose from his grip, I said, "I'll go get us some drinks."

I watched as Rick exchanged phone numbers with several women while throwing out the line, "Okay, but don't tell my wife!" I must have heard him use that same joke twenty times during the night. In all my celebrity encounters, I had never seen one man receive so much attention. It almost made me ashamed to be a woman.

Returning with the drinks, I heard one fan say consolingly, "Only time can heal your pain."

Turning toward the small pack of spectators, Rick yelled, "And a blow-up doll wouldn't hurt, either!" There was no doubt that Rick was a stand-up comedian. Everything he said and did seemed rehearsed and unnatural, as if he were performing in front of an audience. I extended a bottle toward Rick, who reached for the neck and took a swig. Grabbing my hand, Rick led me to a table in the back corner of the bar.

"Thanks for rescuing me," he said.

I shifted into the horseshoe booth. "I had no idea your life would be like this."

"Me neither." He motioned toward the bar for another round of drinks. I had yet to take a sip of my first. With '80s cover tunes blaring in the background, Rick began to share what had happened during his honeymoon with Darva and the events that led to the annulment of their marriage.

"You know, it's just too bad I never had a chance to show her my bedroom magic." Rick made it sound like a bit in his stand-up comedy routine.

"What do you mean?" I asked, probing for more information.

Rick inched his way toward me. "I'm no Wilt Chamberlain, but let's just say I've had my fair share of experience. You see, Marlise, two things need to exist to make a marriage work: laughter and good sex. If you have those qualities, then it's sure to succeed."

His plan sounded so easy, as if humanity could survive off of the scientifically proven nympho-clown theory.

"I hate to brag," Rick continued. "But I'm absolutely amazing in bed."

Easy, tiger. I pushed the beers beyond his reach.

"During the day, I'm hyper and sometimes even goofy, but at night, I become a calm and gentle teddy bear."

Did I just hear a grown man refer to himself as a teddy bear?

"There's nothing I enjoy more than spooning a woman between the sheets. Genetically, I have an abnormally high body temperature. My skin gives off a soothing heat because I work out so much."

Reaching over, Rick touched his hand to my cheek. "Can ya' feel that?"

"Yep," I nodded. "Kind of like an oven mitt."

"I like to think of myself as a Dr. Jekyll and Mr. Hyde," he continued. "Two totally different lovers."

It wasn't a stretch to imagine.

"I can gently nibble on a woman's ear, but then I can also be an animal and rip off her clothes with my teeth."

I recoiled as I stared at his jagged chompers. The thought sounded painful.

Rick leaned forward, pursed his lips, and asked with a nod, "Are you following me here?"

Trying to stay professional to gain insight into his life, I realized that our conversation had gone completely overboard. Sliding out of the booth, I excused myself and headed to the restroom. I looked into the mirror and tried to press the flushed color out of my cheeks. When I returned, I found Rick drumming his hands on the table to the beat of the music. It was nearly one in the morning and the bartender was ringing the tavern triangle to announce last call for alcohol. Rick caught me yawning.

"No way, missy, you're not going anywhere until we dance."

Tugging me by the arm, he led me to the dance floor like a child dragging a floppy rag doll. The band was playing "Come On Eileen." I had never quite figured out how to dance to songs from the '80s. With Rick's first gyration, our twenty-year age gap suddenly became apparent. I moved my hips and stayed more or less grounded, while Rick kicked his feet straight out in front of his body like a Radio City Rockette. I could tell we were both trying to relate to the other's dance steps, but I just couldn't seem to pick up the same beat as Rick.

"Great moves, Marlise," Rick cheered with approval. "You really know how to groove. The only problem is that your pants are falling down."

I looked at my low-waist pants and realized that my attempt at trendy fashion didn't seem to jive with Rick's polyester suit. Before I could justify my ensemble, Rick grabbed my hand and spun me around in a series of erratic circles. I was dipped, twisted, yanked, and wrenched around the floor, nearly losing my footing because my long hair kept covering my face and blinding my vision.

"No, let me lead," Rick yelled above the music as he suddenly switched to the waltz. "This will work a lot better if you just relax."

"You're a maniac on the dance floor, Rick," I said, clearing the curtain of hair that hung between us. When I slowly backed away for fear of personal injury, Rick didn't even seem to notice I was gone. He closed his eyes, bit his bottom lip, and sort of shimmied around the club alone for the remainder of the night. On our way out, Rick stopped at a parked cop car and pretended to urinate on the bumper. I didn't know how much more I could take.

"So are we on for a workout tomorrow?" he asked.

Suddenly I thought about Edward and the fact we needed photos for our story. I had taken several shots inside the club, but nothing that could support a headline.

"Sure, I'll call you in the morning." As I reached out my hand, Rick pulled me toward him and kissed me on the cheek.

"So, are you getting paid to seduce me?" he whispered into my ear. His hot breath smelled like beer.

"No, not really." My story was turning into the assignment from hell.

At nine the following morning, Edward and I met Rick at his home in Encinitas.

As we waited, Edward pointed toward a rusted truck in the driveway and asked, "Might that be Rick's lorry?"

"I think so," I whispered back. "But he insists he's getting a new Lexus next week."

Suddenly the front door of the house was flung open and Rick came jogging out, humming the theme song from *Rocky*. He was dressed in white shorts and a black tank top that drooped at his chest and armpits.

"Hello, sunshine," I said, somewhat surprised by his endless energy.

Rick stretched upward toward the sky before springing into a series of jumping jacks. "I hope you two are ready to get your hearts pumping."

After my brief introduction, Edward held up his camera and said, "Well, I'm afraid I'll have to leave the workout to the two of you."

Rick insisted we drive in one car—mine—for ecological reasons. While he climbed into the backseat, I rolled my eyes at Edward. During the drive, Rick mentioned his future Lexus at least three times. That morning, our plan was to work out at Frogs Club One in Solana Beach. We found it odd that Rick claimed he had been training there six days a week but couldn't remember where the gym was located. Once inside,

Rick filled out a visitor's pass rather than showing a membership card like everyone else. His $10 entrance fee was waived and he was handed a free club T-shirt.

"I'm going to hit the StairMaster for a thirty-minute cardio," Rick said, tossing a towel over his shoulder. "I'll meet you guys back at the barbells." Sure enough, Rick was a stallion among the best of hard bodies. Women kept interrupting his workout for autographs and even offered to give him advice on love. Watching from afar, Edward and I wondered how a man like Rick had been able to hit the pinnacle of fame overnight. Although I was already staring straight at him, Rick suddenly whistled from across the gym as if to get my attention.

"I guess that's my cue," I mumbled to Edward.

There was sweat rolling down the center of Rick's hairy chest and he seemed a bit pinkish in color. "Can you spot me on the weights?"

I nodded without giving a verbal response.

"And don't get too close," he added. "I'm a bit gamey."

My weak little chicken arms started to shake as I attempted to help Rick pump iron on almost every machine in the gym. We finished off at the punching bag, where Rick lightly thumped the base with his pointed toe. He looked more like a ballerina than a boxer.

"Oh, do hold that pose," Edward coaxed, snapping dozens of shots one after the other. "Now, Mr. Rockwell, can you give it one more hard wallop for the camera?"

With a single nod of compliance, Rick delicately toe-punched the bag. Lowering his leg to the ground, Rick then clapped his hands and announced, "Okay team, let's hit the showers."

Edward and I looked at each other, wondering who on earth he was talking to. Thirty minutes later, we regrouped for an early lunch at Del Mar's Poseidon restaurant. Rick suggested that I park at a meter on the side of the road. I told him I was low on quarters and might need to change some bills inside.

"There's no need to," he said. "I have a few quarters here somewhere."

While I waited expectantly, Rick turned his back, conveniently ignoring me as he gazed toward the sea. Scraping through my purse, I eventually threw in nickels and dimes to bring the ticking meter to the one-hour mark. All I wanted now was to get through the beachside brunch and head home.

"Do you want to split an omelet?" Rick asked, glancing at the menu.

"Get whatever you want," I told him. "This one's on me."

At that cue, Rick ordered a smoked salmon omelet, a side of potatoes, a fruit platter, two slices of wheat toast, and a glass of freshly squeezed orange juice. As usual, our conversation focused on the single topic of money. He repeatedly called the waitress by name after glancing at her name tag and periodically said, "Wonderful, Kristine. Thanks a million." Rick mopped his plate with the crust of his bread.

"There's a big tip coming for you, Kristine," he said, handing over the spotless platter. Keeping my promise to pick up the tab, I paid both the bill and the "big tip."

When we returned to my car, there was a $50 parking ticket on the windshield. If only Rick had given me a quarter, he could have saved me this hassle. Instead, he just shook his head at the ticket and said, "Gee, I feel really bad about that. Let's just forget all about it and take a stroll on the beach."

Like the paparazzo he was, Edward had a plan from the start. "Mr. Rockwell, could you demonstrate your proposal techniques for the camera?"

As if a film crew were on hand, Rick knelt in the sand, grabbed my hand, and said dramatically, "Marlise Kast, will you marry me?" He held the pose while Edward snapped a series of shots. "Actually, it's not that far of a stretch," Rick continued. "I already know you much better than I know Darva."

By this point, I was so bored that I just laughed off his comment. By two o'clock on Saturday, I anticipated that our lingering date had finally come to an end. Instead, Rick shamelessly reminded me that his kitchen cupboards were bare. "I intend to hold you to your promise to go shopping with me," he said.

As soon as we arrived at Henry's Marketplace in Solana Beach, Rick grabbed a cart and started filling it with potted plants and garden supplies from an outside display. Holding up a pot of purple flowers and one of white flowers, Rick asked a salesgirl, "Which one is your favorite color?" When she did not respond, he smiled and said, as he put them in the cart, "I like them both, too."

Even before we entered the store, Rick had stocked up on two house-plants, a bag of topsoil, and a three-pound sack of nectarines. While Edward and I trailed behind, Rick headed straight for the wine aisle.

"Do you see any Merlot over there?" Two bottles of Merlot and three bottles of Chardonnay later, Rick then tossed in honey turkey breast and roast beef. The cart started to overflow before my eyes.

"Do you need some help, Rick?" I asked.

He was too busy digging into a barrel of trail mix to notice my sar-casm. At first I thought Rick was playing some kind of joke as he shoveled ten scoops of trail mix into a plastic bag. He then twisted the bag shut and threw it into the cart on top of his blueberry pie, chocolate chip cookies, fig bars, and deli sandwiches.

"I love this stuff," Rick said as he ripped off another Baggie. "I just can't get enough of it." To my surprise, he then filled a second bag with the peanut mixture, grabbing seven pounds of trail mix in total.

"Careful there, Rick," I warned. "One scoop of trail mix can lead to flatulence." Rick didn't seem to notice my warning. He was too busy looking for the cracker aisle.

"Hey, do you like hummus?" he asked, as if my taste buds could somehow affect his selection. Just then, two containers of garlic hum-mus came whizzing past my head, landing in the cart.

"Heads up!" Rick yelled, throwing a packet of pita bread across the aisle like a Frisbee. Finally we made our way to the register, unloading the goods and watching them skate across the conveyer belt.

"Is your name Breann?" Rick flirtingly asked the checkout clerk. "Am I reading your name tag right? Breann?"

She nodded.

"You're a regular pro with that laser scanner, Breann. I love how you make it look so easy."

She remained silent and only looked up to mutter the final total. Only once during the course of my two-day assignment did Rick offer to pay for anything, and even then, it was only a beer. Ultimately, *Globe* picked up the grocery tab, too, because Rick couldn't seem to dig into his pockets fast enough. Every time I took out my wallet, Rick stared at my wad of cash like a kid in a candy store. He seemed to be counting the bills with his eyes as I fanned them out in front of me.

After dropping Edward at the hotel, I took Rick back to his home to unload his fifteen bags of groceries. As I climbed over the rear seat for the last load, Rick yelled from the house, "Check the floor to make sure nothing fell out. I sure wouldn't want to leave anything behind."

Once in the kitchen, Rick started unpacking the bags. The cupboards were literally bare except for a collection of half-empty bottles of hotel lotion and soap. His fridge had a single glass of water on the shelf, most likely the one that I had failed to finish the day before. Struggling to be polite, I said, "Let me know if I can help."

Rick was busy emptying bags of trail mix into a used, cardboard Quaker Oats container. A few almonds and chocolate chips slipped from the bag and landed on a tattered dishtowel that covered the yellow-tiled countertop. Rather than shaking the towel over the sink, Rick carefully folded the rag in half, cradled the mixture in the center and then shook the loose bits back into the box. At one point, a single peanut fell onto the floor and rolled into the corner. Bending down, Rick picked it up and tossed it back into the container.

"So, am I everything that you expected me to be?" Rick asked. With a lick of his finger, he pressed down on several stray oat flakes before flicking them into the cereal box.

"Actually, you're much different than I had imagined," I said.

He opened his fridge and eyed his new stock of goods. "What do you mean, 'different'?"

"Don't take this the wrong way, Rick, but you don't really seem like a millionaire."

Suddenly he seemed to get defensive. "Just because I'm rich doesn't mean I have to be wasteful or flashy with my things."

"I couldn't agree with you more," I said. "All I'm saying is that you're not at all like the guy everyone saw on TV."

"Well, that's showbiz for you," he said, with a laugh. "Come on, I'll walk you to your car."

It seemed that our date had finally come to an end. I reached out to shake Rick's hand and this time, he gave me a friendly farewell hug.

"Good luck with everything," I said.

"Thanks, Marlise. I can't wait to see how the article turns out."

Me neither.

That Sunday, I typed through the night until I had written every detail of my weekend with Rick. Not quite sure what the editors wanted, I abandoned the typical tabloid lingo and wrote the article as a first-person account. It was four in the morning by the time I faxed my sixteen pages of copy to the editors. Edward had also processed his pictures and had transmitted them to Florida during the night.

Three hours later, my phone rang.

"Marlise, this is brilliant."

"Good morning, Madeline," I said, trying to hide my scratchy voice. "Did Florida get my story?"

"Get it? They loved it! You had the entire *Globe* staff in hysterics this morning. You should have heard them during the conference call. Honestly, Marlise, I had no idea you could write."

Her comment caught me off guard. After all, I had been writing tabloid stories for nearly two years. It was sobering to realize that even *Globe*'s editors did not regard tabloid reporting as legitimate writing.

"They want to keep the piece as a first-person account," Madeline continued. "It will run as a cover story called 'My Nightmare Date with *Millionaire* Groom.' What do you think?"

"Sounds good," I said. "As long as I can keep my anonymity."

Madeline laughed. "Marlise, we chase celebrities. We don't become them."

The next week as I stood in line at the grocery store, I glanced at the magazine rack and was startled to see my photograph on the cover of *Globe.* There had to be some explanation. Grabbing the issue, I read the headline "*Millionaire* Groom Proposes to New Gal on First Date." Inside were six photographs of Rick with me, including an eight-by-five of us together on the beach. Utterly embarrassed, I flipped the entire stack of magazines face down and dialed Madeline from inside the store. "So, what happened to my anonymity?"

She was laughing on the other end. "Oh come on, Marlise. You look great. What's the big deal?"

"The big deal is that my face is out there now. I'll never be able to sneak into weddings or parties or funerals again."

"Don't flatter yourself," she said. "Fame is brief. A week from now, no one will remember this."

She was wrong. That month, I received phone calls from people I hadn't seen since junior high. Relatives, friends, and even members of my father's church commented on the article. The worst call came from my mother, who first learned of the story while standing in line at a supermarket counter. "How far do you plan on digging yourself into this bottomless career?" she asked.

"I don't know, Mom," I told her. "I honestly don't know."

Note:

In April 2002, Tonya Harding was cited for violation of her 2000 probation. On October 23, 2005, she and her boyfriend, Christopher Nolan, were involved in a fight for which he was charged with assault. The former skater is currently pursuing a career in boxing.

According to his Web site (www.rickrockwell.com), Rick Rockwell self-published a book about his fake marriage, *What Was I Thinking?*

CHAPTER 16

The Tabloid Mafia

There was a tense feeling at *Globe* that no one could quite explain. Madeline's door was suddenly closed more than it was open. Sharmin kept receiving calls from people with high-powered names that she would transfer to Madeline in a whisper. Editors began flying back and forth between LA and Florida, but never stayed long enough for us to determine the reason for their visits. Something major was about to go down at *Globe*. We could sense it, but no one was bold enough to probe. We just kept going about our daily routine, waiting for the inevitable explosion.

"Whatcha working on?" Pete asked, leaning toward my computer.

"'Burt Reynolds Bankrupt,'" I told him. "And you?"

Pete glanced back at his screen. "'Oprah Packs on Sixty-Five Pounds.' Hey, while you're up, can you grab me the Oprah archives from the file room?"

I was sitting down. "But Pete, I'm not up."

"I realize that," Pete said. "But I just assumed you would get up at some stage."

Sharmin spun her chair toward Pete. "Go get it yourself, lazy ass."

"I would," Pete said, "but I'm obesity-challenged."

Sharmin shot a rubber band at Pete's head. "All the more reason."

I pushed my chair away from the desk and stood up.

"Don't do it, Marlise," Sharmin warned. "Don't you go waitin' on Pete. That's how slavery got started."

I was already on my way to get the Oprah file. "What's in it for me, Pete?"

"My sweet loving," Pete said.

Sharmin and I couldn't help bursting out laughing, knowing the office rumor that Pete was a closet homosexual. Walking into the file room, I noticed that the green light was blinking on the communal printer. "I'll bring your copy, too," I called to Pete. "It's coming out right now."

Misunderstanding me, Pete yelled back, "I don't want coffee. I only drink hot cocoa!"

Grabbing the paper from the printer, I flipped over the pages and yelled, "Pete, it's your copy on—"

Suddenly my voice dropped off as I realized I wasn't looking at Pete's article, but rather at Madeline's resume. Frantically, I tried to shove the pages back into the feeder. Turning quickly, I ran directly into my editor.

"Madeline!" Instantly, I knew that she knew I had just seen her resume. "I . . . I . . . can explain," I stuttered. "I thought it was Pete's copy I was grabbing, but then, umm . . ."

Pete's voice echoed from the other room. "I already told you, I don't drink coffee!" The floor shook slightly as he came ponderously down the hall toward us. "What in the Sam Hill is taking so long? There'll be no loving for you tonight, missy!"

Snatching her resume from the printer, Madeline turned to walk out of the file room, instead slamming right into Pete's belly.

"Oh. Hello, Madeline. I didn't realize you were in here."

Now all three of us were crammed into the closet-sized file room. Pete studied our faces while Madeline rolled her resume into a tube. "What's going on in here?" he asked.

Our voices sang in unison. "Nothing."

Sharmin's voice hollered from around the corner. "Hey people— don't leave me out here all by my lonesome!" Her quick footsteps pattered toward us. "What are you two doing in there? Is it time for our *ménage à trois* already?"

Pete inched toward us to make room for Sharmin, who said, "Good morning, Madeline. What brings you to the servant's quarters?"

Madeline held up her roll of papers. "The printer. Mine seems to be jammed."

Everyone stood silently, waiting for someone else to interject.

"Why do you three look so guilty?" Sharmin asked, speaking slowly.

Pete raised his hands in the air as if being held up at gunpoint. "I'm not guilty."

"Neither am I," I said, following his plea of innocence. "I just came in here to grab the Oprah file."

"What are you two working on, anyway?" Madeline asked, trying to change the subject.

"Hold on," Sharmin interrupted. "Will someone just tell me what's going on?"

Madeline lowered her head. "Fine. Everyone in my office. Now."

Like a row of ducklings, we waddled behind Madeline into the confinement of her nest. She closed the door behind her. "Okay, what I'm about to say goes no further than this office."

We all nodded in agreement. "There's a rumor circulating that *Globe* is on the verge of a buyout. Now, nothing is for certain, but I heard that the owner is shopping it around."

"What happens to us?" Pete asked. "Do we have to move to Florida?"

"You know as much as I do," Madeline explained. "All I'm suggesting is that we should all dust off our resumes."

Sharmin was biting her nails. "They couldn't fire us, could they?"

"Well," Madeline said, turning toward her. "If *Globe* were under new ownership, they could do whatever they wanted."

"Maybe there'll be a severance package," I blurted with perhaps too much excitement in my voice.

"You're not going anywhere, Marlise," Madeline said. "You produce the most work and earn the least amount of money in the company."

Ouch. That hurt.

"So that explains what's been taking my contract so long, huh?" I asked.

Madeline nodded. "I imagine that if the company sells, then your contract would still be offered even though it would be under new ownership. But, as I mentioned, this is only speculation. There's no need to panic. And whatever you do, don't tell anyone until it's final."

We returned to our desks and immediately called everyone we knew. Pete told his roommate, Sharmin told her lovers, and I told my family.

Sharmin also wrote up an office memo for Caelan and Karen, inviting them to join her and her daughter at Chuck E. Cheese's for some "fun and office gossip."

Karen canceled at the last minute, but Caelan showed up to give his input on the possible sale of the tabloid. Since joining *Globe*'s LA staff, Caelan had spent most of his time on the road as our roving editor. Despite his frequent absence, it was obvious that he already had an inkling of what was going on.

"I'm not all that bothered, either way," Caelan said, biting into a pizza slice. "Perhaps new ownership would be good for *Globe*. Who knows? We could all be getting a wee bump in pay, ye know."

Grease was dripping down his elbow onto the checkered tablecloth. Reaching forward, I brushed away a thread of cheese dangling from his chin. Both Sharmin and Pete did a double take at my unusual comfort level with our editor. Caelan kicked me under the table and suddenly I realized what I had done.

"Since we're on the subject of surprises," he said, unexpectedly. "You might as well both know that Marlise and I are dating."

I balled up my napkin and pegged it at him. "Caelan, I thought we weren't going to tell anyone."

"Well you're the one messing about and picking cheese bits off me face," he scolded. "You canna expect me to keep this a secret forever. Besides, Pete and Sharmin are family."

Sharmin was shaking her head. "Well, well, well . . . who would've guessed an office romance, right under our very eyes?"

Pete congratulated us both, as if our ability to keep it a secret had been more of an achievement than the relationship itself. "How long have you two been together?"

"Ten months," I answered. Sharmin's daughter, Ryann, was now running over from the Skee-Ball machine.

"Did you hear that?" Sharmin said, plopping Ryann onto her lap. "Marlise and Caelan will be your new parents if Mommy dies."

Ryann clapped her hands together and cheered, "Yippee!" Standing up, she grabbed my hand and begged me to join her in the ball pit.

I turned back toward the table. "Only if everyone comes."

Together, we climbed into the cage of rainbow balls, burying our bodies beneath the colorful mounds to avoid being pelted by our co-workers. Madeline would have died had she seen her prized staff diving into this infantile play pit. But this was us, the tabloid family that stayed together even through times of change. I glanced at each of them, Sharmin and Ryann, Pete, and of course, Caelan. In the end, it was because of them, all of them, that I decided to stay a little longer.

As the weeks passed, rumors of the buyout began to morph into reality. We all knew *Globe* was going to be sold. It was just a question of when and to whom. Caelan was convinced that a company buyout would rob the lowly employees of their accrued comp days. Undoubtedly we would be appropriately compensated for our paid vacation days. It was our deferred days for overtime that we were fearful of losing. I didn't take his fears too seriously until Caelan began making travel plans.

"We're going to Hawaii," Caelan said, holding up a stack of air tickets.

I snatched them from his hand. "What do you mean 'we'? As in Sharmin, Pete, the whole lot?"

"No, luv. As in you, me self, and me mates from Ireland." He was referring to his five friends who had immigrated to LA from the British Isles. "Unless we cash in our days now, who knows if we'll ever get another holiday?"

It took a bit of negotiating and planning but, just like that, the seven of us were off to Maui. My stress level began to dissipate the moment we boarded the plane. Caelan had organized our entire trip, including accommodations, a four-hour hike to the Seven Sacred Pools of Kipahulu, and kayaking at Turtle Bay. Kayaking took more coordination than I had anticipated. Caelan had hay fever and kept suffering from attacks.

"Stop sneezing or we'll tip over," I warned, trying to balance the rocking boat.

Our kayak was surrounded by three-foot turtles that gracefully turned circles and somersaults like birds underwater. As I peered at them over the edge, the kayak capsized, dumping all of our belongings into the sea. I watched as our things faded into darkness. While I flipped the boat upright, Caelan took a dive, barely catching our snorkel gear between his outstretched toes. Whipping his leg over the edge, he flung the rescued masks back into our yellow canoe.

"Rose! Grab me hand!" he said, quoting a scene from *Titanic*.

Readjusting my bikini top, I called back, "No, Jack, save yourself!"

By the time we washed ashore, a crust of sand had caked onto our skin like breadcrumbs on chicken patties. Somehow our Irish friend, who was to pick us up, had driven to the wrong beach, leaving us stranded for two hours. By the time he arrived, we were perched on our overturned canoe. Having apparently forgotten to apply sunscreen, our friend was so charred and frustrated that we could hardly understand his angry brogue.

"So tell me then, where in the world 'ave you two been hiding yourselves?" he said, acting blameless as he waved his hands in the air. "I've been lookin' all over for you."

The following afternoon our entire group unintentionally snorkeled onto a nude beach. Sunbathers bounced up and down the cove, playing paddleball, Frisbee, and soccer. It was a massive sea of floppy flesh. Caelan mumbled, "I'm feelin' a bit insignificant here, like a calf among the bulls."

Day by day, nature fed our nomadic desires. We explored bamboo forests, climbed volcanic domes, and traversed raging rivers. We showered under the spray of cascading waterfalls and bathed in the freshness of cool ponds. We survived on pineapple and bananas, stopping only to replenish our bodies with coconut milk before trudging further. Each day, we hiked until the night blindfolded the sun. I stared at the sky as if it were my first time out after dark, gazing as dusk scattered the stars like confetti. "It looks like God tripped on his way to empty his hole-puncher," I commented, pointing toward the dots littering the heavens.

I think, perhaps, it might have been another Life Day.

No matter what the calendar said, I wasn't ready to leave Hawaii. Worse yet, I wasn't ready to return to *Globe*. This therapeutic outlet that Caelan had arranged seemed to drastically clash with my life back at work. Dully, I returned to the same office, sat at the same desk, and worked with the same editors whose patterns never seemed to change. I looked down at my manicured hands as they typed away, while all I really wanted was to scale mossy rocks with bits of green stuck under my nails.

Caelan would often catch me staring out the window at nothing in particular. The only thing that could bring me back to the moment was the sound of a story file being slammed onto my desk. I had never felt such a sense of sorrow. Perhaps no one would have noticed my new mood had it not contrasted so sharply with my usual extreme optimism. I had once been full of life, and now I was drained of it.

Caelan asked, "So, where's Marlise, then?" I told him I had left her back in Hawaii. I was not sure if I should embrace or reject this foreign sadness. As much as I wanted the feeling to pass, part of me wanted it to stay. Somehow, I needed to understand what was happening to me and why.

Making matters worse was the lull in celebrity news. This Hollywood drought kept me chained to my desk with virtually no reason to travel as I had in the past. It was during this time that Trenton Freeze decided to bring new blood into the LA office. He was convinced that such a move might give *Globe* the comeback for which he had been hoping.

After months of futile hunting, the editors had managed to poach a British tabloid reporter by the name of Daniel Taft. The thirty-two-year-old had previously worked with Trenton when they had both freelanced at England's *Daily Mirror*. Now, Taft would be sitting in Keith Harden's old chair, two desks in front of me.

With dark red hair, Daniel Taft wore gold-rimmed glasses, pleated slacks, and dress shirts that appeared to have been pressed at the cleaners rather than self-ironed. Against his pasty skin, Daniel's raspberry cheeks looked dry and irritated. The editors thought Daniel was brilliant. In addition to his British accent, he gained points by introducing technological advancements like walkie-talkie cell phones, Palm Pilots, and digital pen recorders. He had a passion for Hollywood's nightlife, hobnobbing at LA's finest locations in order to build his list of celebrity contacts.

Within weeks of Daniel's arrival, he was sent to San Francisco on his first out-of-town assignment. For $50,000, *Globe* had purchased a series of photographs pertaining to Don Johnson. Unfolding like a slideshow, the first picture showed the actor kissing his wife, Kelley Phleger, in front of their San Francisco home. The second shot showed her strolling away from the mansion with their two-month-old daughter, Atherton Grace. The third was of Don driving his blue Land Rover toward San Francisco's

Tenderloin district. The fourth snapshot captured him entering the Art Theater porn shop. Forty-five minutes later, he was photographed exiting with a large brown paper bag. The final shot in the series was of Johnson checking into the Coventry Motor Inn. Daniel's task was to follow up on this pictorial evidence.

According to the photographer who sold the series to *Globe*, Johnson had stopped at a gas station on his way to the motel. There, he allegedly unpacked the shopping bag, unwrapped the products, and discarded all of the packaging into a trash can. The photographer later returned to the same garbage bin to find the box covers of several sex videos. The most unexpected item, however, was the packaging from a rubber replica of a male sex organ. Ironically, it was marketed by a company called Doc Johnson.

Despite the visual proof in the photos, there still was an enormous amount of investigation that needed to be done. The photographs were considered unprintable unless a firsthand source was willing to go on the record. Daniel's assignment was to locate a witness and determine if Johnson had been inside the motel alone or with someone else.

After three days in San Francisco, Daniel had managed to track down the name of the porn shop employee who had sold the merchandise to Johnson. *Globe*'s research department had been able to find a San Francisco address to match the name of that employee. After hearing Daniel's tabloid pitch, however, the female employee immediately notified her boss, who then banned Daniel from the shop. Without the saleswoman's firsthand account, *Globe* could not credibly report that Johnson had, in fact, bought the items. That's where I came in.

Caelan had been helping run the story out of the LA office. Up to this point, he had done all he could to keep me from getting involved. When matters in San Francisco grew increasingly complicated for Daniel, the Florida editors requested that I move in as backup. Torn between his personal and professional obligations, Caelan tried to convince the editors that the pornographic nature of the story was not fit for any young woman to cover, especially not for a minister's daughter. Ultimately, Trenton Freeze won the conference-call debate, convincing the team that a woman would appear less suspicious.

So, off I went to San Francisco. My first stop was at the home of the saleswoman who, only hours before, had reported Daniel as a stalker. Knocking on her door, I was met by a woman with soft eyes and cornrow braids that hung to her shoulders. She wore ripped jeans and a tie-dyed shirt that flared at the sleeves. Greeting me through the screen door, she had a familiar accent that I immediately recognized. Her dialect would be my point of connection to establish trust and to create a comfort level between us.

"Are you from South Africa?" I asked.

She hesitantly nodded. "Yes. Why do you ask?"

"Well, my father was a missionary in Lesotho for ten years," I said. "Oh, I'm sorry. How rude of me. My name is Marlise."

Quickly she unlocked the door and reached out to grab my offered business card. Glancing at it, the girl suddenly looked terrified. "I do not want to talk to you people. Your friend already came to my work and my home many times. Please do not bother me anymore."

I pretended not to know what she was talking about. "My friend? Are you talking about a British man with round glasses? Someone named Daniel?"

She nodded hesitantly.

"He's not my friend," I continued. "Actually, he's my competitor. Daniel is a freelance reporter who is trying to sell this story all over the world. I, on the other hand, work for a magazine that can assure your protection through this confidentiality agreement."

I pressed the source agreement up against the screen door. "You do know that this actually has nothing to do with you, right?"

The wooden beads in her hair tapped together lightly as she shook her head from side to side. And so, I started over from the beginning, explaining the identity of her famous customer and why it was so important that she sign *Globe*'s agreement.

"With or without your help, Daniel will print your name," I explained. "But if you give me your signature, I guarantee I will not use your name. That will then push the competition out of the running. And, for all the trouble this has caused you, I will also give you ten thousand dollars by the end of the day."

"I am sorry, I want to help you very much," she said, turning the lock on the screen door. "But I am not supposed to be here. I am from Africa."

"Those things don't matter to us," I told her, as she began to close the wooden door. "Wait, please. All I need is a signature."

No matter how much cash we dangled, the woman was not going to risk deportation. The editors were furious when they heard the news. Without a substantiating story, they were stuck with useless photographs for which they had paid $50,000. Daniel Taft and I were both ordered to take the first flight back to LA. Suddenly, I found myself becoming assertive with Madeline.

"Wait," I protested. "Don Johnson has been living in San Francisco for over five years. The city is jammed with sex shops. He must have visited at least one other store at some point or another."

And so the hunt began. With Daniel at the wheel, we drove in silence down the seedy streets of San Francisco. He would pull curbside and wait for me as I ran into one porn shop after another. From nine that evening until four the next morning, I passed through the doors of more than twenty sex shops. Each time I crossed another threshold, the walls of my sheltered childhood cracked a little more. It was the most disgusting way to be introduced to porn, something to which I had never before been exposed.

In an effort to strike up conversations with staff members, I inquired about things I had not known existed until twenty-four hours earlier when I began this assignment. By the time I left San Francisco, I was an expert. My *Globe* expense report was filled with humiliating purchases. Out of the twenty porn shops, I found three that would confirm they had been visited by Don Johnson. The following morning I phoned Caelan to tell him the news.

"Okay, so I made small talk with the employees and found out that Johnson is a regular customer at Adult Media and Golden Gate #4. I didn't give the full tabloid speech or anything. I thought I would talk to you before asking people to sign source agreements."

There was a long pause before Caelan responded in a monotone. "I suppose the editors will be thrilled. I'm just sorry you had to go through all this, luv. So, how are you holding up?"

"Well," I said, "it's only six in the morning and I've already taken two showers."

"I feel like this is all me fault. I promise to get you outta there today.

You just hold tight until I can have a bit of a chat with the editors."

By ten o'clock, I was back at Adult Media, roaming the aisles crammed with X-rated videos, sex toys, and magazines. The man who had previously been working the night shift had been relieved by another employee. I would have to start my script all over from the beginning.

"Can I help you, miss?" The man asked, looking up from his newspaper.

"Umm . . . yes . . ." I quickly scanned the shelves for something not overly offensive. Digging into a plastic tub, I answered, "I'll take three of these and two of these and just one of those up there behind you."

Embarrassed, I looked away as he grabbed them off the counter and began punching numbers into the register. "Will that be all?" he asked.

Trying to appear casual, I imagined that I was purchasing produce at a grocery store. "Yep, I think that about does it for me. . . . You know, it's funny. I'm visiting from out of town and thought, what the heck, I'm in San Francisco. Why not buy a few gag gifts? Right?"

Fanning out a paper bag, the man dropped the items inside. "Where are you from?"

"LA," I said, leaning onto the counter. "Hollywood to be exact; land of the rich and famous. But it seems these days, more and more celebrities are moving to the Bay Area. Have you noticed that?"

Handing me the receipt, he nodded. "Well, I see a few of them in here from time to time."

"You're kidding me," I said. "Like who?"

"That *Nash Bridges* guy comes in here and buys all kinds of gay porn. You know, Don Johnson. He used to be on *Miami Vice*."

Did he just say "gay porn"?

Reaching into my pocket, I pulled out my press pass and flashed him my ID. "I know this may sound strange, but I'm actually a reporter. I would be willing to pay you a substantial amount of money for your story."

He started to laugh.

"No," I said, misinterpreting his reaction. "I'm dead serious."

"I know you're serious and I know who you are. I was just wondering how long it would take before the tabloids finally came in." Reaching beneath the counter, he pulled out a shoebox and lifted the lid. "I've got a security video from the last time Johnson was in here, plus his credit card receipts. How much are they worth to you?"

"A lot," I said, peering into the box. On top was a receipt for $664, listing Johnson's recent purchases, including gay videos and a blow-up doll. "Give me five minutes and I'll have an offer for you."

I ran out to the curb where Daniel was parked in the middle of Chinatown's traffic. "I'm about to get a ticket," he said. "How much longer?"

"You won't believe what just happened," I told him, excitedly. "This guy has everything we need to run the story. We're talking security video, receipts, everything. I haven't mentioned a contract yet, but I'm sure he'll sign for the right amount."

Dialing Caelan, I explained the latest developments. "Good work. Put Daniel on the line, then," Caelan said. "He's to go into the shop and finish off the deal."

"What?" I said, hoping Daniel hadn't noticed the frustration in my voice. "Why?"

"If Daniel comes back to the office empty-handed, he'll probably be sacked. Remember luv, this is his story. Now, put Daniel on the line and I'll discuss it with you later."

Fuming, I handed over the phone, anxious for the moment I could speak with Caelan alone. After the call was over, Daniel went back into the porn shop and made an offer to the employee. For $2,500, he obtained the surveillance video, the credit card receipts, and a first-person interview.

From the car, we called the editors to tell them we had gotten what they wanted. Back at the hotel, I made a private call to Caelan and told him how frustrated I felt about being stripped of my work. "I saved this assignment," I said, justifying my fury. "I spent hours porn-shop hopping while Daniel slept in his car. If it weren't for me, this story would have died. This is the first time in months that I've felt like I was really doing investigative reporting. How could you do this to me?"

"Hold on just a second," Caelan said, calmly. "First off, *Globe* works as a team, you know. You shouldna care who gets the credit, so long as everything comes together in the end. Secondly, I'd hope that you aren't honestly pleased with your work. You've just spent the past two days inside of sex shops to report that Don Johnson likes gay porn. If anything, you should be ashamed. And thirdly, you aren't going home empty-handed. I've assigned Daniel to write the entire story, and you'll be sharin' the byline. Finally, I thought you might want to relax and spend some time with your varsity mates. So, it's been arranged for you to stay on in San Francisco through the weekend."

Obviously, Caelan had been giving this a lot of thought. His explanation seemed to put everything into perspective. He was right: suddenly I was no longer proud of my work. Doing as I was told, I tried to drop the matter and enjoy the weekend with my friends. Meanwhile, Daniel spent his weekend typing up our cover story, titled, "Don Johnson's Gay Double Life."

As a result of our investigative work, *Globe* was finally able to publish the original photos that had set this chain of events in motion. The editors considered the $50,000 they had paid to the freelance photographer money well spent. When the article hit the newsstands, I became a hero to the editors, an embarrassment to my family, and a shame to myself.

Back at the office, I left my porn-shop purchases on the desks of my colleagues. After all, I had bought them with *Globe*'s money. "Thanks for the souvenir," Madeline said, walking out of her office holding up a suggestive lollipop.

Sharmin walked by, crunching on her candy stick. "Come on Madeline, think of it as a Tootsie Pop."

Trying to cover her laugh with a fake cough, Madeline said, "Well, whatever it is, I don't think I want to be seen eating it."

Pete held his Jawbreaker Booby Bombs in the air. "Would you rather have my boobies?"

"Okay, enough already," Madeline said. "I believe this sort of dialogue goes against company policy. Can we all get back to work, please? Marlise, I have a new assignment for you."

I looked down at my desk and read the lead sheet, "Madonna Fat. See photo."

"What's this about?" I asked, holding it up.

"Oh, we just bought a photo of Madonna," Madeline said, handing me a copy of the picture. "Trenton wants to run a cover story about her gaining twenty pounds."

I glanced at the photo. It showed Madonna walking down the street, dressed in pink silks embroidered with gold lacing and sparkling jewels. Her flat stomach peered beneath her open top and beads were dangling between her protruding chest bones.

"I need it by the end of the day," Madeline said, turning away from me.

I took a closer look at the picture. Madonna's face appeared distorted, as if it had been pulled like taffy. "This negative has been stretched," I remarked.

Madeline stopped in her office doorway and turned back to face me. "Excuse me?"

I held the photo up to the light. "I'm sure of it. Madonna's face looks abnormally wide. Plus, I know she's heavily into yoga now, which would only make her body more slender and toned than before. I'm telling you, this negative has been stretched."

The office fell silent, as all the staff members stopped typing to look up from their computers.

"Well, I don't care if it is or not," Madeline said, her voice becoming increasingly loud. "If Trenton wants you to write that Madonna weighs five hundred pounds, then that's what you'll write."

I looked over at Sharmin, who was now biting the tip of her pen.

Suddenly, without thinking through what I was saying, I stood up and looked Madeline in the eye. "No. I'm not writing it."

No one in the office moved except for Madeline, who took a step closer toward me. "What did you say?"

Oh no. What did I say? Be strong, Marlise. Don't back down.

"I said I'm not going to write the story. If you want to claim that Madonna is fat then you'll have to write it yourself."

I had no idea what had come over me. Neither did Madeline. She immediately called me into her office, shutting the door behind us. The sound of that door closing signaled the tabloid guillotine. I had heard it countless times, but until now, I had never been on the other side. I could practically see the smoke coming from Madeline's ears.

"Don't you ever speak to me like that again," she commanded. "If you have a problem to discuss, then you address me in private and with respect. I expect to have that article typed and on my desk no later than noon today. If you can't get it done, then I'll find someone who can."

With a single nod of compliance, I left Madeline's office, relieved that I still had a job. As I passed Sharmin's desk, she tried to lighten the mood by asking with a smile, "Would ya like a glass of water to wash down your foot?"

Returning to my desk, I wrote the article according to Madeline's guidelines. It was on her desk long before the deadline. Madeline told me to go home and get some rest.

At the time, I didn't want to go home. Home was the one place where I would have time to think. Instead, I drove to the art store for charcoal pencils, brushes, and clay. I didn't know the first thing about art, but felt I had to do something to keep my mind occupied while at home. From the art store, I went to the hardware store and bought two buckets of paint and rollers. Finally, I headed home. Chantal was at a wedding in Rhode Island, Heidi was at a science conference, and I was alone.

I put on my baggy overalls that were reserved specifically for house painting and car repair, neither of which I had ever done. Uncertain of what to create, I dipped the brush into the glossy mixture and splattered the stark whiteness of my bedroom wall. Sinking the brush even deeper into the pail, I smeared again and again, feeling my heart beat a little faster with every new spot of color. I was angry and sad and confused, all at the same time. My vision blurred as tears filled my eyes, clearing only after the first drop rolled down my cheek.

Suddenly there was a knock at my door. I remained silent, not moving, refusing to let anyone else into my world. "Marlise? 'Tis Caelan. Come on, luv. Please open the bloody door."

"Go away," I shouted. "I'm not home."

He knocked again, as if I hadn't heard him the first time. "I ain't going anywhere 'til you let me in. I'll sleep out here if I have to."

Hesitantly, I unlocked the door. Caelan was holding a single red rose and a candle that had the word "joy" written in Chinese. I knew I didn't deserve a boyfriend like Caelan. He was much too kind, continually bringing me roses while I repeatedly searched for thorns.

"Please, just go," I begged, rubbing my eyes. "I'm sad and I don't know why. Look at me, I'm crying for no reason. Just let me deal with this alone. I'm probably contagious."

Caelan lifted my lowered chin. "'Twould be impossible for you to make me sad."

Pulling me toward him, he wrapped his arms around my entire body, almost seizing my pain. Instantly, I lost control of my emotions, heaving uncontrollably into his chest.

"It ain't that bad, you know," he said. "After all, you still have your job."

"I'm not crying about what happened today," I sobbed.

Caelan pulled a Kleenex pack from his back pocket. "Well, what 'tis it then?"

Blowing my nose into a tissue, I searched for the perfect answer to his question. I couldn't find one. "I don't know," I told him. "I'm just sad."

That night I lit my new candle and stayed awake drawing, painting, and writing in my journal. By morning, the word "joy" had melted into a pool of wax.

Heidi returned from her trip on Sunday afternoon to find that I had painted my entire bedroom charcoal gray. She knew something was terribly wrong. As I had done with Caelan, I pushed Heidi away, allowing the inner fits of anguish to break within me. She bought me soothing remedies like green tea, St. John's Wort, collections of short stories, empty journals, and the Holy Bible. I shoved them all under my bed for fear they might work. That would only confirm that I did, in fact, have a problem.

And so I ran away, from everything and everyone who longed to pull me out of my door-less room. Days were spent at the office, evenings at the gym, and nights under the covers, crying myself to sleep. My sister would kneel at my bedside and say, "I just want you to be happy, Lise." I would turn away from her and cry harder into my pillow.

This was my first exposure to unrelenting depression. It was a feeling that I could not describe, justify, or cure. A heavy, inexplicable sadness enveloped me, stifling the vibrancy of the normal me. Although

I tried to hide my pain at work, even there I became emotionally overwhelmed. I would smile at my desk and sob in the restroom.

The fantasy world into which I had escaped at *Globe* seemed to have vanished with my spirit. I dreaded going to work. I dreaded going home. I dreaded facing life. My parents were worried. Their phone calls were seldom returned. Letters were left unopened. Friendships were dropped. I became a recluse. I didn't like who I was, but was too fatigued and powerless to change. The worst part of all was that I could not be helped. I wanted someone or something to give me a sign. Until then, I would keep wading in the river of my own depression.

During this stage, time passed slowly at *Globe*. Everyone at the office seemed to be withdrawing. Laughter was virtually nonexistent and conversations became exclusively work-related. Our energy and enthusiasm were drained. By this time, Madeline was spending more time alone in her office, secluded behind her closed door. Her communication had become terse and impersonal.

Breaking stories were now such a rarity that eventually Madeline called all the reporters into her office for a brainstorming session. Despite my recent mental detachment from work, I instinctively began pitching ideas. "How about we do a cover story on 'Diva Catfights,'" I suggested, going through the motions. "We can focus on Whitney versus Mariah."

Madeline scribbled the title onto her notepad. "I think it's been done, but I'll run the idea by Trenton tomorrow." Picking up the phone, she dialed Sharmin's extension. "Sharmin, can you please bring the new book arrivals into my office?" She was referring to an assortment of new releases that had been sent by the authors to *Globe* for publicity. Seconds later, Madeline was doling out celebrity books for each of us to read as homework. "Maybe you guys can find a line somewhere in these books that can be developed into stories."

Pete smiled, happy to have been assigned Tim Allen's latest release.

"I'll trade you," I said, holding up a book by Joan Collins titled *My Friends' Secrets*.

"Well, I'll be on vacation," Karen said, laying Larry King's book, *Powerful Prayers*, back on Madeline's desk. "The last thing I want to read on vacation is a book about celebrities who pray."

Like the hands of a clock, Madeline pointed the book in my direction. Having let Karen off the hook, she glanced at me with a smirk. "I believe this subject is right up your alley, Marlise."

Without saying a word, I grabbed the book and resigned myself to having accepted two story assignments. Flipping through a binder of approved lead sheets, Madeline looked up and asked, "Marlise, did you ever start the celebrity roundup we discussed, called 'Hollywood North'?"

"Well, I tried," I explained. "But there didn't seem to be enough stars living in Santa Barbara to justify a two-page spread."

Madeline jotted down a number onto a scrap of paper. "This is the phone number of my Santa Barbara realtor. She'll be your main source for the story. Try to have the article finished today." Madeline looked at her watch. "Any questions before we all get back to work?"

"Yeah, whatever happened to my lead on 'Gladys Knight Donates Millions for Diabetes Research'?" I asked. "I know she'd do an interview with *Globe* if it would help raise awareness for diabetes."

Everyone else was already walking out of the office. Avoiding my gaze, Madeline commented, "I killed that story. It just wasn't going anywhere." Her drastic action seemed somewhat premature, especially considering I hadn't even started the assignment. Leaning forward, I picked up the lead sheet binder from her desk and began flipping through the pages. "And what about my idea on 'Stars Torment Their Bodies for the Big Screen'? With before and after photos, a story like that could easily fill two pages."

"Oh, Trenton wasn't interested in that assignment," Madeline told me offhandedly.

I flipped to another stagnate lead sheet. "What about my . . ."

Madeline grabbed the binder from my hand. "Marlise, don't you have work to do?"

Standing up, I left Madeline's office and never mentioned the subject again. Less than a week later, Sharmin handed me the latest issues of *Star* and *Enquirer*. On the top cover, Sharmin had written a Post-It note reading, "Look familiar?" As I thumbed through the pages of our competing magazines, I finally realized what had become of the ideas I had submitted. Several of my so-called "killed leads" had been sold to the enemy for the going rate of several hundred dollars per lead. When I told Caelan that I suspected Madeline of double-dealing, he reminded me that dozens of other *Globe* employees had access to those same files.

"All I know is that there's a backstabber in our office," I told him.

"Face it, Marlise," Caelan explained. "There're only a few of us in this business who aren't holding knives."

I wasn't sure whom I could trust. In fact, I wasn't sure if I could trust anyone. Even those within the immediate tabloid family started to turn on each other. An air of suspicion permeated everyone in the office, including short-term freelancers like Donald Lott. In an effort to gain points with the editors, Donald tattled on Sharmin about her using *Globe*'s research programs for her personal use. Apparently, she had been running criminal reports on the men she had been dating.

In retaliation, Sharmin searched Donald's computer files and found suggestive photos of barely legal schoolgirls. Without hesitation, Sharmin made sure everyone in the office knew about Donald's dirty little secret. Caelan, who was in charge of the office at the time, realized things were getting out of hand. He gave both Donald and Sharmin stern warnings and advised them to keep their distance.

As much as we tried to keep things the same, there was no denying the fact that inevitable changes were taking place around us. In the midst of our plummet, we were hit with news that would irrevocably change the future of *Globe*. We heard about it through Madeline, who walked out of her office like a doctor after surgery. Leaning her back against the wall, she inhaled deeply and announced, "*Globe*'s been sold to the owner of *Star* and *The National Enquirer*."

A few months before our buyout, David J. Pecker had paid $850 million for American Media Inc., which included the magazines *Star* and *The National Enquirer*. Now, in an effort to build his own tabloid empire, Pecker had offered *Globe* Communications Corporation $105 million for the rights to our magazine. In the midst of this tabloid-market monopoly, Pecker paid an additional $350 million to health-and-fitness publisher Weider Publications. There seemed to be no end to his goals.

I took the sale of *Globe* as a sign. This was my chance to break free from a career in which I had become much too comfortable. The only problem was, I didn't know how or when to leave. I had never quit a job without having somewhere else to land. I was not about to start now.

Coincidentally, around this time, I received a call from my former contact Rick Schwartz, who was still working at *Extra*. He told me that the TV show now had an opening for an investigative reporter. He thought I might be interested in the job. *Extra* still had my resume on file from the unsolicited job application I had submitted months before. Now they were also asking for samples of my published work. With some embarrassment, I sent them my least offensive *Globe* articles, knowing that I would be knocked out of the running the moment the package arrived.

Apparently I wasn't the only one at *Globe* looking for change. Nearly everyone in the office was busy devising a backup plan. Our future had never been more uncertain. Although *Globe*'s employees kept begging for reassurance, it seemed no one could provide answers. Even those at the top appeared to be unsure of what was going on. The only one who knew the master plan was American Media's CEO, Pecker. And he was keeping it to himself.

Word had spread that Pecker had plans for major consolidation and company cutbacks. Those at the top of the food chain had the most to fear. Now that all the tabloids would be operating under one publishing house, Pecker wanted to reduce overhead costs by functioning from one central location. No one was quite sure what that would mean for us.

The Florida office took the first blow from these ownership changes. Literally overnight, twenty jobs were cut. Notice was given of the intent to chop eighty more jobs. Dedicated employees were forced to defend their positions. They did so through self-critiquing report cards and telephone interviews with people they had never met. Veterans seemed to be the first to go, forced to clear their desks within months of retirement. Almost every day, I would call a Florida extension only to hear an unfamiliar voice telling me that the person I was trying to reach no longer worked at *Globe*.

The week following the announcement, Pecker's associates paid a surprise visit to the LA office. "What happened to casual Friday?" I whispered to Sharmin, looking at the trio in their three-piece suits. I was wearing jeans and a T-shirt, my hair still dripping from my recent shower.

"Look busy," Madeline mumbled, pointing toward my blank computer screen. "These men will determine your future."

Madeline put on quite an impressive performance, walking up and down the aisle, pretending to have some sort of influence over our work in progress. From across the room, Madeline called, "How's that assignment coming along, Marlise?"

Glancing down at my calculator and expense report, I answered, "Just fine, Madeline. I'll have it to you by deadline."

By the end of the day, many of our questions had been answered. Pecker's visiting representatives called us together for an official announcement. Trenton Freeze would be the new editor-in-chief for both *Globe* and *Star* for the time being. Madeline and Caelan would keep their editorial positions at *Globe*. Cathy Tidwell in Florida would become the executive editor for *Star*. We were also informed that both tabloids would operate their LA headquarters out of one central location. I couldn't believe what I was hearing. It was hard to wrap my mind around the idea of suddenly embracing our long-term competitors as our newfound colleagues.

Karen timidly raised her hand and asked one of the men, "Do you know where that might be and when it might happen?"

Staring at Karen, one of the men replied, "As soon as editorial cutbacks are put into effect, *Star's* LA staff will move into this office with the rest of you. Everything should be settled within approximately four to six weeks."

Where will we all fit? What will become of our Globe family? Will I actually be working alongside the competition?

Fortunately, Madeline offered to take Pecker's disciples to lunch. This gave the rest of us a chance to discuss the buyout.

"I'm packin' my bags," Sharmin announced. "I'll walk away before I let them fire me. Who's coming with me?" She looked at Karen. "Come on, where're my girls at?"

"Sorry," Karen said, pausing to sneeze. "I've got the easiest job around here. I sit in my corner, mind my own business, and get paid to write about soap stars. I'd be a fool to quit."

Donald Lott entered the conversation. "Karen does have a point."

Sharmin held her hand in the air as if blocking his face. "I don't think anyone asked for your opinion, Donald-Peep-A-Lott. We know you ain't goin' nowhere, unless of course you have your lips surgically removed from Trenton's ass."

Pete's calm voice interrupted the intense conversation. "Well, I for one am going to start looking around."

Caelan could be heard from the back of the office. "Actually, 'tis not such a bad idea, everyone."

"I'm already looking," I piped up. "One day they're calling you the 'Tabloid Prodigy' and the next day you're shining shoes."

Sharmin waved her finger in the air. "Hell no, girlfriend. We ain't goin' down like that. It's time to stand up for our rights and start a revolution."

"Easy there, Malcolm X," Pete said. "Don't forget *Globe* is the one putting food in your baby's mouth."

"Leftovers, more like it," Sharmin interjected. "If they think I'm gonna sing 'Kumbaya' beside some cheerleading secretary from *Star*, than they can think again. I would rather go out remembering *Globe* for what it is now."

And just like that, she was gone.

Sharmin simply packed her bags and moved to Arkansas. Along with her belongings and my godchild Ryann, she took part of my joy. Sharmin's departure left my spirit void of all the color and laughter she had helped to create. The office became dreadfully bland as Pete and I typed in silence. We both knew that Sharmin's absence signaled the end of *Globe* as we knew it.

After Sharmin left, Pete applied for a reporting position at Warner Bros. He turned down the job after *Globe* countered their offer with a six-figure deal. "I'd be lying if I said it wasn't about the money," Pete told me. "But if I earned a penny less than what *Globe* is paying me now, I'd leave the tabloids and never look back."

I took Pete's words as priceless advice. In the back of my mind, I had always considered the job at *Extra* to be my safety net. Picking up the phone, I dialed the human resources department at *Extra* to find out the status on the reporting position. "I'm sorry," the woman told me. "That job has already been filled."

Just when I was ready to jump, my safety net had been yanked out from under me. Somehow I had unintentionally become a lifetime member of the Tabloid Mafia. More than anything, I wanted out of this world but was convinced no one else would want me.

Caelan also was trying to break free and had worked his way to the third stage of interviews at CNN. When he received their disappointing rejection letter, we both faced the possibility that life outside of *Globe* might not exist for us. With nowhere else to turn, we put our heads down and continued at our jobs as loyal and faithful servants.

Week after week, it seemed things were only getting worse. Less than half the employees were still left on the payroll. The few of us who remained were doing twice the amount of work. Pete, Karen, Daniel, and I were punching out two to three stories a day. Even Caelan was writing articles along with his editorial tasks, just to keep the rest of us from cracking. At least once a week, we received memos announcing further employee cutbacks.

As difficult as things had become at *Globe*, I had heard that they were much worse at *Star*. The majority of *Star* employees were now being transferred to their new headquarters in New York. Those who remained were preparing for their upcoming move to *Globe*'s LA office.

Less than a week before their transfer however, eighty-five staff members protested Pecker's decision by handing in their letters of resignation. It was a mass walkout. Those who had once felt safe on the corporate ladder suddenly realized there would soon be no one left to govern.

Overnight, the tone of office memos changed from threats and demands to rewards and praise. In the midst of deadlines, we received e-mails of encouragement and phone calls of appreciation. Within one eight-hour span, I had three separate calls from editors telling me to "keep up the good work." They were convinced I was going to quit just like the others.

While many of those at the bottom were suffering blows from the tabloid guillotine, I received an unexpected call from Trenton Freeze. "Hello, Marlise," he said, in a rather upbeat voice. "It's not too often that we get a chance to chat. You see, the reason I'm calling is in regards to the shifting that has been occurring as of late. My hope is for you to start working under the direct management of *Star*'s editor, Cathy Tidwell. I'm sure that you are fully aware that Mr. Pecker has chosen *Star* to be his protégé of sorts. He will be heavily investing in the future of *Star*, turning it into a glossy, top competitor of *People* magazine. It would be in your best interest to accept this honorable position as a staff reporter with *Star*."

I was numb.

"Congratulations, Marlise," he continued. "Now, I'm going to hand you over to Cathy, who will be giving you further instruction. Cheerio!"

"Welcome to the team," Cathy piped into the phone.

"Wow, Cathy," I said, my voice flat. "I honestly don't know what to say."

"I'm so excited that we'll be working together," she continued, without giving me time to process the news. "Okay, first I need you to work on a couple of leads. Start with 'Whoopi Finds Love Again,' then move onto 'Suzanne Somers Stole My Weight Loss Secrets.'"

Either I was extremely tired or completely confused. "Wait, Cathy. I don't fully understand. Do you mean I'm already working for *Star*?"

Cathy took a deep breath. "I realize this may seem a bit strange, jumping from one tabloid to another, but everything should be organized by the end of the month. Your two-year *Globe* contract will simply roll over to *Star*. In the meantime, I have a magazine to run and you have one to write."

"But what about all the current stories I'm writing for *Globe*? I'm in the middle of an exclusive on Michael Douglas and Catherine Zeta-Jones' wedding plans. It just wouldn't feel right to hand it over to *Star*."

I could sense frustration in her voice. "Marlise, you're working for *Star* now. Finish off that article and I'll see if we can squeeze it into next week's issue."

"Of what magazine?" I asked.

"Of *Star*," she nearly screamed. "I'm sorry . . . I apologize, Marlise. It's just that these changes are difficult for all of us right now. You have to trust me, they're for the best. For the time being, we're a bit short on staff so I'll be expecting at least one new lead from you each day. Procedures will continue the same as they did at *Globe* until you are given further notice."

That following week, my name began appearing on the masthead of *Star* magazine. Despite the fact that we all worked for the same boss, I couldn't help feeling like a traitor. For years I had served *Globe* and suddenly I had been forced to change religions. Pete, Karen, Daniel, and Caelan were all still working for *Globe*. Meanwhile, there I sat at my same desk, writing articles for *Star*, the magazine I had grown to loathe while at *Globe*.

It took weeks before I could break my habit of submitting leads to Madeline. "What do you think about an election story called 'Battle of the First Daughters'?" I asked her. "'Al's Gals vs. Bush's Beauties'?"

Waving me away, she said, "Marlise, we don't work together anymore, remember?"

Not only had I lost Sharmin from my life, but I had also lost the entire *Globe* staff. I was an outsider inside my own office. I didn't care if *Star* was going to become the next *People* magazine. I wanted things to go back to the way they had been. I cranked out articles like a factory machine, never quite knowing where they would land. Within a four-week span, nine of my articles were published in *Star* and eight in *Globe*. Three of them became cover stories.

By my third week with *Star*, Cathy began handing me assignments that were far outside my league. I was asked to hunt down a man who claimed that at the age of fifteen, he had been sexually abused by Dolly Parton. Apparently, what allegedly began as pedophilia eventually became a twenty-year affair between consenting adults. A lawyer had originally leaked the story to *Penthouse* magazine in the '80s after he had drafted a confidentiality agreement between Dolly and the boy's mother. Although the story had been told before, my job was to convince the now 33-year-old victim to tell his first-person account of the romance.

This was one of my most frightening assignments. The address Cathy gave me led to the man's rundown home in a squalid section of LA County. Boards covered the windows and weeds grew out of cracks in the driveway. I rang the doorbell and waited nearly five minutes before someone finally answered. Opening the door slightly, a man squinted into the blinding sunlight.

"What do you want?" he asked, in a deep, raspy voice. His thin, wavy hair touched the top of his shoulders. He stood at least a head taller than I did. A rancid odor seeped from the house, as if something were decaying inside. I couldn't help noticing his uncanny resemblance to Buffalo

Bill in *Silence of the Lambs.*

"I want to offer you money," I said, handing him my business card. Grabbing it from my hand, he suddenly slammed the door in my face. Screaming into the splintered wood, I continued my pitch as if the door were still open. "I know all about your affair with Dolly Parton. I also know that she paid you fifty thousand dollars to keep silent. It looks to me, sir, that you got the bad end of this deal."

Placing my ear to the door, I heard someone stirring on the other side. "My intention is not to run away with your story," I continued. "In my hand, I'm holding a contract stating that nothing will be published until we've reached a mutual financial understanding. If you sign, I will also guarantee you full copy approval on the final story."

The movement stopped. As I began to walk away, the handle turned and the door opened forty-five degrees. "My mother needs surgery," he said, resignation in his voice. "The only way I would do this is if I could get sixty thousand dollars to pay for her operation."

I stepped closer. "The only way I can tell you what it's worth is if I know the entire story, in detail."

Over the next three days, I returned to that same dark house to listen to the man share his version of the sordid affair. With my tape recorder beside me, I sat on a stained mattress that he had dragged from another room. According to his version of the story, the country singer had started sexually abusing him while his mother was employed as her makeup artist. At the time, he was only fifteen years old. His graphic details of Dolly's sexual proclivity seemed entirely implausible.

"Other than your word, do you have any proof that what you're saying is true?" I asked.

Reaching behind him, he lifted a large cardboard box onto his lap. "Oh, I have proof. I just thought you were more interested in hearing the story." He spent the next few hours showing me love letters and copies of personal checks signed by Dolly. There were also thirty photographs of the two of them together, kissing and holding one another as a committed couple would do. Dolly had dedicated several of her albums to him. "Here's the ring she gave me during our secret wedding," he said, handing me the piece of diamond jewelry. "It's inscribed with the title of a song I wrote for her."

Even more unsettling was listening to their taped phone conversations in which Dolly asked him to publicly deny their affair. As I left the house, I assured him that the editors would buy the story for close to his $60,000 request. "Just between you and me," I advised him, "don't back down on the dollar amount. I know what tabloid stories are worth, and this one is priceless."

Returning to the office, I phoned Cathy and told her what had happened during my first-person interview. I also told her I had everything recorded on tape to back up my detailed conversations.

"Type it up and send it to me as a memo," she demanded. "This story is hitting us right in the middle of budget cuts, so go back to him and offer five thousand dollars."

I laughed, thinking Cathy was making a joke. After the line went dead, I knew she had been serious. When the source learned of *Star*'s insulting offer, he did as I had suggested and decided to keep his secrets tucked inside the corners of his mind. So did I.

Despite the fact that the source would not accept our offer, my performance and pace on the story had caught the eye of editor Trenton Freeze. He had asked Cathy to arrange a meeting for me to meet with upper management in Florida.

"Trenton thinks it would be a good idea for you to spend some time at headquarters," Cathy explained. "You can see how we run the operation, finally meet the team, and maybe even have a chat with David Pecker. If things go well, who knows, perhaps there's a future for you in Boca Raton."

Boca Raton?

Suddenly my mind imagined a nightmarish future limited to bingo and dominos and friends over sixty-five. As a California girl, it had taken me a while to try to find my niche inside LA's shallow world of plasticity.

"When do I leave?" I asked.

"Next week," Cathy answered. "I imagine we'll have you out here for about a month during this transition period. Can you believe we'll finally be meeting face to face?"

The idea of all those commanding voices actually having identities seemed virtually impossible to grasp. "No," I said. "I can hardly believe it."

Hanging up the phone, I sat in silence, visualizing what two more years in this spin cycle might do to me. Where would I go and who would I become? Over the years, I had served the industry, disguised as everything from a wedding guest and tennis player to a school girl and florist. Now, as I tried to remove my latest mask as a tabloid reporter, I realized that the face beneath was no longer my own.

Without this identity, who would I be? As my insecurities built, so did my fear of the unknown future. That night as I lay in bed, I tried to imagine life outside of my journalistic career. As much as I wanted to leave, I felt a sense of guilt, as if the industry had become my sacred house of worship.

"I want to quit the tabloids," I told my sister. "But I think it'll be a big mistake."

"Well, if it does turn out to be a mistake," Heidi said. "Then it will be the best one you've ever made. Lise, don't worry. Everything will be okay."

I buried my head into my pillow. "How can you say that? I'll be unemployed, depressed, single, and broke."

Reaching under my bed, she pulled out a Bible and tossed it at my feet. I kept waiting for her to say something profound, but wisely, she just walked away. Looking down at the familiar book, I noticed there were fingerprints where her hand had gripped through a film of dust.

I sat up and pulled it toward me, brushing away the dusty evidence with the back of my hand. Idly flipping it open to the book of Job, my eyes fell on the words, "What I feared has come upon me; what I dreaded has happened to me. I have no peace, no quietness; I have no rest, but only turmoil."

Since when did this ancient book become so relevant?

Randomly flipping a few more pages, I read on. "Submit to God and be at peace with Him. In this way prosperity will come to you."

More than anything in the world, I wanted peace.

The following morning, I sat down at my desk and opened a blank document on my computer. Without hesitation, I typed out a letter of resignation, giving AMI two weeks' notice. I believe it was the best writing I had ever done at the tabloids.

Despite the fact that Madeline was no longer my superior, I felt she should be the first one to receive the news. Knocking on her door, I poked my head into her office with the letter in my outstretched hand.

Madeline looked up from her desk. "I've already told you to take up all matters with Florida."

I continued walking toward her. "No, Madeline. This has nothing to do with *Star* or *Globe*. It has to do with me."

With a heavy sigh, she grabbed the page and began to read. As her eyes scrolled back and forth across the words, her expression suddenly changed from annoyance to panic. "No, Marlise. You can't do this. Not now. Please, not now."

I looked down at the carpet for fear that eye contact might weaken my resolve and make me change my mind. "I'm sorry, Madeline. It's been a good run but I have to move on. There are so many changes taking place here and I'm not sure I want to be part of this company's future."

She took off her glasses and pinched the bridge of her nose with her fingers. "Will I be losing two people in your move?" she asked.

I gave her a puzzled look. "What do you mean?"

"I mean, will Caelan be leaving with you? Oh, come on," she continued, studying my overstated look of confusion. "You didn't think you could hide your relationship from me, did you?"

I knew I was blushing. "No, Madeline. Caelan has no intention of going anywhere."

Looking back down at my letter on her desk, she asked, "What if we doubled your salary and gave you a new title?"

I shook my head. "It's not about the money or the position. It's about my happiness."

Madeline put her glasses back on her face. "Are you sure about this?"

For the first time in weeks, I felt a genuine smile creep across my face. "I'm absolutely positive."

"Oh, wait," Madeline said as I walked toward the door. "I've got one more question. Where are you going next?"

I took one last look at her. "Home, Madeline. I'm going home."

Note:

Don Johnson and his third wife, Kelly Phleger, have been married since April 1999. They have three children.

Madonna's December 2003 marriage to Guy Ritchie has produced one child, Rocco. In 2006, they adopted a boy, David, from Malawi.

CHAPTER 17

Loading Zone Good-byes

From the perspective of the editors, it was unthinkable that anyone would voluntarily walk away from the tabloids, much less quit without the prospect of greener pastures. Perhaps it was understandable that during my final two weeks at AMI, I would be expected to work every day, including weekends. After receiving my letter of resignation, it was decided that I should report to both Madeline and Cathy in order to maximize my remaining time on the payroll.

Those final weeks in the office were rough. Most mornings started off with sporadic spurts of doubt and regret. A war was raging inside my head, with little grenades of remorse exploding each time I landed another story. As an incentive to remain committed to my decision, I stuck Post-It notes on my computer screen, marking the countdown to the finish line. Acting as my committed fan club, Sharmin, Heidi, and my parents would phone my private line to reassure me to stay focused on this new path of promise. Madeline and Cathy made matters even more difficult by habitually appealing to me to reconsider my resignation. At times, I had to leave the office for fear of a relapse.

Admittedly, it was far from easy to walk away. During the past few years, the tabloids had become my home and my colleagues had become my family. Despite the ups and downs of the job, it felt good to belong. Now, I would simply be defined as me, rather than as the Tabloid Prodigy.

More than anyone, Heidi seemed to understand what I was going through. She knew my resolve was weak. I told her I wanted to run away to a place I knew nothing about, and to a place that knew nothing about me. And so, overnight, my sister changed her life for the sake of mine. Heidi made an effort to be home when I walked in the door, even if it meant returning to the UCLA lab after I fell asleep. She threw out my tabloids and bought me books like *The Catcher in the Rye* and *Traveling Mercies*. She cooked us tomato soup and grilled cheese sandwiches, intently sketching diagrams of her latest bio-chem discoveries on paper napkins while we ate. On Friday nights, we munched on popcorn and watched classics like *Breakfast at Tiffany's* and *Singin' in the Rain*. On Saturday mornings, we made banana pancakes, flipping them in the air and catching them on our plates. Neither of us were normally into comfort food. But now, nothing was normal and I needed comfort.

Together, Heidi and I spent an entire afternoon baking honey bread for our neighbors, secretly dropping off tin-foiled loaves on every doorstep. Our identities remained a mystery until we discovered that the stirring blade from our bread machine had disappeared. Apparently, the blade had dislodged during the kneading cycle and been baked directly into the rising dough. Suddenly we found ourselves pounding on the door of every neighbor, begging for the return of our baked goods. In exchange, we promised to deliver something less lethal. Fortunately, by the fourth door we were able to retrieve the missing blade.

Time with Heidi proved to be restorative. She tried to make me laugh, often settling for a smile that would peak at grin level before melting into tears. Although still far from happy, it seemed I was slowly coming to grips with my decision to leave the tabloids. If only I could have packaged Heidi's love in a bottle and taken it to the office, things would have been easier.

Eventually, I also began relying on her to accompany me on my investigative assignments. After more than three hundred bylines and months of futile pleading, I finally convinced Heidi to act as my new partner in crime.

My sister only agreed to go along on these assignments on two conditions: one, that the stories be uplifting, and two, that she could remain a silent spectator. The first adventure began after one of my sources gave me complimentary tickets to Hollywood's Magic Castle. Until then, I had always associated magic with my dad's quarter-behind-the-ear trick. Built in 1908, the mansion housing the exclusive club was also the home of The Academy of Magical Arts. Such authenticity amplified how naïve and out of place Heidi and I must have looked within this circle of sorcery.

Restricted to professional magicians, the only way to gain access to the private club was by the personal invitation of a member. My source was a gay hairdresser whom I had featured in the article "Catwoman Julie Newmar's Beauty Secrets." My source's partner was a regular performer at this club and provided my two guest passes in appreciation for the publicity generated by my article. Although visiting Magic Castle was not specifically an AMI assignment, the editors encouraged me to utilize the tickets, confident that I would gain some sort of lead in the prestigious setting.

At the time, Heidi and I had no idea that a strict dress code was enforced at The Castle. As usual, my sister was appropriately dressed in a black cocktail number. When the *maitre d'hôtel* took one look at my black pants *sans* "matching jacket" however, we were asked to leave the premises.

"Oh, well," Heidi said, somewhat relieved. "Guess it just wasn't meant to be."

Our twenty-minute drive home was one of constant bickering, ending only the moment Heidi agreed to give The Castle a second try. After my quick wardrobe change, we headed back. This time, I was wearing the required matching jacket.

"I'm not a huge fan of hocus-pocus," Heidi said, trying to justify her reluctance. "Why aren't you going to The Castle with Caelan?"

"I already told you," I explained, as the valet opened my car door. "Caelan's working on 'Gay Blackmail Scandal Hits Hollywood.'"

Overhearing my comment, the valet gave me a double take. "Okay," Heidi agreed unwillingly. "But we better be out of here in one hour. I still have to feed my lab cells tonight."

As we handed over our invitations, the *maitre d'hôtel* gave me a quick scan and said, "You must be over twenty-one to enter The Magic Castle."

Pulling out my driver's license, I smiled confidently as I handed him my ID. By now, Heidi was rolling her eyes, clearly annoyed by the complexity of the evening. Glancing back and forth between my card and me, the man returned my license and pointed us toward a wall of books that extended from floor to ceiling. "Go ahead," he ordered. "You may enter."

Unable to locate the mysterious point of entry, Heidi and I looked at each other in utter confusion. "What's he talking about?" I mumbled under my breath.

My sister bit her bottom lip and shook her head. "I have absolutely no clue."

I could hear the sound of impatient fingers drumming on the podium behind us. "You have to say the magic words to enter," directed the *maitre d'hôtel*.

Heidi studied the title of books on the shelf while I turned to face the annoyed employee. "I'm sorry," I told him. "This is our first time here—"

"I gathered that," he interrupted. "The magic words are 'Open Sesame.'"

My sister snapped her fingers and spoke to no one in particular. "I knew it had to be something simple like that." Turning toward me, she added, "Okay, say it."

"No," I contested. "You say it."

"Fine," she agreed. "We'll both say it."

Taking one step closer to the wall, we whispered the magic words in unison. Nothing happened. At this point, the voice behind us became even more agitated. "You need to speak directly to the stuffed owl on the middle shelf," he instructed us. "And you'll have to speak louder than a whisper."

Embarrassed, we both eyed the owl and chanted a forceful, "Open Sesame!" Suddenly the entire bookcase spun around and we found ourselves inside the castle walls.

"Was that not the coolest thing you've ever seen?" I cheered, offering my hand in a celebratory high five. Heidi left me hanging.

"Try to blend in," she whispered, as we entered a pack of men wearing black capes, white gloves, and top hats. "Those must be the magicians," Heidi added. "Let's stay clear of them."

Staying close together, we moved through rooms filled with velvet couches and antique tables that held dripping candles and tasseled lamps glowing with red light. We noticed private theaters and secluded dining halls where guests were eating oysters on the half shell or plates of *paella* veiled beneath silver domes. Suddenly we found ourselves in a museum filled with glass displays of magic props and works of art that "came to life" after midnight. To one side was a musty library with worn carpets and tattered books, all with titles of wizardry and conjuring that neither Heidi nor I could recognize.

"Someone's playing the piano," my sister said, turning toward a wooden hallway. "I could use a bit of classical music to calm my nerves."

Fearful of interrupting a private performance, we tiptoed into the open room from which the sound was coming. Oddly enough, we were the only people in there. Directly in front of us was a player piano, the keys moving eerily to sound out Beethoven's "Moonlight Sonata." I studied the bobbing foot pedals while Heidi hesitantly peered behind the back of the piano.

"I dare you to sit down on the piano bench," I said.

By now, Heidi was busy pulling back drapes and looking below the sofa. Daring me back, she asked, "Why don't you sit down?"

Slowly reaching toward the bench, I karate chopped the air and waited for some sort of haunted reaction from the ghostly pianist.

"Look at that," Heidi said, pointing toward a sign on the wall. "I guess this is Invisible Irma's room. It says she takes requests. Do you think she knows any Elton John?"

"Probably not," I responded with a grin. "But I'm sure she knows the theme song to *Titanic.*" Suddenly, the keys fell silent. Both Heidi and I took a step backward and watched in disbelief as the intro to "My Heart Will Go On" began to fill the room. Turning toward the door, we both rushed out and down the hall, the sound of music echoing behind us. Returning to the grand salon, Heidi exhaled deeply and suggested we keep to well-lit areas.

We passed through an English pub where distinguished-looking bartenders served cognac, bourbon, port, and Scotch in Swarovski crystal glasses. "You want a drink?" I offered.

Heidi shook her head and joked, "Not on a school night."

Pointing toward a theater entrance, I asked, "How about a magic show?"

Heidi was already pushing her way through the velvet curtain. "Sure, just as long as we can stay inconspicuous."

Inside, about fifty guests focused on the center stage. Apparently, the magician had just completed a trick involving his cape. Heidi learned toward me and whispered, "He's busting the ole' dove-in-the-cape trick again."

Leaning toward the microphone, the magician announced, "And for this next trick, I'll be needing a lovely assistant. How about you, at the back there?"

Suddenly Heidi and I were blinded by the circle of a spotlight. We both pointed toward each other, uncertain to whom he was referring. With every eye on us, the man continued. "Yes, you there with the dark hair—I'm sure your sister won't mind if I borrow you for a moment."

I let out a sigh of relief as Heidi slowly shuffled to center stage. Without realizing how close she was to the microphone, we could all hear Heidi earnestly ask, "How did you know we were sisters?"

The man waved his wand in the air and answered, "Is it magic? Or is it resemblance?" I could tell she was blushing now. Fortunately, the act involved nothing more than pulling a few cards from a deck and showing them to the crowd. After Heidi's brief performance, we agreed to call it a night. As we started to leave, I suddenly remembered that I was walking away empty-handed. I had no source, no celebrity gossip, and no new lead to follow up. It was sobering to realize that, for a brief moment, I didn't even care.

Linking my arm in hers, I asked Heidi, "Now, that wasn't so bad now, was it?" She shrugged her shoulders as I continued, "I think you're getting the hang of this tabloid thing. If you can cut out the demands, the deadlines, and the depression, then it's really a piece of cake."

At the mention of cake, Heidi blurted, "Oh no! I nearly forgot! I promised to make a checkered cake for my chemistry lab tomorrow." As the valet opened her car door, she continued, "Our lab is celebrating the successful breeding of our first FXR transgenic mouse." This time, it was Heidi's turn to be on the receiving end of the valet's double take. After getting back to our condo, we stayed awake until four in the morning baking a three-layered cake. It was the first night in weeks that I didn't cry myself to sleep.

Several weeks before giving my notice to AMI, I had scheduled a few hours out of the office to have my wisdom teeth removed. Although my appointment had been approved on the company calendar, the editors had apparently forgotten about my meeting with the oral surgeon. All morning long, Madeline had been incessantly calling my cell phone. There I was, my gums pumped full of Novocain while my cell phone kept ringing in my handbag beside me.

"Would you look at this!" the surgeon exclaimed, poking me with a dental probe. "You have a thirty-third tooth back here." The next thing I knew, an entire medical team was peering into my mouth in search of the freak tooth. "This little bugger just doesn't want to come out," the surgeon commented, his knee propped on the arm of the dental chair for added leverage. I could see his muscles flexing as he turned and cracked the roots of the stubborn fang. Following surgery, the dental assistant handed me my teeth in a Ziploc bag as he gave me a prescription for Vicodin. "Now remember," he warned me, "no driving for the next two days."

Through a mouthful of gauze, I let out a muffled "Okay," before walking to the corner to hop on my bike. It was mid-afternoon by the time I could bike the ten miles to *Globe*'s office. During my ride, the cotton pressed between my gums had become saturated with blood and the gauze was now hanging in soggy shreds from my mouth. Madeline took one look at my puffed cheeks and gasped, "Wow, you've had better days, haven't you?"

Staring blankly at my computer screen, I swallowed a Vicodin and shoved a new strip of gauze into the empty pockets where my wisdom teeth had once been. I wondered just how productive my remaining workday would be. Three hours later, Madeline ordered me go home and get some rest. "You can make up the extra hours tonight," she added. "We've got a tip that Vanna White and her husband, George Santo Pietro, are having marital problems. I need you to go out to The Wine Merchant restaurant in Beverly Hills. It's owned by one of George's best friends and he's in there all the time. Ask around and see if you can find out what's going on."

Unable to talk, I scribbled on my notepad the words, "But I can't drive."

Glancing at my note, Madeline looked up briefly and said, "Take a cab."

When Heidi returned home, she found me in tears. Swollen and exhausted, I was afraid to rely on painkillers to get me through the night. "Just tell Madeline you won't do the assignment," Heidi said matter-of-factly.

"You don't understand," I mumbled, pulling the cotton from my mouth. "I don't ever want to be accused of giving anything less than one hundred percent. If I can just make it through one more week with the tabloids, I can always look back and know that I fought to the end."

Heidi sat down on the edge of my bed and handed me another tissue. "No one is questioning that you're a fighter, Lise. We're only wondering if you're a survivor."

Blowing my nose, I tossed the tissue toward the wastebasket and missed. I didn't have time to dwell on my sadness. I had to go to work. Throwing back the covers, I walked to the mirror and started to get ready for one of my last nights out in Beverly Hills.

"Fine. Go," Heidi said, following me to the mirror as she started applying a coat of gloss to her lips. "But I'm coming with you. After all, you can't drive, right?"

I sniffled and nodded without saying a word. By the time we arrived at the restaurant, I realized how torturous my night would be with such a tantalizing selection of gourmet foods, none of which I could eat. Heidi suggested we stick to liquids, like soups and sodas. I told her to order whatever she wanted so that I could live vicariously through her taste buds.

Under the circumstances, it would take a good deal of effort to land a source. My cheeks were the size of balloons and there seemed to be a constant rivulet of drool between my numb lips. Heidi did most of the talking that night, innocently chatting with our Cuban waiter, Ricky. We made a habit of speaking through a chain of command. I would mumble to Heidi, who would then translate my garbled jargon to Ricky, who would then answer me directly. Somewhere in the course of our tag-team conversation, Ricky fell madly in love with Heidi, insisting she try a glass of the Redstone Reserve.

"I don't make a habit of drinking on school nights," she said, swirling the dark wine in her tasting glass, "But considering you're from Cuba and all, I guess I could make an exception."

Less than half a glass later, Heidi began fanning her face, claiming to be "buzzed" and "somewhat intoxicated."

Every time Ricky passed our table, she would cover the rim of her glass with the palm of her hand to pace the frequency of his refills. Our initial plan of "soup and soda" evolved into a four-hour dinner of crab cakes, smoked salmon, shrimp, and salad. I poked and prodded and mashed my mountain of appetizers, hoping that I could somehow beat them into a digestible whip. Ricky pointed toward my plate and asked in broken English, "You don't like?"

"Oh, she likes it," Heidi said, answering for me. "She's just afraid of dry sockets."

Ricky waved his finger in the air as if scolding a child. "We serve no Hot Pockets at The Wine Merchant." I held my hands flush to my cheeks to keep from laughing. The pain was intense.

"No," Heidi explained, between sips of wine. "Not 'Hot Pockets.' They're called dry sockets. You know—it's when food dislodges the formation of the blood clot. This might delay the healing process and exacerbate the pain."

Ricky winced and nodded at her scientific explanation as if he understood what she was talking about. Suddenly grabbing an empty chair, he flipped it around and straddled the chair at our table. With his arms folded over the back rest, he leaned toward Heidi and smiled.

I could tell she was nervous. "Oh, hello, Ricky. Welcome to our table. Can I offer you a crab cake?" She held out the warm platter.

Ricky pushed the plate aside. "You are so very beautiful, Heidi. I want to cook for you in my home."

I readjusted a cotton ball in the back of my mouth and waited for her reaction. Taking a final sip of her wine, she held the empty glass in the air and said, "How about you start with another Redstone on the house, Mister!"

"But of course," he said, reaching for her hand. Lightly kissing the top of her knuckles, he added, "Anything for you, *princessa.*" Within seconds we had refills on wine and a side bottle of Evian, which I'm convinced he delivered as an alcohol pacer.

"You know what I love about American women," Ricky said, topping off Heidi's glass. "They know how to eat. Look at how much you are enjoying your food."

I glanced down at my seafood goulash while Heidi dug her fork into the corner of a crab cake. "Well, Ricky," Heidi said. "Most women wouldn't really consider that a compliment. But I guess I'll take it as one. Thanks."

Ricky seemed pleased with himself. "Oh," he continued. "You must try our tiramisu. We are famous for our tiramisu." Glancing at me for a split second, he added, "I think you can eat it too. You want a straw?"

I shook my head. Amidst all the talk of dessert, I realized the night was coming to a close and I had yet to bring up the subject of Vanna White. Trying to form intelligible words around my swollen gums, I threw out my regular tabloid speech. "Hey Ricky, do you ever see anyone famous in here?"

Puzzled, Ricky turned toward Heidi who translated my incoherent speech. "She wants to know," Heidi explained, "if you ever see anyone famous in here?" Before Ricky had a chance to answer, his attention was drawn away by another customer who was waving from a table at the back. In Ricky's absence, Heidi reached across the table, cupped my hands in hers and pleaded, "Lise, just let it go. You have exactly one week left in that place. You've just got to let it go."

She was right. Why did I feel such a need to deliver? By this stage, the pressure to succeed in my career should have been lifted. After all, I had already given AMI my notice. My eyes started to well up at the thought of finally letting it all go.

When Ricky returned to our table, I muttered, "On second thought, we'll take the tiramisu."

The following day, Madeline asked how things had gone at The Wine Merchant. I told her I had exchanged phone numbers with a few of the employees, none of whom knew anything about the marital status of Vanna White. Although I was somewhat disappointed by my fruitless efforts, Madeline did not press the issue any further.

Changing the subject, she said, "You do know that you're on duty this weekend, don't you?" I nodded as Madeline continued. "It will probably be the last time you'll have to sacrifice a weekend for the tabloids."

The thought seemed foreign to me. "Right now the books are clear," Madeline explained, "but keep your phone on just in case a story breaks in the next few days. By the way, Cathy wants to know how far you've gotten on your wrestling story for *Star*."

At the time, World Champion Wrestling was on the rise and Cathy felt that tabloid readers needed insight into the private lives of professional wrestlers. "I have an interview scheduled with Diamond Dallas and his wife, Kimberly Page, later today," I answered. "I'll file the story by the end of the day."

Returning to my desk, I typed out the background information on the wrestling couple, plugging in their quotes following my interview with them later that afternoon. It was 4:30 by the time I faxed the copy to Florida. When I returned from the fax machine, *The Joshua Tree* by U2 was resting on my keyboard. Stuck to the back of the CD was a Post-It note written in Caelan's handwriting, "Weekend plans?"

Over the past few days, Caelan and I had seen each other only briefly at the office and never outside. With all of the changes taking place at AMI, Caelan had flown to Florida twice, despite still being expected to maintain all of his duties as a reporter and managing editor. We were drifting further apart by the day.

I dialed his extension. "So, are we going to a U2 concert or are you taking me to Dublin to meet Bono?"

Caelan laughed quietly. "When you put it that way," he said, "my plan doesn't sound all that exciting. I was thinking somethin' more along the lines of hiking in Joshua Tree. What do you say?"

"But I'm on duty this weekend," I explained. "What if a story breaks and I'm stuck in the middle of the desert?"

"Don't worry, luv," he assured me. "I'm the editor in charge this weekend. I guarantee it'll be a quiet one. Plus, we really need to get away for a bit. We hardly ever see each other anymore."

He had a point. "So when do we leave?" I asked.

There was a brief pause before he answered, "I'll pick you up at six o'clock."

The two-hour drive to the Mojave Desert was quiet, neither of us saying anything other than to comment on Caelan's music selection or the scenery. Free of any plans or agenda, we stopped midway at Jeremy's Coffee House for a drink and a game of dominos. It was sunset by the time we entered the national park, where silhouettes of pompom-like clusters sprouted from the limbs of the famous Joshua trees. Colors in the sky turned from yellow and orange to purple and black. As wild coyotes howled in the distance, we counted shooting stars and mosquito bites. We munched on sunflower seeds and beef jerky. Clearly, we were no longer in LA.

That night, few words were exchanged between Caelan and me. He picked up Thai food while I stayed inside the Sunset Motel, reading *Condé Nast Traveler*. When he returned, we both continued reading our magazines, eating in silence and enjoying the stillness of the night. Neither of us spoke of the tabloids, or celebrities, or the fact I was quitting my job with no future plan in sight.

Shortly after midnight, a storm passed through the desert, sending bolts of lightning and cracks of thunder just outside our door. The electrical power went out and we spent the rest of the night reading by candlelight. I fell asleep to the sound of raindrops pounding on the windowpane.

That night, I had the most bizarre dream. I dreamt I was walking alongside a freeway with a railroad track running down the middle of four lanes. Traffic was whizzing past when suddenly, a blue truck crossed the tracks and flipped across two lanes of oncoming cars. As the truck rolled, an object flew out of the window and landed on the side of the road. In my dream, I initially thought the object was a baby. When I stopped my car and got closer, I realized it was actually the driver's leg.

Picking up his leg, I ran toward the driver, who was pinned inside his truck. Holding his hand, I tried to keep him calm by telling him that the ambulance would be there soon. The man in my dream was shaking uncontrollably, claiming he had been on his way to a plastic surgeon to have a birthmark removed. Although he was terrified, he did not cry. Instead, I cried for him. The man asked me why I was crying, and I told him, "Sir, don't you realize that your vanity has cost you your life?"

In my dream, the paramedic arrived and carefully took the severed limb from my hands, placing it in an ice-filled compartment of the ambulance. Turning to me, she asked that I help to stop the man's bleeding. As I pressed his stump into my chest, she grabbed him under the arms, and together we lifted him into the ambulance. To stanch the flow of blood, I pressed his stump even harder to my chest. Awaking from my dream in a cold sweat, I could hear Caelan yelling, "Get your knees out of my chest, would ya, luv? You're pressing so hard that I can hardly breathe." Letting go of Caelan's arms, I realized I was curled up in the fetal position.

Never before had I put much credence in dreams, but this particular nightmare seemed to be filled with symbolism. Was this dream just another indication of how repulsed I was by Hollywood's value system? Or, was my dream a subconscious urgency to try to rescue those who were victims of their own vanity? If Hollywood's superficiality was now haunting my sleep, what toll must it be taking on my waking hours?

The following morning, Caelan and I hiked the muddy trails of Hidden Valley. I scaled jagged boulders and towering cliffs, while Caelan stayed below, begging me to come back down. There were snakes and scorpions, jackrabbits and beetles, reminding me that the only animals I had seen in LA were dogs and cats. Driving home, we stopped at The Country Kitchen restaurant for roast beef, mashed potatoes, apple pie, and homemade ice cream.

Although the weekend did not seem to strengthen our fading relationship, it did strengthen me. After that getaway, I sensed that LA would no longer be my home. During those hours in Joshua Tree, I had inwardly made a decision to move away, far away from California. Wherever I would end up, I wanted to be surrounded by nature. I wanted the sun to be my clock and the seasons to be my calendar. I wanted stars to be my streetlights and fields to be my freeways. Just as we approached Santa Monica, I asked Caelan if he would ever consider leaving everything behind.

"Sure, luv," he said. "I would be willing to start over again. Do you fancy giving New York a try?"

His question hung unanswered between us. Looking at him intently, I wondered if he was serious or simply testing my reactions. Whatever the case, it was clear we had reached a crossroads.

That Monday morning marked the start of my final week with AMI. The countdown note on my computer read "5." That meant I had very little time to wrap up my pending leads. Before I even had a chance to begin researching those stories, however, my private line rang at my desk.

"Marlise, it's Cathy."

I wondered how she had gotten my private number. "Hi, Cathy. How can I help you?" Already I was dreading the yet-undefined assignment for *Star*. Considering that this was my final week with the tabloids, I assumed the editors would probably be loading me with tasks that no one else would be willing to accept.

"I want you to stop whatever it is that you're working on," Cathy explained. "We have reason to believe that Kurt Russell is cheating on Goldie Hawn—"

"Haven't we checked on this rumor before?" I interrupted. "Their relationship is pretty solid, right?"

"Well, we don't actually have all the details yet," Cathy continued. "Our source is telling us that Kurt was spotted in Canada with another woman. I need you to check it out."

"Sure," I agreed. "When and where do you want me to go exactly?"

"I need you to be on the next plane to Vancouver," she explained.

Glancing at the clock, I noticed it was 9:05 a.m. "Okay. Do we have a specific location in Vancouver?"

Cathy sounded totally unprepared. "No, nothing yet. Just check into one of the nicest hotels you can find. Ask around and see what you can learn."

This assignment had no direction. "And before you go," she added, "drop by Madeline's office. She has something important to tell you about this story."

Shutting down my computer, I grabbed the Kurt and Goldie files from the copy room and headed for Madeline's office. I knocked on her open door. "You wanted to see me?"

Looking up from her desk, Madeline immediately stopped what she was doing. "Yes," she said. "Come in and please close the door behind you."

Suddenly, I had flashbacks of the first time I had stepped inside that office. I wondered how different my life would have been had I then listened to those pleading paparazzi photos on the wall.

Madeline leaned forward on her desk and said, "So, I hear you're off to Vancouver."

I nodded, waiting impatiently for the point of our conversation.

"Have you ever been to Canada?" she continued.

I had no idea where Madeline was going with this. "No," I answered. "This will be my first time there."

Madeline's voice dropped to a whisper. "Here's the deal, Marlise. One of the new bigwigs at AMI doesn't yet comprehend the concept of 'reliable sources.' Now he has passed down an extremely weak tip that 'someone saw Kurt with a mystery woman in Vancouver.' We have no time, no date, no location, no identity—nothing. Pre-David Pecker, we never would have checked out such an unsubstantiated lead. I know it's not valid and practically everyone in Florida knows it's not true. Still, out of respect for those at the top, we have no choice but to check it out." There was a slight grin on Madeline's face. "Are you following me?"

I nodded, becoming somewhat more enthusiastic.

Madeline continued, "Considering it's your final week with us and considering that you've done fairly well over the past few years, Cathy and I agreed that you should be the one to cover the assignment. Now, I'm not saying that you can just go over there and have a vacation on *Star*. The fact is you'll definitely have to return with something. Florida will be checking your expense report, your list of new sources, and any other material that you will file once you're back in the office."

Confused, I stared at her in puzzlement. "But Madeline," I hesitated, "if the lead isn't true, how on earth am I supposed to come back with a story?"

Madeline shook her head at my naiveté. "Marlise, I'm not saying you have to try to manufacture anything on Kurt and Goldie. Maybe you can find another story while you're there. Shows are always being filmed in Canada because of the low production costs. In fact, four major film companies are located in Vancouver. I'm sure you can put together a few short pieces on some celebrities to run on the gossip page."

I couldn't believe what I was hearing. Madeline and Cathy were actually rewarding me with a semi-contrived assignment to Canada. "And remember," she added in a whisper. "This stays between the two of us."

I gave her a genuine smile. "Thanks, Madeline. I really needed this—"

"Now go on," she interrupted with a wave of her hand. "Hurry up, before I change my mind."

And just like that, I was on my way to Vancouver. Somehow, Air Canada had overbooked and had given away my seat on the noon flight.

To compensate for the inconvenience, the airline gave me first-class seating plus meal vouchers and access to the flight lounge.

When I went to pick up my rental car at the Vancouver airport, I was instantly upgraded to a midsize vehicle simply because the Alamo employee said, "I dig your eyes." On Caelan's recommendation, I checked into the Wedgewood Hotel, voted the best hotel in Vancouver. As I pulled up to the curb, I was met by a bellman dressed in a blue uniform with gold buttons, white gloves, and a top hat. Opening the door to the lobby, he welcomed me to the Wedgewood, motioning for someone to carry my bag. Perched on a mahogany table directly in front of me was a lavish floral arrangement. A crystal chandelier gleamed overhead, while regal red velvet chairs formed a circle beneath it. Jewels dangled from the rims of antique lamps, casting prisms of light on the hardwood floors.

My private-terraced room overlooked Robson Square. It had limestone floors, a lit fireplace, and a marble wet bar. Dining at the hotel restaurant that evening, I felt and looked utterly alone.

"Will someone be joining you?" my waiter asked.

"No," I replied. "I'm here on business."

Taking the bait, the waiter continued to pry. "What sort of work brings you to Vancouver? Are you in production?"

Out of nowhere, I could hear myself saying that I was a food critic from the *Los Angeles Times*. To this day, I'm not certain why I felt a need to lie. Perhaps masquerading had become so much a part of me that I did not know how to stop. It would have been just as easy to tell the truth, but lying had become second nature to me, even when it was unnecessary for my job.

Before giving me a chance to place my dinner order, the waiter started producing samples of dishes, including ahi tuna, *pâte de foie gras*, and quail in Cabernet sauce. Dessert consisted of homemade sorbets. Creamy scoops of strawberry, mango, raspberry, and blood orange were crowned with a caramelized dome. The tabloids had taught me to never underestimate the power of words, even if they're not true.

Each day, I would collect bits of information for the gossip page, eventually landing three items that were later published in *Star*. Each night, I would search for anything remotely Kurt and Goldie related.

Despite the fact that everyone considered the lead to be false, I knew I would be a hero if I could bring home a cover story. I was never able to get the coveted exclusive because there was no Kurt and Goldie gossip to report.

On the second evening, I hung out at the Sutton Place Hotel. The clientele included countless actors, many of whom looked vaguely familiar and none of whom I could quite place. The only one I recognized was Tony Danza. Wearing a zippered track suit, he walked past while I was standing at the bar. Awkwardly, he dropped his straw in front of me. When we both bent to pick it up, he said, "No, I've got it. I just wanted to make sure you wouldn't trip over it." I smiled, wondering what on earth he was talking about.

Locating a table in the corner, I tried to look as inconspicuous as possible. It was useless. Why would a young, single girl be dining alone in such a restaurant? Reprising my speech from the previous night's success, I told my newest waiter, "Actually, I'm a food critic from the *Los Angeles Times*." I thoroughly enjoyed my full-course salmon dinner.

The following morning, I walked to Stanley Park, through the woods, over a suspension bridge, and under a waterfall. I photographed Vancouver at sunset, grateful to the tabloids for allowing me to experience this crisp city during my final week as an undercover reporter. Inhaling deeply, I thought about how much I had changed since working for the tabloids. Good or bad, these changes in my life had forced me to grow. Looking back on my time at *Globe* and *Star*, I had no regrets. That chapter of my life was ending as it was meant to end, blending both work and pleasure, city and nature, torment and peace.

By the end of day three, I had chatted up nearly every bartender in downtown Vancouver and ordered enough fruity drinks to kill an orchard. As relatively "unproductive" as this assignment had been, it still cost the publishers a $1,700 plane ticket, a thousand dollars in hotel costs, and another thousand for food and entertainment. It was worth every penny.

After completing the three gossip pieces from my Vancouver trip for *Star*, I only had two days left at the tabloids. I spent my final hours filling out expense reports, closing pending leads, and cleaning out my desk. For as much time as I had spent in the office, it was surprising to see how little there was to pack. The process was swift until I began un-tacking the pictures on my bulletin board. Slowly, I looked at the images of the people who had so dramatically impacted my life. There was a photo of Sharmin, Pete, Karen, Adam, and me, dressed in our Halloween costumes just moments before Madeline had walked through the door. There was a photo of the *Globe* staff celebrating our team's success at William Shatner's wedding. There was a photo of Randal and me riding through the Egyptian desert at sunset. There was a photo of the *Globe* family playing in the ball pit at Chuck E. Cheese's. Placing these treasured memories in the top of the last box, I closed the lid and walked away.

I had no intention of saying good-bye to anyone at the office. Pete, who was now working full-time from home, had arranged for everyone to get together for dinner in Santa Monica. It was a fiasco. One can always tell the true feelings of co-workers by the number of people who turn out for a farewell bash. Sadly, the announced "dinner" turned out to be nothing more than a few martinis at Flint's Bar with Caelan, Karen, and Pete. Madeline showed up late for one drink. Tossing a twenty-dollar bill on the table, she wished me luck and walked away.

Several weeks later, I learned why Madeline might have been so uncomfortable at my farewell gathering. Apparently, shortly after I had given my notice, someone had searched my computer files for any unpublished stories. During that process, all of my pending articles were discovered, including the notes of my interview with the Dolly Parton source. One month after I left the tabloids, the full article appeared as a *Globe* cover story, titled "Dolly's Affair with 15-Year-Old." It was published without the consent of the source and without my knowledge or byline. Neither he nor I benefited from the long days we had spent discussing his past with the country singer.

My farewell party had drawn to an abrupt close soon after Madeline walked out of Flint's Bar. I could tell Caelan was embarrassed by the brevity of Madeline's visit. He ended up paying the rest of the tab. After everyone else left, Caelan took me to Rick's Bar in Santa Monica. Surrounded by ivy walls and live jazz, he asked what I planned on doing with my life.

As if Caelan had no choice in my decision, I spontaneously

answered, "I think I'm moving to Europe." The flippancy of my sudden response shocked us both.

Caelan choked on his wine. "What?" he said, thumping his chest. "Surely, you canna be serious."

Even after nearly two years of commitment, neither of us seemed to have a clear sense of who the other was.

I nodded slowly. "Yes, Caelan. I'm serious. My mom recently phoned to say she heard about someone who might need a nanny in Switzerland."

Caelan reached into his pocket for a cigarette. "So, are you just moving to the Alps to become a nanny then?"

"I don't really know." I shrugged. "I haven't decided yet. I just need to get away for a while. My parents seem to think a change of scenery might do me good. I don't know too much about the job except that the Swiss family is looking for someone to travel around Europe with their four kids."

Caelan thumbed the wheel of his lighter. "Four wee ones, eh? Come on, luv. You don't know a thing about being a mother."

I felt insulted. "Well, what else am I supposed to do?"

As if in answer, Caelan reached into his pocket and pulled out a small turquoise velvet pouch. As he slid it across the table, I knew it had to be jewelry, something I had always considered symbolic of commitment. With quivering hands, I untied the purse and emptied the gift into the palm of my hand. Exhaling deeply, I smiled at the silver necklace carrying a cross of diamonds.

"It's beautiful," I said, staring in disbelief. "Caelan, I don't know what to say."

Reaching across the table, he clasped the necklace beneath my hair. "Say that you'll stay."

Pressing the cross to my chest, I stared at the table to avoid looking into his eyes. "Caelan, you know I can't stay. It's time for me to start over."

"I understand that, luv," he said. "But why do you have to go so bloody far away? Why couldn't we give it another try, perhaps in New York or something? You know we could have our very own news agency? Between the two of us, I reckon we know a fair bit about celebrities."

The thought of leaving one bustling city for another one sounded incredibly unappealing to me. "You could come to Europe with me instead," I blurted. "Maybe you could deejay full-time over there—"

Even before I had finished describing my ridiculous plan, Caelan was shaking his head. "I doubt they need a club deejay in the Swiss Alps," he interrupted. "And besides, I'd be miserable over there, freezin' me arse off and all. Why do you think I left Scotland?"

Realizing neither of us was willing to sacrifice to save our relationship, our conversation virtually came to an end. "Look," Caelan said. "Go spend some time with your folks in Monterey. You can give my New York idea some thought there and let me know what you decide. I really think it could work out for the both of us."

The next day, I loaded up my Karmen Ghia and drove eight hours along the California coast to Monterey. My parents ran out to meet me in the driveway, hugging me tightly as if they were grateful to see me still alive, rather than just glad to see me. Prior to my arrival, my mother had scheduled a meeting for me with the contact whose brother in Switzerland was searching for an au pair for his children. My brief meeting with this liaison consisted of no more than her giving me a written offer from her brother together with a photograph of the four children. "The girls are four and nine years old, and the boys are eleven and thirteen," the woman explained. "It would do them good to learn another language."

Visions of the Von Trapp family danced in my head. "You mean none of the children speaks a word of English?"

"No," she explained. "They speak High German at school, Swiss German at home, and French in the village."

Suddenly I felt rather bland. Looking down at the offer, which was written in German, I handed it back to her, asking for a translation.

The woman continued, "It says that they are prepared to pay for your open-ended ticket to Geneva, plus all of your living expenses while you're there. I don't think there is any pay, but you can discuss that with them while you're there. It would start out as a two-month trial period, just to help out while their chalet is under renovation." She placed the faxed offer on the table and looked up. "The kids are pretty self-sufficient, so I imagine it would be fairly easy."

"When would they need me?" I asked.

Folding the paper in half, the woman tucked the photograph into the folds and answered, "In ten days."

Knowing absolutely nothing about this family, except that it had four children who needed me, I impulsively responded, "Okay, I'll do it."

Becoming an au pair in Switzerland was about as far as I could get away from my life as a tabloid journalist in LA. The decision seemed to fit into the pattern that my life had sketched as a woman of paradox.

When I shared the news of my decision with my parents, they were confronted by conflicting emotions. They were relieved that I was making a new start, but were hesitant to let me wander so far from home. The next five days were crammed with preparatory tasks like organizing plane tickets, paying bills, packing for Switzerland, and memorizing basic German vocabulary words. My dad and I managed to squeeze in a fishing trip, while my mom and I settled for a leisurely walk on the beach. They begged to see me off from the Los Angeles airport, but I told them it was something I would prefer to do alone. The truth was that I hated good-byes.

During that final hug, my father whispered the exact words I had been longing to hear ever since I had joined the tabloids: "We're proud of you," he said. "Really proud of you."

When I got back to LA, I realized that my mother had stashed a parting gift on the backseat of my car. Inside the bag were seashells that we had collected during our beach walk. There was also an umbrella, a rather appropriate gift for the Mary Poppins-like job I was about to undertake in Switzerland. Attached to her gift was a card that read, "The only thing that amazes me more than how incredibly you have turned out, is how you have survived some of my misguided attempts at parenting. It is almost impossible not to feel overwhelming pride when I think of you. I'll love you forever. Mom."

From Monterey, I had called both Heidi and Caelan about my decision to accept the offer in Switzerland. When I got back to LA, it was obvious that Heidi had taken the news about as well as my parents. She knew that the change of pace would be therapeutic for my soul. "Maybe I can come visit you in Switzerland sometime," she suggested. "We could do a road trip through France or even go into Spain." For Heidi, the most difficult part of my plan was the uncertainty of my return.

"It's just going to be for two months," I kept assuring her.

Unconvinced, she nodded and handed me a card. "Don't read this until we're apart," she told me. Later, I opened the envelope and read:

"Dear Little One, letting you go is one of the hardest sacrifices I have had to make. I have so enjoyed our nightly conversations and the fact that our lives are enmeshed. You bring so much joy and inspiration to me. I am still amazed at all of the hurdles you have had to overcome over these past few years. Your reality is beyond comprehension. That is what makes you so incredible and unique. Through all of this, you have stayed true to the woman you were meant to be. Don't ever lose sight of that as things begin to escalate in your life. Go trek through this world, inhale deeply, and love to live. Write with reckless abandon, Little One, because that is what God has created you to do. I could not possibly love you any more than I do. Your adoring fan. Heidi."

I knew it was not easy for her to let me go, especially considering the weakened state in which I had been for the past few months. But Heidi was a giver. She was willing to let me go, hoping that something new would start happening in my life.

Caelan, on the other hand, seemed unable to come to terms with my decision to leave. Like Heidi, he also knew that I would need longer than two months to heal. He never again mentioned the New York idea. During my last days in LA, we agreed to dwell in the present and ignore the fact that I would be leaving. For the next seventy-two hours, we lived life as we always had. He spun records in his loft, while I did yoga on the living room floor below. We ordered Chinese takeout and walked along the back canals of Venice Beach. We shopped on Melrose Avenue and listened to live jazz at the Los Angeles County Museum of Art. We shared red wine and watched independent films. As always, Caelan told me he loved me, and I told him I loved him too.

On that final day, we said our good-byes at the loading zone of the Los Angeles International Airport. Caelan always said that loading zone good-byes were less painful than Terminal B farewells.

"I'll be waiting here if you ever decide to come back," Caelan promised.

"And I'll be waiting here, even if you don't."

Fighting my emotions, I waved good-bye and walked away, forcing myself to look straight ahead. Burying my hands deeply into the pocket of my jeans, I pulled out a movie ticket faded from one too many trips through the washer. The ticket stub dated back to my second evening out with Caelan. Crushing it like a dying cigarette, I picked up my bag and moved closer to the terminal.

There I was, alone by the curbside, preparing to move to a country I knew nothing about, to work for people whom I had never met. I would be leaving behind everything familiar, all my comforts and all my corners of refuge.

In my quest for peace, I desperately needed to go to a place where no one would know me as the Tabloid Prodigy. There, I would burn my masks and start again. Stripping myself of those blackened identities, I would at last strive to be seen for who I truly was, wholly and completely me.

Epilogue

Heidi Kast-Woelbern: Soon after I left the tabloids, my sister received her doctorate in molecular biology from UCLA. She accepted an offer from a pharmaceutical firm and began conducting research in the fields of cancer and diabetes. Heidi currently resides in San Diego with her husband, Matthew, and their two young children.

David and Gretchen Kast: In 2005, my parents moved to San Diego to be closer to their children. Defying the laws of retirement, my father has launched a successful landscaping business while my mother devotes herself to her grandchildren. In keeping with their passion for missions, my parents currently focus their energies on part-time volunteer work in Romania.

Chantal Layne: After obtaining her teaching credential, Chantal accepted a position at Beverly Hills High School. She continues to reside in the Los Angeles area with her husband and daughter.

Darin Leverett: Darin's marriage to Marlene lasted less than six months. Following his divorce, he passed the bar exam in three states, specializing in tax and contractual law. Traveling extensively, Darin spent several months in Mexico and Europe, during which time he and I made a road trip together through Italy and France. Darin lives in Seattle, where he works as a contract attorney at his father's law firm.

Sharmin Bryles: After leaving *Globe*, Sharmin returned to her home state of Arkansas, where she became an administrative assistant in a medical facility. Currently completing her master's degree in rhetoric and urban studies, she resides in Little Rock with her husband, Billy, and daughter, Ryann. Despite the miles that separate us, Sharmin and I have remained the closest of friends.

Pete Trujillo: On January 2, 2005, Pete suffered a massive stroke and passed away unexpectedly. His death came as a shock to everyone at *Globe*, where Pete had continued to work until the time of his death.

Caelan Dunmore: Six months after our loading zone good-bye, Caelan left the tabloids to open his own New York based news agency. Today, his company is one of the world's leading suppliers of celebrity news and photographs. In 2006, Caelan married a book editor with whom he makes his home in New York.

James Churchill: Putting his paparazzo reputation behind him, James moved to New York to begin a successful career as a studio photographer. Today he is in high demand by some of the leading names in the entertainment industry. James and his longtime girlfriend reside one block away from the news agency of his old friend, Caelan Dunmore.

Adam Edwards: After leaving the tabloids, Adam returned to his home state of New York. He currently holds the position of night producer for CBS radio.

Madeline Norton, **Trenton Freeze**, **Cathy Tidwell**, **Karen Glaser**, and **Daniel Taft** all remain with the tabloids through their association with American Media Inc.

Marlise Elizabeth Kast: My initial short-term position with one of Switzerland's most influential families led to an offer to become their permanent au pair. My adventures escalated there as I moved from the red carpet of Hollywood to the playpen of the Alps.

Ultimately, though, my twin passions for travel and writing led me to become a freelance journalist, focusing on sports, business, and travel publications. After leaving Switzerland, I resided briefly in Central America, the Dominican Republic, Spain, and Costa Rica. My insatiable hunger for cultures and languages took me on a thirteen-month surfing and snowboarding expedition through twenty-eight countries. I am now based in San Diego near my family. As an author and freelance journalist, I continue my search for liquid mountains and untracked terrain, wandering the world with blissful contentment.

Acknowledgments

Mom and Dad, thanks for being there every step of the way, through late nights, writer's block, laughter and tears. Dad, thank you for your words of encouragement, your prayers of hope, and your unconditional love. Mom, had it not been for your motivational spirit, this book never would have happened. It is as much yours as it is mine.

Heidi, thank you for your moral support and for reminding me that the life of a writer is never easy. Somehow, in the midst of motherhood and lab experiments, you still managed to find the time for my needy heart.

Jennifer Marshall and Amy Basha, my endless gratitude goes to both of you, my dear friends. During my moments of doubt, you urged me to follow my dream and "just keep writing."

Jeremy Hughes, thank you for being my special young friend on the bike. Though your words remain trapped and unspoken, you have inspired me to discover and release my own.

Sharlene Martin, I am extremely grateful that, as my literary agent, you chose to believe in me from the first query letter to the final published product. Your determination and tenacity have inspired me to strive for excellence. Thank you for daring to explore my potential and for never giving up on *Tabloid Prodigy*.

Lisa Clancy, I consider myself tremendously fortunate to have worked with such an amazing editor as you. Thank you for making this collaborative process both manageable and rewarding.

Running Press and Perseus Books Group, I am indebted to you, my publisher, for embracing my vision and for giving a new author the opportunity to share her voice.

The entire *Globe* staff, thank you for introducing me to the harsh realities of celebrity reporting and for giving me so many fond memories. Without you, this book would never have come to fruition.

Finally, to you, the reader, thank you for hearing my story and sharing this journey with me.

Select Index